Settler

√ n. 1130 (233)

√2 arbitration

BC 159

GWKS 21, 113, 159 599
pension 160-1
widows 160,167-8/169,171-2,200
univ appd (car) 160-1/169
poor children 160-1, 164
poor & sick 161, 164
poor families 161-2
poor 169

RM & enclosure/commons 51
√charity of tenants 50, 53
steward & bailiff & damwork 25
√native / f&F & estate interests 28, 44, 46
Charwomen or nurses

wpx dom husbandry 56, 58-9, 60, 64

Parliament 136-591

church etc 17-18
scattered estates
estates & land 20, 57
manor & fees 32
√ militia 118
fees 120-2

√ schools 43, 160-1, 165-6-7, 174
medical 170-1

unstatute 193

mines 231
Cartland Co. 235

The landed estates were one of the fundamental structures of early modern England. They were omnipresent, for they were not confined to the country-side but penetrated into every borough and city. English society was composed largely of landlords and tenants. It follows that to understand the nature of this society the relationship between the two must be studied, and in particular the role of the man who linked them: the estate steward.

Stewards, Lords and People analyses the role of the estate stewards in the social mechanisms of later Stuart England. It is based on many years of research among more than 10,000 letters exchanged by stewards and their masters about estates as widely distributed as Northumberland and Corn-wall, Cumberland and Sussex. Professor Hainsworth shows that the stew-ards' labours tended to promote social harmony as they mediated between lord and tenant, between town and country, and between 'national' and provincial culture. No mere rent collectors, the stewards were entrepreneurs exploiting mines and forests, mills and quarries. They were election agents, almoners for their lords' charity, builders and developers of their mansions and gardens, ambassadors among their lords' neighbours, and conduits of their lords' patronage. Their regular reports, and their masters' responses, provide a vivid and detailed picture of the social and political life of England in the late Stuart era.

Cambridge Studies in Early Modern British History

STEWARDS, LORDS AND PEOPLE

Cambridge Studies in Early Modern British History

Series editors

ANTHONY FLETCHER
Professor of Modern History, University of Durham

JOHN GUY
Professor of Modern History, University of St Andrews

and JOHN MORRILL
Lecturer in History, University of Cambridge, and Fellow and Tutor of Selwyn College

This is a series of monographs and studies covering many aspects of the history of the British Isles between the late fifteenth century and the early eighteenth century. It includes the work of established scholars and pioneering work by a new generation of scholars. It includes both reviews and revisions of major topics and books which open up new historical terrain or which reveal startling new perspectives on familiar subjects. All the volumes set detailed research into our broader perspectives and the books are intended for the use of students as well as of their teachers.

For a list of titles in the series, see end of book.

STEWARDS, LORDS AND PEOPLE

*The estate steward and his world
in later Stuart England*

D. R. HAINSWORTH

*Associate Professor of History,
University of Adelaide*

Published by the Press Syndicate of the University of Cambridge
The Pitt Building, Trumpington Street, Cambridge CB2 1RP
40 West 20th Street, New York, NY 10011–4211, USA
10 Stamford Road, Oakleigh, Victoria, 3166, Australia

First published 1992

Printed in Great Britain by Redwood Press Limited, Melksham, Wiltshire

A catalogue record for this book is available from the British Library

Library of Congress Cataloguing in publication data
Hainsworth, D. R. (David Roger)
Stewards, lords and people: the estate steward and his world in
later Stuart England / D. R. Hainsworth.
p.   cm. – (Cambridge studies in early modern British history)
Includes bibliographical references and index.
ISBN 0 521 36489 2 (hardback)
1. Real estate management – England – History.   2. Landlord and
tenant – England – History.   3. Manors – England – History.   4. England
– Social conditions – 17th century.   I. Title.   II. Series.
HD604.H35   1992
333.3′22′0974209032 – dc20 91–30371 CIP

ISBN 0 521 36489 2 hardback

CE

For Margaret Laura

CONTENTS

PREFACE

This book is the end product of a long and complicated project which owes much to a great number of people. At a chance meeting at Manchester University in 1977 Professor T. S. Willan helpfully suggested that I should approach the British Academy with a proposal to edit some of Sir John Lowther of Whitehaven's correspondence with his stewards. I considered these letters were potentially an invaluable source for social and economic historians and so gratefully embraced his suggestion and that project began the following year. In 1979 my colleague Wilfrid Prest, knowing that the letters I was editing were largely stewards' correspondence, courteously invited me to contribute an essay on estate stewards to a symposium he was organising on the professions in early modern England. Here I was in a quandary. I knew quite a lot about Lowther's stewards. I knew nothing about the stewards of any other landowner. My wistful suggestion that my colleague might welcome a 'case study' based on the Lowther stewards was firmly declined. What was wanted was a synthesis. I soon discovered that on the subject of stewards in seventeenth-century England there was virtually nothing to synthesise. Two or three articles had been published on eighteenth-century stewards but they were rather too late for my purposes. If the essay was to be written I would have first to do the fundamental research and then try to synthesise what I had discovered. Collecting materials occupied me for the next seven years (indeed I have never really ceased from doing so), although well within that span I had to write my synthesising essay. I fear that in many ways the essay was rather like a tour of an English garden in winter during which your hosts describe all the lovely blooms that would have been there if only you had arrived in summer. Nevertheless it helped to organise my ideas as the collecting went on and to reveal to me what I lacked and what I must redouble my efforts to find.

In the search I had the help of many generous people. Colin Phillips of Manchester University, a good friend for more than twenty years, led me to the Cheshire Record Office where I found the Cholmondeley Papers which proved to contain a cache of more than 3,000 steward 'in-letters'. Mrs Irene Cassidy, my department's London-based research officer, tracked down numerous collections of letters and accounts, and especially some 1,100 items of estate correspondence in the Fitzwilliam Papers at Northampton. Prior to the project's inception I had already arranged for the Barr Smith Library of the University of Adelaide to purchase the Thynne (Marquess of Bath) Papers on microfilm, together with the Seymour, Devereux and Whitelock Papers, and since then it has acquired the Hastings (Earl of Huntingdon) Papers on microfilm from the Huntington Library. Before the project was so much as thought of I had already collected the several hundred Lowther letters I was still editing for the British Academy, and in addition had the 1,800 or more letters of the Lowther–Tickell correspondence, together with account books and legal papers. Before long I realised that I was amassing sources on a formidable scale and that the labour of reading several thousand letters drawn from estates scattered across the length and breadth of England (together with other documents) deserved more than an essay as the end product, particularly since the essay had been drafted well before much of the material came to hand. In the end the project became three-pronged, two volumes of edited documents and this monograph. In 1983 appeared *The Correspondence of Sir John Lowther of Whitehaven 1693–8* (British Academy/Oxford University Press, 1983). This was followed by *The Correspondence of Lord Fitzwilliam of Milton and Francis Guybon His Steward 1697–1709* (Northamptonshire Record Society, 1990) which was jointly edited with Cherry Walker who, as my research assistant, had earlier made a major contribution to the Lowther volume. This project reaches completion with this monograph, *Stewards, Lords and People*.

Among those many people who have helped me over the past dozen years I should like to thank in addition to T. S. Willan and Wilfrid Prest (for the contributions and encouragements already referred to), Irene Cassidy for much devoted travelling around the counties of England successfully ferreting among archives and arranging vast photocopying projects on my behalf; Cherry Walker for ten years of equally devoted service as my assistant, during which, among many other helpful activities, and with the invaluable advice of Bob Jones, she helped me crack the problem of how to organise such a mass of data by introducing the use of a main-frame computer to someone who was about as naturally fitted for the world of computers as Captain Ludd; similarly I must thank Dr Adrian Graves, a former student and at the time a visiting Research Fellow in my department, for giving up his valuable research time to introduce me to personal computers; also the Master and Fellows of Corpus Christi College, Cambridge, who made me the beneficiary of their enlightened and generous

Senior Research Scholars scheme in 1983, and who have hospitably welcomed me back to their college on several occasions; the Council of the University of Adelaide and its History Department for granting me leaves of absence in 1979, 1983, 1987 and 1990 so that I could hunt down stewards' records in various regions of England; all those who hospitably welcomed me under their roofs during such expeditions and especially Edgar and Christine Bailey (Bristol), Tony and Jane Wood (Liskeard), Bill Hall (Ludlow), Colin and Jan Phillips (Little Leigh, Cheshire), Jim and Nan Thomson (Banks, Cumbria), Bill and Mary Scott (Carlisle), David and Dorothy Widdess (Lancaster); Colin Phillips who has always shared with me his unrivalled knowledge of the north west in the seventeenth century and particularly of the Lowthers and their estates, and who, with his colleague Ann Hughes, has several times invited me to give seminars at Manchester University; Michael Graves of Auckland University for three times inviting me to conferences in New Zealand to present papers which became two related articles and a chapter of this book; my departmental colleagues, especially Austin Gough, Frank McGregor, Lynn Martin and Vivien Brodsky, and successive heads of department, for much encouragement and support; Professor John Beckett for courteously sending me copies of most useful articles when he discovered the theme of my project; my long-suffering general editors, Donald Coleman and Edmund King, for invaluable help and advice in the production of the two complementary volumes of records, and John Morrill, with his fellow editors Anthony Fletcher and John Guy, for much advice and encouragement; Brian C. Redwood, the now retired Chief Archivist of the Cheshire Record Office for drawing my attention to the Marquis of Cholmondeley's papers there and labouring to have them copied on my behalf; Bruce Jones, the former Chief Archivist of Cumbria and his successor Sheila MacPherson and their staffs for great help and co-operation in photocopying a range of records but especially of the Lowthers of Lowther and of Whitehaven and of Sir Daniel Fleming of Rydal; and for similar assistance the Chief Archivists of the record offices of Cambridgeshire, Clwyd, Essex, Gloucester, Kent, Norfolk, Northamptonshire, Northumberland, Nottingham, Rutland, Shropshire, Staffordshire, Warwickshire, Wiltshire, together with the staffs of the British Library Manuscripts Room, the John Rylands Library of Manchester University, the Nottingham University Library and the Librarian of St John's College, Cambridge. I am also indebted to the Duke of Devonshire, the Marquess of Cholmondeley, the Marquess of Northampton, the Earl of Lonsdale, the Countess Fitzwilliam, Sir William Lowther of Erbistock Hall, the late Lord Howard of Castle Howard, Sir Charles Graham of Netherby and the Master and Fellows of St John's College, Cambridge, for the opportunity to copy archives in their possession or on deposit. I am also much in the debt of my postgraduate students, Dr Christine Churches and Tania Jefferies, together with Dr Sara Warneke, and Dr Miriam Collins, for research assistance at vital times, and to the secretarial staff of the History Department over several years.

Finally I must acknowledge the contribution of a self-sacrificing wife who cheerfully accepted and indeed encouraged my long absences in pursuit of the data for this book, which, most suitably and gratefully is dedicated to her.

ABBREVIATIONS

AHR	*Agricultural History Review*
Barrett-Lennard	Barrett-Lennard Papers (including Earl of Westmorland), Essex CRO (Chelmsford)
Bath 4	Historical Mss Commission Reports, Marquess of Bath, 58, *Mss of the Marquess of Bath*, vol. 4, *Seymour Papers 1532–1680*
Beckett, *Aristocracy in England*	J. V. Beckett, *The Aristocracy in England 1660–1914* (Oxford, 1986)
BL	British Library
CWAAS	Cumberland and Westmorland Archaeological and Antiquarian Society
CWAAST	*Cumberland and Westmorland Archaeological and Antiquarian Society Transactions*
Cholmondeley DCH	Archives of the Marquess of Cholmondeley, Cheshire CRO (Chester)
Churches, 'Lowther and Whitehaven'	Christine Churches, 'Sir John Lowther and Whitehaven 1642–1706', unpublished Ph.D thesis, University of Adelaide 1991 (copy held Cumbria CRO (Carlisle))
Commons 1715–1754	Romney Sedgwick, ed., *History of Parliament: the Commons 1715–1754*, 2 vols. (London, 1970)
Commons 1660–1690	B. D. Hemming, ed., *History of Parliament: the Commons 1660–1690*, 3 vols. (London, 1983)
CRO	County Record Office
Davies, 'Country Gentry'	M. G. Davies, 'Country Gentry and Falling Rents in the 1660s and 1720s', *Midland History*, vol. 4 (1977)

Davies, 'Gentry Payments'	M. G. Davies, 'Country Gentry and Payments to London, 1650–1714', *Econ. HR*, 2nd ser. vol. 24 (1971)
Devonshire	Archives of the Duke of Devonshire, Chatsworth
DNB	*Dictionary of National Biography*
Eaton Letters	J. Wake and D. C. Webster, eds., *The Letters of Daniel Eaton to the third Earl of Cardigan, 1725–1732, NRST.*, vol. 24 (1971)
Econ. HR	*Economic History Review*
Fitzwilliam	Archives of the Earl Fitzwilliam, Northamptonshire CRO (Northampton)
Fitzwilliam Correspondence	D. R. Hainsworth and Cherry Walker, eds., *The Correspondence of Lord Fitzwilliam of Milton and Francis Guybon his Steward 1697–1709, NRST*, vol. 36 (1990)
Fleming	Fleming of Rydal Papers, Cumbria CRO (Kendal)
Galway (Arundel)	Lady Arundel of Trerice Papers, Galway Papers, Nottingham University Library
Hainsworth, 'Essential Governor'	D. R. Hainsworth, 'The Essential Governor: the Estate Steward and English Society 1660–1714', *Historical Studies*, 21, no. 84, (April, 1985)
Hainsworth, 'Estate Steward'	D. R. Hainsworth, 'The Estate Steward' in W. R. Prest, ed., *The Professions in Early Modern England* (London, 1987)
Hainsworth, 'The Mediator'	D. R. Hainsworth, 'The Mediator: a Link Between National and Provincial Society in Seventeenth Century England', *Parergon*, n.s., vol. 6, 1988 (Festschrift for Sir Geoffrey Elton)
Hastings	The Hastings (Earls of Huntingdon) Collection of Manuscripts, the Huntington Library, California
Hirst	Derek Hirst, *The Representative of the People? Voters and Voting in England Under the Early Stuarts* (Cambridge, 1975)

Holford	Sir Richard Holford of Westonbyrt Papers, Gloucestershire CRO
Holmes, *Augustan England*	Geoffrey Holmes, *Augustan England: Professions, State and Society 1680–1730* (London, 1983)
Hopkinson	Robert Hopkinson, 'Elections in Cumberland and Westmorland 1695–1723', unpublished Ph.D. thesis, Newcastle Upon Tyne University, 1973
Howard	Fielding Correspondence, Howard Papers, Norfolk CRO
Isham Papers	Archives of the Ishams of Lamport Hall, Northamptonshire CRO
Kerridge, *Trade and Banking*	Eric Kerridge, *Trade and Banking in Early Modern England* (Manchester, 1988)
Kishlansky	Mark A. Kishlansky, *Parliamentary Selection: Social and Political Choice in Early Modern England* (Cambridge, 1986)
Leconfield	Archives of Lord Leconfield, Cockermouth Castle muniments (obtainable through Cumbria CRO (Carlisle))
Leveson-Gower	Archives of the Duke of Sutherland (Leveson-Gower), Staffordshire CRO (Stafford), (for Lord Gower)
Lonsdale D/Lons	Archives of the Earl of Lonsdale, Cumbria CRO (Carlisle)
Lonsdale D/Lons/W	Lonsdale Archives, Lowther of Whitehaven branch
Lonsdale D/Lons/L	Lonsdale Archives, Lowther of Lowther branch
Lowther Correspondence	D. R. Hainsworth, ed., *The Correspondence of Sir John Lowther of Whitehaven 1693–1698: a Provincial Community in Wartime*, Documents in Social and Economic History, n.s. vol. 7 (British Academy, 1983)
Musgrave	Musgrave of Edenhall Archives, Cumbria CRO (Carlisle)

Nicholas	Nicholas Family Papers, John Rylands Library, Manchester
North	North Family Papers, Bodleian Library, Oxford
Northampton (Warwickshire)	Marquis of Northampton Archives, Warwickshire Estate Correspondence, Castle Ashby (microfilm copy held at Warwickshire CRO)
NRST	*Northamptonshire Record Society Transactions*
Paget	Papers of Lord Paget of Beaudesert, Marquess of Anglesea Archives, Staffordshire CRO
Portland (Newcastle)	Duke of Newcastle Papers in the Archives of the Duke of Portland, Nottingham University Library
Radnor	Ashe Family Papers, Radnor Archives, Wiltshire CRO
RHST	*Royal Historical Society Transactions*
Richards, 'The Land Agent'	Eric Richards, 'The Land Agent' in G. E. Mingay, ed., *The Victorian Countryside* (London, 1981)
Sackville	Sackville of Knole Papers (including Earls of Middlesex and Dorset and Countess of Bath), Kent CRO (Maidstone)
Savile	Papers of the first Marquess of Halifax and of Sir George Savile, bart., Nottinghamshire CRO
Stone, *Crisis*	Lawrence Stone, *The Crisis of the Aristocracy 1558–1641* (Oxford, 1965)
Thirsk, *Agrarian History* 4	Joan Thirsk, ed., *The Agrarian History of England and Wales*, vol. 4, *1500–1640*
Thirsk, *Agrarian History* 5	Joan Thirsk, ed., *The Agrarian History of England and Wales*, vol. 5, *Agrarian Change 1640–1750* (Cambridge, 1985)
Thynne, Longleat	Archives of the Marquess of Bath, Longleat
Trevor	Trevor of Glynde Papers, Clwyd CRO (Hawarden)
TSAS	*Transactions of the Shropshire Archaeological Society*

Turner, 'Northampton Estates'	H. D. Turner, 'George, fourth Earl of Northampton: Estates and Stewards 1686–1714', *Northamptonshire Past and Present*, vol. 4, (1966–7)
Wordie, *Estate Management*	J. R. Wordie, *Estate Management in Eighteenth Century England: the Building of the Leveson-Gower Fortune* (London, 1982)
Wynn Papers	*Calendar of the Wynn (of Gwydir) Papers* (Aberystwyth, 1926)

Introduction

'tis a great trust

Sir Henry Parker, 1693

Seventeenth-century England can be seen as a series of distinct, although overlapping, structures. The central structure of the government and the legislature overlapped the structure which consisted of a patchwork of counties and their governments. In turn these structures are overlapped by a third for the realm can also be perceived as an array of towns and villages directly or indirectly connecting with one disproportionately large city, London. Yet another structure was the church with its dioceses and hierarchies, its jurisdictions and its complex patchwork of lands and livings. There was a further underlying structure of great significance: England was made up of landed estates, predominantly owned by the nobility, the gentry, the church and the Crown.[1] These estates were omnipresent. They were not confined to the countryside for they penetrated into every borough and town and, indeed, into the very capital itself. English society was composed of landlords and tenants, and some English landholders were both. It naturally follows that one cannot understand the workings of English society without studying the relationships between landlords and tenants. At the interface between them stood one man whose activities were of crucial importance to both: the estate steward.

Stewards make useful witnesses for modern historians because of two characteristics shared by many landowners among the nobility and greater gentry: absenteeism and an insatiable curiosity about the estates from which they were absent. For a Sir John Lowther of Whitehaven, a Lord Fitzwilliam of Milton, a Lord Weymouth of Longleat, absence of body did not imply absence of mind. For the men who were charged with caring for the estate few matters were considered too trivial to draw to the attention of the most august of landlords. Nor need they fear rebuke for troubling him

---

[1] Three other groups of landlords were smaller but still significant: the Oxford and Cambridge colleges, the great London companies and the endowed grammar schools.

1

with trifles. It is true the curiosity and concern of landlords varied widely. There was a vast difference in the degrees of concern for their estates and the region in which they stood between a Fitzwilliam or a Lowther, both of whose concern with local detail was limitless, and that unamiable employer, the second Viscount Cholmondeley, whose mind seems to have been dominated by the fruits of his estate, the shortcomings of his servants and the management of his racehorses. Nevertheless the difference is more of degree than kind. The social or economic historian will still find the near 2,000 surviving letters Cholmondeley sent to his chief steward an invaluable resource, whilst the mere handful of his steward's letters which have survived from the hundreds the steward must have written can only lead us to contemplate wistfully the great archive that might have been. In general stewards were likely to be rebuked if they sent less than a letter a week, and even then could be rebuked if they were less detailed than their masters deemed appropriate. It was in no way remarkable for the new steward of Longleat to promise his kinsman-employer that he would not fail to 'give an account of your affairs here' by 'the return of every carrier (and oftener if occasion be)'.[2]

It naturally follows that the survivors from the constant flow of letters the stewards wrote can provide historians with a window on provincial society, a society which included about 90 per cent of all English people, and no other provincial source which historians could study is quite as rich in detail or all embracing in subject matter.[3] The historian of the nineteenth century can turn to a much wider and diverse array of sources, including, of course, the numerous body of provincial newspapers. The historian of provincial France can turn to the detailed and conscientious reports of an army of officials, especially the intendants in their provinces during the *Ancien Régime*, and the prefects in their departments throughout the nineteenth century. For the historian of seventeenth-century England such sources are lacking, and the reports of stewards, however variable in quality, however fragmentary or haphazard their survival, assume great significance. It is the purpose of this book to examine the role and activities of the steward in some detail, not primarily in order to understand how seventeenth-century estates were managed, but rather in order to increase our understanding of the workings of seventeenth-century society. The

[2] William Thynne to Sir James Thynne, 27 September 1658, Thynne ix, fo. 47.
[3] The obvious alternative is court records, always a rich source for historians, but court actions possess drawbacks as a source of information about the normal workings of society since, whether at the county or the metropolitan level, they are by their nature exceptional. Most Englishmen and women never saw the inside of a court above the level of a court leet, and a majority of those who did would have only been spectators. Most problems and disputes were solved without litigation. Indeed it was one of the functions of the steward to seek to achieve this.

records they have left to us serve such a purpose admirably. When we read their letters, reports, memoranda and accounts we find ourselves contemplating English society through the eyes of men who were peculiarly well placed to observe that society in action.

The steward's prime function of running an estate, of managing the relations between a landlord and his tenants, together with his second, 'ambassadorial', role of serving as his master's voice, as well as his eyes and ears, in the affairs of the region or county in which the estate stood, gave him a particular significance which was unintended and of which he was probably unaware himself. We cannot understand the workings of English society in the early modern period if we do not understand how the capital interrelated with the local community, politically, administratively, socially, culturally. The estate steward played a crucial role at the interface between the 'Great Society' of metropolitan London and the local community. It was not a role he was employed to play, but rather a role which fell to him because of the unusual position he occupied locally. He was the indispensable link between the small but socially, economically and therefore politically powerful propertied elite, and the rest of society, between the governors and the governed. The steward, therefore, was a 'mediator' in the anthropological sense of the word. He was perfectly placed to act as the vital 'broker' between the metropolitan society with which he was constantly in touch, and the local community in which he lived. Often a man of considerable ability and usually of wide experience, he tended to be more knowledgeable of the world beyond the confines of his region than his neighbours, not least because he was the beneficiary of a flow of intelligence from the capital not merely from his master but also from members of his master's London household, his goldsmith, London lawyer and other metropolitan residents. On the other hand his year-to-year residence in his region, his day-to-day contacts with tenants, neighbouring gentlemen and clergymen, magistrates and lawyers and his frequent visits to its urban centres at times of sessions and assizes, markets, fairs and parliamentary elections, gave him a far wider and yet more detailed knowledge of his provincial fiefdom and the surrounding region than even its owner could possess.

The role of the steward as a 'mediator' between governors and governed, between capital and province, between the 'great society' and the 'popular' culture of the local community, is sometimes explicit but always implicit throughout the following chapters.[4] Here it is only necessary to offer the briefest of summaries. The stewards were the conduit through which flowed from the centre a variety of intelligence concerning national events,

---

[4] For an exploration of the steward's mediating role see Hainsworth, 'The Mediator'.

politics and policies, impending elections, taxation and legislation, whether actual or proposed, the danger of war and the prospect of peace. These wider concerns would form part of a more constant flow of instructions relating directly to the estate: leases, fines, a variety of other tenancy matters, seasoned from time to time with instructions relating to patronage, benevolence and simple charity. In return the steward was a conduit not simply for reports about the estate and requests for instructions and decisions, but also for a flow of intelligence about local reactions to national affairs: legislation, taxation, elections, county and borough politics, wages and prices, natural disasters, the impact of disease or the weather, the problem of the poor. If communities felt moved to draw up and sign a loyal address congratulating the monarch on escaping assassination or on making peace with France, it was often the steward of the district's leading landlord who was asked to transmit it to London. If the community had been sluggish in displaying its loyalty it was the steward, prompted by his master, who stirred its members to action. The role of the steward as his master's 'ambassador' and intelligence gatherer is discussed at length in Chapter 6. All appeals for charity, benevolence, forbearance, a variety of patronage, passed through the conduit of the steward to the landlord, that potent but distant focus of influence. The names of candidates for bedesmen's places, for the occupancy of almshouses, for incumbencies of vicarages, however selected locally, were transmitted by the steward to the landlord and his decisions conveyed by the steward to the beneficiaries and to the community concerned, roles explored in Chapters 8 and 9. The steward even served as the medium by which architectural fashions and horticultural innovations leaped the gulf between capital and province as he supervised the remodelling of his master's mansion or assisted such horticultural and landscaping specialists as London and Wise to develop the mansion's orangeries, gardens and parks, functions discussed in Chapter 13.

His function as the interface between landlord and tenant is explored in detail in Chapter 4. Here it is only necessary to emphasise that this was his chief mediating role. He had to keep his master's lands let. This meant not only that he had to find tenants for vacant farms, since all landlords had a horror of having lands come 'in hand', but had to strive constantly to hang on to good tenants. Since desirable tenants were increasingly scarce in the agriculturally depressed second half of the seventeenth century this was no easy task. The understandable desire of the landlords to see their rents increase was regularly confronted by an equally understandable demand from the tenants that their rents should fall. The steward had the onerous duty of mediating between these and other conflicting claims. He knew his master's lifestyle, indeed his very status, was dependent on his income which must, therefore, be sustained. On the other hand harmony and consensus were more likely to achieve this than confrontation, tenant resistance and, ultimately, abandoned farms. Elsewhere I have described estate stewards in this period as 'governors', not simply in the 'vice-regal' sense but in the sense employed by engineers; that is, devices which operate to smooth out irregularities in the beat of an engine and sustain its smooth, even operation.[5] Without the stewards' constant mediating between otherwise irreconcilable extremes, the mechanisms of English society might have broken down during the period between the Restoration of Charles II and the death of Queen Anne, years marked by frequent wars abroad and agricultural depression and political turmoil at home. On the other hand, the stewards' role as surrogate landlord was of great significance to the nation as a whole. The governing elite of the realm, whether in Parliament, holding the great offices of state, in ambassadorial posts, or in the army or navy, could not have fulfilled that governing function if they had been confined to their estates engrossed with the day-to-day detail of running them. Their stewards set them free to discharge wider, public, responsibilities. How the stewards did this is the concern of the following chapters.

[5] See Hainsworth, 'Essential Governor'.

1

The rise of the estate steward

Land is more precious than to be lost for want of looking after.
Charles Agard, steward, 1659[1]

The estate steward had been a familiar figure in rural England for centuries before the Stuart era saw him rise to a greater prominence. In Ely Cathedral stands a rude stone monument commemorating Ovin, steward to the eighth-century queen, St Etheldreda. Ovin was more likely a household majordomo than an estate administrator, but there is no need to penetrate the gloom of the Dark Ages in search of such shadowy figures. The mediaeval period provides ample evidence of identifiable men pursuing stewardship as a career. In the thirteenth century manuscript texts appeared describing the duties of a manorial steward, notably the anonymous *Seneschaucie*, which covered the duties of all estate servants, while Walter of Henley's *Husbandrie*, although concerned with farming rather than the techniques of estate management, appears to have found its audience in part among stewards. Many other texts 'were reference books of experienced estate stewards who probably acted as teachers in their profession'.[2] Lay stewards and bailiffs became a feature of monastic estates during this century, partly as a result of the injunctions issued by Archbishop Peckham who was determined that monks should not live outside their monasteries. However, this was a great age of demesne farming, and with the decline of demesne farming later in the mediaeval period the popularity of these texts declined and it may be that the office of steward became less significant.[3] Nevertheless the office survived. In fourteenth-century Gloucestershire several estate stewards prospered to such a degree that they founded gentry families of their own, whilst during the same century men who were already

---

[1] To the Earl of Dorset, 1 December 1659, Sackville U269/C63.
[2] Dorothea Oschinsky, 'Mediaeval Treatises on Estate Management', *Econ. HR*, 2nd ser., vol. 8, no. 3 (1956) (hereafter Oschinsky, 'Mediaeval Treatises'), 308. For a fuller discussion of these texts, together with the edited texts themselves, see Oschinsky, *Walter of Henley and Other Treatises on Estate Management and Accounting* (Oxford, 1971).
[3] Oschinsky, 'Mediaeval Treatises', 304, 309.

6

members of gentry families served as steward for manors of the Duchy of Lancaster.[4] In fifteenth-century Norfolk a socially less-distinguished steward, Richard Calle, had the audacity to aspire to marry his master's daughter, and Margaret Paston had so little regard for filial piety that she defied her parent's strenuous objections to the match – a melodrama familiar to readers of the Paston letters.[5]

Misalliances aside, there can be no doubt that some men had found in stewardship a career open to talent earlier than the early modern period. Such opportunities must have expanded after the English Reformation with the acquisition of substantial but scattered monastic estates by the laity and the Crown. Sir Thomas Thynne, whose harsh, not to say brutal, acquisitive features gaze sombrely down on us from the wall of his elaborate and beautiful mansion, Longleat, seems to have used his position as steward to the Earl of Hertford (subsequently Protector Somerset) to found the fortunes of a gentry family which subsequently entered the nobility.[6] The fact that at least 190 Members of the Parliaments of Elizabeth I had been, still were or were destined to become stewards is an indication not simply that in the sixteenth century stewardship was a respectable calling, but that it could be a means of climbing the ladder of degree.[7] The status of the steward naturally varied with the status of his master. Men of humbler station served landlords of humbler status and performed a more restricted range of duties. Nevertheless, during the first decades of the Stuart era some stewards at least can be observed discharging wide responsibilities on behalf of absentee landlords. Examples would include Richard Marris on the Yorkshire estates of the first Earl of Strafford or even earlier that notable antiquarian John Smyth of Nibley, the long-serving estate steward of the Lords of Berkeley, and in less exalted station such men as Thomas Crewe and his successor John Peck supervising the Denbighshire and Flintshire estates of Sir John Trevor, or William Vernon at Rufford serving Sir George Savile.

In summary then, the full-blown estate steward discharging wide and varied responsibilities who was a conspicuous figure in every shire during

---

[4] Nigel Saul, *Knights and Esquires: the Gloucestershire Gentry in the Fourteenth Century* (Oxford, 1981), 64 ff.; Michael J. Bennett, *Community, Class and Careerism: Cheshire and Lancashire Society in the Age of Sir Gawain and the Greene Knight* (Cambridge, 1983), 72–3.

[5] H. S. Bennett, *The Pastons and Their England*, 2nd edn (Cambridge, 1968), 42–6.

[6] Thynne died in 1580. His great-grandson, Sir Thomas Thynne, who inherited Longleat on the death of a cousin, was raised to a viscountcy by Charles II in 1682.

[7] Some of this 190 were undoubtedly stewards-of-courts (for the latter see below), not estate stewards, but it is difficult to disentangle the two from the source used (particularly as some men almost certainly were both). However, courtiers and officials holding Crown sinecures have been excluded; based on *The History of Parliament: the House of Commons 1558–1603*, ed. W. Hasler, 3 vols. (London, 1981).

the later Stuart period, had already emerged during the sixteenth century and was becoming more numerous before the Civil War. Nevertheless as a feature of the provincial landscape he does not seem to have seized upon the imaginations of contemporary writers – certainly not of those who produced the fashionable 'character books'. Of the seventy-seven essays in John Earles's *Micro-cosmographie* (c. 1627) not one is devoted to the estate steward, and other similar works are equally silent.[8] Perhaps as a consequence of this neglect by contemporaries he has met with a similar neglect from historians, even those devoted to the study of English social and economic life in the early modern period. It may be significant that historians have paid far greater attention to the sixty or seventy years prior to the Restoration of Charles II than they have to the sixty years succeeding it, and the former is much less rich in steward records than the latter. This may have contributed to the tendency among modern historians to consider the steward as only emerging as a significant professional functionary during the eighteenth century. A pioneering historian of the professions in England has observed that stewards 'had staked their claim to professional standing' by 1730 and that landowners during the first half of the eighteenth century who possessed large or scattered or potentially rich estates 'discovered' that they needed full-time salaried agents to tend them. 'By the beginning of George II's reign they had become an accepted part of the landed community in every part of England.'[9] This summarises the process well but places it too late. The statement would be more accurate if James II or even Charles II were substituted for George II, while 'discover' is hardly appropriate to a situation with which the grandfathers and great-grandfathers of early Georgian landowners had been equally familiar. There has been a tendency to consider stewards in the seventeenth century as little more than rent collectors. Professor Clay has asserted that it was in the eighteenth century that stewards acquired the skills of surveyors, a knowledge of land law, and acquired the technical skills needed to improve their masters' estates through various forms of agricultural innovation.[10] Clay has also observed that the movement towards 'ring fence' estates owed a good deal to 'the increasing professionalization of estate administration as the period wore on' and 'the increasing tendency to employ the modern type of land steward, who saw his task not just as that of a mere rent collector but as an active manager whose business it was to improve his employer's property to the utmost'.[11] Again he appears to be referring to

---

[8] Interestingly, of the 1,000 or so titles drawn from the Elizabethan and early Stuart periods and printed in facsimile in *The English Experience* series, not one is specifically devoted to the duties of a steward. See further my essay 'Estate Steward'.

[9] Holmes, *Augustan England*, 24.

[10] Christopher Clay, 'The Management of Estates', in Thirsk, *Agrarian History*, 5(ii) 243.

[11] Thirsk, *Agrarian History*, 5(ii) 180.

the period 1720–50, and even beyond, rather than the period 1660–1720. If by 'improve' he refers to 'agricultural innovation' then this time frame is no doubt well judged. Historians who examine the records which stewards left behind them during the seventeenth century will find scant evidence that they were involved in agricultural improvement. This is hardly surprising since many of the improvements in agricultural practice were not discovered until the eighteenth century, and the vast majority of their masters were not themselves involved in farming or even stock rearing. It would be a mistake, however, to assume that a lack of technical expertise in improved agricultural methods inevitably downgraded or restricted the significance of stewards and their functions.[12] As to surveying, stewards had an increasing body of surveyors to call in at need (when they were not expert surveyors themselves as was Lord Cholmondeley's William Adams), and where their knowledge of the land law did not stretch or could not be augmented by their master's library, they could mobilise their master's local lawyer or have their master take counsel's advice in London, and they often did. At least as early as the second half of the Stuart period men with wide knowledge, great experience and a determination to expand and develop the resources of the estates entrusted to their care can be found across the English shires. Any implication that in the seventeenth century stewards were confined to routine tenant concerns like collecting rents and fines and negotiating leases is mistaken, as this and the succeeding chapters seek to demonstrate. Professor Beckett has written that 'in the world of 1660 the chief management tasks involved collecting rents and overseeing established farming methods'.[13] In fact the chief management tasks then and for years after would have involved struggling to keep old tenants and finding new ones, and few stewards whose records I have examined devoted their time to overseeing farming methods other than to police the provisions of the tenants' leases relating to care of the soil's fertility. Certainly the duties of the steward were passing through a gradual evolutionary process during the seventeenth century, probably most clearly observable in the activities of stewards as election agents, and certainly the degree of professionalism and the variety of functions and responsibilities varied widely from steward to steward and estate to estate. It is the contribution of the stewards on the more complex estates to the rich texture of provincial life which this work will particularly examine. Whilst emphasising that eighteenth-century stewards discharged a variety of functions Professor

---

[12] Joan Thirsk has identified stewards as influencing the more positive attitude to their estates which landowners displayed as early as the later seventeenth century. Thirsk, 'Large Estates and Small Holdings in England', in P. Gunst and T. Hoffman, eds., *Large Estates and Small Holdings in the Middle Ages and Modern Times* (Budapest, 1982), 74.

[13] Beckett, *Aristocracy in England*, 142.

Beckett has observed that 'despite their acknowledged importance rela-
tively little is known about individual eighteenth century stewards'. This
statement would be even more appropriate if it was applied to seventeenth-
century stewards.[14] This neglect has been unfortunate because the steward
played a rich variety of roles which took him into practically every aspect of
provincial life, not simply in the rural areas where his prime responsibilities
lay, but also into every country town.

As an occupation of profit and some prestige the office of estate steward
was familiar enough to rural society in early modern England, and certainly
well before the Civil War. The word steward had in fact already three
different meanings, denoting different, although sometimes overlapping,
functions: household steward, steward-of-courts and estate steward. In
noble families since at least mediaeval times 'steward' had been the title
given to the officer charged with the responsibility of organising and
administering the lord's household. It was in large households an onerous
but very prestigious position, sometimes occupied by a kinsman of the lord,
often by a member of a gentry family. Households were often peripatetic
between castles and mansions standing on widely separated estates. The
steward moved with, or ahead of his master, setting up the household in
whichever of his centres of authority the lord chose to spend the succeeding
weeks. A typical household steward was Sir Henry Heydon (obit 1503) the
son of a prominent lawyer with estates at Heydon and Baconsthorpe,
Norfolk, who was steward to the household of Cecilia, widow of Richard,
Duke of York.[15] When a lord became accustomed to dividing his time
between one rural estate and a town house in London, and particularly
when the latter became his established base with only occasional, if regular,
rural visits, the structure of his household inevitably changed. London
households were more expensive to maintain for much of the goods and
services, and especially food, which sustained them had to be purchased.
The size of the lord's 'family' diminished because fewer servants were
employed. The significance of the household steward correspondingly
shrank. He was, indeed, during the succeeding centuries to decline in status
and significance to that plebeian if imposing majordomo, the Victorian

[14] John Beckett, 'Estate Management in Eighteenth Century England: the Lowther–Spedding
relationship in Cumberland', in J. Chartres and D. Hey, eds., *Land and Society* (Cambridge, 1990), 56, 57. I am indebted to Professor Beckett for his kindness in sending me a
copy of this article. Professor Clay wrote his invaluable two-volume synthesis of English
economic life during the period 1500–1700 without any reference to estate stewards
significant enough to bring them to the attention of the index. This is in no sense a
criticism. Works of synthesis cannot synthesise what has not been done as this writer
discovered early in this project (see Preface above). C. G. A. Clay, *Economic Expansion
and Social Change: England 1500–1700*, 2 vols. (Cambridge, 1984).

[15] See entry in *DNB*.

butler. This declension was aided by a second factor. Rural households shrink even when the lord was long in residence on his estates. The profitable leasing of the demesne lands, often including the very 'home farm' which stood close to the major house, encouraged a marked reduction in household size, as no doubt did the increasing tendency to convert a varied range of feudal obligations and payments in produce to payments in cash. As we shall see these household changes had their effect on the position, status and functions of the estate steward.

The office of steward-of-courts was destined to last much longer, indeed as long as manorial courts survived.[16] His modern equivalent or descendant is the retained lawyer of an estate, whether the estate be controlled by a magnate, a company or a board of trustees. The mediaeval steward was expected to possess legal knowledge, and significantly thirteenth-century treatises on estate management are normally found bound with legal treatises. Indeed 'it is certain that by the end of the thirteenth century estate stewards on large manorial estates were trained lawyers.'[17] In the seventeenth century a steward-of-courts similarly looked after the legal business of the estate, appearing on its behalf in the county court or at assizes, engrossing leases, suing recalcitrant tenants and tradesmen or encroaching neighbours, but in addition he presided over the courts leet and courts baron of the manor. The estate steward would always be present at meetings of the manorial courts and usually kept a record of the proceedings. If the estate steward was himself a lawyer then he would usually combine both functions as William Gilpin did at St Bees-Whitehaven for Sir John Lowther from 1693 to 1698.[18] After Gilpin ceased to look after the day-to-day running of the estate, confining himself to such larger roles as maintaining the Lowther political 'interest' and serving as the estate's lawyer he was replaced by a man of lesser status who was not a lawyer and so Gilpin, who had moved to his home, Scaleby Castle, near Carlisle, regularly rode over to Whitehaven to keep Lowther's courts.[19] Gilpin's predecessor, Thomas Tickell, who served as steward from 1666 until his death in 1692 was not a lawyer and usually had either Lowther's brother-in-law, Richard Lamplugh of Ribton (a local squire with legal training) or

---

16 Much information on stewards-of-courts is to be found in C. W. Brooks' invaluable monograph *Pettifoggers and Vipers of the Commonwealth: the Lower Branch of the Legal Profession in Early Modern England* (Cambridge, 1986), although Dr Brooks tends not to distinguish between estate stewards and stewards-of-courts if lawyers (or the same lawyer) discharged both functions.

17 'The development of law under Edward I made it essential for stewards and bailiffs to have a good legal education, or else for lords to appoint professional lawyers if they were engaged in litigation'. Oschinsky, 'Mediaeval Treatises', 302, see also 300–1.

18 Although the previous steward-of-courts, lawyer Ewan Christian of Unerigg insisted on Lowther's sending a formal discharge. *Lowther Correspondence*, 13.

19 *Lowther Correspondence*, 'Epilogue', 661.

some Cumbrian solicitor to preside on court day. In theory Tickell could hold courts without a lawyer present for at an unknown date, but probably about 1680, Lowther copied into a notebook an undated appointment of James Bird, a Westmorland lawyer, and Thomas Tickell 'jointly and each of them severally stewards and steward of all ... my courts, as well leet as baron', with authority 'jointly or severally' to summon and hold them. However, St Bees-Whitehaven was remote, was in 1680 an estate of modest size, and Lowther probably simply wanted to ensure that his courts were kept without being interrupted simply because on some occasion a formally qualified lawyer could not attend them. In practice men with legal training regularly attended, although Tickell was always present in court and the court record is uniformly in his handwriting throughout his stewardship.[20] The majority of estate stewards were not lawyers, however, and to be a steward-of-courts was simply a branch of normal legal business. Many London-based lawyers fulfilled this function, at least for manors in the Home Counties. Further afield lawyers who divided their time between local practice and the London courts appeared for their local magnates. Lord Cholmondeley's chief steward, William Adams, regularly feed a leading Cheshire lawyer, Sir Francis Manley, to keep his master's courts at Nantwich, Malpas and Bickley for a fee of £10.

If during the seventeenth century the relationship between estate stewards and stewards-of-courts was normally one of either harmonious co-operation or combination of roles, the connection between estate stewards and household stewards was more like that between two men on a see-saw. As the position of the household steward declined – the very title becoming almost extinct – the position of the estate steward correspondingly rose. Stewards who in earlier days might have been mere rent collectors and seekers after tenants, usually combined with a supervisory function over the operations of the demesne farm, were now transformed into officials charged with supervising increasingly elaborate estates whose function was to sustain their master's status, and, if their masters were politically active, their public careers. Moreover, the steward at the principal estate of a nobleman or gentleman possessed of several scattered estates would find himself transformed into a 'chief steward', that is, one responsible for overseeing and instructing, albeit at a distance, the activities of 'understewards'. Good examples of such men in the latter half of the seventeenth century are William Adams for Viscount Cholmondeley, Andrew Clayton at Welbeck for the Duke of Newcastle and James Whildon at Chatsworth for the Duke of Devonshire. However, the most potent influence on the emergence of the steward as a man of diverse and

---

[20] See Lonsdale, D/Lons/W, Commonplace Books (list 5), Untitled Notebook, c. 1661–1680s
D/Lons/W1/30, fo. 30; D/Lons/W, St Bees Court Book.

far-reaching responsibilities was the increasing absenteeism of his master. Estate stewardship as a complex and highly responsible function evolved slowly over time. No revolutionary shift is suggested here. Nevertheless, increased absenteeism amongst a whole class, the nobility and greater gentry, would greatly affect the institution of stewardship not only in its day-to-day functioning and responsibilities but in its perception by others. When the lord was resident on his estates the estate steward was an 'adjutant'. When the lord was absent the steward became a 'viceroy'. He was then a surrogate lord, feared, resented, courted, closely observed, a man who could influence the opinions of others merely by confiding his own. The prolonged absence of the lord enhanced the status of the steward in the eyes of his neighbours, even though, *au fond*, that status was governed by the status of his employer. Like the moon he shone by reflected light, and the moon is most imposing when the sun is absent. When his lord appeared on the estate his own light correspondingly dimmed.

Just such a shift in the pattern of residence and absenteeism appears to have occurred about the time of the Restoration of Charles II in 1660. Landlords during the second half of the seventeenth century spent much more time in London than had their fathers and grandfathers. London had served as a magnet for the nobility long before the Civil War.[21] Indeed Charles I had sought to inhibit absenteeism by ordering landlords back to their estates and heavily fining the disobedient. It is a measure of the shift in practice and opinion after 1660 that such a policy would not only have been considered impractical under the later Stuart kings, it would have been deemed unthinkable. After 1660 long and regular Parliaments, the growth of the public service, the navy and the army, the steadily growing significance of London as a marriage market, a financial market, a land market and in general as a social and economic focus for the governing class, together with the lure of the law term, all combined to persuade great and moderate-sized landlords to occupy London lodgings for a portion of each year, and for some to rent, purchase or build permanent town houses.[22] Their absenteeism thus became a permanent part of their way of life, and this threw a heavier burden of responsibility on the shoulders of their rural surrogates, the estate stewards. It may well be that the dislo-

---

[21] During the reign of Elizabeth, however, courtiers tended to leave their wives to manage their estates in rural obscurity while they sought influence and the rewards of office at court, Hainsworth, 'Essential Governor', 359.

[22] See F. J. Fisher, 'The Development of London as a Centre of Conspicuous Consumption in the Sixteenth and Seventeenth Centuries', *RHST*, 4th ser., vol. 30 (1948), reprinted in E. M. Carus-Wilson, ed., *Essays in Economic History*, ii (London, 1966). For a useful corrective to the idea that a majority of the gentry regularly visited London before the Civil War, see Alan Everitt, *Change in the Provinces: the Seventeenth Century* (Leicester, 1969) and his 'The County Community' in E. W. Ives, ed., *The English Revolution 1600–1660* (London, 1968).

cations of the Civil War, with parliamentary landlords during it and exiled Royalists after it cut off from their estates for years at a time, may have given stewards substantial experience of discharging their responsibilities with little direction from their employers. However, for every landlord cut off from his estate by his service in the Long Parliament or the Parliamentary armies, there must have been another confined to his estate by the inaccessibility of London for landlords with Royalist sympathies. After the Restoration London was open to all and very large numbers of English landowners took full advantage of this opportunity. Some came initially to make their peace with the new regime, some came to seek compensation for heavy losses suffered in the Royalist cause, some simply to attend Parliament, some to seek profitable places for their sons or suitable husbands for their daughters, some to please their wives and some to please themselves, but whatever their motives come they did and in numbers never seen before. In 1669 Samuel Pepys, that inveterate Londoner, found himself conversing with a country gentleman, one of a small party enjoying the hospitality of Lord Crew. Referring to the supposed menace of London and its expensive temptations to county families, the gentleman quoted 'the old rule' that a family might survive 50 miles from London for a century. If situated 100 miles from London it might survive two centuries, 'and so, farther or nearer London, more or less years'. The gentleman also told the party that he 'hath heard his father say that in his time' (that is, before the Civil War) 'it was so rare for a country gentleman to come to London that when he did come, he used to make his will before he set out'.[23]

The new habit of London residence, once acquired, became settled for many of them. Their periods of residence became regular and for longer periods of each year. Some backwoodsmen, usually for reasons of economy, never acquired the habit, preferring to shun London throughout their mature lives, as did the Westmorland squire Sir Daniel Fleming of Rydal Hall. However, an equally extreme example on the other side is provided by Sir Daniel's kinsman and friend Sir John Lowther of Whitehaven, a permanent London resident who only visited his Cumberland estates during nine years within a period of thirty-two years.[24] Nor was this freakish. Sir Joseph Ashe of Waghn, Yorkshire, who was also lord-farmer of Downton, near Salisbury, under the Bishop of Winchester,

---

[23] *The Diary of Samuel Pepys*, ed. Phillip Latham and William Matthews, vol. 9 (London, 1976), 550.

[24] In 1666, 1670, 1675, 1676, 1678, 1679, 1682, 1685, 1687 and then finally and permanently in 1698. Even this final 'retirement' was unplanned and involuntary. His poor health never permitted a return to London. (The visits amounted to eleven since he visited twice in 1675 and 1679.) The paucity of his visits is all the more striking since he was Member for Cumberland in every Parliament elected during those years. See *Lowther Correspondence*, xviii, note 21.

seems to have visited these widely separated estates rarely, preferring to live in his mansion at Twickenham. Lord Cholmondeley usually found time to visit his Cheshire estates during the summer, but his visits were often brief and by no means invariable, whilst Lord Fitzwilliam left his mansion, Milton, abandoned to the care of his steward, his housekeeper and his chaplain for years at a time.[25] Thus while there were still stewards who were 'adjutants', closely under their master's eye and there to transmit his orders to the other estate servants and to the tenants, as John Banks was to Sir Daniel Fleming, the 'viceroy' steward became a familiar figure, busily about his absent master's affairs in every English shire.

It was not just the magnet of London which ensured that the absenteeism of landlords would persist, become indeed a commonplace of provincial life. Landowners continued to own and acquire estates widely scattered across different counties. Out of a total of £14,636 worth of land which Sir Harbottle Grimstone purchased in Essex between 1631 and 1646 £12,176 worth was acquired from absentee landlords. Much of this absenteeism was probably due to residence on chief estates elsewhere rather than to residence in London. Grimstone himself had his principal estate in Hertfordshire, and it is true that in the 1650s he sold off part of his Essex lands but this was at the dictates of financial exigency, not from a desire to consolidate his holdings into one county. After he became Master of the Rolls during Charles II's reign, and thus more affluent, he began buying land in Essex once more as well as around his Hertfordshire 'head quarters', and once again the sellers were absentee landlords.[26] Lord Cholmondeley's chief estate was centred on an old half-timbered mansion, Cholmondeley, in Cheshire but he also owned properties in Shropshire, Flintshire and Somerset. Through his wife Lord Fitzwilliam, whose chief estates were in the Soke of Peterborough, was landlord of modest but substantial estates in Norfolk. George Compton, fourth Earl of Northampton, in 1681 inherited major estates in Warwickshire based on the old Tudor mansion of Compton Wynyates in addition to his chief holdings based on Castle Ashby, Northamptonshire. He also possessed an estate in Somersetshire and lesser but still substantial properties in four other counties.[27] When Lord Cavendish employed William Senior, one of the earliest professional surveyors, to compile a complete account of his estates in 1609, an account which enumerated every house, field, tenement and

[25] For the latter see *Fitzwilliam Correspondence*. Fitzwilliam planned to come down virtually every summer after 1687 but did not do so until 1709.

[26] Christopher Clay, 'Two Families and Their Estates: the Grimstones and the Cowpers from c1650 to c1815' (unpublished Ph.D. thesis, University of Cambridge, 1966), 5, 11–13.

[27] Three of the latter, however, did not come to him until he inherited the jointure estates of his mother. They were in Middlesex, Huntingdonshire and Buckinghamshire. Turner, 'Northampton Estates', 97.

occupant, Senior found the estates comprised some ninety-seven manors covering about 100,000 acres of which only fifty-seven were in Derbyshire, the remainder being scattered among at least twelve other counties.[28] Subsequently, through purchase, marriage settlements and the vagaries of inheritance these ancestral estates of the Duke of Devonshire were still further augmented. The Savile estates, much expanded by the first Marquis of Halifax, included besides the 'headquarters' estate of Rufford, Nottinghamshire, properties in Lincolnshire and vast holdings in the West Riding of Yorkshire. The estates of the Duke of Newcastle were no less scattered.

Nor were scattered estates confined to the nobility. Sir Thomas Thynne held estates which were ample enough to sustain a peer's rank years before Charles II ennobled him as first Viscount Weymouth in 1682. By inheritance, purchase and marriage Thynne acquired estates in Gloucestershire (Kempsford), Shropshire (Caus Castle-Minsterley and Church and Little Stretton) Warwickshire (Drayton and Tamworth), Herefordshire (Ross-on-Wye), Staffordshire, and in Ireland. On the unexpected death of a childless cousin, Thomas Thynne, who was murdered by Count Koenigsmark, he inherited the chief Thynne estate in the West Country based on Longleat. Spending much of his time in London, making Longleat his rural base, Weymouth rarely visited his other estates. Rather he relied on the regular letters and annual accounts of an array of stewards whose detailed reports are now invaluable to social, economic and political historians.[29] Weymouth's brother-in-law, Sir John Lowther of Lowther, ennobled in 1696 as Viscount Lonsdale, had inherited substantial properties in Westmorland, Cumberland, Yorkshire, Lancashire and the bishopric of Durham from his grandfather and acquired others by lease or by purchase further south. Yet his grandfather, a professional lawyer in his youth, had only been a baronet, and that reluctantly.[30] Such examples could be adduced indefinitely. The point is that such properties needed permanently resident stewards to run them, for their owners were always absent from some of

[28] Yorkshire, Lincolnshire, Lancashire, Nottinghamshire, Leicestershire, Staffordshire, Suffolk, Buckinghamshire and one each in Gloucestershire, Somerset, Hertfordshire and Huntingdonshire. George R. Potter, 'A Note on the Devonshire Papers at Chatsworth House, Derbyshire', *SAJ*, vol. 4, no. 2 (1970), 127.

[29] These letters, held in the muniments at Longleat, are now available to historians on commercially marketed microfilm.

[30] He was 'persuaded' to purchase it for more than £800 by the government of Charles I. A similar fate befell his younger brother Christopher, originally trained to be a merchant, the father of Sir John Lowther of Whitehaven. For the Lowthers see D. R. Hainsworth, ed., *Commercial Papers of Sir Christopher Lowther 1611–1644* and C. B. Phillips, ed., *Lowther Family Estate Books 1617–1675*, respectively vols. 189 and 191 of *Surtees Society Soc. Trans.* (Durham, 1974, 1976–7); *Lowther Correspondence*, Introduction, *passim*; J. V. Beckett, *Coal and Tobacco: the Lowthers and the Economic Development of West Cumberland, 1660–1760* (Cambridge, 1981); Hugh Owen, *The Lowther Family* (Chichester, 1990).

them, and indeed, since the mediaeval custom of progressing from one property to another at different seasons of the year had long been abandoned, they were permanently absent from some of them. This perpetual absence was sometimes disquieting to their stewards judging from their occasionally frantic, always eloquent pleas for them to pay a visit. 'It would be better with us here if your lordship were not so great a stranger to ... [your] Shropshire concerns' writes Samuel Peers plaintively to Lord Weymouth from Minsterley in 1686. 'Besides I fear the distance makes [you] quite forget us and some of your own interest too'.[31] He urged in vain but his fear was groundless. Weymouth was a typical seventeenth-century landowner for whom absence of body did not mean absence of mind.

I have already sought to distinguish between estate stewards, household stewards and stewards of courts. Before considering the manner of men landlords chose to be their estate stewards, and the responsibilities they shouldered, there are further distinctions to draw. These lie between stewards, 'understewards' and bailiffs. There were many different kinds of estate steward in the seventeenth century. Terms like 'steward' and 'bailiff' were used very loosely by contemporaries, which makes classification difficult, and so does the fact that such positions shaded into one another. Grey areas abound. The unambiguous distinctions defined by orders of rank, as in a modern army, are quite absent. The historian, therefore, has to define his terms yet remain well aware that the definitions he is using would not necessarily have been recognised by the men he is writing about, although the distinctions he draws between degrees of status and responsibility undoubtedly would. However, a useful distinction can be drawn if we confine the use here of 'bailiff' to a minor estate official who was responsible for collecting rents and other payments and for ensuring that persons who ought to appear at the manorial courts actually did so. This was essentially a part-time job, indeed only a 'fractional' appointment. A classic example of such an official was Lancelot Branthwaite of Whitehaven whose principal day-to-day occupation was 'bankman' at Sir John Lowther's chief colliery. A bankman was a type of undermanager responsible for the surface operations of the pit, and particularly the bank of coal beside the pithead. With this full-time job Branthwaite combined the position of bailiff of St Bees manor of which the township of Whitehaven formed a part, collecting rents at quarter days and dues from stall-holders on market days, and presenting tenants on court days. The office brought him a stipend of £2 a year. For these duties his immediate superior was the estate steward.[32] For his duties at the colliery his immediate superior was

---

[31] Thynne xxii, fo. 290.   [32] *Lowther Correspondence*, see p. 672.

Lowther's colliery manager, himself a species of steward, although of a distinctive and uncommon type. Lowther himself would have recognised the distinction drawn here between 'steward' and 'bailiff' for when he drew up the articles of appointment of a local attorney, George Fothergill, as steward of his small outlying manor of Waitby, Westmorland, while referring to Fothergill as 'steward' he specifically authorised him to appoint 'a fit and convenient person to be bailiff'.[33] By 'convenient' Lowther probably meant a man who either lived on or close to the manor, and by 'fit' a man of good reputation and sufficient substance to be entrusted with the collection of his master's rents, and perhaps possessed of the ability to keep a primitive account.

'Understewards', a term only rarely employed by contemporaries, were sometimes called 'bailiffs', sometimes 'stewards' by their employers. Essentially they were men charged with the responsibility of looking after an outlying estate, or a portion of a very large estate, under the overall supervision of a chief steward who was based at the administrative centre of his master's principal estate. Thomas Whitehead, understeward of certain manors in Northumberland for his master, the Duke of Newcastle, in the 1660s might write an occasional letter to his employer but normally would have communicated with and through Andrew Clayton, the chief steward who resided in his master's mansion, Welbeck Abbey, Nottinghamshire.[34] The same relationship can be discerned in the letters of the Reverend William Eratt, understeward of at least one of the Duke of Devonshire's Yorkshire properties, to James Whildon, steward at Chatsworth.[35] The estates of Lord Cholmondeley in the north west together with his distant Somerset outlyer were largely administered by understewards who were responsible for specific rent collections but the overall supervision of the estate, including the Somerset manor, was under the overall direction of the chief steward, William Adams, at Cholmondeley Hall. The term 'bailiff' was sometimes applied to stewards of small estates, men earning perhaps £10 or £20 a year, and who usually combined this function with yeoman farming or a career as a country attorney, as also to stewards of the individual members of widely scattered estates who were not responsible to a chief steward because their master did not choose to have one, preferring to rely on some London-based receiver to gather in the threads. The stewards of the Earl of Dorset, like Charles Agard in Warwickshire, Edward Raynes at Lewes and Christopher Smith at Buckhurst were functionaries of this more modest type.[36]

---

[33] Memoranda Books, Untitled Notebook 1661–1680s, Lonsdale D/Lons/W1/30, fo. 25.
[34] For a collection of Clayton's in-letters from both tenants and understewards see the file of Clayton correspondence, Portland Pw1.
[35] For Whildon correspondence, see Devonshire, E. xlviii.
[36] See Sackville U269, various bundles.

A further type of steward worth noting briefly was the 'amateur' steward. The 'amateurs' were men who played the part of stewards, usually on behalf of institutions but occasionally on behalf of ordinary landowners, but appear to have received no official appointment or stipend. A good example is the Reverend Jonathan Bernard, vicar of Ospringe, Kent, who frequently played a steward's role on behalf of St John's College, Cambridge. A former fellow of the college he had been appointed to his living by the master and fellows, probably at the time of his marriage, and laboured mightily on behalf of those he considered his patrons. Some of his letters are preserved in the college archives and show him seeking tenants, negotiating the renewal of leases, and finding purchasers of timber from college woods within Ospringe manor. After one such successful sale of timber the college senior bursar, who was in effect the college's estate steward, begged his 'acceptance of a guinea for a pair of gloves'. Bernard declined this tactfully phrased offer, remarking that 'as I expected none, so I desire no reward for any service done to the college . . . and do assure you I shall be always ready to serve you'. However, it is soon clear that Bernard has in mind a different recompense for his efforts for in a postscript he observes that he has a fourteen-year-old son he intends for the university 'but by reason of my poverty can only enter him as a sizar'. Bernard asks whether he may hope for a proper sizar's place, an exhibition or any other help from the society. He particularly wishes that his son may be accepted into the master's service. This patronage for his son he successfully achieved two years later.[37]

Another amateur was also a clergyman, the Reverend Charles Usher of Kirkandrews-on-Esk, Cumberland, who seems to have been an unpaid over steward to Sir Richard Grahame of Netherby. Grahame had a paid steward, but Usher seems to have supervised his activities during Grahame's protracted absences.[38] Similarly at Lamport Hall, Northamptonshire, the Reverend Richard Richardson, vicar of Brixworth and chaplain to the Ishams of Lamport, and Gilbert Clerk, scholar and mathematician, together kept an eye on the activities of the Ishams' estate steward, John Chapman, when first Sir Thomas Isham and then his younger brother and heir Sir Justinian Isham were successively in Italy on the 'Grand Tour'. Clerk especially reported regularly and at length on estate affairs, awarding praise or blame to the steward according to his estimate of the effectiveness of Chapman's efforts. Chapman himself was something of an anachronism.

[37] Archives of St John's College, Cambridge, Series D, Letters 1 to 40, and for quotations letters 12 (16 July 1706) and 1 (2 August 1706); see also Henry Fraser Howard, *The Finances of St John's College, Cambridge, 1511–1926* (Cambridge, 1935), 11.
[38] See a group of uncatalogued estate letters at Netherby Hall, Cumbria written during the 1670s.

Called 'the bailiff' or even the 'baillie' by his employers, a word one would expect to find employed in seventeenth-century Scotland rather than North-amptonshire, he seemed to have played the role of an old-fashioned steward running the demesne farm and stocking his master's lands with cattle for commercial sale rather than seeking tenants for the Leicestershire and Northamptonshire lands. The first Sir Justinian Isham (1611–75), his origi-nal employer, had at times complained that keeping lands in hand was proving less profitable than letting them, and after his death Clerk made similar complaints of Chapman's overstocking, keeping lands in hand and dilatoriness in finding tenants. Clerk's regular reports to his patron abroad provide much fascinating detail about the problems of running an estate during the later Stuart era.[39] However, Clerk and Richardson were observers and reporters, not as actively engaged in the running of an estate as was Usher or even Bernard. They only fulfilled one of the steward's functions: to serve as a conduit for intelligence and advice.

Sir Henry Parker, deputy lieutenant of Warwickshire to the Earl of Northampton, was more actively engaged in stewardship than any of the preceding amateurs, at least during 1693. In that year Northampton parted with the unsatisfactory steward of his Warwickshire estates around Compton Wynyates. He was 'between stewards' for several months until a replacement could be found and Parker, his close friend and confidant, diligently filled the breach. As his letters show Parker sought tenants, negotiated leases, disentangled the old steward's affairs from those of Northampton, sought out and interviewed potential stewards on his friend's behalf. It is significant that a Warwickshire squire with concerns of his own, an active county MP and important member of the county government should have found nothing demeaning, or indeed remarkable, in fulfilling the role of an estate steward, albeit temporary and amateur, during that busy summer. Parker kept a wary eye on his friend's Warwick-shire concerns even when Northampton had a professional steward manag-ing the estate.[40]

However, the most striking of all the 'amateurs' encountered in this study must be Archdeacon John Gery of Swepston, a village close to Ashby de la Zouch and to Donnington Park, both Leicestershire estates of the Earls of Huntingdon. Gery served as an overall steward to Theophilus Hastings, seventh Earl of Huntingdon, from at least the mid 1670s to at least the late 1680s as is shown by their extensive correspondence during

---

[39] See Sir Gyles Isham's introduction to *The Diary of Thomas Isham of Lamport 1671–1673* (London, 1971), especially pp. 20–1, and the estate correspondence in the Isham Papers, particularly Isham IC 659, 1178.

[40] Turner, 'Northampton estates', 100 and note; for Parker's letters, Northampton (War-wickshire).

that period. Huntingdon appears to have regarded Gery as a friend rather than a servant and they paid overnight visits to each other's residences. Mrs Gery, assisted by a wetnurse, cared for the Huntingdons' baby daughter, Lucy, at Swepston until she was weaned. It is unlikely that Gery received a regular salary, but could always count on Huntingdon's patronage in his clerical career, while his role as Huntingdon's spokesman locally and especially in Leicester doubtless rendered him a powerful figure in his region. Probably Gery considered these indirect and psychic rewards recompense enough. Nevertheless, the tasks he carried out for his exalted friend were those of a more conventional steward. In just one letter Huntingdon asks the archdeacon to investigate a tenancy in which he is convinced a tenant's death has been concealed by the other lessees and to instruct his salaried steward at Ashby, Jaquis, in the matter; he is to ensure Jaquis hastens up an account of workmen rebuilding a weir; he is to oversee the drawing up of a contract for certain workmen to build the Lough-borough Market House and send it up for Huntingdon to take legal advice on in London; he is asked to supervise the 'covering' of Huntingdon's mares at Donnington; he is asked to 'speak effectually' to a debtor who owes £50 and whose only 'pretence' for not repaying it when due was Huntingdon's lack of the security which was in the archdeacon's hands; he must check if Mrs Harvey has quitted all the Huntingdon lands she formerly held; he must pay the vicar and churchwardens of Ashby a legacy of £10 bequeathed by Huntingdon's sister, Christiana, to the poor there, Huntingdon enclosing a form of acquittance for Gery to copy out for them to sign; he is to inform a tenant that Huntingdon dislikes his intention of using a house as a barn which would spoil it as a dwelling; and when the archdeacon next passes Donnington Park his lordship wishes to know how many of the new-planted trees flourish and how many are dead. This seems a formidable list of tasks for a cleric who was no more than an amateur steward, particularly when Huntingdon had a professional steward on the ground. However, the burden was discharged without complaint and probably, judging by Gery's performance on other occasions, with speed and efficiency.[41] These were minor matters, however, compared with the delicate and important negotiations concerning the surrender of Leicester's borough charter to the king and Huntingdon's securing of the coveted position of Recorder which he was to entrust to the archdeacon later that year.[42]

In brief, therefore, the term 'steward' during the seventeenth century did not describe or define a very distinct, precise type of official in the way that we might expect. Most were professionals in the sense that they were

[41] Huntingdon to Archdeacon Gery, 22 May 1684, Hastings HA6030.
[42] See below Chapter 6.

salaried but some were amateurs. Some were totally committed to their duties, some combined them with other careers. However, the stewards and their careers as stewards must now be considered in more detail.

2

The steward's career

'tis a great trust, and a man of temper, with abilities and good experience will be of
great service to your lordship's estate and interest.

Sir Henry Parker to the Earl of Northampton, 1693[1]

[I] hope as I am willing to show myself a gentleman towards you in all my actions,
so you [will] give a testimony you love a gentleman's interest more than the clowns'

Viscount Cholmondeley of Kells to William Adams, 1679[2]

If absenteeism persuaded more and more landowners to entrust their estates
to stewards, rather than relying on 'mere' bailiffs or rent-collecting
managers of the home farm, in what manner of men did they choose to
place their trust? Once appointed, stewards, as we have seen, enjoyed a
social status which reflected their employer's rank. As one steward, after
successfully negotiating the release of an estate servant from the press gang,
succinctly expressed it to his master: he had observed 'much respect to you
and to me for your sake'.[3] Inevitably the steward of a senior nobleman
carried far more weight than the steward of a mere gentleman or even a
baronet, however wealthy. Nevertheless the men who were employed had
their own status before they were hired. In general it can be said that
landowners sought men of substance, education and experience drawn
from the ranks of gentlemen, or at least from the substantial yeomanry.
Professor Holmes has observed that 'a hallmark of the professional man in
eighteenth century England was that he was entitled to nothing less than the
prefix "Mr", and that, in favourable circumstances, he might enjoy the
rank of "esquire" or at least rough parity with esquires'.[4] This attempt to
pinpoint the professional man socially does not work for the seventeenth-
century estate steward, certainly in the second half of the century. Few
physicians and even fewer schoolmasters, academics and clergymen could

---

[1] Referring to the Compton Wynyates estate, Warwickshire; 3 September 1693, Northampton (Warwickshire).
[2] 18 November 1679, Cholmondeley DCH K/3/1.
[3] Samuel Wood to Sir John Trevor, 25 March 1639, Trevor D/G/3276.
[4] Holmes, *Augustan England*, 9.

claim 'rough parity' with esquires, and few stewards of large estates could not. As for the prefix 'Mr', a mere bailiff whose only duty was to present tenants at his master's court and collect rents might aspire to that modest distinction, although not all would achieve it.

Nevertheless it is true that stewards came from a broad range of social backgrounds. Former army officers, younger sons of the gentry, traders in provincial towns, yeomen farmers, county attorneys, sons or nephews of retired or deceased stewards who had 'inherited' the office, men whose fathers or at least grandfathers might have been 'simple', men whose grand-fathers might have been noblemen, can all be found managing estates of varying size and complexity. The more exalted the rank of the landlord, however, the more exalted was likely to be the social background of the steward. It is not surprising that landowners should prefer gentlemen when they were seeking stewards. A gentleman, preferably one who was himself a landlord, was much to be preferred to a man who was only a tenant. Tenants might be too sympathetic to the interests of tenants if those inter-ests were their own, and, as local men, would be too much subject to peer pressure from their neighbours. A landowner-steward, however modest his own estate, would tend to share the interests of his employer. This point of view was expressed with brutal clarity by the first Viscount Cholmondeley of Kells when in 1679 he appointed William Adams to be the chief steward of his estates, which were mainly in Cheshire. There must have been an interregnum between stewards at Cholmondeley and the viscount had been compelled to run his estate through understewards each of whom was responsible for only a portion of it, and who, perforce, reported directly to their master in London. These understewards, termed 'bailiffs' by Chol-mondeley, were not gentlemen of property but substantial tenants with the interests of tenants. Some months after Adams's appointment Cholmon-deley wrote to him remarking that he hoped that as he was willing to show himself a gentleman towards Adams in all his actions, so Adams would demonstrate that he loved a gentleman's interest more than that of 'the clowns'.[5] This broad hint was made even more explicit eleven days later when Cholmondeley explained that when he had delegated the fixing of rents to the 'bailiffs' they had 'effected to beat down' the value of his estate, and not improve it, 'being against their interest', but he expected better from Adams who as a gentleman would 'effect the gentlemen's interest' and scorn that of the 'clowns'.[6] No doubt Cholmondeley's confidence that Adams shared his own attitude toward the interests of landlords and tenants was soundly based. A member of an armigerous family in Shropshire Adams owned a small estate at Longdon worth about £300 a year.

---

[5] See footnote 2 above.   [6] 29 November 1679, Cholmondeley DCH/K/3/3.

Sometimes a steward might not only be a gentleman but even a kinsman of his master, as were Charles Agard, steward of Croxall, Derbyshire, for the Earl of Dorset and his brother Francis who served in Dorset's London household, probably as a receiver. A member of a Derbyshire gentry family Charles Agard was dismissed by his master after many years' service but in his last full year at Croxall, when relations were already becoming soured, Dorset appealed to his steward in terms of his status as well as his kinship, writing that he did not believe Agard had committed any 'wilful fault' for he knew him to be 'too much a gentleman to deceive any man's trust' to whom he was 'so nearly related'.[7] Gentlemen stewards were not exceptional on the Sackville estates. A collection of letters of attorney to stewards shows that on the Sussex estates gentlemen were the rule not the exception.[8] Similarly Francis Guybon (pronounced 'Gibbon'), the long-serving steward of Lord Fitzwilliam, was a member of an armigerous Norfolk family.[9] For several years Lord Weymouth's steward at Drayton, near Tamworth, Staffordshire, was a Captain Morgan Powell, who appears to have been a former army officer and a member of a minor gentry family from the Welsh Marches. Powell was one of the two 'bailiffs' of Tamworth who were joint mayors of the borough and a power at parliamentary elections. Weymouth gradually grew to distrust Powell and replaced him in 1688 with John Mainewaring, who was not only a gentleman but was probably a member of the Shropshire family of Mainewaring or Mainwaring who were kinsmen of the Thynnes.[10] As a kinsman-steward Mainewaring was not unusual on the Thynne estates. Thomas Hawkes, steward of Weymouth's estates about Church Stretton, Shropshire, was a close relative of his master, being the nephew of John Thynne of Egham, Surrey, and Inworth, Essex (whose marriage to the daughter of Sir Henry Mainwaring of Ightfield, Shropshire, is one of the family connections between the Thynnes and the Mainwarings.) In 1658 Sir James Thynne of Longleat appointed William Thynne, most probably a younger son of a cadet branch of his family, to be chief steward of his West Country estates.[11]

[7] Dorset to Agard, 28 September 1675, Sackville U269/C64.

[8] To 'Robert Brookes of Marsfield ... gentleman' (1657), to 'Nicholas Cheesman of Framfield ... gent.' (1661), to 'John Raynes of Lewes ... gentleman' (1671), Sackville U269/E154.

[9] For the Guybon pedigree see G. H. Dashwood, ed., *Visitation of Norfolk*, pt 1, Norfolk and Norwich Archaeological Society, 178–89; for Guybon's career, see *Fitzwilliam Correspondence*, Introduction.

[10] At the time of his appointment he had already served Weymouth for at least three years for his earliest surviving letter is dated 1685. The superseded Powell, a dedicated Jacobite, was a thorn in the side of Weymouth in Tamworth's turbulent, factional politics until the Revolution of 1688 reduced him to political impotence. For Powell's letters to Weymouth as steward, Thynne xxviii. See also *Commons 1660–1690*, vol. 1, 390–2; and Chapter 7 below.

[11] Hawkes had served Weymouth's father, Sir Henry Frederick Thynne, before him. The letters to Weymouth cover the period 1671–93 and are chiefly in Thynne xx–xxiii, *passim*.

Not only noblemen employed gentlemen stewards. Indeed not only noblemen employed kinsmen. Charles Leigh, a Warwickshire squire, thanked his brother-in-law, Sir Justinian Isham of Lamport, for recommending a potential steward, a Mr Farrington, but apologetically observed that while he had also heard well of Farrington from Warwickshire neighbours, there was 'a very deserving brother to that most disconsolate family of my Cousin Littleton's to whom I could not deny my stewardship there'.[12] Sir John Lowther of Whitehaven employed only two estate stewards between 1666 and 1698 although he also successively employed several colliery stewards. The first, Thomas Tickell, who served from 1666 until his death in 1692 was a member of a family of very borderline gentility, although he served as a Royalist officer during the Civil War. His uncle, Richard Tickell, with two Cumbrian associates, was a partner with London merchants in a lead mine in the Vale of Newlands, with Thomas apparently employed in the company since his signature occurs on documents associated with it. Richard Tickell described himself in lead-mine agreements as 'of Cockermouth, gentleman', although his two Cumbrian associates were 'yeomen'.[13] Tickell, although he at one time operated his own small coal mine during his stewardship and had interests in shipping, was a tenant of one of his master's farms. It is perhaps significant of his comparatively modest status that at one time he begged unsuccessfully for a maid's place for one of his daughters with Lady Lowther, although his two sons were clergymen, as was a son-in-law. Lowther always used his influence where possible to further the interests of his steward and of his progeny. Nevertheless there is little evidence of affection or regard in Lowther's letters to his long-serving steward, rather an icy detachment which chills the reader even today. By contrast Tickell's successor William Gilpin was a member of an old Westmorland family, as was Lowther himself although his 'clan' was incomparably wealthier, and all gentry families in what is now Cumbria tended to be interrelated. Gilpin was a practising lawyer with a public appointment as 'Steward of their Majesties' Courts Upon the Borders' when Lowther first persuaded him to take up the stewardship of the St Bees-Whitehaven estate, and had had experience as a Crown prosecutor at Carlisle assizes. Writing to Gilpin about an unsuccessful attempt to exercise patronage on Gilpin's behalf, Lowther remarks that he will leave no stone unturned since delays and disappointments 'cannot be more your trouble

---

William Thynne appears to have served for more than twenty years, and was finally 'inherited' by Lord Weymouth. See his letters, Thynne ix (for Sir James) and xx (for Weymouth) *passim*.

[12] Leigh to Isham, 1673, Isham IC 797.

[13] The mine was leased from the Earl of Northumberland during the late 1640s. See Newlands (Goldscope) lead-mine papers in the Northumberland (West Cumberland) estate papers, Leconfield D/Lec/81.

than mine' for without Gilpin's entitlement to Lowther's efforts as a servant, he might claim on his '*own account* and upon the ancient respect' Lowther had always had for Gilpin's father for what he was able to do.[14] Lowther's 'ancient respect' for Gilpin's father is a trifle odd for the elder Gilpin had been on the opposite side in the Civil War to Lowther's own father, was a puritan clergyman with the temerity to refuse a bishopric from Charles II, partly it is said, because his grandfather had similarly refused Elizabeth I, preferring to go off to Newcastle to operate an illegal dissenting conventicle. However, Gilpin senior had purchased the manor of Scaleby Castle in the 1650s from a kinsman who was a sequestrated cavalier and thus Lowther's steward was heir to a moderately valuable landed estate.[15]

While gentility was a prized quality in the steward of a substantial estate it was not of itself a qualification. Landlords sought men of experience and knowledge. A young gentleman with little more experience of life than that attained at the gaming table, in the hunting field or the fencing academy was hardly to be entrusted with an estate which might yield several thousands of pounds a year from rents, dues, and the profits of its forests and other capital assets. It was a characteristic of stewards that they had usually had experience in other kinds of business. As we have seen some were lawyers like William Gilpin. Some were farmers on a substantial scale. Gervas Jaquis who was steward to the Earl of Huntingdon at Donnington, had been a maltster and a substantial farmer until he abandoned those occupations to serve the Hastings family full time.[16] Some had military experience, others were or had been surveyors. Others had been involved in such varied enterprises as mining or milling or commerce. William Adams owned a small estate but had been a leading surveyor in his region, one of his clients being Sir Thomas Thynne, the future Lord Weymouth, before his appointment as Lord Cholmondeley's steward in 1679.[17] The chief steward of Lord Gower at Trentham, Staffordshire, for many years was a clergyman, the Reverend George Plaxton.[18] Tickell, apart from his military and lead-mining experience had been a customs officer at Newcastle before the Civil War. The steward of the Wiltshire estates of New

---

[14] My emphasis. *Lowther Correspondence*, 431. Lowther's correspondence with Tickell between 1666 and early 1692, is remarkably complete and amounts to more than 1,800 items. Lonsdale D/Lons/W2/1/1–27.

[15] See William Jackson, ed., *Memoirs of Dr Richard Gilpin* by Reverend William Gilpin, CWAAS (1879) and DNB, 'Richard Gilpin.'

[16] See Jaquis to Huntingdon, 29 January 1684, Hastings HA7732.

[17] For Adams as surveyor see E. G. R. Taylor, *The Mathematical Practitioners of Tudor and Stuart England* (Cambridge, 1970), 276. He almost certainly continued to practise as surveyor at least in a restricted way after his appointment.

[18] See his letters in Leveson-Gower.

College, Oxford, was also the Chancellor of the diocese of Salisbury.[19] Some were attractive to their new employers because they had already accumulated experience as stewards to other landowners, and some even served more than one master at a time. William Elmsall had served Lady Frances Leicester of Tabley, Cheshire, for her Yorkshire manors near Pontefract, and at the time of his appointment as chief steward of the Yorkshire estates of Sir George Savile was still responsible for the Yorkshire affairs, chiefly mining royalties, of the Duke of Leeds.[20] The qualifications looked for in stewards were also sought in men appointed as understewards. When one of Lord Cholmondeley's understewards died suddenly in 1706 a cousin of William Adams, the chief steward, wrote at once to recommend his son-in-law, who was 'a very ingenious young man in business, bred up at London with a money scrivenor and a merchant'. He had lately managed a copper mill which was now 'at a stand for want of ore'.[21]

On very many estates, indeed all of any substance, wide experience was not simply desirable, it was essential. Estate management was England's largest collective business and it extended its tentacles into most industrial and commercial undertakings: mining, quarrying, flour-milling, fulling-milling, forestry, wool and textiles, urban house-building, moneylending, draining of marshes and other forms of land reclamation, and even ship-owning, shipbuilding and trading voyages. Stewards also had an important role as the ambassadors of their absentee masters, maintaining good relations with sometimes powerful neighbours, preserving networks of friendship and interest, and thereby playing a crucial role in county and borough parliamentary elections in which they often functioned as election agents.[22] Moreover, it was one of their functions, where possible, to oversee the expansion of the estate through the purchase of neighbouring properties. All decisions to purchase new ground, however small its dimensions, were always made by the master, but he relied heavily on his steward's reports and advice before taking the plunge, and he was utterly reliant on his steward's capacity to persuade his neighbours to sell desirable properties to improve the estate, and to sell them at prices the master would consider appropriate. It required experienced men possessed of managerial skills and judgment to discharge these increasingly complex responsibili-

---

[19] His name was Spencer. Henry Parker to the Earl of Northampton, 5 May 1694, Northampton (Warwickshire).

[20] Elmsall to Savile, 15 April 1711, Savile DDSR/211/2. For the Leicester appointment see the Leicester of Tabley Papers, Correspondence, John Rylands Library, Manchester University.

[21] Chrisopher Adams to William Adams, 26 October 1706, Cholmondeley DCH/L/29.

[22] All these functions are analysed in detail in later chapters.

ties. The estates about Compton Wynyates in rural Warwickshire seem to have been reasonably straightforward, but Sir Henry Parker had no doubt what kind of man was needed to manage them. Writing to his friend Northampton he observed that many would desire the post and apply to be Northampton's servant, but it was 'a great trust' and needed 'a man of temper, with abilities and good experience' for such a man would be of great service to Northampton's 'estate and interest'.[23]

Men who were experienced, knowledgeable, with a head for business as well as conscientious and honest, not surprisingly, were hard to find. The death of a steward in office was often succeeded by a period of some months before a permanent replacement could be found. As a result landlords did not part with their stewards for light cause. On the other hand, stewards did not move from employer to employer. It was common for a steward to spend the whole of his career with the same lord, or at least the same family. Thomas Tickell's quarter century with Sir John Lowther was not exceptional, nor was the fact that he died in his service. Mr Caudle's twenty-two year stewardship at Horsford, Norfolk, for Dacre Barrett was only ended by his death in 1719.[24] Guybon, aged and enfeebled, died in Fitzwilliam's service in 1710 after thirty-two years' service, and seems to have served Lady Fitzwilliam's uncle before him, so that his career must have lasted about fifty years.[25] Similarly Gervas Jaquis served the Hastings, Earls of Huntingdon, for more than forty years.[26] William Elmsall of Thornhill discharged the complex and onerous duty of chief steward of Sir George Savile's Yorkshire estates for more than thirty years. Thomas Smith cared for Savile's Nottinghamshire and Lincolnshire estates, together with smaller holdings in Shropshire, for a similar period. Charles Agard appears to have served Lord Dorset for more than thirty-five years before his dismissal in 1676. Agard's earliest surviving letter is dated 1645, but in 1671 he refers to his service to Dorset and his father as stretching over '30 and more years' and in 1673 implied in a letter to the Countess of Dorset that he had succeeded his 'Uncle Curzon' who died in 1639.[27] Similarly

23 See footnote 1 above.

24 Letters of Robert Britiffe to Dacre Barrett, Barrett-Lennard D/DL C3/10 and C3/29.

25 Guybon was described as 'of Setchey, gentleman' in a power of attorney dated 1663 which empowered him to act for Sir John Cremer to recover certain debts. Cremer was Lady Fitzwilliam's uncle, and Fitzwilliam may well have 'inherited' Guybon as steward of Setchey when Lady Fitzwilliam inherited the manor at her uncle's death. See Fitzwilliam, Misc. Papers F(M)C 1035, and Introduction to *Fitzwilliam Correspondence*.

26 'I am sorry to find that after more than forty years service (in your most noble family) I should lie under such severe censures.' Jaquis to Huntingdon, 8 September 1685, Hastings HA7758.

27 31 July 1671, 30 July 1673, Sackville U269/C63.

Robert Hawdon, the steward of Milcott, Warwickshire, had already served the Earl of Middlesex almost a quarter century in 1645.[28]

Stewards did occasionally retire but when they did they were usually of great age, and too enfeebled or physically handicapped to carry on. William Atkinson, steward of Sir John Lowther of Lowther, the uncle of Lowther of Whitehaven, was 'inherited' by Lowther's grandson, the future Viscount Lonsdale, along with the estate. Subsequently Atkinson did retire, full of years and crippled, probably by arthritis, but even in his eighties was occasionally consulted by the family or his successor on matters relating to events dating from his early years which nobody but himself could remember. Moreover, if stewards were disinclined to leave their master's service, it was rare for masters to send them packing. In general stewards found their masters swift to chide and slow to bless but for all their grumbles very reluctant to dismiss them. Deliberate dishonesty flagrantly revealed, disputes about arrears of rent alleged to have been paid to the steward but withheld from the lord, long-running disputes about accounts, could, as in Agard's case, lead to dismissal but this was surprisingly rare.[29] The Earl of Thanet was greatly dissatisfied with his steward at Appleby, Thomas Carleton, blaming him for the low rents on the estate there among others things, but shrank from dismissing him for at least seven years until he finally took the plunge in 1723.[30] Otherwise disputes between lord and steward were restricted to rebukes, sometimes tactfully, sometimes abusively expressed, on the part of the employer and to plaintive but respectful defences on the part of the steward.[31] Stewards and lords, once reasonably suited, clung tightly and clung long.

Why lords wanted stewards is no mystery, particularly those who intended to be long absent from their estates or only seasonal visitors to them. It is pertinent to ask, however, why did the stewards become stewards and why did they devote their lives to the occupation? There can be no doubt that stewardship of a valuable estate was considered to be a plum appointment. In 1651 Ellis Lloyd, a Welshman of armigerous family, was jubilant at the prospect of obtaining 'a very good place as a steward to a gentleman of £4,000 or £5,000 per annum'.[32] Security of employment, security of status,

---

[28] 'I have received . . . that sad message of the loss of your dear father, and my good lord and master, to whose commands (I bless God I can truly say) for this 24 years I have been faithfully obedient.' Hawdon to Middlesex, 28 August 1645, Sackville U269/E249.

[29] Lord Dorset also dismissed Arthur Walker, his chief steward of the Sussex estates, in April 1673 for being found 'faulty in some accounts of my rents to me'. Stewards Appointments, etc., Sackville U269/E154.

[30] Beckett, *Aristocracy in England*, 154.

[31] The relationship between lords and stewards is examined in Chapter 14 below.

[32] Lloyd observed that he would be holding the place already but that he 'wanted money' to set himself up 'in such equipage' as was necessary for such an employment, and urged his

an assured income, the inducements were an interesting blend of psychic and financial rewards. It has to be admitted that both forms of reward are difficult to assess today. The psychic rewards of being a steward to a wealthy gentleman, and especially of being chief steward to a wealthy peer or to a baronet whose estates were as vast as were Sir George Savile's must have been very real. The steward was not simply his lord's agent in a purely day-to-day business sense but his ambassador to his region.[33] The more wealthy and influential his master, the more he was courted by local gentry, clergy, substantial yeomen, members of borough corporations and indeed anybody with a local axe to grind or a favour to ask. In a great age of patronage he was recognised as a conduit to a potential fountain of patronage.[34] As we have seen, his own status in the region was enhanced by the status of his employer. In an era dominated by rank these were potent rewards indeed.

It might be thought the financial rewards were much easier to assess, since the salaries paid to stewards frequently appear in stewards' annual accounts of receipts and disbursements and sometimes in the lord's instructions to stewards set down at the time of or shortly after their appointment. In fact it is impossible to say what financial rewards stewards received for their labours, for we can be sure that the salary they received was only a fraction of it. Mere collectors of rents, bailiffs in fact, were paid no more than £2 or £3 a year. The salaries of stewards were more substantial but varied greatly. Lord Dorset paid the stewards of his Sussex estates no more than £15 a year. From his appointment in 1679 William Adams received £100 a year from two successive Lords Cholmondeley. Sir John Lowther of Whitehaven originally paid Tickell £20 a year but, fearing that his steward might leave him and recognising that the salary was inadequate for so onerous a position, he subsequently doubled it to £40. Tickell's successor, Gilpin, despite his slightly higher social status and legal qualifications, received the same salary, as did Fitzwilliam's Guybon. In fact £40 was a very common salary for a chief steward in this period. In general the salaries of stewards seem niggardly, and it is difficult to believe that they would have been eagerly sought, in spite of the psychic rewards already referred to, if there had not been other financial inducements. All stewards enjoyed various perquisites, including a range of fees paid at the engrossing

---

half-brother to do his utmost to help him accomplish this 'not inconsiderable employment'. In fact he was never destined to secure it. A law student at the outbreak of the Civil War, Lloyd had served as a Royalist officer under Sir Ralph Hopton. Lloyd to Richard Griffith, 3 April 1651, B. E. Howells, ed., *A Calendar of Letters Relating to North Wales 1533–1700*, University of Wales History and Law Series, vol. 23 (Cardiff, 1967), 101.

[33] See below Chapter 6.

[34] For a discussion of the steward's role as such a 'conduit' see Hainsworth, 'The Mediator'.

of leases, the receiving of 'fines', at the transfer of a tenancy from a deceased father to his son, and so on. Although a feed lawyer usually conducted the manorial court the steward was responsible for summoning the court and the ordinary working of the court and fees associated with such working usually fell to him. Other stewards might be rewarded by the lease of a farm at a favourable rental which might be operated as a commercial farm by the steward or his family, as Thomas Tickell did near Whitehaven, or might be sublet on terms favourable to himself. Somewhat beyond our period the Earl of Cardigan franked letters written by his steward, Daniel Eaton, to his sister to relieve her of the burden of paying postage, and provided a rent-free cottage for Eaton's widowed mother.[35] These perquisites were all legitimate because the landlord knew of them and indeed had consented to them.

There were others much more dubious which usually we can only guess at simply because they were matters about which the steward would never inform his master. If the steward was a mediator between the local region and his absent master, and if, because of that influential position, he was a conduit to patronage in an age when patronage was vital to the well-being of many, it would have been remarkable if supplicants had not sought to buy the steward's favour. However, evidence for such greasing of the wheels of patronage is hard to come by and this is scarcely surprising. The steward would have taken care to keep such payments from his master's notice, and it is the correspondence of masters and stewards, and the stewards' accounts, which constitute the chief archival source for steward activities. Nevertheless, where a steward's in-letters have survived occasionally we receive a hint. When the Reverend Samuel Caldecott of Sutton sought the help of the Duke of Newcastle's chief steward, Andrew Clayton, to have himself transferred to a more comfortable parish from one in which the congregation was 'so infected with presbytery that a man cannot fix the least point of honesty or humanity upon them' he concluded his letter with the carefully worded promise that 'my care shall be that you shall never repent of your so doing'. Less discreetly ambiguous was a gentleman seeking a lease three years later who bluntly offered cash to the steward 'or a good gelding to the value of it'.[36] These perquisites could better be described as 'semi-illicit' rather than illicit because the landlord must have assumed that such *douceurs* were commonplace and would only have troubled himself about them if they adversely affected his own interests. It was perhaps this semi-illicit type of perquisite which William Elmsall had

---

[35] Beckett, *Aristocracy in England*, 153.
[36] Caldecott to Clayton, 1662, Portland Pwl 434; William Meynell of Bradley to Clayton, 24 January 1665, Pwl 468.

in mind when he assured his new employer, Sir George Savile that he would 'eschew' all perquisites as 'pernicious'.[37]

There were undoubtedly other sources of illicit income which masters most certainly would not wink at, and which were sometimes betrayed to them by other estate servants, who were determined to accomplish a steward's removal, perhaps because of jealousy for his privileges or because he bore too heavily upon them when they sought to exploit the estate to their own advantage in petty ways. One of these was for the steward to agist cattle or horses on his master's park for his own profit, often to the detriment of the deer it was intended to sustain. This was an accusation levelled at Captain Morgan Powell by his enemies on the Drayton Bassett estate.[38] Another would have been to persuade his master by some deceitful argument to lower rents, or at least not raise them, at the renewal or issue of leases in return for a bribe from incoming tenants. A sudden and unexpected change of stewards could inadvertently flush out illicit perquisites. Sir John Lowther had long grumbled about the costs of operating the horse-drawn gin which pumped out his chief coal mine, and of which Thomas Tickell had held the contract. Shortly after William Gilpin had replaced his deceased predecessor he found himself in a fierce dispute with Lowther's colliery steward, John Gale, as to who was entitled to 'inherit' this lucrative contract. In pressing his claim to his distant master Gilpin assured him that if he did not the inhabitants of Whitehaven would believe his master esteemed him less highly than his predecessor in not allowing him the same valuable perquisite. This ingenuous letter only confirmed Lowther's suspicions that he had been cheated on the gin contract all along. This perquisite was worth about £50, or at least that was what Gilpin expected would be saved when his wrathful master replied demanding that the gin contract in future be let to the lowest bidder.[39]

Probably the commonest as well as one of the most valuable perquisites possessed by stewards (and for that matter, by many understewards and bailiffs) was the fact that in an era of very low liquidity they held in their hands substantial sums of money, sometimes for weeks or even months at a time, and rarely was this money allowed to gather dust while in their possession. It is significant that in their accounts stewards showed sums of money received by their master as a 'debit', sums expended by their master, or on his behalf, are shown as a 'credit'. This apparent paradox is easily resolved when one realises that a steward's accounts were viewed as *his*

[37] This, however, was in 1711 when salaries were improving. Elmsall to Savile 15 April 1711, Savile DDSR/211/2.
[38] See Morgan Powell's letters to Lord Weymouth 1687–8, Thynne xxviii, *passim*.
[39] Lowther's letter has not survived but its tenor can be deduced from Gilpin's highly embarrassed reply. *Lowther Correspondence*, 27–8.

accounts even when they were devoted entirely to his master's affairs and not intermingled with his own which they sometimes were. Thus income was a 'liability' in the sense that he had to pay the surplus of it to his master, and all outgoings on behalf of the estate were a 'credit' in that they represented sums for which he, and in the event of his death his estate, would not be liable. This accounting practice is symbolic of the fact that all the income of the estate passed through the steward's hands, whether it departed directly to his master's purse in London or to his London gold-smith or whether it went to pay for the multifarious services the estate needed or the expenses it incurred. These expenses were often modest enough, but on particular estates at particular periods, such as during the rebuilding or extending of the mansion, the creation of new gardens or the building or rebuilding of farmhouses and outbuildings, they could be very heavy indeed, and on some estates the expenses could be continuously heavy. For example Sir John Lowther's estate had continuous expenditure on the labour force who extracted the coal underground and on the 'leaders' which bore the coal on their ponies to the waiting ships. Other expenditures at Whitehaven involved millwrights, expert miners brought in to solve particular problems and men involved in capital works for either the town or the port.

Since stewards had to meet all expenses from estate income their dealings with their master's revenue was far from a simple matter of taking in rents, fines and dues and transmitting that money to London. The money was in their control, and substantial sums must have lain on their hands for lengthy periods of time. Skilfully used, money breeds money and there can be little doubt that stewards took what advantage they could of this situation. Charles Agard was dismissed because of disputes about accounts, including rents paid but never either transmitted or satisfactorily accounted for. Lord Dorset was not the only master who felt from time to time that his revenue was not flowing to him down an unimpeded channel. Indeed the second Lord Cholmondeley felt that almost continuously, and his letters are a long, continuous litany of complaints, threats and protest, twice angrily asserting that his chief steward and his minions kept him to the income of 'a squire of no more than £300 a year'. (Cholmondeley was never a master of tact. His chief steward was himself a squire of £300 a year.)

It may be that not all stewards who were suspected by their employers of feathering their own nests by short-term speculations in their master's money actually did so, but some undoubtedly took full advantage of their opportunities. Since such a charge would certainly be vehemently denied by a steward accused of the practice, and his accounts, which were usually audited by the landlord himself, would certainly never betray it, what indications suggest that it ever happened at all? One clear hint is derived from those occasions when a steward or understeward died in office or, for whatever cause, abruptly left his master's service, perhaps summarily dismissed or rendered incapable of service by severe illness or accident. Often the servant died owing his master money. Much to his indignation Lowther suffered setbacks twice with his colliery stewards. The first, Thomas Jackson, was discovered to be heavily in Lowther's debt for the profits of the mines, and other creditors were found to include the coal-miners employed in Lowther's pits, and to such a degree were their wages in arrears that they were behind in their rents to their employer.[40] His successor, Richard Bettesworth, died in office in 1677, also in debt to his master although not on a Jacksonian scale.[41] The chief steward bore the brunt of his master's indignation on both occasions because he had allowed the colliery steward to run so far behind in his payments of the profits of the mines. Certainly Lowther and Tickell, in trying to recover more than £700 of arrears from Jackson, amounting probably to about thirty to thirty-five times his annual salary, found themselves reluctantly but increasingly intertwined in Jackson's own business affairs, which included the management of two colliers in the Irish trade, owning at least half of one of them, a wholly owned vessel and cargo already Virginia bound, and a wholly owned coasting vessel, as large as the 'Virginian', bound from Whitehaven to London. He also leased a coal mine. Certainly Jackson as steward did not let his master's money lie idle in his hands as the harried Tickell comments rather confusedly: ' . . . his humour and temper carrying all trade before him, tempted thereto especially when he hath the command of moneys, and this makes him always poor in purse and in arrear with everybody'.[42] Whether Jackson's use of Lowther's money for his own purposes amounted to embezzlement technically (as the law then stood) is doubtful, but that he had long delayed its payment and profitably misapplied it is certain.[43] Jackson remained in debt to Lowther for many years after he quit, or was dismissed from, his service early in 1675.

Mr Idle, the steward of Lord Gower's Yorkshire estate of Stittenham, the ancient seat of the Gower family but long abandoned in favour of

---

[40] Lowther found this aspect of the crisis peculiarly galling, not least because Tickell, as the overseeing steward, and responsible for all rental accounts, should have spotted this alarming symptom long before. He did not find Tickell's defence that his master should have been able to observe the situation from the regularly dispatched accounts at all persuasive. It was Tickell's duty to remedy the situation, not wait until his master chanced to spot it. Lowther to Tickell, 26 January 1675, Lonsdale D/Lons/W2/1/10. The Jackson affair can be traced in the surviving correspondence from 6 November 1674 to June 1675.

[41] Tickell to Lowther, 12 August 1677, D/Lons/W2/1/12.

[42] Tickell to Lowther, 30 November 1674, D/Lons/W2/1/9.

[43] Tickell refers to Jackson's receipts as 'I fear to[o] much converted to his own use, having lately sent a new ship of about 40 tons and all the cargo on his own account into Virginia.' Tickell to Lowther, 6 November 1674, *ibid.*

Trentham, Staffordshire, died in late December 1707 or early January 1708, at which time he had not returned a penny of Gower's Michaelmas rents, although most had been collected weeks before. He had also failed to pay the half year's rent of £25 on the farm for which he was Gower's tenant. In 'a declining condition' for several years before his death Idle left a personal estate worth less than £500 and bonded debts and other liabilities to about £1,300. It is difficult to believe that he could have become so heavily involved if he had not had both the prestige of being Gower's steward and money constantly in his hands with which to create a deceptive appearance of solvency. William Whytehead, a senior estate servant sent to investigate reported that in 1707 Idle had paid Gower's Lady Day rents with the rents collected for Michaelmas 1706, 'and this has been his practice for several years, always getting what moneys he could of the tenants as soon as the rent day was past and keeping it in his hands to supply his occasions for four or five months after he had received it'. It is clear, incidentally, that Gower had little hope of ever recovering his missing £225. The parson of Bulmer, Idle's home parish, had disingenuously informed Fairfax, Gower's lawyer for the Yorkshire estates, that Idle had died 'in good circumstances' which had lulled him into a sense of false security and bought time which Idle's son, who appeared to have little to learn from his father, usefully employed in driving off all the stock from his father's farm so that Gower could not distrain on it to secure at least part of his missing rents.[44] The correspondence of landlords immured in London is full of complaints about funds too long withheld, with demands that copies be made of account books and sent up so that the beleaguered master could see his financial position with his own eyes.[45] Masters were so conscious of the fact that large sums of money were, at least temporarily, in the hands of their stewards, that it was the usual practice for a steward to sign a bond, backed by 'sufficient' sureties who, at least in theory, would guarantee the master against financial loss. Such bonds often provided only feeble and inade-quate security, however.[46]

The advantage of acting as a temporary 'bank' for his master's money had all the more significance because the nature of the steward's employ-ment ensured that he had profitable affairs of his own to conduct. In a sense all stewards were to some degree part-time employees, although the phrase

[44] William Whytehead to Lord Gower, 24 January 1707, Leveson-Gower D593/Add. 4/1. For a fuller discussion of masters' anxieties about accounts and the stewards' anxiety to have their accounts passed, see below Chapter 14.

[45] Money was bound to lie on the hands of even the most conscientious of stewards because of the practical problems involved in transmitting it to London by 'returns', since there was no banking system, and masters would rarely permit specie to be sent for fear of highwaymen. This problem is examined in Chapter 5 below.

[46] For these bonds and their effectiveness, or lack of it, see below Chapter 14.

would have had no meaning for contemporaries. It is not that stewards as an occupational group were incorrigible 'moonlighters'. Their masters knew they had other sources of income than their bounty, and indeed would not have employed them on any other basis because it meant that as their servants were not wholly dependent on their salaries for their livelihood those salaries need not be overly generous. Conversely a landlord could afford to employ a man to be his representative whose rank, dress and manner of life would require a much larger income than the bare salary he was paying could possibly sustain. As we have seen, some stewards were surveyors and kept up their professional activities, as did those who were lawyers. Others were squires in their own right, some were merchants or shipowners like Thomas Jackson or his successor John Gale at Whitehaven. The steward of Lord Fitzwilliam's Norfolk estates, King, was a substantial yeoman farmer. Stewards, although servants, occupied a privileged position in a landowner's 'family' just because, unlike other household servants, the whole of their time was not at the disposal of their masters. Their duty was to oversee their masters' estates and fulfil a number of duties some of which were specified in their terms of employment and some of which were not, but they were professional men rather than servants in that they decided how they would carry out those duties, when they would do so and, within commonsense limits, how much of their time they would devote to it.

It is significant of the profitable possibilities of stewardship that other men tended to assume that all men who had long been stewards of large estates were men of affluence. This was particularly true of their relatives, and especially those who eagerly awaited the reading of a deceased steward's will. Soon after Francis Guybon's death Lord Fitzwilliam received a letter from Guybon's nephew enquiring about his uncle's financial affairs which referred to the 'expectation of the rest of the relations running pretty high from the common report of my uncle dying very rich'.[47] Sometimes such expectations were grievously disappointed. In 1677 Lowther's collieries steward, Richard Bettesworth, died in his service with his estate encumbered with debts to Lowther for receipts he had failed to surrender to his master's purse. On hearing the news Lowther, with gloomy prescience, predicted that if Bettesworth's debt to him was greater than the £87 of Bettesworth's money he chanced to have in hand he would have no redress at law and if so he would have 'clamour from his relations' who would not believe that 'he could spend his salary much less any of his stock'. Sure enough both Thomas Tickell and Lowther himself found themselves the target of suspicion and resentment, thanks to the disappointed expectations

---

[47] Thomas Guybon to Fitzwilliam, 18 September 1710, Fitzwilliam F(M)C Box 22, Unnumbered Correspondence 1710–44, no. 85.

of the deceased's brother, a London resident who could not be persuaded his brother was not a man of affluence.[48] However, Bettesworth's opportunities for self-enrichment were limited because he was only the colliery steward, and that only from 1675 to 1677.[49] Very different must have been the outcome for any expectant heirs of Richard Beardsley, long the steward of the Warwickshire estates of the Duchess of Somerset. Her lawyer reported after Beardsley's death that it was said the steward 'was worth but £1,000' on entering her employment, and died worth at least £30,000, but 'the man is dead, I shall make no inference'.[50]

In considering the rewards of stewardship there is one which probably loomed very large in the minds of almost all who undertook the position, whether it be the stewards of a group of small manors for a wealthy country squire or the chief steward of a nobleman with scores of manors under his supervision. For that matter it loomed as large in the minds of understewards and even mere bailiffs on a couple of pounds a year for very part-time duties. This was the potent but unpredictable possibility of patronage. All stewards, whatever their rank or salary, whether they commanded many subordinates or none, whether their responsibilities were wide-ranging or restricted, were members of their master's household, of his 'family' as the word was then understood. In an age in which there were no social services to provide a safety net for those who fell from fortune's wheel the members of that privileged group were guaranteed a protection which the less fortunate could rarely hope to achieve. Moreover it was not simply a matter of continuity of employment, housing, diet and so on, desirable though these might be for those with very limited resources outside their employer's bounty, but rather the power and influence which a wealthy noble or gentry landlord could mobilise on behalf of those he believed to deserve his intervention. Thomas Tickell within months of taking up the post of steward of St Bees-Whitehaven dreamed briefly of seeking his fortune in London within the apparatus of state. His letter confiding this to his master has not survived, but Sir John lost no time in dissuading him from such a course. Firstly, he urged the difficulty he would have in replacing Tickell from such a distance 'when I can neither judge of the person nor can instruct any in my business'. Secondly, he threw cold water on Tickell's hopes, for, he argued, if there were more posts in London than elsewhere 'there is ten times the proportion of persons who both want and wish it with the greatest desire' and many who have been 'bred to

[48] Lowther to Tickell, 25 August 1677, and other succeeding letters, D/Lons/W2/1/12.
[49] Hainsworth, *Lowther Correspondence*, Appendix D.
[50] Thomas Gage to the Duchess of Somerset, 23 August 1669, *Bath*, vol. 4, 266. Although referred to here as 'the bailiff' Beardsley was a real steward, however dubiously acquisitive.

employment here' and have the help of friends 'can scarce get bread, so much does the persons here exceed business'. He assured his steward the new taxes 'do not afford any place worth the owning' in London. After this cold draught came the sugared words: a firm promise to continue his efforts to get Tickell a place in the Customs House at Whitehaven. He also grudgingly conceded that so far as Tickell's salary was concerned he might 'stretch a little upon my own account'. As we have seen he subsequently doubled Tickell's salary although this was not until 1679, twelve years later.[51] Tickell agreed to remain, although he spiritedly asserted that his London 'friends' were as well able to find him work there as any. Significantly it was the promise of influence to be exerted, not the dubious half promise of some minor increase in salary, which was decisive. He declared he esteemed his employment at Whitehaven worth more than mere payment, even 'at half salary', nor was he hoping for an increased salary from his master but rather Lowther's aid in obtaining a Customs place.[52] The latter he argued, would redound to Lowther's honour as well as Tickell's profit for while Lowther's service would never be neglected because of Tickell's public duties, Tickell would cut a better figure as Lowther's servant with the additional income from his Customs House salary and perquisites for, he concluded: 'a poor servant is but a pitiful one. Riches as well as abilities to manage make men to be best regarded.'[53] Tickell's reward was long in coming but worth the wait, and although his Customs career had its setbacks, particularly during the reign of James II, his master's influence over the long haul was able to sustain him. This successful appeal to patronage may well, after the death of its beneficiary, have encouraged William Gilpin to move his family to the Cumberland coast and endanger and ultimately lose his public appointment in Carlisle, for while nominally he moved only to take up Tickell's stewardship he also was ambitious to achieve the same Customs House post that Tickell had so long enjoyed, or a still better one.[54] If so he was disappointed for despite Lowther's best efforts he was never able to achieve for Gilpin what he had achieved for Tickell, perhaps because the Customs House directors had no desire to revive such a monopoly of power as existed when the landowner

[51] See Tickell to Lowther, 1 April 1679, D/Lons/W2/1/14.
[52] The reference to 'half salary' is obscurely expressed but Tickell appears to mean that if his salary was half what it was it would not greatly concern him so long as he could live on it.
[53] Tickell's letter is, as usual a draft, and 'manage' was substituted for 'govern', and 'regarded' for 'obeyed', as if he felt that using such words of command was inappropriate in a letter from one who was only a surrogate 'governor' to the man who really had the hegemony. Lowther to Tickell, c. 28 January 1667, with Tickell's draft reply, 5 February, Lonsdale D/Lons/W2/1/2.
[54] Hainsworth, *Lowther Correspondence*, 661 and note, and the letters *passim*.

owned the port and its facilities and his obedient steward effectively controlled the Customs House.

Patronage could take many forms and did not simply apply to the servant himself, but also to members of his family. Tickell's sons and a son-in-law obtained preferment in the church thanks largely to Lowther's efforts on their behalf. 'Your excessive industry to introduce my son through so many difficulties to Bridekirk shows your power and worth to my admiration for which I do most jealously thank you' Tickell acknowledged.[55] Sir John Lowther of Lowther obtained a place in the Salt Works worth £40 a year for the son of his steward Atkinson.[56] Lord Cholmondeley acted beneficially both as a member of the House of Lords and an officer of influence at the court of Queen Anne to get William Adams's Private Member's Bill concerning the settlement of his estate on his grandchildren, his son having predeceased him, through all legislative stages to the royal assent.[57] He also intervened on behalf of Thomas Hinckes, who was no more than Adams's nephew, although less successfully and Cholmondeley did not really approve of this beneficiary of his influence. For his part Hinckes had the impudence to complain to his uncle that the fact that Cholmondeley did not exert himself sufficiently on the family's behalf (he had not got as good a Customs post as he had sought) suggested he did not sufficiently value Adams's services as steward.[58]

Even a temporary amateur steward might mobilise a nobleman's powers of patronage. Sir Henry Parker, looking after the Earl of Northampton's Warwickshire estate when his lordship was between stewards, besought Northampton to obtain a fellowship at New College, Oxford, for his son. The son was next on the list and while there was no vacancy one of the fellows was holding an outside living worth £250 a year in contravention of the statutes and could be dislodged if the earl uttered 'one word' on the subject.[59] Scapegrace sons were rescued from the consequences of their folly, respectable daughters were received in London when seeking a place in a noble household or while seeking a suitable husband with the help of their fathers' powerful patrons. Sometimes masters were mobilised to

---

[55] Tickell to Lowther, 3 May 1680, Lonsdale D/Lons/W2/15. Just how 'excessive' Sir John's industry had been can be examined below in Chapter 9.

[56] Lowther to Atkinson, 20 April 1694, Lonsdale D/Lons/L, Agents Letters 1/4.

[57] 'Your bill has passed the House and his lordship will speak (or make interest) to the Queen that what more is to be done in it may be perfected.' Chritchley to Adams, 2 April 1702, Cholmondeley DCH/L/49. For the bill, GB Parliament, *House of Commons Journals*, vol. 13, 4 February 1702 (Petition of William Adams); also 13, 19, 23 February, 10, 17 March, 2 April, 6 May 1702.

[58] See various Hinckes letters to Adams particularly 27 March 1708, but also 12 February and 18 March 1708, and Hinckes to Cholmondeley, 27 March 1708, Cholmondeley DCH/L/29, L/30.

[59] Parker to Northampton, 5 and 16 May 1694, Northampton (Warwickshire).

protect their stewards from unwanted burdens as when John Peck asked Sir John Trevor to help him escape the onerous and unwelcome office of sheriff.[60] Sometimes it was to obtain a beneficial lease or a favourably assessed fine from a neighbouring landlord. 'The favour, sir, you shall show [Thomas Tickell] I shall own as done to myself' wrote Sir John Lowther on such an occasion.[61] Jobs, places, preferment, commissions in the army or navy, aid in vexatious lawsuits, deliverance from the press gang for a young kinsman, all were of the stuff of patronage and all could be assisted by the exertions of the steward's master, and although a favourable outcome could never be guaranteed, when help was sought it was not sought in vain.

Finally since stewards were servants, using the word not in the menial sense of today but rather in the seventeenth-century sense in which even a duke could be a servant if his master was a king, and therefore members of their master's family, they enjoyed one privilege which was greatly valued. Where the employer was a Member of Parliament, whether as an elected member or as a peer, members of his family, that is, his household, could not be arrested for debt during the life of a Parliament. The debtors' prison was a menace which could imperil men and women of all ranks and this benefit was a very real one. Lord Cholmondeley, who as an Irish peer had this privilege as a member of the Irish Parliament, confided to his steward on one occasion that a Cheshire neighbour in financial difficulties had sought a position in his household, but he had already taken one broken gentleman into his family as an understeward and would take no more for fear he would become 'notorious for it'.[62]

There were, therefore, many inducements to make a man seek a position in stewardship beyond the financial security which was furnished by a modest salary which for many stewards was probably the least significant inducement of all.

[60] Peck to Trevor, 14 and 17 November 1649, Trevor D/G/3276. The office was avoided. Peck also requested favours for his son and further favours for himself on 1 and 21 December 1649, D/G/3276.

[61] Tickell had spent only months in Lowther's service at that time. Lowther to William Kirkby, 19 June 1666, Lonsdale D/Lons/W2/1/1.

[62] Cholmondeley to Adams, 8 February 1694, Cholmondeley DCH/K/3/10.

3

The whole duty of a steward

If I had a thousand eyes, hands and hearts I should use them all in your employment and account them too little to express my engagements to you and to testify myself, sir, your obliged and faithful servant,   William Thynne[1]

Since 'tis from you alone that I can have any punctual account of the progress of my work so from you only 'tis that I hope for any life in my business; though I know 'tis not your proper employment . . . I know how to value service that depends upon punctilios of order. That will never do me nor no master good.

Sir John Lowther of Lowther[2]

Considering the multiplicity of duties and responsibilities which confronted many stewards they might well have thought at times that William Thynne's thousand eyes and hands were hardly extravagant qualifications for their employment. Inevitably, stewards' experience of their employment varied greatly from estate to estate and employer to employer. Some estates were very large, comprising several dozen manors, and required the watchful care of a chief steward with several understewards and a small army of estate servants to carry out his orders. Some consisted of but one small manor and the stewardship could be carried out on a very part-time basis by a country attorney as part of the ordinary business of his legal practice. It was not just a question of size, however, but rather the degree of complexity. Sir John Lowther possessed in St Bees-Whitehaven a very modest estate in acreage, minute by comparison with the estate of his cousin and namesake at Lowther with manors stretching across several counties, and that estate in turn was dwarfed by the Devonshire estates based on Chatsworth. Nevertheless, the puny size of St Bees-Whitehaven masked an operation of remarkable complexity which came to involve salt-making, coal mining, ship-owning, the Virginia tobacco trade, several manufacturing ventures (including textiles and vitriol), the planning and

[1] William Thynne, steward of Longleat, to Sir James Thynne, 18 October 1658, Thynne ix, fo. 52.
[2] To his steward William Atkinson, 10 February 1694, Lonsdale D/Lons/L, Agents Letters 1/4.

laying out of a 'model' town complete with what today would be called 'planning regulations', the building of a church and a school and the appointment of clergymen and schoolteachers, and maintaining, improving and operating a substantial port. All these responsibilities, and that list is very far from exhaustive, were in addition to what are considered the 'normal' duties of a steward: collecting rents, dues, and fines and negotiating leases.[3]

The basic core of a steward's duties were spelled out in his letter of appointment or his master's letter of attorney or in some set of general instructions which his master signed. Sometimes the master drew up the document, sometimes the incoming steward drew it up himself and submitted it to his master for his approval and signature, as William Adams did for Lord Cholmondeley in 1679. Lowther of Whitehaven possessed several small Westmorland manors, originally part of his mother's dowry. In 1680 his need for a steward for the isolated manor of Waitby provides an archetypal example of the small, very limited stewardship which could be carried out by a local attorney as part of his ordinary legal business – in this instance, the Westmorland lawyer George Fothergill. Lowther signed a power of attorney which empowered Fothergill to receive or sue for and recover all rents and dues and debts from Waitby's tenants; to appoint a 'fit and convenient' person to be a bailiff (who would presumably actually collect the rents); to keep the manorial court and sign legal documents in Lowther's name; issue receipts and acquittances, keep accounts and pay the surplus to Lowther in London at regular intervals. Fothergill, in brief, was to 'exercise the place and office of a steward' and 'to perform as fully in every respect ... as I myself might or could do I being personally present.'[4] Here is encapsulated the fundamental duties of a steward. Some stewards charged with the management of far larger estates received instructions in their power of attorney that were only marginally more detailed than were those of Mr Fothergill. Lord Dorset's power of attorney to Robert Brookes of 1661 to be 'steward, collector and receiver' of more than a score of manors in Sussex empowered him to collect 'farm rents, rents of assize, quit rents, amerciaments, profits of courts, and all other rents, duties and profits whatsoever'; to summon the several manorial courts; to seize for his master's use all 'heriots, waifs, strays, felons goods'; to pay such sums to whoever his master appointed to receive them; and to account for them at Dorset's half-yearly audit. He was finally authorised to 'take distress' for arrears of rent. All this is really only Mr Fothergill's duties spelled out in a

---

[3] This rich mix of responsibilities at Whitehaven can be observed in detail in William Gilpin's letters to his master in *Lowther Correspondence* and in Churches, 'Lowther and Whitehaven'. See also below Chapter 12.

[4] Memoranda Book 1671–82, Lonsdale D/Lons/W1/31, fo.25.

little more detail, although they were much more onerous because of the number of manors and courts involved.[5] In addition the document appointed Brookes to be 'wood reeve', charged with preserving Dorset's woods, preventing theft and waste and maintaining the fences.

Both William Adams at Cholmondeley and William Gilpin at St Bees-Whitehaven drafted their own letters of attorney and sent them to their employers. This may explain why they are both rather more detailed and wider in their definition of responsibilities. Adams in his draft described himself as 'of Longdon, Esquire' and categorised himself as 'agent, steward and overseer' for his master's estates in Cheshire, Shropshire, Flint and Somerset. The fact that from the first he would have an array of understewards under him charged with the care of discrete areas of the estate was reflected in his responsibility for calling Cholmondeley's 'bailiffs, rent gathers [*sic*] and under-agents' to account for all receipts from the tenants, whether rents, fines, heriots, services or sales of timber, and to issue receipts and acquittances. Adams was to keep complete accounts of all receipts and disbursements, and to return all surpluses to his master in London. Not only was Adams authorised to oversee the under-agents to ensure the efficient management of their parts of the estate, it was his function to pay them their salaries along with all the other household and estate servants and reimburse their expenses. Finally Adams inserted an 'enabling clause' which seems to have covered all matters not specifically described in the document: 'and in all other things relating to and concerning my ... estate to behave himself in such sort as shall be most to my advantage, and as I shall from time to time order and direct'. By this document Adams was placed in charge of an estate with a purely rental income of about £4,000 a year, but which also included mills, forests, salt works, a mansion, several manor houses and at least one deer park.[6] The Adams power of attorney was unusual in that there was no mention of the manorial courts, although Adams did summon such courts and feed a lawyer to preside over them.

William Gilpin's power of attorney contained no general enabling clause as such, but was still a more detailed document, appointing him Lowther's 'true and lawful attorney and commissioner' and referring not merely to farms and tenements but also 'mines and delves of coal, iron, lead or other minerals whatsoever, boileries of salt, wood and underwoods, fairs, markets, tolls, franchises, liberties and heridaments', and when it

---

[5] The document appears to be a draft amended by Dorset himself who filled in the steward's name, and inserted in the margin the names of the manors. Stewards Appointments 1658–75, Sackville U269/E154.

[6] Draft dated 2 October 1679; Cholmondeley DCH/M/32 Misc. A marginal addition to the draft stated that Adams was to receive a salary of £100 out of the 'profits' of the estate.

authorises Gilpin to make leases of Lowther's properties limits such leases to no more than twenty-one years and specifically excludes all coal mines and other minerals 'which are not to be leased'. The letter also refers specifically to the keeping of 'all manner of court leets and view of frankpledge, court barons, customary courts and demises, courts of pie powder within ... the manors, lordships, fairs, markets', and the power to appoint attorneys to use and prosecute any actions on Lowther's behalf. Gilpin drafted his letter of attorney and sent it to Lowther, observing that he had 'only sent it as a form, which your honour may diminish, enlarge or qualify, as you see cause'.[7] The only obvious 'qualification' Lowther made was to deny Gilpin the authority to lease coal mines, something it would never have occurred to him to do without his master's direct order.

Although powers of attorney are useful the duties and responsibilities of stewardship cannot be discerned from those which have haphazardly survived among estate papers. They only describe in very general terms the basic duties, the core responsibilities, and if these were the only surviving evidence our knowledge of the role of the steward both on his master's estate and in the surrounding region would be feeble and incomplete. They provide no more than a skeleton which other sources must flesh out. It is from the correspondence of stewards, and their surviving account books, that we can perceive the amplitude and variety of their responsibilities and activities most clearly. Later chapters describe a range of responsibilities at which the letters of attorney scarcely so much as hint. Among these was their role in financing their lords' absenteeism, returning money to London by a wide variety of expedients to which they were driven by the absence of any system of provincial banking; their role as 'ambassadors', acting as their lord's surrogate in maintaining relationships with neighbours of all ranks whilst negotiating with tax assessors and commissioners, and serving as their masters' surrogates in militia matters. They also fulfilled another ambassadorial function: supplying intelligence on a wide range of topics, but particularly with regard to the possibilities of increasing the value of the estate by purchases of land and other assets from neighbouring owners, and negotiating those purchases on behalf of their masters. They had the vital function of maintaining their masters' political influence and, as an early form of election agent, mobilising it at county and borough parliamentary elections. One should not forget their role of advising and assisting their masters in the vexed and sometimes controversial matter of supplying ministers to churches whose advowson was part of the estate they administered. They served also as their masters' surrogates in the distribution of charity and in other ways put into effect their masters' benevolent impulses,

---

[7] Gilpin to Lowther 29 March 1693, *Lowther Correspondence*, 7. Copy of letter of attorney in Lowther Notebooks, Lonsdale D/Lons/W1/33, fos. 200–3.

from something as small as the provision of a pound a year pension to an old servant to something as large as the construction of a new school or an almshouse for the aged. They even suggested suitable beneficiaries for his bounty, whether individuals or needy groups. They were charged with the defence of the estate against predators from within (for example, recalcitrant tenants) or without (for example, poaching gangs and woodstealers) and with the defence of their masters' rights and privileges within his manors. They organised the exploitation of the estates' resources of timber, minerals, quarries and other commercial and industrial possibilities. They acted as 'clerk-of-works' both in their masters' rebuilding or remodelling schemes for their mansion, and indeed for all building activity connected with the estate, and supervised the modelling of the gardens and grounds which beautified the country seat and they dispatched to London the fruits of those gardens and the venison from the deer parks which were their responsibility to maintain, along with other local foodstuffs, to help sustain their masters' London households. All these varied functions will be examined in the following chapters.

The truth is that the steward could never say that such and such a task formed no part of his duties. He was there to do everything that his master's absence prevented him from doing for himself. Sir John Lowther of Lowther, subsequently first Lord Lonsdale, would have had no patience with the demarcation disputes beloved of modern union officials, as his remarks to his steward quoted as an epigraph to this chapter make clear. Lowther conceded it was not Atkinson's 'proper employment' to supervise the rebuilding of Lowther Hall, but he knew 'how to value service' that depended 'upon punctilios of order'. That would never benefit him nor any master.[8] Even where a master had stewards, as Lowther's cousin at Whitehaven did, one for the estate, one for the collieries, the estate steward could not draw a line between his responsibilities and his colleague's specific duties. 'All my business seems in a strange posture' grumbled Thomas Tickell's master on one occasion, insisting: 'Mr Bettesworth may do that part belonging to the shipping but the directive part, as to pits or workmen I expect from your care.'[9] Later Lowther acquired John Gale, a much more skilled (and sober) colliery steward, whose duties included both the oversight of the sale of coals to the ships and 'the directive part' (managing the coal mines) as well, but this successful appointment made no difference to Lowther's perception of his estate steward's responsibilities: he must be ever active in inspecting the mines, taking part in all major decisions about new levels, new drainage schemes, purchases of mines or

---

[8] See epigraph to this chapter and footnote 2 above.
[9] By 'shipping' Lowther meant the sale of coal to ships' masters. Lowther to Tickell, 23 November 1675, Lonsdale D/Lons/W2/1/10.

mining rights, or in matters relating to the workforce, and in general being a vigilant and omniscient presence about every aspect of Lowther's multifarious concerns.

The fact that stewards had to do for their lord just about everything he would have done for himself had he been present on the estate explains why a steward's duties varied greatly from master to master. William Adams might have known little or nothing about managing race horses in his days as a well-respected surveyor, but as the second Lord Cholmondeley's chief steward he must have become better informed. Unlike Thomas Tickell or his successor William Gilpin at Whitehaven, who must have known about as little about coal mines as any other lawyer prior to his appointment, Adams did not have to concern himself about coalmining, but, like his Whitehaven counterparts he did not have to acquire a knowledge of salt-making and marketing.[10] Francis Guybon at Milton need not trouble himself about managing mines or saltpans, and his master's interest in horseracing was nil, but he had to have a memory well stored with information about fenmen and their rights because Fitzwilliam's estates stretched across the Soke of Peterborough into the fens. The lawyer steward of Lady Arundel of Trerice was almost as well informed about copper mines as Thomas Tickell was about coal mines, as befitted the steward of a Cornish estate. In Wiltshire the steward of Sir James Thynne at Longleat knew nothing of such concerns as these. Rather his days tended to be dominated by his devotion to his master's deer park and forests, supervising keepers, tracking down poachers, training dogs and hawks, and supervising the stables as he directly managed his master's substantial stock of horses.

It is clear then that stewards on substantial estates lived rich and varied lives, and the notion that they could slumber in bucolic torpor between their Lady Day and Michaelmas collections could not be more mistaken.

---

[10] Sometimes even so august a figure as Adams could be charged with a task which appeared quite menial, as when he was asked to order a housemaid 'to brush my lord's embroidered waistcoat that is in your custody and take care that the worms doth not get into it'. However, this simply reflected the overall responsibility of the steward for his master's mansion, the contents of it and for the overall direction of the staff that maintained it. Michael Laroche to Adams, 5 May 1690, Cholmondeley DCH/M/27.

4

Between lord and tenant

Gentlemen must be kind and abate rents and give leave to plough or else it will be worse for landlord and tenant.   Francis Guybon, 1708[1]

I assure you, my lord, several tenants in these parts keep landlords in a kind of awe for fear they should throw up their land, so the world is thrown upside down since I knew Croxall.   Charles Agard, 1674[2]

Such ungrateful people as these no persons can oblige for condescensions whet their litigious appetites, never to be satisfied or quieted until they fall into their primitive dust.   Thomas Tickell, 1677[3]

However varied a steward's duties and functions might be his chief concerns, his day-to-day tasks, related to his master's tenants and to those parts of the master's estate which they rented or leased. These properties were predominantly farms but could also be additional pastures, rabbit warrens, fishing rights, houses, or such industrial undertakings as flour or fulling mills, mines or quarries. Everything that the steward did, every action performed, every policy pursued or solution devised, should ideally have helped to secure one fundamental objective: the prosperity of the estate and thereby of his master, his family and his posterity. The surest way to achieve this was by promoting harmony between landlord and tenant, playing a mediating role. To have a disaffected tenantry, involved in outright confrontation and full of bitterness and hostility toward the landlord, could only obstruct his achieving that objective.[4] Moreover, if lands came in hand as a consequence of mass desertion by tenants the income from rent would plunge, the lord's complaints would grow increasingly bitter and the final result would be a disgraced steward out of employment. It was, therefore, as much in the interests of the steward as of

[1] To his master Lord Fitzwilliam of Milton, 23 February 1708, Fitzwilliam F(M)C 1645, *Fitzwilliam Correspondence*, Letter 552.
[2] To his master, Lord Dorset, 22 August 1674, Sackville U269/C63.
[3] To Sir John Lowther, referring to the latter's Whitehaven tenants, 22 February 1677, Lonsdale D/Lons/W2/1/12.
[4] For an analysis of the steward as mediator which borrows its basic concept from the anthropologists see Hainsworth, 'The Mediator', *passim*.

the lord that harmony should prevail. Not only would it make his tasks less burdensome, it would increase his lord's trust and dependence on him, and a steward who enjoyed his lord's complete confidence possessed a stature and influence in his local region which transcended his nominal wealth or rank.

Inevitably this situation of contented landlord and happy tenants living in a harmonious relationship, however desirable to all parties concerned, was an ideal which stewards found it extremely difficult to translate into reality. The interests of landlord and tenant never coincided so neatly and all too often were perceived to be adverse to each other. In any conflict between landlord and tenant, therefore, the steward would appear to be in a hopelessly compromised position since he was the salaried servant of one of the contending parties, a senior member of the lord's household even if perpetually at a distance from the lord's permanent residence. How then could the tenants possibly trust him and if they did not trust him how was he to resolve disputes? On the other hand, since he was a member of his lord's family, his lord had a right to expect that he would always promote his interest rather than the interests of the tenants. In fact many masters suspected that their stewards were too sympathetic to the interests of the tenants, pursuing polices which favoured them rather than their employer.[5] Such suspicions were sometimes justified, although less frequently than employers tended to imagine. Nevertheless one cannot ignore the psychological effect on stewards of the fact that many of them lived amongst the tenants with whom they dealt day by day. A man's life is pleasanter when he lives with some degree of harmony with his neighbours. Even Thomas Hawkes in Shropshire, who was a gentleman and indeed a kinsman of his master, Lord Weymouth, appears to have felt this subtle but continuous pressure. In 1687 the tenants were distressed and infuriated by woodcutters dragging their loads constantly over their lands as Weymouth exploited his Stretton woods and Hawkes reported that the Thynne estate servants had had a 'most tormenting' time with the tenants and *'especial[ly] myself that live amongst them'* with their constant complaints about the 'many rude workmen' and 'so great timber carriages'.[6] The problems of Hawkes remind us that another element related to rank: stewards were often

---

5 'Where you take a kindness you care not what I suffer and lose to gratify your friends.' Lord Fitzwilliam's angry reproach is a classic of its kind. Fitzwilliam to Guybon, 29 May 1707, Fitzwilliam F(M)C 1582; *Fitzwilliam Correspondence*, Letter 504. Richard Pollard's defensive remarks from Tavistock to Rachel, Countess of Bath, were a response to this suspicion: 'I humbly beseech your honour to believe that I value more the least esteem or respect from your honour than the greatest praise or love this country can afford me'. 25 March 1642, Sackville U269/C276.
6 My emphasis. 'I speak them fair and encourage them with the shortness of the time.' Hawkes to Weymouth, 7 August 1687, Thynne xxiii, fo. 188.

gentlemen. The vast majority of tenants were 'simples'. It was not only Lord Cholmondeley who preferred to have as his chief steward a gentleman who would prefer a gentleman's interests, rather than those of the 'clowns'. A steward of 'simple' rank, especially one who was a tenant farmer himself, would have the 'wrong' perspective. However, this was two-edged. The tenants might well prefer the reverse, and might distrust a man of superior rank, perhaps a landlord himself like Lord Cholmondeley's William Adams, who would be unlikely to sympathise with their concerns.

At the interface of landlord and tenant, therefore, the stewards had a mediating role which was very difficult. They could not afford to antagonise their master whose instrument they were. Yet if the estate was to avoid debilitating confrontations they must gain the trust and respect of the tenants, however grudging or tinged with underlying suspicion. Moreover, during the period contemplated here, the last fifty or sixty years of the Stuart era, the stewards' difficulties were compounded by the fact that tenants were in a position to resist too harsh an assertion of the lord's hegemony simply because there was a shortage of tenants. Landlords, through their stewards, were competing for them. In such a situation stewards could not afford to simply follow the commands and demands of their lords in blind obedience if such demands were likely to be strenuously resisted by the tenants. The latter were all too likely in the last resort to vote with their feet and throw up their tenancies in favour of better terms elsewhere.[7] There were two ways in which they could do this: either surrender the farm at the end of the lease or at Lady Day of the following year if they were 'rack' or 'half-rack' tenants, or if they were in arrears and lacked the means to pay them they would simply abscond. The latter method was the more feared because it was rare to obtain any satisfaction from the absconder or even to track him down.

It was unusual for landlords in this period to behave with brutal callousness toward their tenants, but significantly in the worst example I have found the steward strenuously intervened to protect the tenants, seeking to reverse what he perceived as a callous and unjust policy. The Reverend Charles Usher of Kirkandrews-on-Esk, Cumberland, was an example of a clergyman who acted as chief or supervisory steward of the Grahame estates. In 1672 he complained to Sir Richard Grahame of Netherby that two men had appeared bearing leases signed by Grahame and were evicting old tenants, many of them good 'rent payers'. Grahame

---

[7] 'Landlords could not for long lose sight of the fact that ... their own interests and those of their tenants at rack rent coincided extremely closely. They could not prosper unless their tenants prospered, and if their tenants were in difficulties they could not expect to remain unscathed.' Christopher Clay, 'Landlords and Estate Management in England', in Thirsk, *Agrarian History*, 5, ii, 231.

was rumoured to have signed other leases which would cause tenants to be evicted, tenants who either were not in arrear for their fines or who had given good security for their payment. Moreover, parts of the commons had been taken from the poor tenants who needed them and enclosed for the benefit of a few who had no need of them – a heinous offence in the eyes of tenants anywhere. Usher reported there was a 'general clamour' against these proceedings, and besought his master to take into his 'serious consideration' those tenants who had paid fines and were yet threatened either with eviction or with becoming undertenants to new landlords 'and consequently mere arbitrary vassals', not simply because 'of the misery you have thrown them too hastily into' but because of the 'blemish' it would put on Grahame's reputation in being 'inconsistent both to your word and hand'. He solemnly concluded: 'Your honour is so dear to me as I cannot but desire you to be just in all your doings.' This was by the standards of this deferential and formal society a blistering rebuke, and only actions which the steward considered to be as unusual as they were undesirable could have persuaded him to utter it. The result of Usher's intervention is obscure, but the mediating role of the steward, seeking to restore a harmonious relationship between landlord and tenants, could hardly be clearer. However, if it was, as I have suggested elsewhere, the stewards' role to act as 'governors' in the mechanical sense, smoothing out irregularities in the beat of the engine of society, their problems lay far more with recalcitrant and obdurate tenants than with callously exploitive masters, at least throughout the second half of the seventeenth century.[8] It was often a wearisome and frustrating labour. Thomas Hawkes in Shropshire complaining of the 'crossness and untowardliness of the people', Thomas Tickell at Whitehaven grumbling about the ingratitude, as he saw it, of the urban tenants whose 'litigious appetites' were only whetted by concessions and never 'to be satisfied or quieted until they fall in to their primitive dust', were only two of the more eloquent sufferers.[9]

One of the more irritating manifestations of the tenants' capacity to resist both lords and stewards was their readiness to play off one against the other, appealing to the lord over his steward's head, insisting that it was the steward's arbitrary and tyrannical behaviour that was hindering negotiations, or telling the steward that the lord had promised certain concessions in their lease or about their rents when he was last in the country or the tenant was last in town. Where estates were within comparatively easy reach of the capital we often find tenants visiting their landlord at his

---

[8] Usher to Grahame, 15 February 1672, in a group of uncatalogued estate letters at Netherby Hall. See also Hainsworth, 'Essential Governor', 359.
[9] Hawkes to Thomas Thynne, 8 April 1673, Thynne xx, fo. 94; for Tickell, see footnote 3 above.

London home in order to negotiate leases or for other purposes, some of which at least were designed to undermine the steward. Others travelled from outlying estates to the landlord's seat, usually preceded by a flurry of warnings from the understeward about the sinister purpose of the visit. We find the infuriated understeward of an outlying Northumberland estate warning the chief steward of the Duke of Newcastle, and indirectly the duke himself, that they would shortly have at Welbeck a female tenant 'whose impudence and boldness with addition of base lies will weary both his excellency and yourself'. His anxiety is that he could be 'baffled by these unworthy people' and so see his authority undermined.[10] Interestingly although stewards were often accused by their masters of being too indulgent toward the tenants, stewards were often nervous that they would earn their masters' displeasure by appearing to treat tenants too severely, particularly over arrears of rent.[11] Certainly tenants were quick to approach the lord directly if dissatisfied with their treatment from the steward and such appeals to Caesar were often successful. William Thynne was horrified to discover the concessions his master had made to the tenant of his rabbit warrens who was heavily in his debt, and protested that if he was left alone until Michaelmas he might sell all the rabbits and abscond.[12] Similarly a Shropshire steward warns that a certain debtor intends to come to his master because the steward demanded security while his master did not, but 'I better know his condition than your worship did . . . his cattle are no more than will pay your arrears.'[13]

This then was the challenging, often uncomfortable milieu in which the steward laboured. As we shall see while he often experienced failure, while his short-term successes often proved ambiguous and indecisive in the long run, over all the labours of the stewards as a group were salutary for society and there was more general social harmony across the country under the later Stuart kings than could have been expected considering the nation's traumas during the first half of the century and considering the often malign and divisive policies, particularly in the sphere of religion, pursued by the post-Restoration Parliament or by the king's ministers, and considering the

---

[10] Thomas Whitehead to Andrew Clayton, 15 April 1662, Portland (Newcastle) Pwl 511; Hainsworth, 'The Mediator', 95 and note.

[11] 'Here is a little arrears now to be had without suit, neither must you be angry if I distrain upon your tenants who are very slow in paying, I being resolved not to let them . . . run in arrears for all their railings against me.' John Peck to Sir John Trevor the younger, 18 May 1650, Trevor D/G/3276.

[12] William Thynne to Sir James Thynne, 7 February 1659, Thynne ix, fo. 87. In an earlier letter, scenting danger, he had remarked: 'I hear he has gone to you as conceiving Mr Gould and I are not his friends' (Gould was Sir James's lawyer). See 24 January 1659, ix, fo. 84.

[13] Samuel Peers, Minsterly, to Sir Thomas Thynne, 29 March 1681, Thynne xxi, fo. 228.

factional politics and the increasing fear of Jacobitism which characterised the later years of the dynasty.

If an estate was to sustain its regular flow of income, particularly its income from rents, the farms and other lands must be kept in the hands of reliable tenants who could be trusted to pay their rents, if not on time at least after only a short delay, and who could be depended on to hold their farms year after year. In the event that such a tenant died leaving no male heir to continue the farm then a new tenant who appeared to be as worthy of trust as the old must be found to replace him. Alternatively the steward might investigate the capacity of the widow to carry on the farm alone, working it with sufficient success to sustain the rent or he might try to find her a suitable new husband. Lord Fitzwilliam was not slow to point his steward toward likely possibilities. In the same letter that Fitzwilliam expresses regret at the death of a tenant, he observes that he had told a potential tenant of the vacancy and that the former tenant's widow 'would make him a good wife'.[14] However, until death intervened every effort must be made to hold tenants to their 'bargains' whether these were leasehold or copy-hold tenancies, whether they were tenancies at will or at half rack. Empty farms yielded no rent and the only crop to be expected was a barrage of angry expostulation from the distant landlord. Even Lord Fitzwilliam who had an unusually affectionate relationship with his old steward, was enraged to discover that Guybon had evicted a tenant long in arrears and taken her farm 'in hand' without his master's knowledge, let alone consent.[15]

The steward, therefore, had a two-pronged task: he had to keep tenants, and, when this failed, he had to find tenants. During the latter half of the seventeenth century both these apparently straightforward tasks often presented great difficulties. These difficulties ensured that throughout this period tenants were often able to exact concessions from landlords, although the stewards at the sharp end of the struggle were naturally more willing to concede them than were their masters, sheltered from the fray by distance and infused by nostalgic memories of more prosperous times, or by a simplistic notion that rents were sacrosanct. Rents, landlords believed, might only rarely rise but should never under any circumstances fall since that would reduce the value of the estate they had inherited and which one

---

[14] Fitzwilliam to Guybon, 1 June 1699, Fitzwilliam F(M)C 1083; *Fitzwilliam Correspondence*, Letter 97.

[15] Writing on 29 May 1707: 'I know you understand not how to manage that farm, not being able to ride about as you have done, that what through want of care servants will be negligent that I am sure to lose half in half of every year I keep it in my hand. I know not how to be angry enough at this great miscarriage of yours.' Fitzwilliam F(M)C 1582; *Fitzwilliam Correspondence*, Letter 504.

day they hoped to bequeath to their heir. Lord Fitzwilliam told a tenant who was seeking a reduction under threat of throwing up his farm that he must 'keep up the reputation' of his rents because his son 'was upon his marriage and it might hinder him'.[16] Faced by low prices, or climatic hazards such as long dry summers or unseasonal rains, both of which were experienced frequently during the second half of the seventeenth century, many tenants faced stewards with a simple choice: either the lord must wait long for his arrears, or he must reduce rents, or both, or they must throw up their leases and depart. The fundamental problem the stewards faced is clear. In the second half of the seventeenth century tenants were well aware that there were in most regions of England more farms to let than there were desirable tenants to occupy them. For tenants it was a seller's market and they were always ready to exploit their advantage. Landlords and stewards were in the unfavourable position of competing with the neigh-bouring landowners for tenants, and finding new tenants was difficult, uncertain, laborious and time consuming, and the stewards, having no stick, needed carrots with which to tempt their prey. The carrots they needed were rents which reflected the depressing impact of the tenant market, supplemented by other favourable terms in their leases. The latter might include a clause that while the tenant should pay 'king's taxes', all local taxes would be met by the landlord, or even in some leases that all taxes would be borne by the landlord. They might include a more generous agreement about the proportion of the farm which could be tilled or mowed, as distinct from grazed.[17]

The crucial problem, however, related to rents and fines, a problem which is reflected in that well-known phenomenon of the later Stuart era, the 'fall in rents'. Usually ascribed to the first decade after the Restoration, in fact the phenomenon persisted longer, although this may not be apparent in particular rent rolls.[18] Stewards' accounts are always a more reliable guide to what rent the landlord really received for a particular property. The 'fall in rents', a phrase coined by contemporaries, has been ascribed in modern times to a decline in the prices of agricultural products but it has been argued that rents could rise even when prices were low, a phenomenon

---

[16] Fitzwilliam to Francis Guybon, 12 February 1708, Fitzwilliam F(M)C 1643; *Fitzwilliam Correspondence*, Letter 550.

[17] However, ploughing was often a very contentious topic between landlord and tenant and is considered in more detail below.

[18] Succinctly expressed by Dr Wordie: 'Over the country as a whole, rents appear to have increased steadily until the 1650s, levelled off in the 1660s and to have actually fallen in the 1670s and 1680s.' J. R. Wordie, *Estate Management in Eighteenth Century England: the Building of the Leveson-Gower Fortune* (London, 1982), 15n. Wordie goes on to say that there was some improvement in the 1690s, but if this was the experience of the Leveson-Gower estates it was by no means universal.

observable during the early eighteenth century, for example.[19] Contemporaries preferred other explanations, including emigration (both from the country to London and from England to the American colonies), high interest rates and the growth of London banking which was believed to drain money from the provinces to London. Ironically a favoured explanation for the 'fall' was the increasing tendency for the nobility and gentry to live in London. This last 'cause', it was argued, had the effect of drawing still more money from the provinces whilst it threw more demesne land onto the depressed rental market.[20] In fact this contemporary complaint does not seem persuasive. Had the landlords remained at home they would have farmed their demesne lands intensively themselves and competed with their produce with tenant farmers both locally and in London, while their permanent absence from London, together with their substantial households, would have thinned the London market for meat and other agricultural produce. Conversely when an absentee landlord returned to his estate to spend a summer the steward would be buying malt for brewing, fodder and oats for the horses, and laying in a great store of provisions, including beef cattle and sheep, all purchased locally, to sustain the lord, his family and the greatly augmented household. These arguments would have made little impression on Sir William Coventry, however, who was an eloquent exponent of the absenteeism explanation.[21]

Whatever the causes of the fall in rents, the phenomenon was real enough to make the mediating role of the steward difficult and laborious. Their letters provide us with a rich source for studying the impact of the 'fall' throughout the country, and demonstrate just how prolonged was the difficulty of maintaining rents and of keeping old or of finding new tenants, for it was still observable, at least in some regions, during the reign of Queen Anne. In 1667 a Cambridgeshire steward observed that he could not get a penny of rent for Lord North. Rather the tenant truculently said that if his rent was not reduced he would abandon the farm 'and this they have to throw at a man's teeth when he asks for money'.[22] Twenty years after the Restoration we find Arthur King, steward of Lord Fitzwilliam's Norfolk properties, warning: 'Mr Barker and Mr Ledington I find will both leave at Lady Day unless your lordship be kind to them' – meaning, by this

[19] C. Wilson, *England's Apprenticeship* (London, 1965), 248.

[20] For an interesting analysis of the rental decline and its possible causes see Davies, 'Country Gentry', 91 ff.

[21] See his 'Essay Concerning the Decay of Rents and their Remedies', written about 1670, BM Sloane Mss 3828, fos. 205–10, reprinted in Joan Thirsk and J. P. Cooper, eds., *Seventeenth Century Economic Documents* (Oxford, 1972), 79–84.

[22] Francis White, steward at Kirtling, to Anne, Lady North, 5 November 1667, North C10, fo. 27. He added ironically that if the local countrymen were to be believed they need no longer worry about these cares for they claimed 'the world is to be at an end within these few days for the sun has refused to give his light above this fortnight'.

euphemism, reduce the rent actually paid. Another man will take a property but only if the rent is cut to £40 the first year, £45 the second year and only achieve the true rent of £55 at the third year. Even then he must be let off some arrears for a previous tenancy and be allowed £5 for his expenses in coming to London to sign the lease. The situation was no different on Fitzwilliam's Northamptonshire estate. In 1671 Francis Guybon gloomily reports that a tenant had renewed his lease 'with much ado' for five years 'but with £16 a year abatement ... I think more of the lands or tenements will fall of the rent they are now let at.' Things were no better fifteen years later when we find him warning his master that if John Wilkinson was not permitted to plough part of his 30 acre field he would leave Marholm on Lady Day. Fitzwilliam must not part with him for tenants were hard to get. He feared they would have 'enough' on their hands at Lady Day, more than would be let. Conditions seem to have been no better almost a generation later for it was in 1708 that the ageing steward urged plaintively: 'Gentlemen must be kind and abate rents and give leave to plough or else it will be worse for landlord and tenant.' As late as 1716 in distant Cornwall a steward was gloomily reporting that while he was labouring to let some of his mistress's farms, the potential tenants were insisting on moderate rents, expensive repairs and no local taxes. Moreover, the tenants were as opposed to what they perceived as high fines as they were to high rents. A steward reports that he had done all he possibly can to 'bring the tenants up' to his master's terms but he could not 'stir them one jot higher than two years value to add one life to two'.[23] His experience, with variations, could be repeated again and again.

Certainly the efforts of landlords to attract tenants seem born of some degree of desperation. So fierce was the competition that landlords were prepared to have their stewards lure tenants from other landlords and indeed resort to even less scrupulous practices. John Chapman, the Ishams' steward, reported indignantly shortly before Lady Day 1680 that he feared they would be 'hard set' to find tenants for land at Shangton for one Daintry, their principal tenant, had been lured to Sir Thomas Haselrigg's where they kept him drunk for two or three days while Chapman was away in London and had finally got him to rent their mill field, so Isham would lose him to his rival landlord for the coming year. Daintry had been 'ready to hang himself ever since he did it'.[24] All this competition had broader implications for the power of the gentles and the capacity for resistance of

[23] King to Fitzwilliam, respectively 19 October and 3 August 1680, Fitzwilliam F(M)C 464, 462; Guybon to Fitzwilliam 18 March 1671, 30 June 1686, 23 February 1708, Fitzwilliam F(M)C 422, 551, 1645; *Fitzwilliam Correspondence*, Letter 552. John Cocke, Redruth, to Lady Arundel of Trerice, 16 August 1716, Galway (Arundel) 12,322. Robert Brescie to William Adams, 31 August 1700, Cholmondeley DCH/L/28.
[24] Chapman to Sir Thomas Isham, 23 February 1680, Isham IC 1238.

the simples and, thereby, for the role of the steward at the interface between them, as will be discussed shortly. The point is that tenants were scarce and they knew that if they surrendered their leases or if the landlord evicted them he might be left with no choice but to take the land 'in hand', that is, farm it himself for what profit he could achieve. This was a dismal prospect for both the landlord and the local steward. Landlords dreaded having land come 'in hand'.[25] As for the steward he knew he was likely to be blamed if the land in hand did not show a profit and what chance was there of its showing a profit? Charles Agard, steward of the Staffordshire–Derbyshire estates of the Earl of Dorset, provided the classic analysis of this problem when responding in 1674 to his master's complaints about arrears and low rents. Agard assured Dorset that his Derbyshire lands were let as high as any in the county, so high indeed that if times did not mend many tenants had grown so poor that they would be forced to throw up their leases. If they did Dorset and other landlords would be forced to stock the lands themselves and if 'poor laborious' tenants could not make this rent, how could landlords who 'understand not the way of grazing' and who would have to employ servants to tend the farms and perhaps have to borrow money to stock them? He concluded grimly: 'I assure you, my lord, several tenants in these parts keep landlords in a kind of awe for fear they should throw up their land, so the world is thrown upside down since I knew Croxall.'[26]

Here Agard is nostalgically looking back more than thirty years across the watershed of the Civil War to a period when tenants were competing for land and therefore were easier to hold in awe. All that was now changed. Tenants were prepared to form combinations not only to oppose any increase in rents but also to campaign for their reduction. In the same year that Lord Dorset was instructed by Agard, Lady Dorset received a report from another agent at Croxall reporting that the bad season had so 'daunted' the tenants that they had appointed a day of meeting and consulted together and the most substantial of them told the steward that having long been tenants there they were loath to throw up their farms but they must certainly do so if her ladyship did not lower the rents.[27] George Crowther, steward at Drayton, had experienced six years earlier the readiness of Staffordshire tenants to combine for, despite 'the seasonal weather and the rise of corn and I believe the goodness of the pennyworth too', he had been unable to let the tithes for more than £130 because there was 'such

[25] The reasons for their dread are cogently analysed in Davies, 'Country Gentry'.
[26] Charles Agard to Lord Dorset, 22 August 1674, Sackville Mss U269/C63. The Croxall estate straddled the Derbyshire–Staffordshire border.
[27] Thomas Brome to David Denham, receiver to the Countess of Dorset, 22 November 1679, Sackville Mss, U269/68.

a combination between the farmers and the takers'. That is, those who were abandoning the lease of the tithes were in close alliance with those who were negotiating to take it.[28]

The letters from tenants to stewards or to landlords often ask the lord to be 'kind' to them, or they write that they will 'stand to his courtesy'. These are euphemisms, coded phrases. They are asking the landlord to reduce the rent covertly by retaining the existing rent on the rent roll while agreeing to accept a lower rent from the tenant. This permitted the landlord to provide rent relief to his tenants during bad times whilst maintaining the nominal annual value of the estate. Lord Fitzwilliam striving to retain a tenant who might otherwise abandon his farm put it with characteristic succinctness that if he ploughed any part of the farm the rent must stand in the books at £60 but he would be 'very kind to him' unless 'the times mended very much', which he did not expect they would for the next two years, but he must not bring his rents too low and undervalue his estate.[29] Tenants had to be coaxed into tenancies, reassured that they would not commit themselves irrevocably to losing bargains by promises that if the farmer could not 'make the rent' the landlord would adjust the rent actually received.[30] Others were so suspicious of making a bad bargain at a time when their fellows were making better bargains, that they had to be convinced that they were not being tricked or lured but rather that they were enforcing their will on the landlord. When Lord Cholmondeley wanted a particular tenant named Whittaker to take a large piece of ground called the Warren Hills which the tenant had earlier talked of renting he warned his steward that he must contrive in his negotiating to make it appear that Whittaker was making the proposals, not the other way round. Cholmondeley knew 'the beast's humour' only too well: he would think there was some trick in it if the proposal did not come from himself. William Adams in fact tackled the problem by using an intermediary as a stalking horse but found Whittaker 'shy in the matter' until he discovered that the tenant had his eye on particularly desirable ground near his landlord's park. Adams seized this opportunity and bargained that Cholmondeley might agree to the latter if Whittaker would agree to the former. Whittaker accepted this but insisted on the following conditions: the bargain was void if he died within the term, he was to be allowed two days of getting 'flag turf', to be tithe

---

[28] George Crowther to dowager Duchess of Somerset, 2 August 1673, *Bath*, vol. 4, 275.
[29] 'I can be kind considering hard times' he concluded. To Francis Guybon, 19 February 1708, Fitzwilliam F(M)C 1644; *Fitzwilliam Correspondence*, Letter 551.
[30] 'My son Egerton ... writes me word he hopes to bring Thomas Downes to his proposal which is that if the times do not mend and upon impartial survey it appears he does not make the rent that then I am to consider him.' (The last was another euphemism for a clandestine reduction of the rent actually received.) Dowager Viscountess Cholmondeley to William Adams, 27 October 1688, Cholmondeley DCH K/3/8.

free, to have a barn of five bays built on the ground, and to be free from heriot for his rack land. Cholmondeley seems to have agreed to all this save the abandoning of the heriot. The precise outcome is uncertain although Whittaker certainly got the ground he wanted to lease. What is clear is that a desirable tenant could drive a very hard bargain indeed. Faced with such hard-bargaining tenants, landlords and their stewards must fight a rear-guard action to at least control the damage. One landlord, for example, refused to let land he had expensively marled other than 'for life', although quite prepared to let unmarled land for terms of years. Thus he would not allow a tenant to take a marled farm for a trial period of, say, two years to determine whether it would make the rent or justify the entry fine demanded, for fear the tenant would leave at the end of two years having simultaneously depleted the soil and given the farm a bad reputation.[31]

The tenants they were seeking were not only 'shy', they were adroit in the way in which they exploited that great enemy of the landlord: time. They would delay and delay as Lady Day approached in the hope of extracting concessions. Henry Vaughan, understeward at Maxey for Lord Fitzwilliam, suspected there was a confederacy among the neighbours to 'beat down the price' of a vacant farm 'because we are straitened in time because of ploughing it.'[32] Sitting tenants whose leases were up for renewal also employed delaying tactics, seeking to delay the renewal of their lease so long that the season would be too far advanced for other tenants to wish to take it 'and then they think to have their own terms' as one landlord indignantly observed.[33]

The correspondence of landlords often shows clearly, sometimes with unconscious humour, the long-drawn-out rearguard action that masters or stewards put up against the demands of stubborn hard-bargaining tenants who are negotiating renewal or potential tenants negotiating their first lease. They also show how often the rearguard action is really only a slow retreat with the tenant victorious at last. A landlord insists that a tenant must pay at least £50 a year and all taxes, and he is not permitted to plough more than 12 acres. The landlord will repair his house and barn but will not

[31] For the Whittaker case see Cholmondeley to Adams, 30 January, Adams to Cholmondeley 7 February, Michael Laroche to Adams 22 February 1700, Cholmondeley DCH/K/3/13 and 14; see also Whittaker's fine of £18 for the park land in Adams' accounts of Bickley collection for 1699–1700, DCH Accounts/1692. For the marling case see Brigadier George Cholmondeley to William Adams, 19 September, 17 October and 9 November 1700, Cholmondeley DCH/L/28.

[32] Fitzwilliam to Guybon, 5 December 1700, Fitzwilliam F(M)C 1154; *Fitzwilliam Correspondence*, Letter 165.

[33] Dowager Viscountess Cholmondeley to William Adams, 27 October 1685, Cholmondeley DCH K/3/6. A few months later she complains again: 'I find its a trick they put upon me to shuffle it off so far in the year till they think I can get no other [tenant] and then make their own terms with me.' Same to same, 23 January 1685, K/3/6.

supply timber to renew fences unless he buy it from him. A week later: if he will pay no more than £40 then he must not plough at all and he must still pay for his timber. A further week: if he will pay only £40 a year and only local taxes then he must not plough and must agree to four boon days a year of free labour on the lord's estate and donate a New Year's gift to the landlord's lady. Later still: well then he may plough 12 acres but the landlord must select the land to be ploughed himself, he must leave it fallow the last two years and sow it with sainfoin grass the last year. Meantime the landlord will donate the timber for the fences gratis. And so on, and so on. Often the many demands originally insisted on shrink to the derisory gift of a goose to the landlord's wife at Christmas. Not even the old traditional boon days survive on all occasions. 'Goody' Thomson defeated Lord Fitzwilliam in this, much to his dismay. She demanded a £4 reduction in rent before she would take a farm, to which Fitzwilliam countered with a forty-shilling reduction, an 'abatement' he declared he would make for nobody else (a hollow declaration in practice), and Guybon must not forget to demand a New Year's gift and boon days and only let it for three years. Alas, his steward bargained for a New Year's gift but no boon days nor any queen's taxes. It was an ill precedent to other tenants in the same parish, his master grumbled, and boon days could be no prejudice to her for he never employed the tenants at unseasonable times and when they had work to do for themselves. It was little consolation that Guybon had managed to persuade the hard-bargaining widow to an abatement of only £3 for at the beginning Fitzwilliam had declared he would never accept less than the full rent, then sworn he would take the farm in hand rather than see it drop more than twenty shillings. An abatement of £3 a year in a rent of £30 seemed a great loss, but, like so many of his fellow landlords, he was compelled to bear it. Early in the negotiations Fitzwilliam had welcomed her interest in the farm because, as he all too presciently put it, 'she is a notable woman'. The steward agreed, and would gladly have let it to her even at a £5 reduction. Better her at such a reduction than a less worthy tenant at the full amount, he argued.[34]

Goody Thomson was not alone in seeking lower rents, nor in attaining them. However, tenants stuck in a long lease who could not persuade their landlord to be 'kind' to them, and who did not wish to throw up their farm and take flight from their bargain, tended to seek another method of weathering hard times and poor markets. Faced with a rent it was impossible or at least inconvenient to pay they simply paid late or not at all. Even

[34] See also the letters concerning Benjamin Burton's farm, between 20 February and 4 July 1706, Fitzwilliam F(M)C 1459–61, 1479–82, 1499, 1500, 1507; *Fitzwilliam Correspondence*, Letters 418–20, 432–5, 446–8.

'good' tenants paying the proper rent did so at their own pace and at their own choice of time. The well-known image of tenants in their best smocks or Sunday go-to-meeting suits rolling up to the manor house at an appointed day, usually Lady Day or Michaelmas or both, and paying their rents across a long table to the agent and then drinking their landlord's health in the beer he had provided dates from a later era. It would have seemed an Elysian prospect to seventeenth-century landlords and stewards. The first Lord Cholmondeley in a grumbling letter to his recently appointed chief steward declared that he expected him 'to bring my affairs to that discreet settlement as my Lord Newport's whose rents are paid infallibly on his court days, has his estate set up a good pitch [i.e. let at high rents] and is reputed a good landlord'. He should have been reputed a prodigy if this claim was even half true. However I suspect that Lord Newport, in this respect at least, was of the nature of Sarah Gamps's 'Mrs 'arris'. As Jasper Helliar, beleaguered steward of the second Lord Cholmondeley's remote Somerset estates, reported in 1685, the tenants mainly disregarded the sittings of the manorial court at rent days, and half the Lady Day rents were still in arrears in August.[35] He should not have been surprised and his indignation was wasted energy for as John Warren, the Earl of Middlesex's Warwickshire steward, could have told him poor tenants had no hope of paying their rent until they had received income by selling their crops.[36] Similarly in Shropshire tenants never paid their rents before Stretton Fair, at which they sold their produce, which was a full two months after Lady Day.[37] This situation was exacerbated if unfavourable seasons – too wet, too dry, situations of over-abundance or of dearth – made it difficult for tenants to market their wool or beef or other crops. From drought-stricken Leicestershire in August 1684 a steward warned the Earl of Huntingdon that many landlords had not even called for their Lady Day rents, by then nearly five months in arrears, not even 'my Lord Chesterfield who is accounted a hard landlord', because 'nothing sells well being no grass either to fatten or keep them'.[38] The steward on this occasion disingenuously offered to arrest the tenants if it was his master's 'pleasure', knowing

---

[35] Cholmondeley to William Adams, 3 December 1679, Cholmondeley DCH/K/3/1. Helliar to William Adams, 17 August 1685, DCH/L/48.

[36] 'Your honour's tenants here think they do well if they pay one half year before another is due ... I think it is better to have a little patience with them than to seize their stock.' John Warren, steward at Milcot Lady, to the Earl of Middlesex, 7 July 1675, Sackville Mss U269/C125/20.

[37] Thomas Hawkes, steward at Stretton, to Thomas Thynne, 7 May 1674, Thynne xx, fo. 138.

[38] Gervas Jaquis, steward at Ashby de la Zouch, 13 August 1684, Hastings HA7739. 'Your honour ... is much offended in my slow returns but it is not mine but your tenants' faults who do not pay me for I am not wanting in calling on them daily, but they cannot pay 'till they make money of their goods.'

that this would be the last thing Huntingdon would want. The tenants knew this also, and exploited their awareness to the full. Lord North was told that a Henry Dear had come to pay £20 off his considerable arrears and, as the steward ironically added, 'according to the custom of the country he will pay the rest as soon as he can'.[39]

Paying at their convenience was a custom firmly adhered to by many tenants in the second half of the seventeenth century, and the landlords were helpless to break them from it. As a consequence there is one subject which is common to all estate correspondence in this period: the vexed topic of arrears. Stewards, however determined to act conscientiously in their master's interests, however determined in their own interest to keep them well supplied with money, found it difficult to extract rents from the poorer tenants. As a result, since there is a natural tendency for things which are difficult but possible to get most attention and things which seem almost impossible to be pushed to the back of the desk, some tenants would run on for years paying little or no rent at all. If the steward was young and vigorous, scarcely a day passing without him saddling his horse for some journey about the estate, such tenants would be few and harassed. If he was old and increasingly enfeebled, or suffering frequent bouts of ill health, the poor payers or non-payers would become an increasing proportion of the tenants as a whole. In his later years Francis Guybon was just such an ageing steward. The poorer tenants of such Fitzwilliam manors as Marholm, Northborough and Etton appear to have taken full advantage of this, and the steward largely gave up the battle and behaved as if he hoped that since the individual rents were small his master would not notice that some of them were missing. In the long run this hope naturally proved vain. Like other landlords Fitzwilliam had firm views on arrears, particularly so far as poor tenants were concerned. No poor tenant should be allowed to run more than a year or two in arrear for their few possessions could not secure the debt. 'They have nothing to pay it with but their cows and then how can they live?'[40] Fitzwilliam, a more-generous-hearted man perhaps than the average landowner, was not unsympathetic to the plight of his poorer tenants, observing on one occasion how 'heartily sorry' he was to hear 'how sad times it is' with them. He was prepared to accept whatever rents they could pay even though well below the rent on the rent roll, so long as he could live from what they paid for 'I care for no more.' However, he believed they should all pay something because he was convinced that too much forbearance made many of them 'careless and begets their ruin'.

---

[39] Francis White, steward at Kirtling, Cambridgeshire, to Lord North, 26 March 1667, North C4 fo. 133.
[40] Fitzwilliam to Guybon, 30 May 1706, Fitzwilliam F(M)C 1490; *Fitzwilliam Correspondence*, Letter 441.

His views on the perils of forbearance were shared by his fellow land-owners.[41]

On some estates landlords faced with years of neglect and arrears no tenants could possibly hope to pay were compelled to 'forgive' the arrears and clear the books, although not usually until after long and strenuous efforts to recover them. The classic instance of this was the Leveson-Gower estate in Staffordshire where the first Lord Gower's father, Sir William Gower, had damaged a fine estate by leaving it in inadequate hands while he enjoyed lengthy London 'seasons'. Inadequate hands because instead of following the example of so many of his contemporaries and employing a chief steward, he simply relied on local tenant bailiffs of the type the first Viscount Cholmondeley had found so unsatisfactory.[42] As Dr Wordie writes: 'these men were tenants, associated themselves with the interests of the tenants, and were expected to do nothing more than collect rents', in return for a modest annual payment. Unhappily, although not surprisingly, even this limited duty was ill discharged, and by 1691 Sir William's heir found his tenants in arrear to the tune of £1,532, whereas the combined arrears for 1668–70 had amounted to only £174.[43] Sir William Gower's income had been cut nearly in half. The fact that this still left him with more than £2,000 a year perhaps explains his complaisant attitude to arrears, always supposing that he grasped that they existed. When under the first Lord Gower the Reverend George Plaxton was given overall control as chief steward of the estates in Shropshire, Staffordshire and Yorkshire, with more substantial understewards to supervise the affairs of discrete blocks of properties, the new broom dreamed of one day reclaiming these arrears but despite prodigies of organisation and efficient estate management over a period of more than a quarter of a century, he finally gave up the struggle and persuaded his master to write off the arrears which had been owing since 1691.[44]

---

[41] 'I will forbear them willingly what is reasonable and fitting for both their good and mine.' Fitzwilliam to Guybon, 2 October 1707, Fitzwilliam F(M)C 1614; *Fitzwilliam Correspondence*, Letter 529. His distrust of forbearing if not his charitableness had been shared by the Earl of Dorset a generation earlier: 'if they be bad tenants it is better to take a course with them at first than let them run on at length, for I never yet knew any tenant the better for forbearing'. Dorset to Thomas Brome, March 1677, Sackville U269/C656/64.

[42] '. . . effecting to beat down my estate and not improve it, being against their interest'. See his complaints of 18 and 29 November 1679, Cholmondeley DCH/K/3/1.

[43] Wordie, *Estate Management*, 18–19. Dr Wordie points out that the figure for 1691 was for the whole estate, whereas the 1668–70 figure was for the Shropshire–South Staffordshire estates only, but this does not materially invalidate the comparison, particularly when it is remembered that the second figure is for one year only.

[44] Wordie, *Estate Management*, 35. Plaxton's excellent management had both increased the income and achieved regular payment of it, but despite all his efforts he could never reduce the arrears he had inherited.

The Leveson-Gower estate problems involved more than just arrears. Sir William Gower had sacrificed long-term financial interest for short-term gain by letting leases for large fines but inadequate rents; usually these were leases for three lives. Leasehold tenants on his estates, as on the estates of other careless landlords, tended to regard their farms as virtually their property and even if supposedly bound by covenants as to how they should maintain the farm buildings and other capital assets, and how they should treat the soil which they leased, would try to ignore the terms of their lease when it suited them. One important covenant which careful landlords would always insist on inserting related to ploughing. The questions of how much land a tenant might be permitted to plough and for how long he should continue to plough it could be contentious issues which troubled that harmonious relationship between landlord and tenant which stewards laboured to achieve. Landlords not only wanted rent from their land, they wanted the land to retain its value, not simply in the sense of holding its rent but also of retaining its fertility. Fitzwilliam might have been absent from his estate for years at a time but nobody took a closer interest in the terms of his leases, prescribing how much and for how many years of a lease land could be ploughed, and for how many years it should be grazed, with the last year sown with sainfoin grass. No landlord was more determined that his tenants should not be allowed to 'plough it out of heart' as he put it.[45] Despite warnings from his steward that 'gentlemen must be kind ... and give leave to plough or else it will be worse for landlord and tenant' Fitzwilliam was determined that no farmer should plough unless his lease permitted it and the lease would specify precisely what land should be ploughed and what should not. When a tenant called Burton insisted on ploughing even though the lease was still not signed or fully agreed Fitzwilliam warned his steward: if Burton 'has not a mind to be ruined let him leave off ploughing for I have law enough of my side and money enough to deal with any pragmatical fellow that will plough my land up whether I will or no'.[46] When the tenant realised he had gone too far and apologised with uncharacteristic humility Fitzwilliam still declared that he must now try at law whether Burton should plough 'my land whether I will or no'. He was too pragmatical and 'must be humbled' for nobody should plough without a lease. In fact nothing happened to Burton, for Fitzwilliam's bark was fiercer than his bite, and the 'pragmatical fellow' seems to

[45] He instructs his steward concerning one tenant: 'Pray be watchful of him and secure my rent without you perceive he begins to plough again and likely to continue. I expect he should lay my land 3 years from ploughing before he leaves which his lease obliges him to.' To Guybon, 29 January 1708, Fitzwilliam F(M)C 1641, *Fitzwilliam Correspondence*, Letter 548.

[46] To Guybon, 26 February 1708, Fitzwilliam F(M)C 1647, *Fitzwilliam Correspondence*, Letter 553.

have got away with his 'pragmatism'. Possibly the steward's mediating influence had taken effect. Even as he reported that Burton was ploughing 10 acres without authority he urged that Fitzwilliam must give more tenants 'leave to plough a little'. Certainly by 15 April Fitzwilliam's threats had shrunk to no more than a petulant: 'Burton having ploughed up my land without first acquainting me I shall build him no barn until I have better considered of it'.[47]

The 'pragmatical' ploughman could be found on many estates. 'Ware the butcher, notwithstanding what I can do hath ploughed both the fields, telling me that he will enjoy his bargain' reports John Peck in 1649.[48] 'I have offered Mr Polden again to let him have his tithe for £40 per annum ... provided that he plough no more than heretofore, but he will not be tied to any such thing. No doubt but he intends to break up the Down before his time be expired' warns Thomas Allen in 1690.[49] Such defiance is a familiar story. So is the alarm among landlords to which it gave rise. In 1684 the dowager Lady Cholmondeley complained to her steward that she had heard that one Richard Downes had had a great bargain at her farm of Carton, and had ploughed 'above 20 Cheshire Acres which is a great deal and will make it worth nothing ... If you make no better bargains than this I shall bring my jointure to very little at last.'[50] Lady Cholmondeley's anxiety was characteristic of landlords who, while they found very tempting the higher rents brought by arable land, nevertheless feared for the long-term value of their estate if their stewards negligently, or worse, connivingly, permitted unrestricted ploughing. A decade later Lady Cholmondeley's son was moved to fury when he received a letter from Orchard, the understeward charged with the oversight of his Somerset estates, in which Orchard proposed to let a farm at a reduced rent because it had been extensively ploughed over many years.[51] As a justification for a lower rent

---

[47] Guybon to Fitzwilliam, 23 February, 8 March, Fitzwilliam F(M)C 1645, 1650; Fitzwilliam to Guybon, 11 March, 15 April, F(M)C 1652, 1660, *Fitzwilliam Correspondence*, Letters 552, 556, 557, 563.

[48] Peck to Sir John Trevor, 5 January 1649, Trevor D/G/3276. Ware was just as defiant in November for 'notwithstanding your son's power of revocation [of his lease] and my persuasions' he had begun to plough his field. 17 November 1649, D/G/3276.

[49] Allen to Lord Weymouth, 6 January 1690, Thynne xxiv, fo. 117.

[50] Lady Cholmondeley to Adams, 17 September 1684, Cholmondeley DCH/K/3/6. It was hard to cure rogue ploughers of their roguery. Three years later, while Downes was renegotiating his lease at Carton, Lady Cholmondeley was surprised to find that her steward had allowed Downes to continue on the farm without first signing a lease 'for I do not intend he shall hold it three years to plough it with what corn he pleases' for he 'thinks to have it as his own terms and keeps all others from taking it'. 3 March 1687, Cholmondeley DCH/K/3/7.

[51] 'He tells me he'll give but £65 per annum for it ... there is near 50 acres of it in tillage and has been so a long while, which has much lowered the value of the farm.' Lancelot Orchard, 7 January 1697, Cholmondeley DCH/L/48.

this was certainly tactless. While the lower rent proposed was remarkable, Cholmondeley thundered, it was still more astonishing that he should employ for an argument an excuse which was only a sympton of his 'negligence if not knavery', for 50 acres could not be ploughed up in a year without destroying both pasture and meadow which was contrary to the covenants in all leases. Cholmondeley felt he had no choice but to take that and another similarly mistreated farm in hand for two years and bear the inevitable loss in order to 'recover 'em a little after this shameful villainous usage', and 'break this combination and knavery that is upon me', even deciding to uproot a minor gentleman in his service 'from his own country, Cheshire', to supervise the farms for a year or two until he could break this 'damned knot of knaves'.[52] This might seem, even for the terrible-tempered Cholmondeley, a strong reaction to an apparently innocent remark about tillage, but it was simply an extreme expression of a common anxiety.

It was the duty of the stewards as guardians of the estate to protect it against such exploitation by the tenants. Cholmondeley was always too ready to believe that every setback he suffered was the consequence of deliberate knavery, with his agents leagued with local enemies against him. However, the least paranoid landlord would have been dismayed and enraged to find that his local agent had stood idly by whilst most of a farm was turned to tillage by its tenant. Orchard's not unreasonable explanation was that the farm had been so tilled for many years before the estate was placed in his charge. It did not save him. He was replaced shortly after. Nevertheless if stewards had to protect property they also had to promote harmony, and this was difficult when their masters wanted as little land turned to arable as they could persuade or compel tenants to accept and the tenants wished to plough as much land as they could get away with. This irreconcilable conflict of interest provided stewards with serious problems. Repeatedly we find stewards doffing their protector hat in favour of their mediator hat, urging their masters to permit this or that tenant to plough, or to moderate their demands for rent of arable land. Thomas Allen urged his master to lower the rent of part of a farm which had been enclosed for pasture between the tenants signing his lease and actually coming to the farm. Although the change was an improvement to the estate as a whole, he points out, it was certainly a loss to the tenant at the time.[53] Stewards would even occasionally mediate on behalf of illicit ploughing, usually on compassionate grounds. Thomas Hawkes reports that two poor men in Little Stretton who have 'great charges of children' had enclosed two small

---

[52] Cholmondeley to William Adams, 23 January 1697, Cholmondeley DCH/K/3/12.
[53] Tactfully concluding 'but if your lordship thinks otherwise you may compel him to hold it by the contract ... which he signed'. Allen to Weymouth, 20 January 1690, Thynne xxiv, fo. 126.

grounds and sowed them with corn which was almost ripe. If his master expected any additional rent from them he must give speedy orders in it. 'I think it a piece of charity to give it them and [I] hope you will please to do it.'[54] Sometimes, however, the stewards claimed to have an eye to the estate's long-term advantage, as when Thomas Wilkinson at Castle Rising urged that the land a tenant wished to plough was overrun with mole hills and it would be a great charge to cut them, and if the land were ploughed for four or five years and then laid down with clover it would improve the farm and be much to the advantage of his mistress as well as the tenant. On occasions the interests of the steward might be directly engaged if he was a substantial tenant himself. Thomas Hawkes presents the uncommon picture of a steward virtually disqualifying himself as an advocate and declaring a personal interest: the tenants at Stretton were importunate with him for permission to plough a field on the common, offering 'the ninth sheaf'. Hawkes had counter-offered the eighth sheaf but, since he would be himself a beneficiary of the new tillage, left it to his master to set the terms if he agreed to the ploughing at all.[55]

There were other occasions when the roles were reversed, when landlords were seeking tenants prepared to take land for ploughing and to pay the enhanced rents which would be demanded. If the rents were deemed too high, at least under the local climatic conditions or the state of the market for grain, then the steward would once again find himself mediating, seeking to persuade his master to accept lower rents. In August 1647 Robert Hawdon warned his master, the Earl of Middlesex, that the latter's 'prices' for land for ploughing were 'so high that men will not hearken thereto' because of the high price which seed corn was likely to bear that year. His mediation seems to have failed for in November he mourns that he is unlikely to let any land to plough for corn, for corn was 'at so great a price for seed that men are fearful to adventure'.[56]

The power which scarcity gave to tenants to resist the hegemony of the landlords during the later seventeenth century did not simply extend to successfully lowering rents or obtaining more favourable terms and covenants in their leases. The phenomenon of tenants adversarially confronting their landlord, either as individuals or in groups, appears over a broad spectrum of issues, and includes circumstances where the landlord appeared to be clearly in the right. Tenants were always supposed to give

---

[54] Thomas Hawkes to Sir Thomas Thynne 14 August 1677; Thynne xx, fo. 337.
[55] Wilkinson to Thomas Matthew, 10 February 1707, Howard 663/349. Hawkes to Sir Thomas Thynne, 14 August 1677, Thynne xx, fo. 337.
[56] Hawdon to Middlesex from Milcott, Warwickshire, 30 August and 27 November 1647, Sackville U269/C249.

long notice of their intention to quit a farm or a substantial piece of land. This was a covenant more honoured in the breach than the observance, particularly among rack-rent tenants who leased by the year. 'It is a maxim among the rusticks that if a man holds from year to year he is not obliged to give notice of his departure', explained a steward who was reporting the unheralded departure of three such tenants.[57] One is struck again and again by the tenants' reluctance to pay their landlords money which is clearly owed, whether in the form of rents, or fines or such unpopular feudal dues as heriots. As we have seen, tenants appear to have taken the view that not only should rents and fines be low they should be paid at the convenience of the tenant. As for heriots, the surrender of the best beast on the farm (or the money value of it) at the death of the tenant by his heirs or executors, the struggles between the stewards and recalcitrant tenants seeking to evade this feudal due will be discussed in more detail later.[58] Suffice to say here that common strategies were either to deny that any heriot was owed at all, or, if the terms of the lease were too clear for that to be a successful tactic, to cheat the lord of the best beast by passing off some inferior one and hiding the best beast or transferring it to some other farm until the danger was over.

Where tenants were debtors they were quick to exploit the law, a weapon which many have too readily assumed was a weapon only employed by the gentles. As estate records repeatedly demonstrate, seventeenth-century lawyers drew their clientele from a wide social spectrum, not simply relying for their clientage on the bigger landlords. When a bailiff seized two horses for two heriots owed at the death of a Mrs Giles, her grandson frightened the official into leaving the horses on the property by threatening to replevin them and to go to trial with Lord Weymouth because, he claimed, his grandmother's life was not in the lease.[59] Moreover, even when tenants did not employ lawyers, they were aware of opportunities the common law provided and exploited them, particularly when they wished to avoid or at least to delay making payments of rents or fines to their landlord. There is an ancient Indian proverb that 'it is the poor grass which suffers when two kings go to war'. However, in seventeenth-century England when two great landowners 'went to war', or at least to law, when disputing the ownership of parts of their estates, the 'poor grass' sat up and took notice, smelling advantage on the wind. In the 1650s such a dispute raged between Sir Henry Frederick Thynne and Sir James Thynne of Longleat and we find the

---

[57] Thomas Allen, steward at Longleat, to Lord Weymouth, 14 April 1684, Thynne xxii, fo. 81.

[58] For the resistance to heriot and the corresponding vigour of the lord's assertion of it see below Chapter 10.

[59] Thomas Allen, steward at Longleat, to Weymouth, 12 April 1690, Thynne xxiv, fo. 202.

Longleat steward writing dolefully to his master that the tenants would pay no rent till the title was clear between his master and Sir Henry, for they claimed, with grim irony, that there could be no security better to them than their detaining their money in their own hands. Similarly when Lord Carlisle acquired lands formerly the property of Sir John Ballantyne, his steward at Naworth Castle reported angrily that the tenants on that land refused to pay their fines because Lord Carlisle had not signed them a bond to indemnify them of any claims by Ballantyne's executors after his death. Carlisle should bring writs against them for they were 'very obstinate fellows' who deserved no favour.[60] The truth is there were a lot of very obstinate fellows among the ranks of English farmers in this period, and not all of them were to be found among the comparatively affluent tenants for the poor were often prepared to assert themselves.

It might seem that tenants, whether versed in the law or not, would be helpless against the landlord if they demonstrably owed him money. He could sue them in the county court or he could haul them before his manorial court, presided over by a steward of courts who was one of his attorneys, and with the proceedings recorded by the estate steward. Such a court could serve notice of eviction or it could authorise the impounding of the debtor's cattle – horses, sheep, cows, pigs – either in the pound or pinfold, which was a manorial institution controlled by the lord and his officials, or if the stock seized was too numerous for such an enclosure he could carry them off to his own demesne lands and could legally charge the debtor rent for the time they remained there. If the debtor tenant still refused to pay his arrears of rents or fines he could send the stock to market and sell the goods to recover his debt. In the final resort he could evict the tenant from the property. Against such formidable weapons what possible defence could a recalcitrant or debtor tenant make? No doubt some tenants did passively give up, but again and again we find stubborn, ingenious tenants fighting long and sometimes successful rearguard actions against such sanctions. In the first place tenants did not take kindly to having their cattle impounded. Some went the legal way and took out a writ of replevin which at least temporarily restored their cattle to them. Others were less subtle. In 1689 Thomas Pope, steward at Kempsford for Lord Weymouth exasperatedly reported that one debtor was 'very poor but very prodigal' (he meant wicked, not extravagant) for he broke almost all orders issued by Weymouth's manorial courts, and if anyone impounded his cattle he had 'tricks to fetch them forth when he please by false keys and other ways'.[61]

[60] William Thynne to Sir James Thynne, 12 April 1659, Thynne xi, fo. 105. James Maxwell to Carlisle, 6 November 1695, Castle Howard Mss J8/28/14.
[61] Pope to Weymouth 7 December 1689, Thynne xxiv, fo. 98.

Some scorned 'tricks' in favour of simply breaking down the pound wall and letting their beasts out.

Another device was to convey cattle into the ownership of some friend or relative. 'Allyn's sister pretends the colts and all his goods are made over to her and upon good consideration' indignantly reported William Thynne in 1659, after he had seized the goods and horses of a debtor tenant wildly in arrears, 'so that he doth not only deceive you of rent but would cheat also by this trick.'[62] Some tenants were ready to thwart their landlord from beyond the grave for when they felt the pangs of death close at hand they took steps to ensure that nothing would be found on the farm which would be worth the seizing. The impulse to thwart their landlord posthumously could take other forms with ancient tenants marrying a 'lusty young wife' who, under the terms of their tenure, would inherit the tenancy which would prevent their lords from recovering the farm at their death and leasing it on an 'improved' tenure.[63] Other tenants fought long delaying battles with their landlords by deceiving the steward as to the extent of the lands they actually held. In an era when accurate surveying of estates was still in its infancy, this could be a more successful tactic than might seem possible today. Lord Fitzwilliam's Norfolk steward had a long-drawn-out battle with a supposed tenant who refused to pay any rent for his land on the grounds, as he claimed, that it did not belong to Fitzwilliam and neither landlord nor steward could find convincing proof that the claim was fraudulent.[64] This explains the readiness of tenants to thwart or at least delay stewards who sought to define and describe more accurately the leasehold and copyhold farms within a particular manor when drawing up a more up-to-date rent roll. Thus we find a Sussex steward blaming his failure to complete a new rent roll on the tenants who were 'so averse and backward therein, unwilling to make out and discover what lands they hold and what rents they pay'.[65]

The landlord's ultimate sanction was eviction, a weapon which they used reluctantly and as a last resort. Even then there were eleventh-hour

---

[62] William Thynne to Sir James Thynne, 24 January 1659, Thynne xi, fos. 83v–84.

[63] To the considerable satisfaction of the steward one example of this scheme backfired, for when the 'lusty young wife' was delivered of a child 'as she was milking her ewes' she claimed it had been fathered by another man 'which hath almost broke the old man's heart but it is a just reward for him'. Richard Pollard to Rachel, Countess of Bath, 1 May 1642, Sackville U269/C276.

[64] This was a long-drawn-out struggle, with the tenant, Rowbottom, refusing to produce his rent until Fitzwilliam produced his deeds; with King declining his master's advice to put stock on the land on the sensible ground that Fitzwilliam had no stock and no other farmer would agist his stock there because Rowbottom would simply impound it for trespass. Arthur King to Fitzwilliam, 9 March, 5 August, 9 September, 30 November 1685, 7 February 1686, Fitzwilliam F(M)C 510, 516, 523, 524, 530.

[65] Edward Raynes, Lewes, to the Earl of Dorset, 2 February 1669, Sackville U269/C58.

reprieves. Tenants would be evicted in a manner heavy with symbolism, turned out onto the road, their cattle with them, and publicly discharged from being tenants with the steward and other estate servants on their horses as potent symbols of the lord's authority and the whole drama witnessed by interested or anxious neighbours. Then, in return for good security for the arrears and with solemn and publicly uttered promises of better payment of their rents they would be allowed back into their home and permitted to drive their cattle back onto the pastures.[66] However, not all tenants were prepared to play their part in such edifying dramas, particularly if they suspected there was little hope of reprieve. Some tenants would barricade themselves in their houses at the approach of the steward and his assistants. In 1651 a steward who was bent on evicting tenants who refused to yield their farms although their leases had been fraudulently obtained, accompanied the sheriff to one house and overcame the resistance of one man, his wife and a maid, and turned them out in favour of caretakers for his master. He then advanced with the sheriff and his men upon a much larger farm, but the news had gone ahead of them and the house was barricaded and 'strongly kept', a gun being discharged from within. The sheriff forced his way in and removed ten men and women and several children. In both places the sheriff read his authority and gave them all three days' liberty to clear their stock from the ground, after which the delinquents saw they had no alternative 'and began to relent and submit'. On the Saturday the steward held court and the evicted appeared and were 'sorrowful for what they had done' and some solicited to remain tenants, which the steward refused. However, a brother-in-law of one of the tenants intervened for his sister's sake, and the steward having 'the pretext' that 'he was an honest and able man' relented. Some at least of the evicted were restored although their fraudulent leases were surrendered.[67]

There were resolute tenants who were prepared to go further than barricading themselves in their houses. Some were ready to use fear as a weapon, usually by the threat of employing a successful recourse to law against the lord's servants, but also the threat of violence and even, occasionally, actual violence against a landlord's officials. In 1651 John Peck found himself contending with 'such a mad fellow'. A debtor tenant named Clanthorne, who had taken care to rid himself of his cattle so that they could not be seized, had taken a neighbour's cattle onto his ground. When Peck sent 'three lusty man' to distrain them the tenant, abetted by his wife and his father, beat them soundly and recovered the cattle. Peck therefore sent a warrant to the High Constable who entered the house with

[66] A typical example was described by Thomas Brome in a letter to a London servant of Lady Dorset, 25 April 1683, Sackville U269/C98.
[67] William Lynne reporting to the Countess of Bath, 13 October 1651, Sackville U269/C277.

his men but Clanthorne took up a 'great cleaver and was like to have killed him' so that the High Constable fled. Finally Peck with a band of men went himself, seized Clanthorne and his father and goods from the house to help pay the debt, but finding that he could get nobody to take the Clanthornes to gaol made an agreement with him that they should be released on condition that the turbulent tenant vacated the premises, which he did and went off, perhaps appropriately, 'to be a soldier'.[68] Even more infuriating for steward and landlord was the experience of the chief steward of the Duchess of Newcastle, Ralph Gowland, who in the autumn of 1716 sent a bailiff to evict a recalcitrant tenant named Hudson from his farm. Hudson bolted the door against the bailiff and when he beat on the door the debtor's wife ran a sword through a knot hole and the bailiff narrowly escaped with his life. Hudson drove off with his dogs any cattle brought onto the farm by his sister and brother-in-law who had agreed to take a lease of it, and meanwhile kept his own stock safe on a neighbour's ground. Gowland bound Hudson over to keep the peace until the next assizes. Three months later Hudson was still forted up in his farm. Although Gowland had succeeded in having Hudson committed to prison, demanding that he be close confined with bail set at the impossible figure of £200, the sheriff had weakly let Hudson out and he had promptly grasped the opportunity to replevin his stock which the steward had contrived to seize during his brief incarceration. Hudson had by then run through a whole range of expedients popular amongst embattled tenants: threats, casual violence, concealment of assets on a friend's ground, repleving confiscated stock, and somehow suborning an official (in this instance the sheriff of Northumberland) who might have been expected automatically to support the landlord.[69]

One of the unusual aspects of that Northumbrian conflict is the fact that the steward had managed to find a replacement tenant. Usually tenant farmer solidarity tended to help the potential evictee. Finding replacement tenants was very difficult, particularly when the recalcitrant tenant could use fear as a weapon. In 1685 Francis Guybon was contending with some tenants called Cooper. They owed long arrears of rent and Fitzwilliam wanted them off his land. This was easier said than done. Guybon found them terrifying figures, who might seek the steward's injury either at law or perhaps by violence. However, he seized all Cooper's stock and drove them to Stamford market where they were sold, providing enough money to cover his arrears and all charges and leave a surplus. However, Cooper

---

[68] 'God bless me from him for I fear the beggarly knave intended me no good.' Peck to Sir John Trevor the younger, 5 November 1651, Trevor D/G/3276.

[69] Ralph Gowland to the Duchess of Newcastle, 28 September 1716, Portland (Newcastle) PW2/544.

refused to receive the surplus or to come to any account, threatening lawsuits against Guybon and his assistants, claiming they had done more than they 'could answer in selling them' but, Guybon anxiously asks, 'I hope your honour will stand by us.' He had been unable to let the farm because the tenants were 'fearful to meddle with it, [the Coopers] are such devilish, dangerous people, and [Cooper] give out words that he will not part with it'. Guybon concluded wistfully that he wished with all his heart that they would leave the town. He warned his master that Cooper intended to visit him soon but Fitzwilliam must not be alone with him for fear he should do him 'some mischief'.[70] Here the Coopers seem to have frightened off potential tenants in order to frustrate the landlord, but it was not at all uncommon for tenants the lord was seeking to evict to peacefully discourage potential tenants who would rarely consent to dislodge a sitting tenant against his will. We find the dowager Lady Cholmondeley writing to her steward to demand that a tenant be turned out of his farm immediately for she finds he 'knavishly puts off others and disparages' the property, claiming, no doubt, to anyone who came to inspect it that the land would not yield the rent and so on – an old trick which landlords bitterly resented firstly, because it was often so effective, and secondly, and more importantly, because it was likely to give such farms a bad reputation and so devalue the estate.[71] Her son was just as enraged when he discovered that a tenant who refused to remain on his farm unless the rent was reduced by £10 had told a prospective tenant that he had no intention of leaving so the other, who would have paid the full rent, had found himself a farm elsewhere. Nevertheless, despite his anger, it is clear that Cholmondeley was considering reducing the rent when he came down in the spring. The recalcitrant tenant seems to have been playing his hand skilfully.[72]

Not just tenants of farms played these tricks; it could happen at mills, or even saltworks. Lord Cholmondeley and Sir Orlando Bridgeman owned a saltworks jointly. The tenant was heavily in arrears and another potential tenant had been discreetly found but the latter refused to sign a lease until his predecessor had official notice to quit, which caused Lady Bridgeman to suspect that the old and new tenant 'hold intelligence with one another'. She supposed the 'design' was to beat down the rental value of the works although she believed it to have been let too low in the past.[73] Millers with

---

[70] Francis Guybon to Fitzwilliam, 22 April 1678, Fitzwilliam F(M)C 441.
[71] To William Adams, 26 November 1685, Cholmondeley DCH K/3/6. 'I am assured he has used me ill' wrote her husband on an earlier occasion, explaining why he never wished to deal again with such a tenant, '. . . endeavouring to bear down my rent and keeping others from dealing . . . In time [I] shall let them know I have noted them who intend to improve themselves by debasing my rents.' Cholmondeley to Adams, 7 February 1680, DCH K/3/1.
[72] Cholmondeley to Adams, 24 October 1689, Cholmondeley DCH M/27.
[73] Lady Bridgeman to Adams, 6 October 1686, Cholmondeley DCH L/48.

their tendency to defraud their customers, or to be suspected of doing it guilty or not, were rarely popular members of farming communities. Yet even they were protected from too hasty eviction by the reluctance of potential tenants to benefit from the eviction of another. In Staffordshire in 1688 Lord Weymouth's steward, John Mainewaring, found great difficulty in ridding his master of a miller hopelessly in arrears. Detested as a cheat by his neighbours who insisted on taking their grain elsewhere, abandoned by his relatives who knew his financial situation only too well, Mainewaring could not oust him because the only potential tenant he could find refused to take the mill if it meant the eviction of his predecessor.[74]

Even this brief summary of the functions and activities of the steward at the interface between lord and tenant demonstrates the problems and difficulties he faced and the laboriousness of the work involved. At the same time it demonstrates that tenants in the second half of the Stuart era could be formidably stubborn, alert to their own interests and capable of defending them against what they perceived as assaults from either landlord or steward. They were very ready to exploit the many remedies furnished by the law; they were adroit at playing off lord against steward and steward against lord; they knew the weaknesses of the steward's position and the strengths of their own and took all advantages of them. The steward could not rely on brute force, or even on the law's kindness to property and its owners, but needed the skills of a diplomat and of a politician, and had to know how to use to best effect the subtle but potent influences of prestige, deference and judicious, if sparing, patronage. In view of the stewards' problems it is remarkable that they were as generally successful as they were, particularly when one remembers that diverse as their activities were at this interface between their employer and his tenants, this was only one area of their duties. For example, equally important in their lords' eyes was the duty of supplying them speedily and regularly with the income from their estates. This vital activity, without which no landlord could have left his estate for the labours of government or the pleasures of the city, presented its own problems which we must now consider.

[74] Mainewaring to Weymouth, 22 August 1688, Thynne xxviii, fos. 226–8.

5

Returns to London

Many come to me ... to leave money with me to have it in London.
                                    Robert Herrick, Leicester tradesman, 1616[1]

though you'll travel all over Cheshire and Shropshire I must one way or other have bills for these £364 ... or else I am undone, for I can no longer keep my credit here without it. Therefore I do expect without any frivolous or nonsensical excuses that without any further delay you get bills for this money, for in short I must be forced else to change hands ... I desire that you would once take it for granted that I am in earnest, else I must be forced to convince you by way much ... against my nature.
                                    Lord Cholmondeley to William Adams, 1701[2]

In the eyes of his master few duties of the steward assumed a greater significance than that of transmitting to him the fruits of his estate. In the eyes of the steward few duties can have seemed more onerous. In an era before the development of country-wide banking institutions, with credit-transfer arrangements still unsophisticated and restricted, and with the roads, especially those radiating from London, infested with highwaymen, securely transferring substantial sums from provincial estates to London-based landlords or their goldsmiths presented very real problems. The struggles of stewards as they grappled with these problems and the ingenious shifts they adopted to solve them, with these struggles going on continuously, month by month, not seasonal or limited to the weeks following Lady Day and Michaelmas, make stewards' records a vital source for Britain's financial system during this period.[3] This was not a new problem in the second half of the seventeenth century although the increasing tendency for landowners to spend some part of each year in London, and some to stay years at a time, increased the scale of the problem

[1] Quoted in Kerridge, *Trade and Banking*, 52.
[2] To his chief steward William Adams, 22 February 1701, Cholmondeley DCH/L/28.
[3] A rich variety of provincial and London-based merchants, craftsmen and manufacturers were also grappling with the same problems but I suspect that the survival rate of their records cannot match the wealth of archives which survive from landed estates in all parts of the kingdom. For some that have survived, see the valuable references and bibliography in Kerridge's *Trade and Banking*. For an important pioneering study of Midlands land-lords and their efforts to transfer money to London see Davies, 'Gentry Payments', 15–36.

whilst making its incidence more widely experienced.[4] Some landowners could receive London income, either from pensions or monopolies paid in London, or could directly sell meat or wool to London markets and receive their profits there, like the Spensers, or sell iron and lead mined on their estates to London merchants, like the Earls of Rutland and Shrewsbury, or receive rents from extensive London properties, like the Earls of Bedford and Southampton, but even these landlords needed to move some income from their rural estates to London. The vast majority of landlords, however, were wholly dependent on their rural resources to meet London expenses.[5]

As early as 1595 the Earl of Huntingdon transferred some of his Leicestershire rents to London by the personal bills of Robert Herrick a Leicester tradesman, drawn on his brother William, a London goldsmith who also acted as agent for Robert's hosiery. As Robert wrote to his brother: 'Many come to me ... to leave money with me to have it in London' thereby unconsciously offering us a definition of a 'return'.[6] This demonstrates how early the inland bill of exchange had appeared to assist the landlord to 'return' his rural income to London. However, it was only one of several expedients adopted even then, of which the most unsatisfactory because much the most hazardous, was to send rural income as specie, that is in gold or silver coins, by road. Despite the hazards of loss by highwaymen this method was occasionally used by desperate landlords and stewards throughout the seventeenth century. In fact there was little gold to be had in the country, so that rents had to be largely conveyed in silver, much of it shilling pieces, which made the parcels both bulky and heavy – disadvantages which eager footpads were happy to contend with, particularly as it made such consignments difficult to conceal. When in 1602 Sir William Cavendish wanted to move the remarkable sum of £13,500 to London he had to engage a body of armed guards to escort the baggage train, the operation costing £43. He had no choice for the country's primitive credit networks could not have handled such an enormous sum in one transaction. Similarly the Earl of Northumberland in 1603 moved his northern rents from Topcliffe to London under the armed escort of seventeen men. In the 1630s the rents from the West Country estates of the Earl of Salisbury were still being sent up by carrier or under the conveyance of his own servants. In 1641 the Earl of Cork was compelled to risk sending £3,300 packed into carts in order to pay a debt, while Wentworth was driven to

---

[4] Moreover, as Stone reminds us, the increasing tendency to draw on London for a wider variety of luxury goods increased the need to transfer safely rural earnings to metropolitan coffers. Stone, *Crisis*, 510.

[5] *Ibid.*

[6] Stone, *Crisis*, 512; Kerridge, *Trade and Banking*, 52 ff. where the Herricks' operations are described in interesting detail.

send recusant fines from Yorkshire in specie with a dozen of his own armed retainers as escort. Detailing these examples of 'money moving', Stone observes that in the sixteenth century direct transfers of bullion were unavoidable and 'even up to the Civil War it was still frequently employed'.[7] If this implies that direct transfers of bullion ceased, or were at least very unusual after the Civil War, or indeed during the second half of the seventeenth century, the implication is mistaken. Indeed, as we shall see, it may have been employed rather more confidently during the last decade of the seventeenth century than earlier.[8]

Stewards charged with the responsibility of maintaining their master's financial lifeline to London after the Civil War were not in a position to engage armed guards. Their employers would never have countenanced such an expense, nor were the sums they were transmitting large enough to justify it. Nevertheless, their masters' needs and the difficulty of finding safer methods of transfer often persuaded the landlords to take the hazard. When they did so they sometimes made use of the lord's own employees or his relatives who were journeying to London, or to lawyers travelling up for the term, or to local officials on London journeys. 'If I can get any more guineas I shall send them up by some of the attorneys' reported William Gilpin in June 1696, and repeated the message the following October. He had also dispatched thirty guineas by the local Customs Collector Andrew Hudleston who had set forward for London the week before.[9] Occasionally stewards carried up the money themselves. Sir Richard Temple's steward, William Chaplyn, took amounts of £50 or more to London on several occasions, and on one occasion a tenant of Sir Richard carried up £132 for him.[10]

By far the most common method, however, was to employ carriers. During the seventeenth century services by carriers increased in frequency and in number and became progressively more widespread. John Taylor's *Carriers' Cosmography* of 1637 shows that by that date most regions of the kingdom had regular carrier services, and during the next seventy or eighty years the number of services more than doubled. While increases in the network supplying the Home Counties accounts for much of the growth, services extended to the remoter corners of the kingdom.[11] At least as early

---

[7] Stone, *Crisis*, 511, 512; Kerridge, *Trade and Banking*, 50.

[8] As Davies remarks, the use of inland bills 'by no means wholly superseded the shipment of specie however much the latter may have been reduced'. Davies, 'Gentry Payments', 18. In 1685 George Plaxton sent Lord Gower £1,100 in four consignments by carrier from Staffordshire which bespeaks some degree of confidence. Plaxton accounts, 3 April, 3 May, 27 June and 4 July 1685, Leveson-Gower D 593/F/2/14.

[9] *Lowther Correspondence*, 3, 10 June, 3 October 1696, Letters 286, 289, 309.

[10] Davies, 'Gentry Payments', 18, note 7.

[11] Alan Everitt, *Change in the Provinces: the Seventeenth Century* (Leicester, 1969), 39–41; J. A. Chartres, *Internal Trade in England 1500–1700* (London, 1977), 40. Northern

as 1670 the remote little town of Egremont, West Cumberland, had a regular service to London although it may not have lasted long.[12] The carriers with their long lines of packhorses, and bawling burly outriders, armed and resolute, were a much respected institution, as much a part of the lives of our seventeenth-century forefathers as is the rural mailman today. An Oxford don writing to Sir Daniel Fleming referred to the Kendal–Oxford carrier, Thomas Burnyeate, as 'our northern ambassador' while another Fleming correspondent had earlier referred to Richard Burnyeate, Thomas's father, as 'the trusty Trojan'.[13] Carriers carried passengers as well as freight, either sitting on the packs or on horses supplied by the carrier. Often such passengers were also armed so that a carrier train was usually a target beyond the scope of all but the most numerous, organised and determined band of highway robbers.[14] The landlords' respect for carriers as resolute men capable of moving goods safely over dangerous roads sometimes persuaded them to entrust parcels of specie to their care. However, both stewards and landlords were very conscious of the risks. Stewards would rarely do so without their masters' express consent, and sometimes protested when their landlords' needs drove them to a reckless disregard of the risks. In 1655 Charles Agard may have taken the risk without first obtaining his master's consent judging by a letter in which he hoped Dorset had his rents 'which I was fain to send up by the carrier for want of safe returns', but this initiative was unusual.[15]

More than a generation later Thomas Allen at Longleat planned to send up £100 in specie hidden in a hamper large enough to take the carcase of a doe. Disconcerted by his master's cancellation of the doe, he feared at first to enclose it in a smaller handbasket containing eight game birds, but finally dispatched it in a 'tin pot' under some butter and four woodcock. The following month he again used a tin pot to send up £100, but this time one which locked, sending the key separately. It is not clear whether he had

counties lacking a service in 1637 enjoyed six-weekly carrier services by 1715; Chartres, 'Road Carrying in England in the Seventeenth Century: Myth and Reality', *Econ. HR*, 2nd ser., vol. 30 (1977), 79–80.

12 'The Eggermond [*sic*, Egremont] carrier lies at Miles Poplinton's on the back of St Clement's in Witch Street against the Half Moon, who is yet in town.' Thomas Tickell, 17 October 1670, Lonsdale/D/Lons/W2/1/5.

13 Dr John Mill and the Reverend Thomas Dixon to Fleming, respectively 28 March 1691 and 11 May 1679, in J. R. Magrath, ed., *The Flemings in Oxford*, vol. 3 (Oxford, 1924), 47, and vol. 1 (Oxford, 1904), 284.

14 Sir John Lowther of Whitehaven carefully noted during the 1670s that Kendal carriers who 'come into London every Thursday afternoon, and go out every Friday noon, and are in Kendal the Tuesday sennight after' charged for passengers 'upon a fardel 20 shillings; a horse to themselves 30'. The packs on their horses weighed 224 pounds, and they charged 3d a pound in winter, 2d in summer. Lowther of Whitehaven memoranda books, D/Lons/W1/14, fo. 2.

15 Agard to Earl of Dorset, 24 January 1655, Sackville U269/C63.

first obtained permission to do so.[16] More typical was the attitude of John Peck, steward of Sir John Trevor at Trevalyn, who in 1652 felt that rents were so 'very hardly come by' that he was 'wary' to venture the dearly won results to carriers. However, a Captain Barber had promised to send £100 for him by 'the next return of the carrier ... in a pack of flannel in case you will run the hazard of it'. Sixty years later the Nottinghamshire steward of Sir George Savile, seeking to return his master £500 wished he had been able to enclose it in one of the boxes he had recently sent up since they had arrived safely but 'durst not' without Savile's order.[17] Sir Ralph Verney's steward, Hugh Holmes, sent his master £60 in 1663, probably because his master insisted that he should, but only very reluctantly and warned: 'Sir, you must needs think of some other way for the money to be conveyed to you. This is not a safe way. It begins to be common.' His last remark suggests that the method was becoming more and more commonplace and therefore that robbers were more aware of the possibilities which robbery of carriers presented. Common it certainly must have been for during the six years 1651–6 £1,370 was conveyed to London from Stowe to Sir Richard Temple all by road and chiefly by carrier, and between late 1657 and 1662 about £1,050 travelled by the same method to the London coffers of Lord Cardigan.[18]

Certainly landowners with estates far distant from London were aware of the risks. Wrote Lowther of Whitehaven in 1668: 'For packing [I] do not approve of it by any means, the carriers being frequently robbed as soon as they come near this town.'[19] However, while he was adamant that his steward, Thomas Tickell, should not send money by carrier in the 1660s and early 1670s, he did not object as strongly when Tickell and his successor, Gilpin employed carriers in the late 1680s and 1690s, which suggests that either carriers had been a safer conveyance than he had thought during Charles II's reign, or that the roads had become safer at least for carriers during the later decades of the century.[20] In September

---

[16] Similarly Francis Guybon sent his master a buck 'and a little white round box with 50 guineas by Clarke' (a carrier). Guybon, 9 August 1696, Fitzwilliam F(M)C 967. Allen to Lord Weymouth, 20, 27 January, 5 February 1689, Thynne xxiv, fos. 126, 130, 132.

[17] Peck to Trevor, 24 April and 11 May 1652, Trevor D/G3276; Thomas Smith to Savile, 4 February 1717, Savile DDSR 211/327/82.

[18] In amounts of from £50 to £250, Davies, 'Gentry Payments', 19.

[19] 25 February 1668, Lonsdale D/Lons/W2/1/3.

[20] I am indebted for this point to my former student Anne S. Robertson. However, this is an argument from silence, for his surviving letters offer no reason for his change of attitude. Dr Davies indeed suggests that the fears of some landowners may have been exaggerated, remarking on the 'striking' absence of complaints of losses from highway robbery in the records of the Midlands landowners which she consulted, Davies, 'Gentry Payments', 19. However, Lowther's optimism must have suffered a check in January 1691 when a carrier called Pearson was robbed of £640 on the road south of Shap, Westmorland, by three mounted men 'with faces covered', which moved Tickell to write on 15 February 1691 that

1694 Gilpin casually remarks that he is sending £100 by carrier 'and so every fortnight so long as I have any to send' but he seems in fact to have sent only one consignment by carrier, trusting the remaining returns to bills on London merchants, perhaps because Lowther had replied that if returns could be had 'any other way 'tis better'.[21] Moreover, carriers themselves could be cautious, particularly if they were travelling separately from their packhorses or wagons. Thus Lord Fitzwilliam received forty guineas in London from a Peterborough carrier which his steward had handed to him in a sealed paper, but fearful of being robbed the carrier had left the money in the country and paid Fitzwilliam 'by way of return'.[22]

Carriers seem to have had two ways of charging for money carried: either by weight or in ratio to the value of the specie carried. Sometimes they carried substantial sums of cash unwittingly, although it is not always clear from the steward's letter when this expedient had been adopted. If the carrier did not know what he was carrying then the secret of its presence would be better kept, but another risk was added for such sums were not the responsibility of the carrier and the loser would have no claim on him for the loss. When Fearey the Peterborough carrier left in the country the sealed paper alleged to contain forty guineas for fear of robbery, preferring to pay it by return, Fitzwilliam had to explain that the paper had really contained fifty guineas which Fearey then agreed to make up.[23] In 1695 Guybon had sent his master £100 in guineas and odd silver hidden in a box of plate 'at the end where the shavings are', explaining that he could not get a return at Peterborough which made him send it this way, which suggests he had not first sought Fitzwilliam's permission. In December he sent a further £100 concealed in a box of apples, and used the same expedient when sending apples up for his master's daughter the following February.[24] Certainly whether the carrier knew it or not the cash was often concealed, travelling hidden in trunks, under butter or in carcases of deer or in bundles of cloth or other cargo. Clarke, the Brigstock carrier, brought up a trunk to

    he would wait to return money by bill 'the carrier's road (since that last great robbery in Westmorland of £600) being unsafe', Lonsdale/D/Lons/W2/1/26; the highwaymen, 'aged thirty-five to forty' were armed with swords and pistols, Westmorland Quarter Sessions, Kendal Indictment and Order Book, Cumbria CRO (Kendal).

21 Gilpin 9 September, Lowther 29 September 1694, *Lowther Correspondence*, Letters 140, 155; see also D/Lons/W, General Estate Cash Books: William Gilpin's Cash Books 1693–9, Estate Accounts 1693–9, D/Lons/W3/13.

22 Fitzwilliam, 7 August 1697, Fitzwilliam F(M)C 1006; *Fitzwilliam Correspondence*, Letter 26. The same carrier a year earlier would only undertake to carry 50s down to Milton in his wagon for he dared not venture them 'in his pocket' as he was leaving late at night. Fitzwilliam, 8 August 1696, F(M)C 967.

23 Suggesting that Guybon may have intended to deceive the carrier of the true value of what he carried in order to save on the charge. Fitzwilliam, 8 August 1696, F(M)C 967.

24 Guybon 4 November 1695, 22 December 1695, 10 February 1696, Fitzwilliam F(M)C 945, 951, 955.

Lord Cardigan in 1659 which contained £250, which Lynwood, Cardigan's steward advised his master to send for. It is not clear whether Clarke was aware of the value of the consignment. John Peck sent up a 'cooke pie' (*sic*) to Bossom's Inn where his master was to send for it. The pie weighed 92 pounds, part of which was due to its containing a sealed linen purse with £14, no doubt in coins of small denomination. Since Peck had only paid a penny halfpenny a pound carriage – that is the pie by weight – the carrier cannot have known he carried money.

Carriers from the Welsh Marches demanded higher rates for specie, for as Peck once rather sarcastically observed to Trevor: 'I would you had enquired of Mr Lloyd the carrier's name he gave the 13s 4d. unto for securing £300 for never a carrier that I know will take his warranty' (he means so low a premium) 'for 300 shillings'. Forty years later the cost had dropped to lower levels than Peck is implying. Thomas Briggs, the Kendal carrier, charged a fee of 1 per cent for carrying coin in the 1690s to London.[25] It may be that the Briggs family had lowered their charges from earlier days. In 1675 they charged Thomas Jackson, a former Lowther colliery steward, 4d per pound sterling, which was a rate of 33s per £100, to carry £25 to London. In 1696 Lord Fitzwilliam considered a charge of 25s per hundred or 1¼ per cent unacceptable.[26] A year later he is still grumbling that Clarke had charged him very unreasonably for the £100 he brought up the previous summer. Now using another carrier, Fitzwilliam observed that unless Guybon could send the cash up 'in a box with something else out of the country' he had better agree with the carrier for 10s the £100 'which I think is enough'. More than a decade later he was still worried by charges. He had found a new carrier, Chatteris, in 1708 but he reports that he had to pay him 5s for the last £200 which he had brought up and Fitzwilliam feared he would expect more in the future, but he resolved to try him once more to see how 'he deals with me'. Fitzwilliam's reluctance to pay for carrying specie may have reflected a quite different concern, for he remarked the same year that it grieved him to see so much specie 'sent out of our parts which will make it scarce'. He hoped that 'good people' would carry money into the country.[27]

Whatever the charge, once it had been paid carriers were theoretically

<hr>

[25] '23rd day of December 1693: Received then by me Thomas Briggs ... from the hands of Will Atkinson in three bags sealed the sum of two hundred pounds which I promise to deliver to Sir John Lowther of Lowther, baronet, at his house in Pickadilly [*sic*], London, at or before the tenth of January next, and likewise received ... forty shillings sterling for the carriage thereof' Lonsdale/D/Lons/L, Letters 1630–1729: 'Letters to William Atkinson 1677–1694'.

[26] 'Send no more money by Clarke for he charges 3d a pound for all he has brought me which he reckons £150.' Fitzwilliam to Guybon, 10 December 1696, Fitzwilliam F(M)C 972.

[27] Fitzwilliam, 22 April 1697, 6 and 27 May 1708, F(M)C 991, 1664, 1669; *Fitzwilliam Correspondence*, Letters 15, 566, 570.

liable for the specie's loss. Thomas Jackson's £25 was robbed from Briggs along with 'a great sum besides' but as he had paid him 4d per pound for carriage Jackson expected 'good payment at London which Briggs promised the next return'.[28] However, such a security would be small consolation to a steward or his master if the carrier's assets were inadequate to meet a loss by robbery. Moreover, carriers do not always appear to have been liable for large amounts. When Sir John Lowther of Lowther lost £200 when highwaymen robbed the Kendal carrier in Craven in 1671 his brother commiserated with him on the fact that since the robbery had occurred after dark the hundred in which it occurred was not liable for the loss. This hardly suggests that old Lowther, one of the shrewdest and most cautious moneymakers who ever kept an account book, had any hope of recovery from the carrier. Significantly Tickell on one occasion referred to transmitting specie by carrier as sending 'without any further security than hazard'.[29]

Lowther's loss reminds us that it was not only the main carrier routes which were under threat so that possible loss from carriers was not the only problem. Fortunate indeed was the steward who had packhorse trains passing his master's gate. Most had to convey their specie to market towns from which carriers began their journeys and this could be miles away over roads little less hazardous than the roads fanning out from London – indeed potentially much more hazardous to an unescorted messenger carrying his master's silver to the carrier's provincial depot. Lowther of Whitehaven long persisted in making returns with some drovers who were maddeningly slow payers, explaining 'the greatest reason which inclines me to them is their receiving it upon the place which I suppose spares you much trouble and some hazard'.[30] A quarter of a century earlier a steward closer to London had feared the dangers of carrying money to market towns in search of returns, remarking 'to carry monies ... either to Gloucester, Worcester or Coventry (and nearer also) I fear may be as dangerous if not more as to London, if not discreetly handled'.[31] Gilpin at Whitehaven was fortunate to have the services of a Whitehaven–Kendal carrier, Edward Bowerbank, who was prepared to carry £100 to deliver there to the London carrier Briggs at a cost of 2s 6d. While this saved Gilpin some anxiety it was far from foolproof, for he had insisted that no other carrier but Briggs must be used, and on one occasion Bowerbank missed Briggs by a day so that the money which Gilpin cheerfully thought was well on its way to London

[28] Tickell, 26 January 1675, Lonsdale/D/Lons/W2/1/10.
[29] 16 July 1672, Lonsdale/D/Lons/W2/1/7. For the Lowther robbery, see Sir William Lowther of Swillington to Sir John Lowther of Lowther, 9 February 1671, Lonsdale/D/Lons/L, 'Misc. Letters 1550–1872'.
[30] 27 August 1672, Lonsdale/D/Lons/W2/1/7.
[31] Robert Hawdon to the Earl of Middlesex, 27 October 1647, Sackville U269/C249.

turned out to be awaiting Briggs's return lodged rather insecurely at the house in Kendal of a friend of Gilpin.[32] The dangers implicit in carrying their masters' silver to the nearest market towns in which carriers had their depots helped to make both masters and stewards eager to find safer alternatives.

Fortunately for the nerves of both stewards and landowners they had another means of transmitting funds which had developed during the sixteenth century. This medium was the 'return'. Some stewards and landlords occasionally used the word return so loosely that they applied it to any process of sending money to London, including specie by carrier.[33] As late as 1675 Lowther of Whitehaven could write: 'Concerning returns the common way is, as you are informed, by pack, but the way proposed is by James Nelson who returns by bill.' However, his steward drew the correct distinction when he wrote a year later: 'I find no returns for which reason I have delivered unto Edward Briggs [the London carrier] the sum of £160 sealed up in two bags of £80 a piece.'[34] Guybon, Fitzwilliam's steward, certainly recognised the distinction, yet on occasions wrote as if he did not. Thus, in 1708 he correctly writes that he will send another £100 by Chatteris the carrier 'for I know not how to return it'. A few years earlier he had reported that he had 'returned' a specific sum yet it is clear from the context that specie is meant for he comments on the quality of the coins. However, this was during the reform of the coinage when coins of various denominations were passing to and fro between London and the provinces as landowners desperately sought to unload bad money before it was too late. Certainly his master had no doubts: 'I hope you will take care to return me some money soon *or* send it me up in specie.'[35]

The return became a significant means for stewards to send money to London-based masters because of London's remarkable capacity to devour the products of the provinces, from coal to pigs, from cloth to corn, from cattle to geese, from wool to cheese. The alternatively muddy and dusty highways converging on London were crowded not merely with wagons and packhorse trains, but by a lowing, bleating, squealing and cackling

---

[32] Gilpin to Lowther, 1 October 1694, *Lowther Correspondence*, Letter 157.

[33] 'Both as a noun and as an adjective its contemporary use can be confusing ... since occasionally it denoted the sending of specie ... and even the bill of exchange itself.' Davies, 'Gentry Payments', 18. Davies discusses the problem of nomenclature more fully on pp. 33–5.

[34] Lowther, 17 March 1673; Tickell, 3 July 1674, Lonsdale/D/Lons/W2/1/8 and 9.

[35] Guybon, 5 April 1708; 28 June 1696, Fitzwilliam, 7 December 1705, respectively Fitzwilliam F(M)C 1658, 962, 1436; *Fitzwilliam Correspondence*, Letters 561, 406.

cacophony of all manner of livestock being driven to the London markets. The need to pay for this gargantuan consumption, which involved a transfer of London wealth to provincial pockets, provided the stewards with their opportunities for returns. There were two types of return, both based on the position that someone in the country was prepared to pay a sum of money there in order to receive in return an equal sum in the city. One of these, to be considered below, was the inland bill of exchange, developed during the sixteenth century and employed ever more widely in the second half of the seventeenth century. The other was a much less formal exchange in which the instrument might be little more than a receipt or an IOU which having been given in exchange for cash in the country, was transmitted to London and there redeemed for cash either by the person who had issued it or by a correspondent who held cash on his behalf. For the issuer of this IOU the transaction was a means by which he could, in effect, move money to the country, for he was paying money in London to have the use of it in the provinces.

However, the neatness of this solution disguises very real problems of which the most worrying for the steward was the scarcity of returns. There always seemed to be more people anxious to move money to London than there were people who wished to move money from London to the country. It was not just squires anxious to enjoy the fleshpots of the developing capital who created this imbalance. The collectors of such taxes as the 'chimney money' in the various counties also needed to transfer large sums to the capital and competed against the private sector. The latter, moreover, included all those local merchants and tradesmen who relied on London for the wares which they retailed or for materials to work up for local sale, although these were to some degree balanced by those who wished to receive cash for locally manufactured goods, like cloth, which had been sold in London. Men of this stamp sometimes took the initiative in approaching stewards in search of reverse returns. In October 1654 the Kendal merchant, Thomas Sandes, informed Hugh Potter, chief steward of the Earl of Northumberland's West Cumberland estates, that he had begun to trade to London again and so had 'occasion for returns'. Having heard that Potter's 'great receipt' was at hand, presumably of Michaelmas rents, he said he would like to return £200 or £300 'at the time you used formerly to give me'. If Potter would inform him how much he would like returned and where Potter's servant should meet him to receive the bill of exchange for the money, the steward need not doubt of 'good payment' in London by his correspondents. The correspondents would be the London merchants who sold his cloth. Subsequently Sandes acknowledged the receipt of £150 at Penrith from Potter's servant, and observed that he hoped that such returns could be arranged again so that money Potter had received in rents and fines would remain in the county for the purchase of wool.[36]

Fortunate indeed was the steward who found himself so approached. More usually stewards found tracking down sources of safe returns an onerous and frustrating task. Returns by local merchants and tradesmen were naturally affected by 'good' and 'bad' times in their markets. Robert Hawdon found himself struggling with this situation in March 1647 for although he had been very 'earnest' with Warwickshire tradesmen who had 'trade at London' to pay their London money to the Earl of Middlesex he found he could obtain no commitments from them because 'their commodities sell not of late'.[37] The same anxiety was inhibiting Northamptonshire farmers a decade or so later. Lord Cardigan's steward found his 'neighbours that drives to London' would not make returns for fear their sales would not cover the bill.[38] John Peck, struggling with post-war difficulties, urged his master to reverse the process; that is, to find money from persons in London who were anxious to receive it in the country or perhaps needed to pay a debt there. While this became a well-established method it was easier recommended than accomplished and nothing came of the suggestion at the time. A month later Peck has sought returns at Chester and Oswestry in vain and proposes to send to Nantwich, telling his master's son that he is much troubled by having to carry the Trevors' money from the manor house at Trevalyn to a house at Meaford because there has been much robbing about the town. Having tried Nantwich with no success Peck the following month was sending to Shrewsbury with no better result. When he finally found a return from Chester he apparently decided he must take full advantage of this long-sought opportunity because £50 of the £400 returned is out of his own pocket as, in effect, a loan to his master.[39]

---

[36] Sandes to Potter 9 and 16 October 1654, Leconfield D/Lec/Correspondence, 69/1654. Sandes observed that while he had allowed only a very short time for the payment of the bill in London should a future return be for a much larger sum he would have to 'bargain' with Potter for a longer time for repayment.

[37] He intended to leave the next day for Evesham in the hope of finding a return of £100. Hawdon to Middlesex, 28 March 1647, Sackville U269/C249. On one occasion he rode 12 miles or more through Warwickshire following a false lead to the home of a Mr Woodward only to find, contrary to what Woodward's kinsman had told him, that far from needing money in the country he needed money in London. Hawdon to Middlesex, 27 October 1647, C249.

[38] William Lynwood to Cardigan, 22 February 1659, Brudenell 1, xiv, fo. 49.

[39] Peck to Sir John Trevor, 24 November 1649, to John Trevor 21 December 1649, 5 January 1650 and to Sir John 25 January 1650. Two years later things were no better for Peck complains that 'Here is neither sale for cheese nor cattle, neither can I get any of the graziers that I can trust to return you £100.' Peck to Trevor, 12 March 1652; all Trevor D/G/3276. Advancing money to the master from the steward's own pocket was not unusual. 'It's no disturbance to me' wrote John Swynfen to his master 'to send a bill (when there is urgent occasion) for some more than is come in'. Swynfen to Lord Paget, undated but probably about January 1681, Paget D603/K/3/4.

Almost three-quarters of a century later stewards were still grappling with the same problem. 'Trading is so dead that returns are very difficult to procure' complains John White from Staffordshire to Lady Gower in 1711, while in 1717 Thomas Smith reports from Nottinghamshire that a pig-dealer, John Greathead of Worksop, who constantly returned for him, had not lately sent up half as many swine as usual because the markets were so dead in London 'he cannot buy them here to answer'. That is, Greathead could not return money for Smith on the scale he had in better times because the diminished London sales meant that he bought fewer pigs and so needed less money in the country with which to purchase them.[40] Nor were Hawdon and Peck alone in having to search far afield for returns by bill. After many local disappointments in West Cumberland William Gilpin finally tracked down a useful source in Newcastle although he had to send £100 there by carrier at a charge of 3s 6d.[41] Stewards often found themselves disappointed locally, sometimes for reasons more unusual than a simple down-turn in trade. On one occasion Gilpin had succeeded in finding a return for his master only to have his expectations dashed when the local shipowner involved had to employ all his London funds to ransom his ship from Dunkirk privateers.[42]

Stewards had to be ingenious and imaginative as they diligently sought returns and quick to seize on any chance opportunity, as Lowther of Whitehaven reminded his steward in 1668, urging him to 'be inquisitive after any who have occasion for money there and can pay it here'. During the 1670s Mr Basil Fielding, a connection of Sir Christopher Musgrave's, was responsible for paying the garrison of Carlisle Castle, and he would accept money from local gentlemen or their stewards in exchange for bills on the Treasury which could be forwarded to London for presentation there. Tickell was inconveniently distant from Carlisle but nevertheless used this method to send his master £100. Sir Christopher Musgrave and Fielding could not oblige him for a larger sum because 'this quarter's receipt in the Custom House being the best in the year will stock them a good while', a clear example of the competition for returns between the public and private sectors.[43] In 1691 a westerly gale compelled a transport

[40] John White to Lady Gower, 5 February 1711, Leveson-Gower D868/9/171; Smith to Sir George Savile, 9 February 1717, Savile 211/227/81.
[41] The return may have been found through his father who was a minister and physician there. Gilpin to Lowther 19 April 1694, *Lowther Correspondence*, Letter 108 and note.
[42] See the reference to Robert Biglands and the *Rainbow*, Gilpin to Lowther, 23 July 1694, *Lowther Correspondence*, Letter 127.
[43] For Lowther and Tickell's correspondence about this Carlisle source, which was in fact spied out by Lowther through his friendship with Sir Stephen Fox, see Lowther, 13 August, Tickell, 22 August, Lowther, 27 August 1672, Lonsdale/D/Lons/W2/1/7. (On the back of this letter Tickell copied a return: 'Sir, ten days after sight hereof I pray you pay to Sir John Lowther Bart. or his order £100, make good payment and place the same to the account of

bound for Ireland to shelter at Whitehaven and Tickell eagerly relieved its captain's need for cash to meet its expenses there in exchange for a bill on the captain's London employer.[44] Another source of returns at the right season were the woolbuyers who went about the farms and the local markets buying wool, and who were not anxious to set out from London carrying large sums of money about them. One buyer received £160 from Lord Fitzwilliam's steward at Milton, bought wool from the Fitzwilliam tenants around Marholm with it and then repaid Fitzwilliam in London. Fitzwilliam was happy to finance the woolbuyer's operation because it meant not only that he had received a substantial and much needed return from the country, but also that no money had left the country, and indeed that it had come into the hands of his tenants who would be the better able to pay their rents.[45]

The difficulties involved in finding regular sources of returns in the north, the west and in Wales induced stewards to exploit the possibilities of drovers. As John Peck succinctly informed his master in 1651: 'It is very hard to get any money returned you but by the graziers when their markets are to send up cattle.'[46] In the north west the drovers received money from the stewards and bought cattle locally or from Scottish drovers at the great northern cattle fairs. They then drove the cattle south through what local Cumbrians still call 'Gallo'gate' (Galloway-gate), that is, through the Eden valley and then either south over Shap or south east through Appleby. Many villages in the Eden valley still retain their ancient structure of houses distributed around a village green which is extraordinarily elongated, narrow for its width but still very wide for a village green. These greens were designed to hold large herds of cattle overnight during the drives. The cattle were sold in London to the butchers of Smithfield and on receiving payment the drovers would call on the stewards' masters at their London residences to repay their debt. Thus the rents of the provinces passed south to the capital 'on the hoof' rather than simply as the transference of an

---

... Christopher Musgrave.' The return is addressed to Richard Kent, esquire, at Sir Stephen Fox's lodging in Whitehall and dated 5 September.) For the Customs House competition see Tickell, 9 September; Lonsdale/D/Lons/W2/1/7.

[44] Lowther, 13 August and Tickell, 9 September 1672, Lonsdale/D/Lons/W2/1/7; Tickell, 11 March and 8 April 1691, D/Lons/W2/1/26.

[45] Fitzwilliam to Guybon, 24 September 1702, F(M)C 1234; *Fitzwilliam Correspondence*, Letter 237.

[46] Peck to Trevor, 7 March 1651, Trevor D/G/3276. '[The drovers'] cash dealings and the security of their cattle led them to perform important intermediate banking services ... The moneys in the hands of the drovers were of great significance at both national and personal level in the mid seventeenth century. The traffic made Smithfield a major market for inland bills for internal trades generally.' J. A. Chartres in Thirsk, *Agrarian History*, 5, ii, 481–2.

obligation acknowledged and transmitted by bill as in the cases of Pay-master Fielding or the master of the stormbound transport. The cattle droves were an old established trade. Camden visited a 'beast fair' at Northallerton where he found buyers who had come from as far afield as Middlesex.[47] In Wales the Trevors' estate based on Trevalyn Hall was only one of many which made use of Welsh drovers. Sir John Wynn of Gwydir returned money to his sons in London by David Lloyd, a local drover, at least as early as 1621, and this association between the Wynns and Lloyd lasted for more than forty years. In May 1661 Sir John Wynn's grandson, Sir Richard, returned £65 by 'old David Lloyd the drover', who was to repay it to Wynn's London correspondent. Nor were officials slow to use drovers to transmit the Crown revenues which they had collected locally. In 1661 one of Sir John Wynn's younger sons, Maurice, who was Receiver General for North Wales, sent bills to the Barons of the Exchequer which were to be redeemed by Welsh drovers.[48]

The arrangement with the drovers was very much to the drovers' advan-tage. They were as aware as the stewards of the danger of carrying large sums of money by road and welcomed the opportunity to transmit safely the proceeds of London cattle sales back to Wales or the north to finance the next drive.[49] This was also true for those drovers who brought fat sheep and cattle up to London from counties in the Midlands. A drover called Miller paid Lord Fitzwilliam £50 which he had borrowed from a Smithfield salesman so that he could receive that sum in the Soke of Peterborough from Fitzwilliam's steward. He would then purchase sheep locally with the £50, drive them up and with the proceeds pay off the salesman, 'allowing interest'.[50] This symbiotic relationship permitted Fitzwilliam to receive a much needed return of £50 at the same time that it permitted the drover to move £50 safely to the country, and it was the security of the transfer which helped to persuade the Smithfield salesman to advance him the money in the first place. Moreover, since the drovers usually received the money from the stewards in advance they were in effect being provided with interest-free loans with which to finance their business. As late as 1710 we find a drover, Joseph Grahame, writing to Sir Christopher Musgrave's steward, Jeffrey Beck, that he was camped with some horses at Hudforth, a site on the Eden

---

[47] Alan Everitt, 'The marketing of agricultural produce' in Thirsk, *Agrarian History*, 4, 540.
[48] For the Wynns' association with drovers see *Wynn Papers, inter alia* Letters 990, 2297, 2347, 2362 and 2645; 155, 365, 370, 372, 404.
[49] In May 1692 a drover from Kaber, Westmorland, was robbed of £144 near Ellerbeck, North Yorkshire, by two highwaymen; reported in North Riding Quarter Sessions, 2 August 1692 and cited in K. J. Bonser, *The Drovers* (London, 1970), 34. I am indebted to my student Anne S. Robertson for this reference.
[50] Fitzwilliam to Guybon, 29 April 1708, Fitzwilliam F(M)C 1663, *Fitzwilliam Correspon-dence*, Letter 565.

near Penrith much favoured by drovers, and soliciting 'a hundred pounds or two to return' to Musgrave in London. If Beck had the money 'by him' it would oblige Grahame greatly for he was bound for Crieff Fair 'to buy beasts'.[51]

There were problems with using drovers for returns. The method was cumbersome, and led to long delays, not least because the Smithfield butchers were remarkably slow payers and until the drovers received payment from them they could make no payment to the steward's master. Not only were the drovers receiving, in effect, interest-free loans, short term but sometimes for very substantial amounts, but the security of the 'loan' was rarely sufficiently substantial to ease the anxieties of the landowner. In view of this the fact that landowners instructed their stewards to persist with drovers for years at a time shows how desperate for returns such landowners were. In 1659 Sir Owen Wynn was constrained to ask his son Richard to obtain six months' grace from a creditor in London because there was 'no safety in sending money by Chester or Shrewsbury in these times there being no drovers'.[52] Alternatives to drovers for returns were never easy to find, and finding them could prove impossible for weeks or even months at a time.

The advantage and hazards of using drovers are well illustrated by the experiences of Sir John Lowther of Whitehaven, whose stewards' correspondence provides an illuminating case study of the problems of returning because it covers an unbroken span of more than thirty years. Lowther employed a family of drovers, the Elletsons, to make the bulk of his returns during the eight years from 1666 to 1674. They presented numerous advantages: they were a large concern and the money seemed in safe hands; they were able to cope with substantial sums because they sold cattle on a considerable scale; they were always prepared to come to Lowther's house at Whitehaven to receive the cash from his steward which meant that the money did not have to travel insecurely over dangerous roads to some centre like Carlisle, Penrith or Kendal.[53] These were very real advantages and much prized and persuaded Lowther to persist with the Elletsons in spite of the drawbacks of using them, of which the worst was their tendency to fail to 'meet their day' for payment. When London-based landowners made use of Midlands graziers it was often possible for the landowner to receive his money in advance, the graziers simply using the device as a means of safely transferring the fruits of London cattle sales to Midland markets so that they could purchase more cattle for fattening. With only

[51] Crieff Fair, Perthshire, was one of the most important annual cattle fairs. Grahame to Beck, 13 September 1710, Musgrave D/Mus/A1/2.

[52] Letter 2186, 22 April 1659, *Wynn Papers*, 352.

[53] Lowther to Tickell, 3 September 1667, Lonsdale/D/Lons/W2/1/2.

two recorded exceptions returns to Sir Ralph Verney between 1679 and 1688 were paid by the stewards of his Buckinghamshire estate only after the cash had been received by Verney or his surrogate in London.[54] Lowther was in no such happy position with the Elletsons. His steward parted with Lowther's money first and then Lowther had to endure long delays before he was paid. In July 1672 Lowther acknowledged receipt of a bill on them for £80 payable the following month but, as he grumbled to his steward, he had no doubt they would fail to pay it on the day 'having but this last week discharged a bill due in December'. This was no isolated instance. As early as 1667 Lowther had complained that one of the Elletsons 'keeps not his day', and in early 1668 reported that the drovers were in arrear for all the bills due 'these four months'. In 1669 he complains that it was usually three or six months before they paid any bill.

Lord Fitzwilliam would have found such a situation intolerable as his letters, with their obsessive cries for ever more and speedier returns, make clear. That Lowther did over such a long period testifies eloquently to the lack of regular alternatives available to West Cumberland landlords and to his reluctance to trust specie to the roads leading to Cumbrian towns. In 1667, while accusing the Elletsons of being 'the worst paymasters' he had ever had to deal with, Lowther insisted that Tickell persist with them for they had no alternative to employ. In 1668 he hesitated to suggest that Tickell should try for other returns from Kendal because getting it there would prove a 'greater hazard than the Elletsons'. In 1673 he was still groping for a solution to the problem. He was tempted by the news that a James Nelson of Kendal returned to London by bill which would be a much better way than using the Elletsons but he still feared the money could not be got to Kendal with sufficient security. Tickell reinforced Lowther's concern, pointing out that Nelson insisted on seven weeks between receipt at Kendal and repayment at London, while they would have to send the money to Kendal 'at great uncertainty' and at their own charge 'and adventure'.[55]

In truth Lowther was even more worried by the possibility of losing the Elletsons as returners than by their tardy repayments. In 1670 he urged his steward to increase his returns by them for fear they might abandon him in favour of the collectors of the chimney money and thus disappoint them in the future. Three years later his attachment is weakening. Tickell must seek some other safe way, not that he must 'decline them wholly', but use other means as often as possible.[56] Lowther did receive some compensation for

[54] Davies, 'Gentry Payments', 30.
[55] Lowther to Tickell, 8 October 1667, 25 February 1668, 10 February 1673. Tickell to Lowther, 29 August 1674, respectively Lonsdale/D/Lons/W2/1/2, 3, 8, 9.
[56] Lowther to Tickell, 7 June 1670, 25 May 1673, Lonsdale/D/Lons/W2/1/5 and 8.

the Elletsons' delays. He instructed Tickell in 1669 that he must insist on the shortest possible time between the drawing of the bill at Whitehaven and the due date for redemption in London and that the Elletsons agree to pay interest from that due date until the date the bill was actually redeemed. To this the Elletsons agreed, for, as Tickell informed his master, they seemed 'much troubled' at their 'failings' and all 'with one consent' agreed that Lowther should be honestly paid with 'compensation', that is, interest, for their delays. Three days later they told Tickell to inform his master of their gratitude for Lowther's generous forbearance 'though they pay for your time'.[57] Lowther in fact was more forbearing than some of their clients for they were several times prosecuted for late payment, but he was aware that the Elletsons were not to blame for their delays, which were chiefly due to slow-paying Smithfield butchers.[58] When in 1667 the drovers were indebted to Lowther on bills to the tune of three or four hundred pounds, while they were always ready to 'acknowledge the bills' they would not offer a firm date when they would be redeemed because they did not know when sufficient funds would come into their hands from their own debtors in Smithfield.[59] All these considerations could move Tickell to remark as late as 1674 that returns by the Elletsons were 'most convenient in every way'.

Certainly Lowther did not abandon the Elletsons. They, in a sense, abandoned him, along with their other clients, when they went sensationally bankrupt owing, according to Tickell, the barely believable sum of £30,000.[60] Lowther had not been so incautious as to trust large sums to the drovers without some security, although they would never allow him as much security as he sought. As early as 1667 he had suggested that it would be convenient for both sides if the Elletsons gave bond for £500 as a standing security for all outstanding bills, and in return he would never press them for payment when it was inconvenient for them to pay it. Lowther frequently urged Tickell to press them for better security and to be forever 'inquisitive into their sufficiency'. In mid 1672 he was urging Tickell to persuade them to add some other bondsmen to themselves for greater security. These anxious suggestions the Elletsons tended to resist, but

---

[57] Lowther to Tickell, 12 October 1669: 'Draw your bills at as short a day as you can get them to accept of, that paying me interest the longer it may make amends for their constant failings.' Tickell to Lowther, 9 March 1668; 2 May 1671, respectively Lonsdale/D/Lons/W2/1/4, 3 and 6.

[58] For such prosecutions see Lowther to Tickell, 9 July and 13 August 1672, Lonsdale/D/Lons/W2/1/7.

[59] Lowther to Tickell, 8 October 1667, Lonsdale/D/Lons/W2/1/2.

[60] His excitement may have misled Tickell into inserting an extra nought. However, Lowther does not challenge the figure in his surviving letters. Lowther informed his steward of the Elletsons' breaking on 19 January 1675; Tickell supplied the details on 26 January 1675. Lonsdale/D/Lons/W2/1/10.

Lowther appears to have been sufficiently secured to save him from serious loss. Nevertheless his fears grew toward the end, observing three months before the collapse that there was little hope for the future and some fear for what was past, all the bills for twelve months being still in arrear. He hardly dare own his anxieties for fear their situation was desperate. When this fear proved well founded Tickell assured his master that such 'sober men' could not possibly have consumed such a debt and must have vast sums owing to them. Certainly Lowther finally recovered all his Elletson debts although it took several years.[61]

For landowners in Lancashire, Cheshire and Shropshire the extensive trade in cheese based on the dairy farms of the Cheshire and Lancashire plain provided a rich source of returns. Much cheese was exported to London during the seventeenth and eighteenth centuries, occasionally by road but more commonly by ship from Chester, Liverpool or lesser ports.[62] Dairy farmers of the area made the cheese and then either sold it for local consumption or sold it to cheesefactors based in such centres as Chester, Nantwich or Northwich. The cheesefactors then shipped it to London to cheesemongers, each factor having one or more whom they regularly supplied. Most cheesefactors supplied several London clients but occasionally there was a family relationship, as with Thomas Dod of Nantwich who consigned cheeses to his brother John. The rural factors who sent up cheese to London mongers needed a means to get the fruits of that transaction back to the country, partly to receive any profit, partly to recover their capital to invest in more cheese. The mongers also needed to have these and other funds transferred to the country because they needed to have cheese purchased on their behalf. It was this double need of mongers and factors to finance cheese transactions which gave stewards their opportunity to return money with reasonable security to their masters in the capital. Historians of rural industry in the Cheshire and Lancashire area or of the workings of the seventeenth-century money market can both be grateful to the chance survival of much of the incoming correspondence and most of the meticulously kept accounts of William Adams, who was chief steward to the first and second Viscounts Cholmondeley over a period

---

[61] Tickell to Lowther, 26 January 1675, Lonsdale/D/Lons/W2/1/10; Lowther to Governor Sir John Linch, 1 March 1683, 'Memoranda and Letter Book (drafts) 1675–1689', Lowther Memoranda Books, Lonsdale/D/Lons/W1/14. Lowther was still pursuing the last £100 in Jamaica in 1685, and his letter to one of the Elletsons, who had become a customs officer there, reveals that a bond for a further £100 had been discharged only after long delay and a costly lawsuit because one of Elletsons' sureties had forfeited his estate.

[62] For the significance of cheese to the farmers of this region see Thirsk, *Agrarian History*, 5, i, 153–4; ii, 361–3, 486–7. See also R. Edwards, 'The Development of Dairy Farming on the North Shropshire Plain in the Seventeenth Century, 1670–1870', *Midland History*, vol. 4 (1978), 3–4.

of about thirty-five years. It is the characteristic of letters that they tend to highlight the occasions when such returns go wrong while accounts set down only those returns which are successfully concluded. However, when both sources are combined much can be learned about both the routines and the problems of this type of money moving.

One problem was common to all stewards who returned by bill: there were never enough sources of returns to meet the demand. Steward competed against steward, landowner against landowner and public officials and tax gatherers against everybody. On the Cholmondeley estates, where gathering the rents, fines and other estate income was divided amongst understewards who were each allocated a 'collection', the understewards might find themselves competing against each other. In late 1682, when the chief steward Adams was spending some weeks in London, and an understeward, Wever, was acting in his place, another understeward named Faulkner found great difficulty in sending money up. He left money with Wever to be returned in a bill drawn by cheesefactor Thomas Dod on his brother John but part of Wever's own collection had come to hand and so Faulkner's was set aside. Nor could Faulkner find an alternative. 'I was with all the factors that were in Nantwich upon Saturday last' he complains 'but could not prevail to have a bill from any of them.'[63] Three days later Faulkner and Wever were anxious to return £160 together but still could not obtain a bill 'amongst all the cheesefactors in Nantwich'.[64] Similarly another understeward, Arthur Manning, found himself riding from factor to factor. Dod had made him a 'fair promise' of a bill for £100 but then performed nothing, and then he arrived at another factor's house just in time to see him 'receive £140 before my face' from another man so that the factor could take no more. Manning feared he would be compelled to carry the money to yet another and rather less reliable factor who was already offended that he had not been Manning's first choice! Nevertheless he would be as 'nimble' as he could for 'her ladyship'.[65] On Christmas Day Wever reports that the bill for £100 he encloses has been obtained only with 'much ado' and with an allowance of a longer time for payment than would be 'well liked of', but it would not have been obtained then if the factor had not just bought a tenant's cheese and had already accepted £40 (of the £100) from an understeward in order to accomplish this.[66] Sometimes stewards'

---

[63] William Fawkner (or Faulkner) to Adams, 13 December 1682, Cholmondeley DCH/L/48.
[64] Peter Wever to Adams, 16 December 1682, DCH/L/48.
[65] Arthur Manning to Adams, 23 December 1682, Cholmondeley DCH/K/3/5. Four days later he hopes Lady Cholmondeley understands that it was Dod's 'unkindness' which had caused his failure to 'return'. Same to same, DCH/K/3/5. He finally found a return the following month. Jonadeb Colley to Adams, 8 January 1683, DCH/K/3/4.
[66] A postscript plaintively begs 'Be not angry with this clownish Quaker', presumably referring to himself. Wever to Adams, 25 December 1682, Cholmondeley DCH/L/48.

would track down returners by discovering from their masters' tenants which factor had recently bought cheese from them and dispatched it to London. They might even engage a tenant to procure a bill for them.[67] Even when a factor who was eager to exchange a bill for cash to go to market with appeared at the manor house or approached the steward in the marketplace, there could still be a problem if the potential returner was a stranger or if he was only too well known to the steward's master and considered unreliable. In the first instance the steward would have to delay the transaction until he had enquired into the repute of the stranger; in the second he might have to delay even longer until he received permission from London to make use of the dubious returner's services.[68]

These were rural problems. More problems could arise in the capital. Having received a bill, the landowner would send a member of his household to present it to the cheesemonger. Usually the bill was accepted but sometimes it was not. Landowners found this peculiarly infuriating. They knew they would have to wait some days, perhaps even three weeks or more, for their money even if it was accepted, but if it was not they had all the delay consequent on sending the bill back to the country. There the steward would either have to obtain a bill on some other cheesemonger which, hopefully, would be accepted, or to get back the money already handed over to the cheesefactor, which he would probably have spent and might not be able to repay at short notice. In any event the money had been long in his hands at no profit to the landowner and the problem of getting the money to London was still confronting the steward, as was his master, angry and embarrassed at being besieged by hungry creditors. Cheesefactors themselves were naturally not keen to see their credit eroded by such refusals. We find a Thomas Williams, a Nantwich cheesefactor begging that Adams will try again with a bill which had been once rejected as 'he had taken course' the bill would be paid in time. If a second bill of £50 on a different cheesemonger was refused he would take steps to see it was paid elsewhere at a shorter time to cancel out the delay.[69] In general cheesemongers would only accept bills for repayment if they had received separate

[67] 'I will send this night to a tenant that has sold his cheese some time ago to procure me a bill from the factor.' William Holbrooke (understeward) to Adams (then in London), 25 June 1698, Cholmondeley DCH/L/41.

[68] 'There was a man with me on Saturday last (one Worsly by name) who hath bought Joe Hocknell's cheese and would return £100 with me on Saturday next. He is a stranger to me but I shall enquire of him better.' Wever to Adams, 4 December 1682, Cholmondeley DCH/L/41. In fact nothing came of this at the time but Adams returned £60 by Thomas Worsley on Jeremy Ives at Newgate Market the following February. See Cholmondeley DCH/Account Books 1682–3.

[69] Wever to Adams, 18 December 1682, Cholmondeley DCH/L/48. The first bill (of £40) seems to have been paid. The second £50 transaction appears to have failed for there is no record of it in Adams's accounts. DCH/Account Books 1682–3.

advice from their client factors, or if they owed them money for cheese purchases or if they were certain that cheese was on the way to them. In 1689 a cheesemonger called Kent made 'some demur' about paying a £25 bill to a member of Lord Cholmondeley's London household until he had an account that his cheese was shipped.[70] Cheesemongers would sometimes honour bills even though they owed the factor nothing, or owed less than the sum the bill was drawn for, but not if they did not like the time allowed for payment. Refusing a bill a Mr Compear 'wondered that Mr Coe would draw a bill upon him at so few days sight, being he owed him nothing.'[71] A household servant is denied acceptance of a bill for a mere £10, the cheesemonger being very 'snappish' with him, because he claimed the bill was 'none of William Salmon's hand', and besides he had received no separate advice. Lord Cholmondeley was furious when a cheesemonger delayed acceptance of a £100 bill for lack of separate advice, particularly as another cheesemonger the same week had declined a bill for only £14 on the grounds that the factor had drawn too much already – a bill, moreover, which had been sent back to Cheshire for nonacceptance once before.[72]

This long recital of refusals, failures and delays may suggest that cheese-factors and cheesemongers were a very unsatisfactory way of returning money. This would be mistaken. The problems described above simply demonstrate how onerous and frustrating stewards could find their prime function of returning money. Such difficulties might be experienced with any returns by tradesmen's bills. There is no mystery as to why stewards persisted with cheesemongers and factors. Reliable cheesefactors drawing on cheesemongers with whom they were in regular and profitable correspondence were an efficient means of transferring money securely. The Adams accounts reveal that in the nine-month period December 1682 to August 1683 Adams returned more than £1,000 to London employing six separate factors and nineteen bills. Again in the brief period 10 July to 11 September 1699 Adams sent up eight bills drawn by three cheesefactors on six different cheesemongers totalling £1,540. All were accepted and all were paid.[73]

The development of the inland bill of exchange during the early modern period has been cogently described by others and needs no extended

---

[70] Mungo Karnes to Adams, 12 January 1689, Cholmondeley DCH/K/3/8.
[71] Lady Cholmondeley's characteristic response was to instruct her steward to concern himself no more with either Compear or the factor for she liked neither them nor their way of dealing, Jonadeb Colley to Adams, 8 April 1690, Cholmondeley DCH/K/3/8.
[72] Edward Mariner to Adams, 12 and 21 November 1700, Cholmondeley DCH/L/28. Michael Laroche to Adams, 20 June 1699, Cholmondeley DCH/K/3/13.
[73] Adams to Laroche, 20 September 1699, Cholmondeley DCH/K/3/13 and DCH/Acco. Account Books 1682–3 and 1698–9.

repetition.[74] The purpose here is to examine what problems stewards faced when they struggled to return money to London, how inland bills helped them to solve these problems, and what difficulties this solution presented to both stewards and their masters. The bills with which the drover Elletsons furnished Thomas Tickell and which they subsequently redeemed from Sir John Lowther in London were not true bills of exchange since they were, in effect, no more than IOUs forming the instrument of a transaction between the drovers and Lowther. They were not transferable to or negotiable by others. The only serious problem they presented was that the Elletsons found great difficulty in redeeming the bills without long delays, and since the men who drew the bills and the men who redeemed the bills were either the same men, or at least members of the same firm, the soundness of the bills depended entirely on the financial stability of the Elletsons. That is why Lowther insisted with growing anxiety on joining other bondsmen to them for greater security. Thomas Greene had even more informal arrangements with some returners, although he took care that his master, Sir John Nicholas, received the money before the returner was reimbursed. On one occasion Nicholas found himself visited at his London home by a man bearing £150. This money came with no warning from his steward because the steward, as he subsequently explained, would not have Nicholas 'disappointed' as he had been on a previous occasion and Greene was far from sure the money would be forthcoming. However, since Greene would not have to pay anything for the return and Nicholas would not have to send a servant through the dangerous London streets for the money, and since his master ran no hazard, he had decided to 'embrace the opportunity'. Now that he knew his master had received the £150 he would take steps to pay the man his money in the country. This was a very informal arrangement, involving no documentation at all beyond Nicholas's letter to his steward reporting the delivery of the money and the receipt he would give the payer to carry down.

The bills which William Adams and his understewards obtained from Cheshire cheesefactors were more sophisticated instruments, true bills of exchange payable to Cholmondeley or his order. Cholmondeley could cash them directly with the cheesemonger or he could endorse them to others to settle debts, or endorse them to his goldsmith who could present them for acceptance and subsequently for payment. Similarly Shrewsbury drapers always drew bills on their London correspondents in favour of the person named 'or order', which, as Thomas Hawkes pointed out to the dowager Lady Thynne, meant that the bills could be paid to whomever she appointed to receive the money in London, whether a private person or a

---

[74] See especially Kerridge, *Trade and Banking*, and Davies, 'Gentry Payments', *passim*.

goldsmith. Hawkes, like many stewards, was grappling with the situation that his mistress lived distant from London in a different county whilst the drapers on whom he depended returned only to London.[75] This was a very useful characteristic of the inland bill, so that some of them were endorsed to other men in London, or endorsed in the country in favour of the steward's master. A good example of the latter was a bill sent to Sir John Lowther of Whitehaven by William Gilpin in 1694. Drawn by Francis Grindall on Anthony Wilks, a London merchant, in favour of Robert Greggs, a Whitehaven resident, Greggs had endorsed it to Lowther in exchange for cash from Lowther's steward.[76] Greggs was rather like a person today who is paid by a cheque but has no bank account and prefers to cash the cheque through the agency of someone who does. There was one drawback to these more sophisticated, endorsable and therefore transferrable bills. Whilst they could be used almost like money, passing from hand to hand, they were also less secure because they could be stolen and false endorsements forged on them. Landlords and stewards feared losing such bills to highwaymen. As late as 1717 Thomas Smith at Rufford did not think his master would approve of his sending up bills by Madam Savile, his master's mother, 'for fear of robbing'. This fear was well founded: 'Have a care of sending up bills of exchange in letters' Lord Fitzwilliam warned his steward in 1698, 'the northern letters have twice been robbed and the bills taken out and the money received by those rogues.' It had been a great loss to several 'merchants and gentlemen'.[77] If for any reason a bill failed to come to hand, the drawer would be asked to warn his correspondent in London not to honour the bill unless it was presented by the beneficiary 'or his order' (and in the latter instance the acceptor would have to be sure that the beneficiary's endorsing signature was genuine).[78]

These bills had, in theory, a legal structure to give them force. While such unsophisticated instruments as the Elletsons' bills would simply state they were payable on a date stated on them, true inland bills usually declared that the bills were to be paid at a stipulated number of days 'after sight'.[79] The receiver of the bill would send it to the tradesman for acceptance, and if he accepted it the tradesman would be expected to pay the money after

[75] 'What money is paid the drapers in Salop upon return they order to be paid in London; now what sums I have ever returned to your son, Sir Thomas, I cause the bill to be made payable to his order.' Hawkes to the Dowager Lady Thynne, 5 April 1680, Thynne xx, fo. 423.

[76] Gilpin to Lowther, 23 April 1694, *Lowther Correspondence*, Letter 112.

[77] Smith to Savile, 4 February 1717, Savile DDSR 211/227/82; Fitzwilliam to Guybon, 29 September 1698, Fitzwilliam F(M)C 1059, *Fitzwilliam Correspondence*, Letter 77.

[78] See as an example William Salmon of Nantwich, cheesefactor, to James Fisher of the Lion and Lamb, Thames Street, cheesemonger, 6 June 1698, Cholmondeley DCH/L/41.

[79] In April 1671 Lowther acknowledged receipt of a bill of £130 'dated the first instant and payable the first of May by the Elletsons'. Lowther 18 April, Lonsdale/D/Lons/W2/1/6.

the passage of the number of days expressed on the bill. Ten, fifteen or twenty days 'after sight' were not uncommon periods on cheesefactors' bills, but the number of days could vary considerably.[80] In September 1674, for example, Lowther of Whitehaven informed his steward that he had received the bill drawn by one William James for £100 'payable eight days after sight', which had been accepted by the tradesman, John Bedell, who would, Lowther supposed, 'pay it about a week hence'.[81] Since payment did not inevitably follow presentation the law had to determine who was liable during the transaction and at what stage such liability transferred. If the man on whom the bill was drawn refused acceptance of a bill the person who had drawn it was liable for the sum stated on the bill. When the acceptor accepted the bill he assumed the obligation to discharge it, which explains why Lord Cholmondeley's London servants sometimes found bills from cheesefactors refused by the cheesemongers on whom they were drawn. Otherwise when a bill was presented for acceptance the acceptor was expected to give his verbal or written assurance that the money would be paid at the time the bill specified. Sometimes an acceptor might refuse to pay on those specified terms, demanding a longer day of payment. If the holder of the bill accepted such a variation then the original drawer of the bill ceased to be liable and it would be up to the holder to sue the acceptor if he subsequently defaulted. As lawyer William Gilpin warned his master on one occasion: 'If [Mr Shallot] do not punctually pay it when it becomes due I desire it may be returned because by giving time you dispense with the drawer.'[82] If holders acted as Gilpin so pithily advised then the liability would remain with the drawer and back would go the bill to him with a demand for the money's repayment or for a fresh bill on a more compliant correspondent.

As so often, however, the letter of the law does not adequately convey the practical realities. In March 1697 Lord Fitzwilliam received two bills from his steward but reported that the tradesman upon whom they were drawn had assured him that 'they deceived me who sent me these bills if I expected the money upon sight' because 'by way of trade they always had two months time after sight to pay them'. The tradesman promised to pay them at such a date if Fitzwilliam 'would have patience'. Since Fitzwilliam knew the man to be reliable, having received bills on him from his Norfolk estate, he 'accepted of the time' and the tradesman then accepted the bills. Even when bills were accepted at a due date, payment was never sure. In the same

---

[80] Thomas Williams provided Adams with twelve bills between July 1681 and December 1682, of which nine were drawn at 'twenty days' sight', one at sixteen days, one 'at sight'. Adams' accounts do not specify the terms of the other two bills. Cholmondeley DCH/Acco., Accounts Books 1680–1, 1681–2.

[81] Lowther 15 September 1674, Lonsdale/D/Lons/W2/1/9.

[82] Gilpin to Lowther, 1 October 1694, *Lowther Correspondence*, Letter 157.

letter Fitzwilliam reported that he had got another bill paid but only after sending many times to the acceptor, while another tradesman could not accept a bill for payment at the specified time, but Fitzwilliam was keeping the bill rather than sending it back to Northamptonshire since he knew the man's difficulties were only temporary.[83] Delays were characteristic of the process rather than rare exceptions likely to give rise to lawsuits. In 1679 the first Viscount Cholmondeley complained to his steward that the bills he was receiving on Jones and Snell, cheesemongers, were at twenty days after sight, which involved a three weeks' delay.[84] His son would have thought himself lucky to be paid so quickly. As late in our period as 1714 Sir George Savile received a bill of £40 from a timber merchant called Hodgson who regularly bought his timber. The bill had been drawn in Hodgson's favour by a ship's captain who had bought timber from him and was carrying it to London. Hodgson asked Savile to 'be easy' with the captain until he had 'got his freight' (that is, sold his cargo) for he did not question that, given time, he would make good payment.[85] Some delays were not so amicably negotiated but were rather the unforeseen consequence of extraordinary events like wars or rumours of war. In October 1688 the prospect of the Dutch invasion set the press gangs to work to man the fleet. This delayed ships in such outports as Chester and cheese remained unshipped, so that at least one London cheesemonger was unable to pay bills which he had already accepted. Lady Cholmondeley sought her steward's advice, enquiring whether to return the bill to Cheshire to try to get the money there, or to have the monger arrested, fearing that if she did she would 'get nothing here but his person'.[86] The legal position was clear enough: the drawer in Cheshire was not liable and the cheesemonger in London was, but it- is possible the factor paid back the money just to preserve his credit with the Cholmondeleys and their steward.

Even in less nervous times than the eve of the Glorious Revolution there was a casualness about bill payments. In 1682 a cheesemonger demanded fourteen days' sight for paying a bill and then did not pay for three weeks,

---

[83] The king owed the man at least £4,000 for purveyance to the royal stables. Fitzwilliam to Guybon, 4 March 1697, Fitzwilliam F(M)C 983; *Fitzwilliam Correspondence*, Letter 8.

[84] Cholmondeley to Adams 26 November 1679, DCH/K/3/1. Interestingly he directed that all bills should be enclosed in letters addressed to his goldsmith, Fowles, apparently because he thought they would be more secure from theft. Same to same, 29 November 1679, *ibid*.

[85] John Hodgson, Hull, to Sir George Savile, 19 March 1714 (enclosed in Smith–Savile correspondence), Savile DDSR 211/227/93.

[86] Lady Cholmondeley to Adams, 27 October 1688, Cholmondeley DCH/K/3/8. Similarly Adams was told to inform one of the understewards that a bill he had returned on a William Farnhead had first been accepted, but now Farnhead refused to pay on the ground that he owed nothing to the drawer. Since the London household feared that Farnhead was in 'but a very low condition' the understeward was to have the bill back again and deal with the matter (that is, presumably, try to recover the money or get the factor to draw a bill on an alternative correspondent). Laroche to Adams, 11 January 1696, DCH/K/3/10.

while another declared when a £50 bill fell due that he had no money 'at present' so that there would be at least a further week's delay.[87] A few months later a household servant begs Adams to seek bills drawn on a particular cheesemonger because he was such a good payer, whereas other bills he found 'very tardily paid and not without abundance of trouble'.[88] A decade later things were no less flexible for the goldsmith John Rogers informs William Adams that a bill drawn on Thomas Compear, cheesemonger, is still unpaid, but he had not returned it to Cheshire because Compear 'from time to time' promised to pay it.[89] (Bankers could be as loathe to part with money as cheesemongers for when a household servant received from a cheesemonger a note for £200 on the goldsmith Sir Thomas Fowles and went there to cash it the 'presize coxcombe' (*sic*) behind the counter said because it was the coronation day he would pay no money until the following Tuesday.[90]) Like Lowther with the late-paying Elletsons Lord Cholmondeley thought to use interest charges as a means to speed up returns or at least obtain some compensation for delay. Discovering in January 1698 as he checked through the accounts relating to the purchase of his new town house that many Cheshire bills were not paid or only part paid well after the due day he demanded that his steward should charge them interest for every day the payments were late. However, the drawers were not cheesefactors, who probably would have laughed at such a demand, but tenants who had signed new leases and the bills were for fine money. They were slightly more vulnerable, although not at law, because as Cholmondeley indeed directed, the steward could withhold their leases until they paid the interest. In general the only sanction London residents had against unsatisfactory tradesmen was to avoid them in the future by declining bills on them.[91]

Some difficulties were mercifully temporary although they seemed all too protracted at the time. The interruptions to the coastal trade provided by the threat of war and the mobilisation of the navy we have already observed. The reform of the coinage undertaken by William III's government in 1696 had an impact which lasted from 1695 to 1697. The reform was a remarkable undertaking to adopt when Britain was at war with France. It was brought to a triumphant conclusion in little more than eighteen months, although not without considerable distress to many of the

[87] Jonadeb Colley to Adams, 11 November 1682, Cholmondeley DCH/K/3/4.
[88] Hugh Beheathland to Adams, 5 April 1683, Cholmondeley DCH/K/3/6.
[89] John Rogers to Adams, 11 February 1692, Cholmondeley DCH/K/3/10.
[90] Robert Eddowes to Adams, 11 April 1691, Cholmondeley DCH/K/3/9.
[91] Cholmondeley to Adams, 13 January 1698, Cholmondeley DCH/K/3/13. Lord Cholmondeley's younger brother, George Cholmondeley, then an undergraduate at Christ Church, Oxford, warned Adams against a particular cheesemonger who had been found in the past to be 'a sneaking, sharking fellow'. 12 November 1682, DCH/K/3/4.

poorer and less well informed of the king's subjects and considerable anxiety and trauma to estate stewards. All the old badly clipped silver coins were to be exchanged for new milled-silver coins, issued at provincial mints as well as the London mint, and the difference in value would be met by a window tax. By early 1697 this process had largely been concluded and the Treasury was only accepting old silver for taxes by weight, although it was allowing 5s 8d an ounce for it whereas in all other transactions old silver was to pass at only 5s 2d an ounce. While this provided landowners with an opportunity of making a profit by gathering up old silver at 5s 2d and paying their taxes, especially the land tax, at 5s 8d, a profit of 6d on every ounce paid to the Treasury, there was a time limit: old silver was not to pass at all after 2 June 1697. The reform of the coinage had an impact on the value of guineas because the parlous state of the silver coins had inflated the value of gold coins relative to silver, so that the ratio between silver and gold in England differed from continental ratios, particularly those of Holland. Indeed this difference was one of the motives for the reform because it tended to encourage clipping and the illegal exportation of silver. Guineas in London were worth about 30s prior to the reform but the production of the new milled-silver coins with their enhanced intrinsic value quickly reduced the inflated value of gold and the exchange rate to guineas fell to about 22s 6d very quickly. Many holders of guineas had their fingers burned and this hazardous period of transition greatly complicated the stewards' efforts to transfer their masters' rural income to London.

In January 1696 Lord Cholmondeley warned his steward that as the coinage reform bills, which Parliament had just passed, allowed no clipped money to pass after 10 February save in taxes to the king, Adams must pay coins which would be sufficiently acceptable to the cheesefactors to persuade them to give bills to the same value on the cheesemongers or he would be 'a great loser'. This was a counsel of perfection. Stewards were in the awkward position that the tenants could not pay in unclipped money because there was very little of it in the realm until the mints could supply it, and if they received no rents the stewards could make no returns. In June 1696 William Gilpin warned his master it would be impossible to 'answer' any bills his master drew on him 'unless it be in clipped money'.[92] Moreover, returns were in shorter supply than usual because people who took up or sent up produce to the capital preferred not to use returns but rather to carry good money down to the country and risk the hazards of the highway rather than receive bad money in the country by way of return.[93] Yet another difficulty was that those who furnished returns by bills to

---

[92] Gilpin to Lowther, 3 June 1696, *Lowther Correspondence*, Letter 286.
[93] See the complaint of Francis Guybon to Lord Fitzwilliam, 2 August 1696, Fitzwilliam F(M)C 964.

stewards had an awkward habit of expressing the amounts in guineas (at a ratio of 28s or 30s to silver) whereas the cheesemongers and other tradesmen in town would not redeem the bills at such a rate now that guineas were being undermined by better silver coins.[94] Even if the bills were expressed in silver, cheesemongers would sometimes endorse them to be paid by their goldsmiths who when presented with the bill would refuse to honour it except in bad silver. One cheesemonger disputing such a bill with a presenter flew into a passion, declaring he cared not what became of the bill for he cared for neither lord nor goldsmith, and as for the goldsmiths and bankers they were all 'a pack of rogues'.[95] By August 1696 with the guinea rate fixed since March at 22s 6d tradesmen would try to fob off presenters of bills with banknotes which were unacceptable because they were discounting at 14 per cent in August (and at 17¾ per cent in September). As one London household servant reported, his master's bills must be designated to be redeemed in cash or the cheesemongers would 'plague him'.[96]

These difficulties, although prolonged, were at least temporary. One final difficulty was encountered over a far longer span of time. Landowners felt that while returners were providing them with a service by moving their money to London they in turn were providing the returners with a service in moving their money to the country. Not unreasonably they deemed it a reciprocal arrangement of mutual benefit. Nothing was more likely to arouse the wrath of landowners, therefore, than demands from returners of a fee or premium or some other additional inducement for involving themselves in returns. Sir Ralph Verney steadfastly refused to pay premiums of even a penny in the pound for returns.[97] As we have seen, landowners like Lord Fitzwilliam were not fond of paying percentage charges to carriers for bringing up cash, but they were quite outraged at the

---

[94] Cholmondeley to Adams, 28 January 1696, Cholmondeley DCH/K/3/10. In February Cholmondeley complains that despite his warning Adams has accepted bad money in the country and has returned 'such uncertain bills in guineas' which he fears will not be accepted by his London creditors, and a week later points out that guineas are already passing on the Exchange at £1 8s 6d, so Adams must only send bills on tradesmen expressed in pounds sterling or he must 'stand the loss of it' for Cholmondeley will not. On 30 March Laroche sends word that Parliament has fixed the rate at 22s 6d. DCH/K/3/10, K/3/12.

[95] Richard Harrison to Adams, 5 and 15 October 1695, Cholmondeley DCH/K/3/10.

[96] 'I think Mr Morgan to be a villain to give you another bill of £50 upon John Boys who is such another as he is for he won't accept the bill but to be paid in banknotes which is next door to nothing for they are at 18 per cent discount. ... no workman will meddle with banknotes.' Laroche to Adams, 23 August, 19 September, 13 October 1696, Cholmondeley DCH/3/12.

[97] Davies, 'Gentry Returns', 28. She discusses this reluctance at length citing other landowners, some who paid, others who did not.

thought of paying fees for returns. In 1709 Fitzwilliam even refused to pay the daughter of a Northamptonshire carrier, Robert Fearey, for bringing him a sum of money, come up by way of return, from her father's London depot, at which she roundly declared he should have no more money from her. (He offered her strong ale to cool her passion but, he reported to his steward, 'nothing would serve her but a bottle of wine for she drank, as she said, no malt drink. Such people are come to a fine way of living.') Her father was equally angry, saying Fitzwilliam should have no more returns by him since Fitzwilliam refused to pay porterage, but Fitzwilliam had no intention of paying fees to have money moved around London for this would 'prove of ill consequence'; others would expect the same and thus make returns 'very chargeable'.[98]

At least Fearey and his redoubtable daughter were providing the service of bringing money to the house. Still more aggravating were those who sought to charge for returns when the landowner sent for the money himself. Some of the charges were disguised. One cheesemonger would only accept a bill of £120 if £40 of it was paid in *louis d'or* at 17s 6d each which was not 'current money'.[99] In 1690 Lord Cholmondeley's secretary drew a bill on the chief steward in favour of a cheesefactor named Baldwyn. As soon as Baldwyn notified his cheesemonger that he had received the money the latter would repay the £95 to Lord Cholmondeley. This 'reverse return', a method considered more fully below, was only obtained for a payment of 2d per pound.[100] Sometimes when needs were urgent premiums could seem less undesirable, and a master might urge a steward to offer as much as 20s for a £100 bill.[101] However, much more typical was Lord Cholmondeley's angrily sending a bill back to the country when a cheesemonger refused to redeem it unless he was paid a premium of 20s, for less, he asserted, would 'not answer the kindness'. The monger, John Ewer, claimed that his factor had been promised that Ewer should have this premium by Cholmondeley himself. Ewer, who said he had no need of money in Cheshire at the time, claimed the factor would not have 'presumed so far' but for Cholmondeley's 'importunity and promise of a reward which', he impudently added, 'must be such as becomes his lordship'. All this received short shrift from the angry nobleman who returned the bill to Cheshire, commanding that there

[98] Fitzwilliam to Guybon, 17 March 1709, Fitzwilliam F(M)C 1731; *Fitzwilliam Correspondence*, Letter 622.

[99] Laroche to Adams, 15 July 1699, Cholmondeley DCH/K/3/13.

[100] Laroche to Adams, 8 April 1690, DCH/M/27.

[101] As when Laroche found himself without resources at the time of year he purchased his master's wine, and urged Adams to get a bill from Salmon, the most reliable cheesefactor, on Joseph Burton, a very reliable cheesemonger, using the inducement of such a premium if necessary. Laroche to Adams, 29 April 1699, Cholmondeley DCH/K/3/13.

should be no more returns from 'that knave' (that is, the factor) in the future.[102]

Stewards would always seek to protect their masters from such premiums. William Gilpin discounted his returns from one local source because the source charged Lowther 20s per £100. He therefore moved to another source who only charged 10s. A year later he observed that a local competitor for returns, the Customs House, seldom gave anything for returns 'there being' as Gilpin delicately expressed it 'usually some willing to requite the favours they receive by gratuitous returns'. That is, the Customs House could move their money without paying charges because the merchant who supplied the return would receive favourable but illicit treatment when he next imported tobacco or other merchandise. Similarly Thomas Greene, steward of the Wiltshire estates of Sir John Nicholas, changed from one returner to another because the change saved 15s on a £150 bill.[103] As late as 1709 John White, steward to Lord Gower, informed his master that he had £250 but could not return it without paying for it which he had never done and was unwilling to begin. Two years later he told Lady Gower that he had managed to return £200 but the only way he could avoid a fee was by conceding a month's grace for payment.[104] By the early years of George I's reign it is possible to see a new professionalism slowly emerging with new routines and the symptoms of the emergence of provincial banking. In 1717 we find Thomas Smith at Sir George Savile's Rufford, sending to Nottingham to see if 'Mr Smith the banker' (no relation) will remit between £200 and £400 without other consideration than letting him have a bill at four or five weeks. However, the steward recognises that 'returning for profit' was 'a trade with him' and he was fearful the banker would only do it for pay. In fact the banker allowed him a bill of £400 without charge but with the concession of thirty-five days to pay.[105]

When landowners were desperate for cash in London and their stewards were unable to find returns in the country, they would sometimes operate a 'reverse return'. That is they would draw bills on their stewards to be paid in the country. This was the old established method referred to earlier. In 1649 John Peck was able to exploit his master's influence as a leading parliamentarian by having his master request £200 for himself and £100 for

---

[102] Cholmondeley had, of course, made no such promise to the factor although it is possible one of the understewards had done so without his master's consent. Cholmondeley to Adams, 1 November 1684, Cholmondeley DCH/K/3/6.
[103] Gilpin to Lowther, 18 June 1694, 22 August 1695, *Lowther Correspondence*, Letter 118 (and note), Letter 230. Greene to Nicholas, 31 October 1698, Nicholas 75/15.
[104] 6 July 1709, 19 May 1711, Leveson-Gower D868/9/58 and D868/9/174.
[105] For a shorter time a penny a pound premium would have been insisted on. Smith to Savile, 4 and 9 February 1717, Savile DDSR/211/227/81 and 82.

his son, from a Captain Taylor, then in London, which Peck would repay in Denbighshire at sight of Trevor's confirmatory letter when the captain came down.[106] For his Michaelmas and Lady Day collections in 1689 George Plaxton returned to Lord Gower £850 by bills on a London tradesman, but £1,167 by bills charged on Plaxton by his master from London, so that reverse returns were 57 per cent of the whole.[107] The beneficiaries of the bills might be local gentlemen who wanted to take money down from town without actually carrying it; they might be local tradesmen or graziers or farmers who had received money in London for goods they had brought up themselves or they might be officials or army or navy officers who were travelling down to the country on public employments and would need funds there when they arrived. On one occasion Fitzwilliam had his steward pay £50 to the wife of a neighbour, Francis St John, who was then in London. On other occasions he had his steward pay cash to St John's steward having received the same amount from St John in London. These were useful returns although in these instances no bill was involved. On another occasion Fitzwilliam writes that he has received a £100 bill from St John in London on his goldsmiths, Sheppard and partners, so Guybon must pay St John's steward when he sees him or carry the money the two miles to St John's manor at Thorpe. He adds that if St John needs money at any time Guybon should pay him 'beforehand' for Fitzwilliam does not doubt the payment of it in London. Sometimes very tempting opportunities came a landowner's way of which he hesitated to take advantage for fear that his steward would be unable to lay his hands on sufficient income to meet the day of payment. In 1700 Fitzwilliam was to lend a man a very substantial sum of which the borrower wanted £600 paid in Stamford. Fitzwilliam anxiously asks his steward in what time he could raise so much out of the rents. For smaller amounts no such anxieties arose. Their tenants would drive beasts, pigs or sheep, to London, sell them and then bring Fitzwilliam their earnings and he would notify his steward to repay them as soon as they reached their homes.[108]

Lord Cholmondeley had no qualms about burdening his steward with bills. One of nature's spendthrifts, he combined this with the unamiable characteristic of believing that if the flow of money diminished it must be because of incompetence or worse on the part of his estate servants rather than the inconvenient fact that not even his estates commanded the riches of Golconda. So we find him drawing bills on Adams for money to be paid to

---

[106] 'Colonel Jones can inform you where to send unto him', he adds helpfully. This was, of course, an example of the informal IOU method of return, referred to earlier, not a formal inland bill. Peck to Sir John Trevor, 14 November 1649, Trevor D/G/3276.

[107] See Plaxton's account, Leveson-Gower D593/F/2/14.

[108] Fitzwilliam to Guybon 16 August 1698, Fitzwilliam F(M)C 1055; see also 1118, 1235, 1236; *Fitzwilliam Correspondence*, Letters 73, 130, 237, 238.

cheesefactors in return for money received in London from cheesemongers. There was nothing wrong in this except that he tended to overdo it and then grumbled when he discovered that his bills were not paid promptly, which naturally eroded his credit. On one occasion an understeward on whom he had drawn bills failed to pay them for up to a year. 'Thanks to him for bringing me under this dog's reputation' he exclaimed indignantly, 'Mr Fletcher's behaviour makes some people believe here I draw bills upon people I have nothing to do with.' As a consequence he solemnly declares he is resolved never more to lose his credit by drawing bills on Cheshire.[109] No doubt this resolve was a considerable relief to his steward, although the relief like the resolve proved temporary. Not only did he use reverse returns he also sought means to anticipate income by in effect using the cheesefactors as bankers and 'overdrawing' his account with them. That is, he obtained bills on credit. As he wrote to Adams on one occasion: 'You must by no means fail me the bills for . . . £250 though you are forced to tick with the cheesefactors.' To encourage this he was prepared to offer the factors 40s premium. He had tried this expedient four years earlier in November 1697 when he needed, he claimed, £1,000 to get his plate out of pawn on his return to town 'to be able to eat at home'. Otherwise he must be 'like a broken merchant', unable to show his head in London. To meet this need he asked his steward to try for a bill from 'Mr Salmon or some other cheesefactor' for £500 or £600 to be made good from monies which were to be paid at Candlemas (2 February) 1698.[110] Like Lord Fitzwilliam, Sir John Lowther of Whitehaven was much more circumspect. On one occasion he would accept only half the money the drover was prepared to offer him for his fear his steward would be unable to redeem the bill. Certainly Gilpin encouraged him to use this method for even though he was out of cash on one occasion when such a bill became due, he nevertheless assured his master that whenever Lowther drew upon him he would find the means to satisfy the bill, simply asking that Lowther give him as much warning as he conveniently could.[111]

---

[109] Cholmondeley to Adams, 10 February 1698, Cholmondeley DCH/K/3/10. Perhaps Fletcher had taken too literally an insouciant directive from his master of 1696. Fletcher, Cholmondeley had written, 'need not think of being exactly punctual in the payment of Laroche's bill drawn upon him' for if it were paid 'a month or six weeks after the time' it would be 'well enough'. Same to same, 19 May 1696, DCH/K/3/12.

[110] In the first instance Cholmondeley was trying to repay a creditor by anticipating fines to come in from leaseholders which they could not pay until Lady Day, and he instructed Adams to tell Salmon it would be a particular obligation which he would return him 'in something of greater moment' when it lay in his power. Cholmondeley to Adams, 21 January 1701, Cholmondeley DCH/L/28, same to same 1 and 6 February, 3 November 1697, respectively DCH/K/3/14, L/28; and L/41. In this instance Adams returned about £900 by 17 November so the tactic may well have succeeded. Richard Harrison to Adams, 27 November 1697, DCH/K/3/10.

[111] Gilpin to Lowther, 19 August 1695, *Lowther Correspondence*, Letter 229.

By such varied means and with these many setbacks and difficulties, a host of seventeenth-century stewards wrestled with their most intractable problem: supplying their masters with the earnings of their estates without lining the pockets of footpads and highwaymen. Inevitably, although unintentionally, their efforts on their masters' behalf made them a vital cog in the financial machinery of the country.

The ambassador

I quite forgot in my last to acquaint you of good Mr Drydon['s] death ... Pray go you to his funeral and present my service to the gentlemen that go down to his burial and let them know I would have been sure to have been there myself had I been in the country and commanded you to be there to perform my last service to my very good friend.

Lord Fitzwilliam to Francis Guybon, 1708[1]

I see with others' eyes.

Sir John Lowther of Whitehaven, 1681[2]

The steward, as his lord's surrogate, was his ambassador to the region in which the estate stood. He was his master's eyes and ears, a vital source of intelligence both open and secret, as ambassadors have always been. He was also his master's voice, in the marketplaces, at the fairs, at the sessions and assizes, in the council chambers of neighbouring boroughs, at the meetings of local gentlemen which preceded elections for knights of the shire and (as we shall see in the following chapter) in parliamentary elections in boroughs in which his master maintained an interest, and even in the meetings of the board of governors of an endowed grammar school.

Sir Joseph Williamson intends some kindness to St Bees School. Order it so that at the next meeting of the governors someone resign so that Sir Joseph may be chosen governor and let the rest sign a letter to him to signify his election which I shall deliver. I do not intend that you shall resign but any of the rest.

It might be thought that Sir John Lowther's instruction showed remarkable faith in his steward's powers of persuasion. In fact his faith was justified for Tickell succeeded in persuading Lowther's brother-in-law, Richard Lamplugh of Ribton, with whom Lowther was then on decidedly indiffer-

---

[1] 15 January 1708. Fitzwilliam F(M)C 1637; *Fitzwilliam Correspondence*, Letter 546. The reference is to John Dryden of Chesterton. A Tory, he was MP for Huntingdonshire from 1690 until his death. *Victoria County History* (hereafter *VCH*): *Huntingdonshire*, vol. 2, 34.

[2] Referring to his stewards in a letter to William Christian, 27 December 1681, D/Lons/W2/16.

ent terms, to resign his governorship.[3] However, its significance lies in its demonstration of the very rich mix of occasions on which a steward might speak with his master's voice. Stewards were expected to address the great with suitable deference, to negotiate and discuss with men of middling rank, and to rebuke or encourage with bluff condescension those of lesser rank. In short, the steward of a substantial estate was a negotiator. It was a crucial aspect of his duties. It was in the interests of a prominent county family that they should remain on good terms with their neighbours, particularly when those neighbours were men of higher rank or their social equals. As we have seen, estates were not definitively surveyed, discrete blocks of land, like a patchwork of neat fields on a Brobdingnagian scale. They were hopelessly intertwined, their boundaries still reliant more on the memories of 'ancient men' than on surveyors' instruments. Inevitably occasions of dispute abounded. Such disputes could be protracted and costly, their principal beneficiaries the lawyers who fought them. Since landlords did not see themselves as existing to benefit lawyers (whatever the perception of the lawyers) most of them preferred to lay the responsibility of making their wishes prevail on the shoulders of the steward rather than engage in an expensive lawsuit of unpredictable outcome. It was often the lord's steward, rather than the lord's lawyer, who found himself first charged with the task of settling disputes about boundaries, feudal rights and feudal obligations, or of warding off encroachers, or of defending tenants against unjust taxes, levies or other impositions.[4] The Duke of Newcastle, speaking through a senior member of his household, Wenman, gave the classic utterance of this perception of the stewards' ambassadorial role. The duke ordered Wenman to remind Ralph Gowland, steward of his Durham estates, that while the negligence of stewards often occasioned 'both charge and trouble to their master ... sometimes good stewards do accommodate and prevent differences'.

The occasion of this letter was Gowland's report that a tenant of the Earl of Carlisle was ploughing some intake moorland within the duke's boundaries. Gowland had decided that it was an encroachment on the basis of a survey of 1576 and on the recollections of aged tenants who had witnessed boundary ridings decades earlier. Unfortunately, Gowland reported, a former understeward had carelessly winked at such encroachments over a lengthy period. However, although Gowland had told the current understeward that he should cut down part of the encroacher's hedge and cut some sods to maintain the duke's right, he had also instructed him to hold off until he had received the duke's instructions. Gowland knew that his

---

[3] Lowther to Tickell, 5 February 1687, Lonsdale D/Lons/W2/22.
[4] The role of the steward in defending the estate against encroachers is discussed in detail below in Chapter 10.

master 'would not have any difference with the earl if it could be avoided'. The duke replied that if Lord Carlisle had a 'prudent steward' Gowland should approach him on the duke's behalf and seek to settle the matter amicably between them, but if he could not persuade the steward that an encroachment had occurred, he must approach the earl himself 'which you can do much better than we can here'.[5]

Lord Fitzwilliam would have thoroughly approved of the concept of the steward as an ambassador whose diplomacy, effectively employed, could ward off expensive litigation. Certainly Francis Guybon was Fitzwilliam's voice in the Soke of Peterborough. He can be observed in this ambassadorial role again and again, speaking for his master in matters trivial and weighty. On several occasions his master instructs him to ward off threatened lawsuits by putting this or that argument to this or that disputatious person. On one occasion Fitzwilliam observes that he has already asked his lawyer, Pemberton, to put a certain argument to the leader of the opposing faction, but fears he has not done so, 'lawyers being willing to have suits go on, it being for their profit'.[6] Fitzwilliam played his steward like a chess piece, moving him across the board of the Soke in pursuit of some particular strategy. Sometimes the steward speaks on behalf of concerns which might appear trivial, although important enough to the protagonists, as when Fitzwilliam enlists Guybon on behalf of the mother of his wife's maid: 'They say the poor woman had the toll of the town out of which she made a pretty livelihood, and it's now taken from her which much troubles her.' Guybon must speak to all his friends to try to have it restored to her. Similarly when a favourite tenant's son appears to be in difficulties with his young wife's portion: he 'must give Charles Duce good words' to persuade him 'to make the matter easy to Joe Bull' otherwise the latter's new wife might not prove 'so good a fortune' as had been hoped. Five years later Guybon was instructed to help a tenant who was likely to be cheated out of part of an inheritance by a 'cross man', one of his wife's relatives. Guybon must tell the tenant Fitzwilliam would stand by him, and that he was prepared to buy the share of the estate the tenant was to inherit if that would help. At least the tenant would be able to tell his oppressors the offer had been made and that alone 'may frighten them'.[7] On other occasions the

---

[5] Ralph Gowland to the Duke of Newcastle, 21 June 1709, with Wenman's draft reply on the reverse, Portland (Newcastle) Pw2, fo. 532a. Wenman is simply passing on the duke's views and instructions, not expressing his own. He may have been the duke's secretary or his receiver.

[6] Fitzwilliam to Guybon, 3 April 1701, Fitzwilliam F(M)C 1165; *Fitzwilliam Correspondence*, Letter 176. For other letters casting Guybon in this ambassadorial role in local disputes see 2, 9 and 23 January, 13 February 1701, F(M)C 1158, 1159, 1160, 1161; *Fitzwilliam Correspondence*, Letters 169–72.

[7] Fitzwilliam to Guybon, 2 July and 17 February 1698; same to same, 3 January 1706, F(M)C 1047, 1030, 1442; *Fitzwilliam Correspondence*, Letters 66, 50, 411.

disputes were more serious, concerning the welfare of a whole community. Lord Fitzwilliam sought to use Guybon as his spokesman in defending several neighbouring villages from being charged with the maintenance of a road which others might use and which would be of little use to those who were saddled with the charge.[8] However when the villagers subsequently went to the sessions to dispute the matter at considerable cost Fitzwilliam, who now had better information, shifted his ground. Every 'town' should mend its own highway and his steward must 'persuade them to peace'.[9]

Of course, in a litigious age like the seventeenth century the steward could not always ward off litigation. When lawsuits were unavoidable lawyers would inevitably be mobilised on the lord's behalf, but this did not mean that the steward's role had ended and that he could now surrender the affair to the legal experts. When lawsuits were afoot the lord's lawyers had three basic roles: firstly, advising the lord (or the steward on behalf of the lord) on how the law stood; secondly, determining what evidences and what witnesses would be needed to fight the case with any hope of success; and thirdly, pleading on the lord's behalf if the dispute ever reached a court. It was the function of the steward to mould the bullets the barrister would fire. In this he acted rather like a modern solicitor supporting a barrister he has instructed on behalf of a client, and also like the private enquiry agent such solicitors occasionally employ. He would seek out witnesses, take depositions and test the recollections of the 'ancient men' of the district where their recollections were likely to be of service. Where a dispute was to be settled by the arbitration of 'commissioners' (usually neighbouring gentlemen or local attorneys) rather than in court he would make firm recommendations to his master as to who should be chosen, and, once he had his master's consent, would approach them on his behalf to secure their services.

For example, in 1680 Thomas Hawkes, steward of Sir Thomas Thynne's Shropshire estates, found he had a dispute which was in a most unsatisfactory state because the commissioners (whom he had not chosen or recommended) were very unserviceable. One was elderly, ailing and disinclined to travel; the other was absent in London. The commissioners of Thynne's opponent, Prince, were much more able and formidable. ('I found that Mr Prince had nominated two cunning snaps [as] his

[8] 'To avoid all suits of law amongst us ... the best way will be to have it repaired out of the public stock of the hundred ... for to my knowledge many a hundred pounds has been laid out for such purposes about the fens and why not for this? Pray propose it to Mr Neale and the rest and tell them its my opinion and withall that I must defend those towns where my estate lies from being oppressed'. Fitzwilliam to Guybon, 13 February 1701, F(M)C 1161; *Fitzwilliam Correspondence*, Letter 172.

[9] Fitzwilliam, 8 and 22 May 1701, F(M)C 1167, 1168; *Fitzwilliam Correspondence*, Letters 178–9.

commissioners that were fit for his purpose' he reports from Shrewsbury.) He therefore took the initiative to fee a local lawyer to discover whether abandoning that commission and starting again with better commissioners would be prejudicial to his master's interests. Learning that it would not, he abandoned the old commission and concluded his report by submitting a list of names of potential commissioners, drawing on his local knowledge of the region. He prefaced his list by observing that since Prince had appointed two attorneys he thought it best his master should do so also and supplied his master not only with a list of local lawyers, but also brief notes identifying them to assist his lord's choice: Edward Smallman, who 'lives in Ludlow' and had married a niece of Colonel Fox; 'Mr Harris your steward' [of courts] 'will not be excepted against among those I name'; 'Mr Samuel Berkley who lives in Bridgenorth and is an attorney and a civil man'; Mr Lancelot Tailor 'your understeward [in Shrewsbury] is an understanding man in his business but I think we must use him as a clerk to take the depositions and see to the business'; 'Mr Edward Pulley who was steward to the late Lord Stafford, an understanding man', concluding with the caution: 'all these or any will expect to be paid'.[10] Meanwhile he visited Prince to explain and apologise for the delay. This courtesy pleased Prince and moved him to suggest a compromise which might settle the matter amicably without further delay and expense, and Hawkes was quick to transmit the offer to his master. In the event this *démarche* proved unsuccessful but the episode demonstrates the possibilities of the steward's mediating role.[11] All Hawkes's activities in the affair demonstrate how much the steward rather than the lord's local lawyer was the true surrogate of the lord when lawsuits and other legal disputes were in progress.

Sometimes the ambassadorial function placed the steward in what would seem to twentieth-century eyes a most extraordinary surrogate role. Fitzwilliam's eldest son, William, died in November 1699 at his father's London home and was buried in the Fitzwilliam vault at Marholm Church exactly a week later. There is no doubt that the Fitzwilliams were deeply grieved at his loss.[12] They and their two sons and daughter appear to have been a warmly affectionate family. Indeed all five seem to have felt a warm affection for their ageing steward at Milton. There was nothing of the cold, insensitive patriarch about Lord Fitzwilliam. Yet when the body was sent down to Marholm from London no Fitzwilliam accompanied it or presided over the interment. Francis Guybon presided in Fitzwilliam's place, ordering the family vault to be opened 'to be clean and sweet against the time',

---

[10] Hawkes to Thynne, 10 January 1681, Thynne xxi, fo. 138.
[11] Hawkes to Thynne, 10 January 1681, Thynne xxi, fo. 138.
[12] Although they were unsurprised. Aged twenty-one, he had long been ill, apparently with tuberculosis. See *Fitzwilliam Correspondence, 1698–99, passim*.

and inviting certain male mourners, nominated by his master from the neighbouring gentry, to serve as pall bearers. On the day of the funeral the steward led a mounted party, which included the gentlemen pall bearers, to a neighbouring village where they were to give the funeral cortège from London an official welcome and escort it to Marholm and where Guybon paid for their refreshment at the inn on his master's behalf. Also in that solemn party were eight strong men from the tenants, chosen by the steward, whose duty it would be to carry the heavy coffin from the hearse into the church and down into the vault below the choir. The eight stalwarts were on foot, and Guybon directed that they should wear gowns and velvet caps and carry long black staves, and after the hearse arrived at Woodson he ordered them to walk beside it to keep off the mob. Guybon approached the steward of a neighbouring gentleman, Francis St John of Thorpe, for leave to pass over his property, Fitzwilliam having decided that this route would be best being 'most greensward all the way'.

There were broader responsibilities which extended beyond the day of interment. On his master's behalf the steward made appropriate presentations: distributing gloves to visiting gentlemen and tenants and three dozen escutcheons among the chief tenants and neighbours. Of the eight silk escutcheons on the pall Guybon gave six to the gentlemen pall bearers, kept one for himself, and returned the eighth to Fitzwilliam. He arranged that Fitzwilliam's chaplain should have eight small escutcheons on his pulpit and cloth for his mourning suit, and gave him fifty shillings to distribute among the poor of Marholm (because, contrary to law, the coffin was covered with velvet and the interior quilted with silk), and sent a certificate to London stating that this distribution had occurred. On behalf of Lady Fitzwilliam Guybon instructed Mrs Bull, Milton's part-time housekeeper, and Mrs Pendleton, the chaplain's wife, not to stir abroad or go to church until their mourning clothes arrived.

If he followed accurately the extremely detailed instructions his master sent him, Francis Guybon did all and more of the things above described.[13] He would have been perceived by the onlookers, whether gentle or simple, as the individual totally in charge of the obsequies. For reasons never explained in his letters Fitzwilliam remained in London, unable perhaps to leave his grieving wife, but through the actions and above all the commands, instructions, invitations and hospitable greetings delivered by his steward Fitzwilliam shaped the rite of passage at Marholm Church. This was not the only time that Guybon represented his master at a funeral, as the epigraph to this chapter demonstrates. The death of Fitzwilliam's old friend, John Dryden of Chesterton, a cousin of the poet, did not draw

[13] Fitzwilliam to Guybon, 28 and 30 November, 7, 14 December 1699, Fitzwilliam F(M)C 1109, 1110, 1111, 1112; *Fitzwilliam Correspondence*, Letters 121–4.

Fitzwilliam from his London retreat but brought the ageing Guybon riding over from Milton to serve as his surrogate. Guybon's role as steward at a funeral was not peculiar to him. In 1667 Gervas Jaquis, steward of the Huntingdon estates in Leicester, was on business in London for the family when an aunt of his master died there. Jaquis arranged for the body of Lady Alice Clifton to be embalmed, wrapped in 'sere cloth' and encoffined, and guarded by relays of her ladies in a room suitably hung in black and decorated with escutcheons. He consulted the heralds on the delicate matter of what degree of state was due an earl's daughter who was not married to a peer and what would exceed her station, and besides watching over the 'lying in state' made all arrangements for the funeral. Finally he reported to the Countess of Huntingdon (the deceased's sister-in-law) on the details of the funeral, who preached and to what text, how many coaches attended the hearse and what members of the nobility and gentry travelled in them. He was also involved over the following weeks in the financial arrangements involved in paying legacies and sundry debts, trying to get back Lady Clifton's coach horses which had been seized by Lord Dacre's guardian as security for a large debt for rent, and various other matters all of which one would expect to be the responsibility of a family lawyer.[14]

One of the heaviest and yet most delicate ambassadorial responsibilities a steward might have to discharge concerned taxation. One can learn much about the operation of national taxation at the local level from stewards' letters simply because they were regularly deputed to speak for their masters in this important business. If the steward adopted a blustering tone of voice towards his master's inferior enemies, and an obsequious, deferential tone toward his master's social superiors, he can normally be found switching to a disingenuous when not downright mendacious voice when confronting the local commissioners of taxation on the estate's behalf. It was, of course, the duty of the steward to protect the estate from 'unjust' taxation; that is, from being assessed at a rate which was more disadvantageous to his master's purse than were those imposed on comparable neighbouring estates. For the loyal steward his master should, ideally, pay proportionally less than comparable landlords and certainly not more. William Gilpin discovered with indignation on taking up his stewardship at Whitehaven that his predecessor must have bungled badly. Far from his master Sir John Lowther paying less than comparable landlords he was actually paying more. Worse, while local recusants like Sir Henry Curwen and William Fletcher of Moresby were assessed as honest Protestants, his Whiggish master had been either maliciously or accidentally assessed as a

---

[14] See six letters to the dowager Countess of Huntingdon and to the earl (then a minor), dated 16 and 30 March, 16 and 30 April, 2 and 7 May 1667, HA7652–7.

recusant. Needless to say, Gilpin moved swiftly to redress the situation although it was impossible to recover the taxes already paid.[15]

In the seventeenth century landlords and stewards did not draw a distinction between 'tax minimisation' and 'tax evasion'. Most landlords single-mindedly pursued the goal of paying the minimum they could get away with rather than the minimum to which they were entitled. For absentee landlords the steward represented his master in confrontations with the local taxation officials. These consisted of the county commissioners, the local assessors who determined what tax the individual property owner owed and the collectors to whom the tax must be paid. Negotiating and minimising taxes were among the most difficult of the steward's ambassadorial duties. During the era of the later Stuarts there gradually emerged the principle of taxation on a quota basis, by which each county was allotted a sum which it had to find.[16] Under such a system if one major landowner contrived to pay less, everybody else would have to pay more. This consideration moved some landowners, Lord Fitzwilliam among them, to help their neighbours by paying in the country certain taxes which they had the option to pay either in London or the country.[17] The quota system, which was certainly the most efficient from the Treasury's viewpoint, could promote harmony if the county's nobility and gentry distributed the burden fairly across their county. If not it could prove very contentious. Francis Greene, steward to Sir John Nicholas, reported in 1698 that the Dorset county commissioners were well agreed at their general meeting that a rate of three shillings a pound would raise the sum charged upon the county but in Wiltshire they were 'mightily divided' for the general meeting of the northern divisions had been too 'hard' on the southern divisions.[18] However, since the local commissioners were themselves landowners and tax payers, a steward would need a remarkably persuasive tongue to convince the commissioners that his master's taxes should be reduced when this meant that others (including probably the commissioners themselves) should pay more. Of course, all landlords minimised their taxes by underestimating the value of their estates. This was a method hallowed by time and the universality of its practice.

[15] Gilpin to Lowther, 26 March 1694, *Lowther Correspondence*, Letter 103.
[16] For the fiscal innovations of the later Stuart governments see especially C. D. Chandaman, *The English Public Revenue 1660–1688* (Oxford, 1975), Chapter 5, 'Direct Taxes', *passim*.
[17] That is, taxes on personal wealth rather than land. In 1697 Lord Fitzwilliam planned to arrange matters with the London taxation commissioners so that his steward could pay in the country, sending a certificate to London to demonstrate this, so that 'my own neighbours may receive the full benefit the act allows'. 22 May 1697, Fitzwilliam F(M)C 994; *Fitzwilliam Correspondence*, Letter 17. See also 'Introduction: Taxation and the Reform of the Coinage', xix–xxi.
[18] 'Some parts of the county will pay 5s per pound, others 14d 'tis believed.' Greene to Nicholas, 11 May 1698, Nicholas 75/5v.

Moreover, if everybody in a particular county did it successfully, but discreetly everybody would benefit for it would help to keep down the total figure of the county's contribution then and in the future. However, here and there we can descry the steward busily pursuing the elusive goal of tax minimisation by more individualistic methods, methods clearly aimed at his master's individual benefit at the expense of his neighbours.

In 1689 John Mainewaring summoned John Scott and John Lucas, the local assessors for the constablewick containing Lord Weymouth's manor of Drayton. He entertained them amid the awe-evoking splendours of the manor house, surrounded by potent symbols of prestige and rank. Having first made sure that neither Scott nor Lucas had read the Act of Parliament imposing the tax, Mainewaring solemnly read them a portion of a letter from his master which showed what 'payments went constantly out of this estate' – expenses, Mainewaring insisted, which ought to be set off against the assessment. The assessors, local men of lower rank, belonging to that broad group of persons whose opinions could be strongly influenced by hearing a greater man confide his own, were no doubt flattered to be taken into the confidence of so august a figure as Lord Weymouth. Nevertheless, scenting danger, they tried to refer Mainewaring to the taxation commissioners of the county. Mainewaring was gently implacable. The assessors had taken the oath and were the men chiefly concerned. The commissioners, he assured them, would not dream of altering what they decided. Moreover, it was hardly fitting that Lord Weymouth should have to publish to so many people as the committee of county commissioners such intimate details of the financial affairs of his estate. The assessors being, as he put it, 'satisfied in their own breast' by Weymouth's letter might moderate the matter as they saw fit, and if the commissioners questioned their assessment, they should point out that his lordship's estates in Tamworth, Anstey and Willimote were to be assessed separately. Finally, no doubt with much head scratching and deep drinking of the ale Mainewaring would have hospitably provided, Scott and Lucas found themselves able to agree that their distant host, one of the richest men in England, should pay just £9 for Drayton which was less than half what should have been due from a manor which yielded an income from rent alone that year of about £480.[19]

Mainewaring then set off to interview the Anstey assessors, fearing he would not 'speed so well there'. His fears were well founded. In vain did he plead the heavy expenses incurred repairing the mills and the chancel of the

---

[19] See Mainewaring's report to Weymouth, 21 October 1689, Thynne xxviii, fo. 239. Scott subsequently told Mainewaring that only one commissioner, Sir Henry Gough, had questioned the low rate on Drayton, and another commissioner replied that the assessors were upon oath, 'and there it rested'. Mainewaring reported that if they had been assessed at the same rate others were, it would have cost £20. xxviii, fo. 241.

church, and the rents his master paid out of the manor. The assessors, better informed than their over-credulous colleagues at Drayton, insisted, correctly, that the Act permitted no 'abatements' and were therefore more severe than the steward had hoped. At the day of appeals Mainewaring rode off to argue his master's case, but in vain. Although he succeeded in persuading one of the commissioners to support his appeal, the chairman of the commissioners, Sir Richard Newdigate, proved obdurate. Mainewaring argued that the expenditure on the estate in repairs that year was greater than the income the Anstey estate had yielded, and that he understood that Parliament had intended that landlords should only be taxed on the 'clear value' of their estates, and thus Lord Weymouth should pay nothing for Anstey or at least a much lesser sum than he had been assessed. Newdigate replied that the steward was mistaken for every estate was to pay according to its normal annual value.[20] Discovering that he could not prevail, Mainewaring hastened to assure the commissioners that anything he had said was on his own initiative with no directions from Weymouth in the matter – a statement almost certainly untrue but as Weymouth's letter, from which Mainewaring had read extracts to the Drayton assessors, has not survived this cannot be established. However, since seventeenth-century stewards were loath to take any initiative without first ensuring that their actions would meet with their masters' approval it is highly likely that Mainewaring's tax-evading tactics were well known to his master, and might have been the result of precise instructions.

With Lord Fitzwilliam we need be in no doubt. In 1697 he wrote a letter to Francis Guybon which was designed to equip his steward to be his master's voice in dealings with both the local assessors and the county commissioners. The instructions were detailed and explicit. Since it was believed the commissioners would be 'very severe' Fitzwilliam remarked frankly that 'it behoves us not to own how much [rent] the tenants pay'. His steward must tell all the tenants not to 'own the full of their rents by a fourth or fifth part'; they could not punish them for 'denying' their rent, but could punish the steward for deception with a fine.

Therefore, I am advised, if they send to you for a rental ... go to them but pretend some business made you forget it. If they ask what such and such a tenant pays, pretend your memory is bad, you cannot remember. Be sure not to name anything, for if you name less than the tenant pays, they will make me pay treble ... if they can contradict us. Be sure to remember nothing they ask you; pretend you are ancient and your memory much fails you.

[20] Mainewaring was not the inventor of the notion that landowners should only pay taxes on 'surpluses'. The notion regularly found adherents in this period and Sir Thomas Clarges expressed the view of many members of the Commons when he argued that 'no man ought to be taxed but for the spareable part of his revenue'. Chandaman, *English Public Revenue*, 139.

If the commissioners taxed Fitzwilliam 'at a venture' and if, propor-
tionately, it did not exceed his rents 'we must be contented'; if it was higher
Guybon must appeal within ten days. The assessors would be chosen out of
the various villages, and would be allowed a small allowance in the pound
for their pains, but, Fitzwilliam grimly observed, he would not recommend
any of them to disoblige neighbours they must live beside all their lives for
the sake of twenty shillings or just to serve the king 'who would hardly
thank them'. The assessors must own what they themselves paid in rents
but could claim ignorance of what their neighbours paid. In general
Fitzwilliam considered the three-shilling tax would be acceptable if it
amounted to the same as the previous four-shilling tax, with one-quarter
deducted. Otherwise 'let them tax what they will we will own nothing for
this may prove a tax of dangerous consequence hereafter'. The steward was
to discuss these matters with certain nominated neighbours on his master's
behalf, and if Guybon believed them trustworthy he was to confide to them
what Fitzwilliam had advised.[21]

In public affairs the steward was often a conduit of advice and instruction to the region which surrounded his master's estate. Lord Cholmondeley was a Cheshire landowner but his property and his family connections stretched into Wales. In May 1707 he wished to mobilise some of his
kinsmen and neighbours to organise the dispatch of addresses of congratu-
lation to the queen on the union with Scotland from the counties of
Montgomeryshire, Caernarvonshire, Merionethshire and Denbighshire.
Rather than writing to all the appropriate gentlemen himself, he chose to
instruct his chief steward, William Adams, to contact such kinsman and
friends as Sir John Wynn and Mr Ellis Lloyd of Pen-y-Lan. Moreover,
Lloyd, who knew that Wynn was seriously ill, and forbidden business by
his doctors and family, wrote in reply not to Cholmondeley but to Adams
pointing out that Wynn might not be able to carry out the affair and
suggesting that Adams should write to 'some other of our chief gentlemen'
on his master's behalf.[22] For a steward to act as a middleman in such public

---

[21] Meanwhile Guybon must keep his master's letter by him, and read it 'over and over again'.
18 February 1697, Fitzwilliam F(M)C 981; *Fitzwilliam Correspondence*, Letter 6. See also
25 February; 4, 11 March; 1, 8 April, F(M)C 982, 983, 985, 988, 989; Letters 7, 8, 9, 12, 13.
Less burdensome than taxation but still not insignificant was the burden of providing
armed and mounted men for militia service or for service in war. Here again stewards
laboured to lessen their master's contribution, or, where unavoidable, furnish horses
which had seen their best days, and arms from the lumber rooms of the manor house
which had last seen active service during the Civil War. 'I have kept you out of providing a
horse and arms' a steward reported triumphantly in 1650. John Peck to Sir John Trevor, 7
September 1650, Trevor D/G/3276. Not all were as successful but it was the duty of all to
protect their master's estate and purse as far as they could.
[22] Lloyd to Adams, 12 May 1707, Cholmondeley DCH/L/30; see also Michael Laroche to
Adams, 8 May 1707, DCH/K/3/21.

business was not unusual. When there were public rejoicings and formal congratulations at William III's escape from an assassination plot in 1696 the town of Whitehaven sent its own congratulatory address which announced that its signatories joined the 'Association' of those who declared that William was lawfully king and that neither James II nor the 'pretended' Prince of Wales had any right to the throne. In doing this the inhabitants acted through the steward of the manor of St Bees, of which Whitehaven was a part, who in turn transmitted the 'association' with its signatures to the lord of the manor, Sir John Lowther. The townsfolk did this because none of them had been given an opportunity to sign the association from the county of Cumberland.[23]

This incident illustrates the point that stewards, like royal ambassadors, did not function in one direction. If they were the voice of their masters they were also the ears. Local people, local interests in a region or a town were not slow to make use of stewards to gain the ear of the great. At some date during the 1670s the Bailiff (that is, the Mayor) of Rugeley, Staffordshire, approached William Swynfen, steward to Lord Paget of Beaudesert, to ask that he enlist his master's help on behalf of the town in which Paget was a substantial landlord. The aldermen wished to revive the town's ancient right to a fair, which had long fallen into disuse. Swynfen saw the proposal as very much in his master's interest and as likely to greatly benefit the town and so obtained Paget's assistance. As a result, as he reported to a subsequent Lord Paget, the fair was revived, and grew to be one of the best in the county, especially for sheep.[24] Similarly in 1717 the townsfolk of Worksop approached Thomas Smith, Sir George Savile's chief steward, begging him to mobilise his master's influence on behalf of some dragoons, probably militia, who had been accused of mutiny by their officers because they refused to surrender their horses at disbandment. The men had refused to do so unless they were shown the alleged order from London which the officers claimed to be enforcing. The dragoons were popular with the townsfolk who took their side, at which the officers threatened to burn the town, claiming it was disaffected. In fact it was the officers who were suspected of Jacobitism and of stirring up trouble for sinister ends. Pointing out that if the dragoons suffered death or imprisonment it would be much harder to enlist soldiers locally at some future emergency, Smith urged his master to apply to the Duke of Newcastle rather than to the Secretary of War or to the officers of the court martial who would be too partial to the

---

23 'It is submitted to your honour's disposal, either to present it as it is, or (if it be too much fouled by going through many hands) that you will ... cause it to be written fair with the same names ... and that you will preface it with an address, or not, as you think fit.' William Gilpin to Lowther, 10 April 1696, *Lowther Correspondence*, Letter 277 (see also Letter 276).
24 Swynfen to Paget, undated but c. 1683, Paget D/603/K/3/4.

officers. Thus Smith did not simply serve as a conduit for the views of the townsfolk, he also urged the merits of the case and suggested the tactics to be adopted.[25]

While stewards were clearly their masters' surrogates in their dealings with their masters' tenants, a role we have already considered at length, it is perhaps surprising to find that on particular occasions they might be asked to assume a more ambassadorial role even with them, although they might sometimes decline to act where they believed the negotiation would do more harm than good. Certainly that was the response Lord Fitzwilliam encountered when he sought to have a farm made more viable at the expense of his tenants' common. In 1699 he had purchased the manor of Maxey, which adjoined his estate in the Soke of Peterborough, with which came Waldrum Hall, a tumbledown farmhouse attached to a ferry on the edge of the fens. It needed more land to make it a satisfactory leasehold farm. With Maxey he had acquired the status of lord paramount of the North Fen, a large area of fenny waste over which his tenants enjoyed common rights. If his tenants agreed to make over 20 or 30 acres of this fen to their lord as a gift Waldrum Hall would be a viable farm. There was even a precedent: the tenants of the Earl of Exeter had presented their landlord with 100 acres of the neighbouring Great Fen a few years earlier. In October 1699 would occur the first meeting of the Maxey manorial court since Fitzwilliam's purchase. Present would be Henry Vaughan, Fitzwilliam's understeward at Maxey, a Stamford lawyer called Burman who as steward of courts would preside, and Francis Guybon, Fitzwilliam's chief steward who was to be his master's eyes, ears and, very discreetly, his voice. In addition Fitzwilliam arranged that Roger Pemberton of Peterborough, his principal local lawyer should also be present. Pemberton, who would on that day be keeping the Northborough manor court, should take some of the principal Northborough tenants over to Maxey to dine with the Maxey tenants at a fitting celebration of Fitzwilliam's first Maxey court. In this affair the 'open' negotiations were to be carried out not by the steward nor the understeward, but by Lawyer Pemberton.[26] Fitzwilliam probably thought that if his chief steward appeared directly in so delicate a matter the tenants would be too much on their guard. Nevertheless the chief steward would be the master spirit. The lawyer, seconded by Burman, would speak

[25] For a fuller account see Hainsworth, 'The Mediator', 99–100, and Smith to Savile 29 November, 1 December and to Madam Savile 2 December 1718, Savile DDSR/227/61.

[26] Burman was not a Fitzwilliam lawyer except for this one function, Fitzwilliam having inherited him from Maxey's previous owner, Lady Sylvius. Although Fitzwilliam seems to have first intended that Guybon should act through him, he probably decided that in such a delicate matter it would be better to employ his principal lawyer, Pemberton. For this affair see Fitzwilliam to Guybon, 30 September, 5, 12, 26 October, 2 November 1699, Fitzwilliam F(M)C 1101–1106; *Fitzwilliam Correspondence*, Letters, 114–18.

as the steward instructed him, and the steward would engage in covert negotiations with individuals on his master's behalf.

Guybon was to instruct the lawyer to wait until the tenantry were 'a little merry after dinner' and then suggest that they should celebrate Fitzwilliam's first court by making their landlord a little present which, Fitzwilliam innocently observed, 'will cost them nothing and signify nothing to any of them'. Pemberton should be told that if his eloquence succeeded in gaining 20 acres Fitzwilliam would give him ten guineas for his trouble, a reward large enough to reveal the importance Fitzwilliam attached to this 'trifle'. If Pemberton found the tenants in 'a good humour' he might then seek to increase their offer, saying that since Fitzwilliam was so 'modest' as to ask so small a present the commoners could do not less than present him with 10 more acres out of their good will. However, Pemberton must do this with great wariness for, as Fitzwilliam anxiously counselled, this might spoil all if the commoners were not well inclined. If Pemberton succeeded in gaining his client 30 acres he was to have twenty guineas, a sum equivalent to a little over half a year's salary of his chief steward. Pemberton should have a document in his pocket for them to sign 'lest they forget their promise afterwards'. Meanwhile Guybon was to ensure that some of the leading men concerned in the North Fen who were not serving on the jury were also invited to the dinner so that they could be in the agreement about the gift, but for all that the business must not be made public until the very day except to some few persons Guybon is sure will 'hold their tongues'. A week later Fitzwilliam, who has as yet heard no comments from his steward about the proposal, writes again urging that if Guybon finds any leading man with considerable influence who is averse to the proposal he should 'whisper in the ear' and tell them he should be no loser; that Fitzwilliam would make him a present when he came into the country, and this to anyone 'you find peevish and averse' but he must not say this to anyone before another person, 'but privately in his ear'.

Fitzwilliam clearly intended that this should be a well-managed affair with nothing left to chance. However, this was a *démarche* which never occurred outside Fitzwilliam's fertile imagination. His steward's replies for this month have not survived but it is clear that Fitzwilliam was flatly told that there was so little hope of success that the request to the tenants must not even be put. No matter how Fitzwilliam grumbles that the tenants should have readily granted him it when 'the thing is so small a matter among them all and would be so convenient for me to make that little farm more commodious', no matter that he belatedly vows that when he came down he would have exchanged some other land in return or given the value of it in money, it was all to no purpose. His plan for a 'decoy for

Waldrum Hall', as he termed it, was dead. His steward knew that neither his nor Pemberton's capacities as orators or negotiators extended to persuading tenants to part with a strip of their commons to gratify their landlord.

A vital role in the steward's ambassadorial activities was played by venison. Those landowners, always a minority, who went to the trouble of maintaining deer parks, did not do so in order to display a status symbol. Deer parks were desirable because they supplied the household of the owner with a much valued form of meat and, because it was so valued, furnished the owner with a means of consolidating friendships. Through a skilful use of his venison a gentleman could hold the loyalty of his equals and inferiors and encourage the friendship of men more powerful than himself because venison belonged to that class of gift which honoured both giver and receiver: the giver won honour by his generosity, the receiver by this demonstration of his worthiness to receive it. Lord Cholmondeley once instructed his steward to deliver a buck to Judge Jeffreys, then on circuit in Cheshire, although the delivery was to be made after dark to the judge's room when he was alone, presumably so that Sir George should suffer no embarrassment.[27] Lord Fitzwilliam's letters show what to twentieth-century eyes might seem an obsessive concern with the disposal of venison, laboriously spelling out who should have a side, who a haunch, who a shoulder, although on other occasions he was prepared to leave it to the steward to choose suitable recipients, which further emphasises Guybon's ambassadorial role. Such gifts went to men who were locally prominent and influential, although not necessarily gentlemen. Usually such men were members of the Fitzwilliam political 'interest' in Peterborough. One of the prime motives for distributing venison was to maintain a landowner's local political interest by rewarding the faithful or by wooing the uncommitted.[28]

As John Peck once cogently advised when his master was about to appoint an understeward:

It behoves you to make choice of one you may confide in as not only to receive the

---

[27] 'The keeper by your lordship's order brought a buck to Sir George Jeffreys upon Saturday last at such time as all company was parted from him late in the evening, who returns his acknowledgment . . . for this kindness', Adams to Cholmondeley, 24 August 1680, Cholmondeley DCH/K/3/3. 'The judge doth to all persons speak very well of your lordship, and doth take the kindness of your buck mighty kindly', Cholmondeley's lawyer reported complacently. John Wybunbury to Cholmondeley, 18 August 1680, DCH/L/50. Jeffreys received the same kindness at the 1682 assizes.

[28] See Fitzwilliam's letters to Guybon in the late 1690s and early 1700s, *Fitzwilliam Correspondence*. The steward's role in maintaining his master's political interest is explored in the following chapter.

rents and return them but also to give you light and intelligence of all things that may redound to your best advantage.[29]

Sir John Lowther of Whitehaven understood this very well, observing: 'I see with others' eyes.'[30] His rueful remark and Peck's sage advice remind us that there was one duty which was common to all stewards on all estates from which the owners were often or invariably absent and which requires more detailed examination: the provision of intelligence. Since stewards were the eyes and ears of their masters they were expected to report fully and regularly on what they saw and heard not simply about the estate itself, but about matters discovered in the county town, at the fairs, at assize courts, at the sessions, at race meetings or hunts, at any place indeed where a landlord's neighbours, both gentle and simple, were likely to be gathered together, and where might be gleaned everything from the merest gossip to such useful pointers as who was ambitious for a parliamentary seat at the next election. Understewards at outlying manors shared this responsibility.

Human nature being what it is some intelligence was no more than gossip. Writes that indefatigable correspondent William Thynne: 'The news here is that Mr Ephraim Westley's son and heir is lately married to a poor ale house wench at Warminster which much disturbs him, especially his wife.'[31] Indeed stewards occasionally apologised for the triviality of the news they thought fit to include, or for the excessive length of their letters. 'My lord, the country affords no better news than this, the city being the theatre where I suppose greater things are acted' Gervas Jaquis apologises to the Earl of Huntingdon, and a similar concern moved William Thynne to observe in what may have been his very first letter to his new master: 'This tedious account of small concernment I fear may be very troublesome to you. If so pray give me notice and I will forbear.'[32] His fear was groundless, and it is highly unlikely Sir James Thynne ever gave him notice to forbear. Sometimes masters were not sure whether intelligence was indeed mere gossip or intelligence with a particular application to their own affairs, as when Sir John Lowther of Whitehaven wondered why his steward had reported the death of a local gentleman. Lowther was not concerned that his steward was bothering him with trifles. He merely thought that his steward might have perceived that this death could result in some beneficial purchase for the estate, but had failed to spell this out clearly. In fact Gilpin

[29] To Sir John Trevor concerning the appointment of an understeward, 2 October 1652, Trevor D/G/3276.

[30] See footnote 2 above.

[31] They were horrified, Thynne reported with relish, 'that so base a born wench should sit in the place of a gentlewoman to the great disparagement of their house'. William Thynne to Sir James Thynne, 10 October 1659; Thynne ix, fo. 155.

[32] Jaquis, Loughborough, 20 November 1667, Hastings HA7658. William Thynne to Sir James Thynne, 27 September 1658, Thynne ix, fo. 48.

had merely wished to keep his master informed of local happenings. Lowther's son, Sir James Lowther, wrote every week long letters to his steward who was expected to reply at similar length.[33] In this he was merely following the example of his formidable father. Stewards who conscientiously reported at length were in no danger of rebuke. Failure to report was a sin. Doing so at length and in detail was not.

Some stewards found themselves acting as a source of intelligence over a far wider area than the environs of their master's estate and on larger issues than acreages and tenant rolls. 'Let me hear something of the thoughts of the country concerning our proceedings' writes Lowther of Whitehaven from the tensions of the Convention Parliament, which had disposed of one monarch and set two others in his place. If Lowther's query strikes an anxious note he should have been reassured by his steward's response, which reported that King William and Queen Mary:

are proclaimed King and Queen of England, etc.' In the presence and auditory of twenty times as many more people at the least than were present for the proclamation of King James the Second, and our guns going off and ships swaggering with their colours, besides innumerable huzzas of the people with great joy, to the full satisfaction of all Protestants who in all places of the country are exceedingly well pleased with your unanimous proceedings.[34]

Thomas Tickell's responsibilities as a gatherer of public intelligence were enhanced in the aftermath of the Revolution for in 1689 Lowther was appointed a Commissioner of the Admiralty and throughout the Irish War Tickell regularly supplied his master, and through him the government, with news of Irish affairs for which the port of Whitehaven proved a good listening post. Runs an early but characteristic report:

Before [Elisha Gale] left Wexford there were two French ships came to Waterford, the one of 16, the other of 30 guns, laden with ammunition and a person of honour supposed to be Mr Fitzjames who was gone towards Dublin with six or seven led horses which makes me despair of a speedy peace in the kingdom.[35]

These early reports became more frequent and more significant as the war in Ireland developed and Whitehaven became an important staging post for the relief of Londonderry and subsequently the campaign which culminated in the battle of the Boyne. On 18 May 1689 Lowther wrote asking what number of horse could be shipped from Whitehaven and Workington and

---

[33] Beckett, *Aristocracy in England*, 151.
[34] Lowther to Tickell, 16 February 1689, and Tickell's reply of 21 February, Lonsdale D/Lons/W2/24.
[35] If by 'Mr Fitzjames' Tickell meant the Duke of Berwick the supposition was premature. *Lowther Correspondence*, xxxiii–xliii. Tickell, 7 February 1689, Lonsdale D/Lons/W2/24. Elisha Gale was a Whitehaven merchant and brother of Lowther's colliery steward, who had safely brought home a new 90 ton 'pink' ('a small square rigged ship, usually with a narrow overhanging stern') which he had just completed at Wexford.

what stock of corn, hay and victuals could be had for these and future transports. In fact Lowther's letter crossed with one from his colliery steward which contained a most detailed report. It listed all available vessels with their masters' names, tonnage and so on, and supplied the number of water and beer casks available, and reported that while provisions were scarce there were 20 tons of butter and 100 tons of biscuit at the Isle of Man which could be brought thence in a week, while the country could supply hay and straw for 400 horses and 1,000 bushel of oats.[36] Sometimes public affairs could have direct application to the more normal estate duties for, as Lowther later nostalgically recalled, Tickell also exploited his secondary post as customs surveyor at Whitehaven to provide his master with valuable intelligence, sending him a monthly account of entries at the Customs House 'thereby the better to judge the state of trade in the place'.[37]

Even in the rural isolation of Longleat William Thynne could provide his master with public intelligence of considerable significance, as when he writes of about a hundred armed men meeting near Lansdowne against 'the present government and public peace'. A terrible storm was raging which caused them to disperse, but neighbouring military units were called out to oppose this abortive rising, and the county militia mobilised. Horses and arms were commandeered from the neighbouring estates, including Longleat. Later Thynne reports which of various suspected gentlemen had been arrested, and although none around Longleat had been so 'secured' he warns his master to stay away until the region is completely peaceful, for if Sir James came, although he might not be arrested, he would certainly be disturbed by investigating soldiers.[38] More than a quarter of a century later his successor, Thomas Allen, sent his master, Lord Weymouth, detailed reports which depict the shadow which fell over Longleat during the perils of Monmouth's Rebellion.[39]

Close supporters of the government of the day were as keen for public intelligence as its enemies. In 1684 we find Archdeacon Gery, who, as a kind

---

[36] Equal to 3,000 Winchester measure. John Gale to Lowther, 20 May 1689, clerk's fair copy, Letter Books, Fair Copies 1684–1694, Lonsdale D/Lons/W1/15. Gale's detailed report was inspired by a query from a government official, Commissary Sales, as to what ships were at Whitehaven 'fit to carry horses, etc., for Ireland', but Gale replied through his master.

[37] Lowther to Gilpin, 29 September 1694, *Fitzwilliam Correspondence*, Letter 155. A naval historian studying William III's war with France would find the letters of Lowther's stewards an invaluable source for the impact of French and Jacobite privateers on the sea-lanes entering the Irish Sea, and especially on Whitehaven's trade with Virginia.

[38] 7 and 25 August 1659, Thynne ix, fos. 137, 143.

[39] Thynne xxii, *passim*. A peculiarly tense moment because one of Monmouth's leading supporters, a Captain John Kydd, the only companion he knighted, was a former Longleat headkeeper during the lordship of Monmouth's old boon companion, Thomas Thynne, and well knew the secrets of the house and of the large quantity of arms it contained. Charles Chevenix Trench, *The Western Rising* (London, 1969), 169.

of oversteward of the Hastings estates in Leicestershire, seems to have served his patron the Earl of Huntingdon at least as devotedly as he served his God, reported that the borough of Leicester was inclining to surrender its charter to the king. Huntingdon received this intelligence with enthusiasm for he was a courtier closely identified with the government and one who wished to earn the favour of the king, and as a magnate with an 'interest' in the borough he was anxious that Leicester corporation should agree to the surrender without resistance and that he should be the medium through which the surrender was made. Gery was the earl's agent in his dealings with the mayor and alderman, urging haste, trying to win over recalcitrants and smooth out obstacles. Meanwhile he was to keep his patron informed of developments, and to give him speedy notice when the decision was finally made and report the date at which the mayor would be in London with the charter. All of this trust and much more Gery faithfully discharged over the succeeding weeks.[40] Huntingdon's relationship with Gery serves to remind us that lords often prompted their stewards to obtain specific intelligence, and particularly political intelligence. Hearing a rumour that a Mr Grey and Sir Robert Shirley had 'combined their interests' to obtain 'a burgess's place' for one of them at Leicester, Huntingdon enjoins Gery not to mention the matter openly but to visit Lord Beaumont or Shirley and 'endeavour possibly from their discourse to find their intentions'.[41]

Finally, since many landowners were members of either the Commons or the Lords, stewards could sometimes be found gathering or furnishing intelligence which their masters could employ when combating or supporting proposed legislation, especially taxes or excises, either in committee or in the House. A particularly striking example of this can be found in Sir John Lowther of Whitehaven's correspondence, where his colliery steward, John Gale, is found supplying his master not merely with data but with very persuasive arguments against a proposal to tax the inland but not the export sale of coal. In doing so he paints a vivid picture of the operation of the West Cumberland coal trade, tracing the coal from the bank at the pithead in the wicker panniers on the horses which 'lead' it to the quayside and thence at low tide across the bottom of the dry harbour to be hoisted up

---

[40] Huntingdon to Gery, Gery's reply, 21 and 31 August 1684, Hastings HA6035 and 3968 and succeeding letters during September. The reports of John Mainewaring to Lord Weymouth on the machinations of the mayor of Tamworth to secure the surrender of that borough's charter against the wishes of the majority of the borough's burgesses in 1688 are equally informative. See Thynne xxviii, *passim*.

[41] 'But that which makes me the more inclinable to believe it is that they do both intend to be at the sessions where I hope to meet you.' Huntingdon to Gery, 3 January 1679, Hastings HA5930. A week later, however, Huntingdon reported that Shirley had been ennobled as Lord Ferrers, Hastings HA5931.

the ships' sides. Showing how the customs officers could not possibly collect the duty unless they accompanied the coal at every stage (to prevent its diversion), and how they would have to keep watch on every pithead; how the expense of collection would be far greater than the return; how, since the inland price of coal would be higher, the pithead banks would be systematically robbed by the local inhabitants; and how the cost of labour must rise with the price of fuel which would hurt other trades and, indeed, other exports by increasing production costs to the nation's loss.[42] Two years earlier Gale had painted a similarly graphic picture for Lowther of the impact of the reform of the coinage of 1696 on the inhabitants of a provincial outport. Macaulay gives a summary of this reform in which, in the course of one of his most brilliant passages, he observes: 'there began a cruel agony of a few months which was destined to be succeeded by many years of unbroken prosperity'. It is this agony which is so brilliantly described by Gale. He takes us into his counting house as he wrestles with the problem of trying to pay wages to the 'leaders' who move his master's coal and the 'haggers' who hew it from the coal face when he has no coins of small denomination which they dare accept. He takes his master to the Customs House as he observes ships' captains and merchants wrestling with the Customs Collector who will accept nothing but milled money or guineas. Of the first there are scarcely any to be had in native English coins whilst the second are fleeing to Ireland where they are valued at twenty-six shillings. We can follow him around the stalls of Whitehaven market where 'one cannot now buy a loaf of bread ... but a jury of inquiry must pass upon the piece of money to be paid for it', for the situation has become so grievous that:

if one produce the broadest old Elizabe·h shilling with both rings and every letter visible, if it will not pass the scale 'tis nonsense to offer it, though never diminished in any other way than by its age. The like may be said of all hammered money, especially sixpences ... I know it may be said to all that a shilling may pass for 10d or 11d as it weighs. This is indeed very true, if we had not to deal with poor ignorant creatures that are so jealous of being imposed on they dare take nothing upon uncertainties. Besides the fractions, in the weight of every piece, are very confounding things to them and do rather administer opportunities ... of being defrauded, nor can a man that sweats for a halfpenny well endure the loss of a farthing.[43]

Meanwhile he warns his master, in words so dangerously indiscreet that he was fearful until he knew the letter was safely in his master's hands, that nothing could more effectively demonstrate the affections of the people to

[42] See Hainsworth, 'The Mediator', 100–1; and Gale to Lowther 10, 17, 24, 27 April and 1 and 15 May 1698, *Lowther Correspondence*, Letters 502, 505, 508, 511, 513, 518, and Lowther to Gilpin, Letter 512.

[43] *Lowther Correspondence*, 318.

William III's government 'than their peaceful temper under their present distraction about money'. If half the like distraction had occurred during the previous reign it would have 'put the kingdom in a flame'.[44]

In general, then, a conscientious steward would not confine his intelligence to matters purely of estate concern. Rather he would seek to keep his master informed of local affairs, including the impact on local people (particularly but not exclusively his master's tenants) of such national affairs as war, governmental policies and parliamentary legislation, political unrest, manoeuvres in forthcoming elections and every aspect of public affairs as it might affect the region in which the estate was set. This aspect of a steward's duties helps to make the correspondence of stewards and their masters an illuminating window opening onto a rich variety of public affairs.

Negotiating, reporting and spying: these traditional roles of the ambassador all came together in the final aspect of the steward's ambassadorial function: the acquiring of property. It was the duty of a steward not merely to manage an estate but to oversee its expansion. When it came to rounding off or otherwise rationalising their estate many masters had the same attitude to land as that old American farmer who declared: 'I ain't greedy for land, I just want what joins mine.' It followed, therefore, that among the matters on which a steward provided intelligence probably none was more eagerly received by his master than advance news of a nearby property which was vulnerable to acquisition. If his master showed interest the steward would investigate the property's extent, potential rental value, likely price, concealed drawbacks and problems and whether there would be any particular advantages to the master if he purchased it. Fitzwilliam spelled out his steward's role precisely: he should inform himself of all particulars before he reported, including owners' names, where they live, yearly rent, how likely to hold it, and whether a good tenant 'thrives upon it', and the condition of the house and outhouses. They were 'great lights' to a purchaser who could bid accordingly. When he discovered that his steward had been misled on some details he commented with some asperity that after giving Guybon such a 'charge' he wondered that he had not ridden over to 'Goody' Thomson of Aylesworth or her son at Sutton to know the truth of everything himself and not trust

---

[44] *Lowther Correspondence*, Letter 314. Gale's reports from Whitehaven grumbling about the impact of the reform of the coinage run from September 1696 to as late as November 1697, which suggests that Macaulay's 'few months of agony' was over-optimistic, particularly as the letters for the twelve months or so prior to September 1696 have not survived. His colleague Gilpin refers to the reform's impact as early as April 1696. *Lowther Correspondence*, Letter 275.

to what he had heard by hearsay from Joseph Chamberlain or some such 'sorry fellow'.[45]

Buying an estate could be a very protracted business ('I have been so tormented with this troublesome business of Maxey for these twelve months last past that I have hardly had leisure to do anything else' grumbled Fitzwilliam on one occasion), but in general landowners were in no hurry to buy, and it was usually the fault of the purchaser rather than the vendor if negotiations stretched from months into years.[46] The sale of estates was not a seller's market for the number of potential purchasers was usually very limited, and even this very restricted field would further diminish, or even vanish altogether, if it became known that a leading gentleman or nobleman was interested in purchasing.[47] The delay was partly caused by the cautious purchaser's determination to discover just what would be acquired and its real worth. The time gained enabled the steward to scrutinise the estate both on paper and on the ground in minute and meticulous detail. If the master decided to purchase, and the property in question was not simply an odd farm but rather a manorial estate with many sitting tenants, the post or a courier from London would soon hasten a 'particular' to the steward. This was a full description of the estate, naming the tenants and the individual plots they held, specifying by what lease they held them, and purporting to show the rents they yielded. The steward would ride over the property with the 'particular' concealed about him and investigate how far it described the reality before him and how far it was a work of creative imagination mendaciously set down by the vendor's own steward or his lawyer. The steward would compare rent rolls with what tenants said that they actually paid, consult the old men of the manor about customs and about obscure leases dating back decades, and seek the advice of substantial freeholders of the district known to be generally well disposed to their master's concerns.[48]

These investigations would be carried out discreetly for fear that foreknowledge of their master's interest would inflate the price. 'I am not willing to be too busy in my enquiry. It would make a jealousy in them that

---

[45] Fitzwilliam to Guybon, 28 October 1697, 13 and 20 November 1707, Fitzwilliam F(M)C 1018, 1627, 1629; *Fitzwilliam Correspondence*, Letters 38, 537, 538. See also F(M)C 1092, 1093, Letters 105, 106.

[46] Fitzwilliam to Guybon, 3 August 1699, F(M)C 1090; *Fitzwilliam Correspondence*, Letter 103.

[47] A London linen draper, prepared to bid as high as £5,500 for an estate, withdrew at the mere rumour that Lord Fitzwilliam was 'in the field', and likely to bid higher. Reverend Jeremiah Pendleton to Fitzwilliam, 17 April 1687, Fitzwilliam F(M)C 566.

[48] Concerning an obscure lease dating from 1651 Fitzwilliam suggested forty years after its signing that: 'old John Burley may remember' it. Remarkably old Mr Burley did. Fitzwilliam to Guybon, 3 August 1699, F(M)C 1090, *Fitzwilliam Correspondence*, Letter 103.

we are over-fond of the purchase' ran a characteristic steward's report.[49] Rather such probings were made as casually as possible, 'accidentally as if in discourse and not as if I bid you do it' as Fitzwilliam, no doubt unnecessarily, coached his steward. He coached Guybon again a few years later, urging that the enquiries about the rent paid by a sitting tenant be made from the tenant's father who was Fitzwilliam's tenant, but 'in ordinary discourse, not as if you came on purpose to ask it and don't talk too much of it at a time, least he guess your meaning, and you may set others over a pot of ale to sift the rest out of him'. What the 'rest' consisted of was spelled out precisely: how many acres of arable and 'lea ground' there was in a field; how many acres of meadow and how it lay; how many acres of several pastures; how much 'Lammas ground' belonged to it, if any; whether small rents were paid out of it and to whom; and 'everything that is proper to know'. The last apparently included the names of the fields where the lands lay, and which were the best pieces and which the worst. It all seems a great deal to extract over a pot of ale, particularly without arousing the suspicion that a purchase was in view. Nevertheless the degree of detail sought was not untypical, although most masters would not have sent such precise instructions for they expected their stewards to know what they needed and how to obtain it.[50]

The topographical disposition or indeed the very existence of a few acres of mixed meadow and pasture could occupy several letters between the purchaser and his steward. On one occasion Guybon was instructed to take 'an understanding country man' with him to ride over some ground offered for sale to discover precisely where three acres of meadow lay; for 'there is a great deal of difference in the lying of meadow'. Similarly Samuel Wood's practised eye scanned some land proffered to his master to ascertain its acreage, but, still unsatisfied, had it surveyed and found it fall short of the claim, a discovery which led to much debate about which land was actually for sale.[51] The steward's duty was here of great importance because the purchase of an overvalued estate could lead to endless difficulties and complications for both master and man which could last for years, quite apart from the obvious financial loss the master would suffer from an imprudent or deceptive bargain. 'If the cottages in my purchase at Castor and Ailsworth are such pitiful things I may thank you for it' grumbles Fitzwilliam to his steward. 'You went into that estate several times by my order to enquire the true rents and see in what condition the houses were, and always gave me encouragement to go on.' Guybon had encouraged the

[49] Thomas Greene to Sir John Nicholas, 11 May 1698, Nicholas 75/3.
[50] Fitzwilliam to Guybon, 1 February 1700, 5 February 1702, Fitzwilliam F(M)C 1114, 1204; *Fitzwilliam Correspondence*, Letters 126, 211.
[51] Wood to Sir John Trevor, 16 June 1639, Trevor D/G/3275/10.

purchase by reporting that the tenants were all 'substantial people', their rents 'a good pennyworth', there was no fear of the rents falling for most of them were on twenty-one year leases, and they paid all taxes.[52]

No less important than establishing the true value was establishing that those who sold the land actually had title to it, or that where several persons shared the title, all had signed the deed of sale. Samuel Wood's careful investigations enabled him to reassure his master that, although land was proffered by a younger son, the eldest had been disinherited by a deed of entail and had later confirmed a release to his younger brother prior to his death without issue. The father was also dead and the vendor and his son and their respective wives would all join in sealing the deed. The honest reputation of the vendor, which he had also carefully investigated, assured him that the estate was free of encumbrances. This was a hazard against which the steward must be especially wary. Charles Agard warned Lord Dorset not to meddle with a property which he had found burdened with carefully concealed encumbrances, a combination of recusancy, delinquency and sisters' marriage portions.[53] Lords were aware of the difficulties a steward could encounter in such intelligence gathering. Fitzwilliam on one occasion stigmatised a vendor as 'too cunning for us to deal with', worrying that some of the land offered was already his own, while one steward's belated search of parish registers revealed that some land already purchased was at some hazard because the younger brother of the vendor was not only under age but declared a lunatic.[54] Certainly these careful, detailed enquiries, required a bloodhound's nose, a total scepticism about the honesty of all vendors, a considerable knowledge of the locality, of conveyancing laws, of the market values in the region and skill in obtaining information from the vendor's neighbours and kinsfolk. A friend advised William Adams to rely on subterfuge and bribery to obtain accurate information about the Hatton estate, pointing out that 'old Will Povey' (a Cholmondeley tenant) was related to the vendor's agent 'and I doubt not will prevail with his kinsman to give a just account', especially if future

[52] 'I have still your letters to produce' he concluded grimly. Fitzwilliam to Guybon, 5 July 1705, F(M)C 1404; *Fitzwilliam Correspondence*, Letter 380. A vendor's mendacious attempts to inflate the value of an estate could sometimes backfire if no sale was concluded. The Earl of Northampton was at loggerheads for years with successive stewards of his Somersetshire estates because he thought that the rents paid should match a rent roll drawn up by a previous steward in 1692, whereas the rent roll had been deliberately inflated in the unfulfilled hope that the estate would be bought by Lord Stawell for a better price than it deserved. H. D. Turner, 'George, Fourth Earl of Northampton: Estates and Stewards, 1686–1714', *Northamptonshire Past and Present*, vol. 4 (1966–7), 103.

[53] Agard to Dorset, 5 July 1656, Sackville U269/C63.

[54] Fitzwilliam to Guybon, 9 May 1700, Fitzwilliam F(M)C 1125; *Fitzwilliam Correspondence*, Letter 137; John Dickson, steward to Richard Hill, see E. M. Jancey, 'An Eighteenth Century Steward and his Work', *TSAS*, vol. 56 (1957–8), 38.

employment for the agent was strongly hinted at.[55] Trying to establish the truth by offering the vendor's servants the bait of continuing employment after the transfer was not invariably successful. When Lord Fitzwilliam purchased the Maxey estate he relied rather too heavily on the information he received from the Vaughans, father and son, who had been stewards for the previous owner. He had assured the Vaughans that he would retain them as his own stewards if he purchased and so was outraged when he began to suspect that they had exaggerated the value of the estate in terms of the potential rents to persuade him to pay a higher price, complaining: 'If they have given me wrong information I have reason to take it worse from them.'[56]

The steward's investigations were necessarily laborious and lengthy, and could help to delay the completion of a purchase for months. William Gilpin began querying a particular title of land with a colliery at Whitehaven in June 1693 but did not triumphantly uncover a mortgage 'industriously concealed' until November 1694, a discovery which brought down the price from £900 to £775.[57] The steward also needed to be aware of local manorial customs or he could fail his master's trust. When Richard Hill bought some copyhold land in a neighbouring manor his steward advised him to do it in his nephew's name, who already held copyhold land there, for no matter how many 'copyhold estates' a man held at his death in that manor no more heriots would be due than if he only held one.[58] These investigations conducted by stewards would one day be displaced by enquiries conducted by lawyers. In our period, however, while lawyers unquestionably had their role it was largely confined to the legal procedures involved in the transfer of property, although lawyers often approached potential purchasers on behalf of vendor clients.[59]

Finally a steward's role in expanding the estate might extend to the pressuring of neighbours to sell to his master, or at least negotiating with them on his master's behalf. Two men who accumulated great experience of

---

[55] John Egerton to William Adams, 22 October 1698. Cholmondeley DCH/K/3/13. Similarly Francis Guybon was urged to discover by a third party the real annual rent of a farm because 'they will conceal the truth from a purchaser', Fitzwilliam, 6 August 1696, Fitzwilliam F(M)C 965.

[56] Because he apparently considered them part of his family and therefore owing loyalty to him rather than to Lady Sylvius, the vendor. In fact they had been part of Lady Sylvius's family at the time of the negotiations and their first loyalty was to her. Fitzwilliam to Guybon, 4 May 1699, Fitzwilliam, F(M)C 1081; *Fitzwilliam Correspondence*, Letter 95. The Vaughans must have persuaded him of their 'innocence' for he retained them for several years, although as understewards they proved an indifferent bargain.

[57] Gilpin to Sir John Lowther, 21 November 1693, 13 November 1694, *Lowther Correspondence*, Letters 29, 172.

[58] Jancey, 'Eighteenth Century Steward', 39. (Letter undated but from 1723).

[59] The owner of the Maxey estate first approached Fitzwilliam as a likely buyer through her lawyer.

negotiating purchases were the successive stewards at Whitehaven for Sir John Lowther, a landowner with an unappeasable hunger for coal-bearing land or at least land through which coal-ways could be made. Since Whitehaven's inhabitants firmly believed that Lowther had too much land already, and all who were involved either in coalmining or in shipping coal to Dublin dreaded Lowther's acquiring a near-monopoly of the supply of coal, both Thomas Tickell and William Gilpin found great resistance to their negotiations. When Lowther wished to acquire a substantial area of ground at the town head from a customary tenant named Hodgson, he found himself baffled by the man's stubborn refusal to sell. Lowther hoped that he might be an employee in his collieries so that his steward might 'endeavour to recall him that way'. Alas, Hodgson was no man's employee, being described on the court rolls as a 'yeoman'. Finally after continual pressure from the steward to sell he added injury to insult by secretly selling the ground to another man, Skelton, for £110. Skelton was a substantial tenant and as loath to gratify Lowther as Hodgson. Tickell kept reminding him of the opportunity he had to 'gratify' Lowther which 'if wilfully lost would never be regained to the perpetual annoyance of himself and his posterity'. These promises and veiled threats had no effect, for, as Tickell admitted, the more he courted him the more intractable he proved. He added wistfully that if they had a press for seamen, with Tickell concerned in it as he had been during 'the last Dutch War', Skelton 'should be sure to march if he did not yield to your demands'. Meanwhile he delayed registering the transfer, and consulted a lawyer about the possibility of eviction or a law suit, although Lowther shrank from such dubious courses. In the end Skelton sold on very favourable terms, and by doing so earned his landlord's gratitude which was still manifesting itself sixteen years later.[60] The negotiations for the purchase of nearby Flatt Hall, which eventually became Lowther's Whitehaven residence, were far more protracted. Tickell must have felt that he had grown old and grey during the eight long years of negotiation and stubborn refusals by the property's owner, a widow and a bitter opponent of her squire, and the purchase when finally completed was very expensive.[61]

Tickell's quest for strategic properties never ceased. On one occasion he advised his master to buy a freehold tenement close by the mill of the neighbouring manor in order 'to gain other dependencies ... especially the mill', and recommended another purchase so as to 'debar others' and 'by

[60] Churches, 'Lowther and Whitehaven', 65–6.
[61] The Flatt was nominally purchased for £1,000 from Sir George Fletcher, (who sold it to Lowther having taken possession himself only the day before) but Fletcher's role was probably simply to inflate the price on behalf of the real vendor. Churches, 'Lowther and Whitehaven', 68–9.

that acquisition to gain more'. A Tickell device which had his master's enthusiastic approval was to offer loans on mortgage to owners of land who would not sell in the hope that the estate would eventually fall forfeit. Both Tickell and Gilpin offered money in this way 'in hopes to hook in' more land.[62] At other times the only way to succeed was to offer more money than the land was strictly worth, a method which caused his stewards much anguish, but which Lowther was often ready to adopt because of the long-term advantages he believed it would bring. Gilpin angrily complained that the locals were imbued with the quaint notion that as Sir John should sell things cheaper than other men, so he should buy at a higher price than other men.[63] This was an old story to Lowther. Tickell had earlier inveighed against the 'insatiable covetousness of silly people' and had even had the temerity to chide his master for yielding to their importunities. It was especially galling to him when Lowther did so because in general his master left such negotiations to the steward, allowing the steward to conclude the purchase without reference to him for fear time lost might mean a lost bargain.[64] He usually contented himself with suggesting other strategies, urging Tickell to use the bait of such future favours as patronage in gaining a Customs House post, employment on the estate, 'kindness' in the matter of a beneficial lease, favourable terms for a building plot in a coveted area of the town or simply a vague promise of being a friend in need in the future.[65]

Certainly the difficulties Lowther's stewards encountered with possible vendors made them preternaturally alert to the possibilities presented by family circumstances such as deaths, marriages, quarrels between siblings or between parents and offspring, financial crises, local feuds, especially feuds among kinsmen, which might affect the owners of property Lowther coveted. No neighbouring family was safe from the steward's prying eyes. 'The man is a silly, vain, drunken man and his wife very sickly and decayed' runs one report. The young heir was still at school and the estate settled on trustees, one of whom was Lowther's tenant. The latter informed Tickell that the estate was not yet for sale, that a neighbouring gentleman wanted

---

[62] Tickell, 15 September, 15 October 1688. This device was used by others. When John Hill urged his master to accept a property on mortgage he explained that if his master complied he would be sure to have the whole estate if it came to be sold, as he believed it would; Jancey, 'Eighteenth Century Steward', 38.

[63] 12 May 1697, *Lowther Correspondence*, Letter 364.

[64] 'In small things of two or three hundred pounds value ... you may contract absolutely if you cannot gain time to acquaint me.' Lowther to Tickell, 8 August 1691, Lonsdale D/Lons/W2/26. See also Tickell to Lowther, 3 December 1690, 9 September 1685, 7 February 1684, respectively D/Lons/W2/25, 20, 19.

[65] 'A reasonable and fair bargain might be much better for him and his family [i.e. in the future] than twice this sum'. Lowther to Tickell, 9 December, 1690, Lonsdale D/Lons/W2/25.

it, but the tenant would give early warning so that Tickell could bid for it. 'Be very inquisitive after purchases near you' directed Lowther in 1688. It was a superfluous direction. In just one letter Tickell reported on five separate possibilities he had been watching closely: a failing gentlemen who might be forced to sell his modest estate; another gentleman's estate (although an attorney was bidding for it); a freehold for sale if the wife and two sisters and their husbands agreed; an heir unable to sell without his mother's agreement, 'but time will bring it about if you and he outlive this old woman'; and some land in Sandwith which might have proved a valuable addition to Lowther's holdings there. (However, it was so dispersed in small parcels with 'ill houses' that he had refused to proceed, and especially 'because it was compassed by suit and not of the righteous [*sic*] heirs'.) Tickell would clearly have completely agreed with Charles Agard when, in reference to acquisitions, Agard told his master that 'land is more precious than to be lost for want of looking after'.[66]

There was one final ambassadorial role for the steward in which we can observe him gathering intelligence, speaking for his master, and negotiating with many kinds and conditions of men on his behalf. This was the steward's role as his master's political agent. However, this duty was so vital and so complex that it must be reserved for fuller treatment.

[66] Lowther, 24 July 1688; Tickell 20 September 1688, Lonsdale D/Lons/W2/23. Agard to Earl of Dorset, 1 December 1659, Sackville U269/C63.

7

Tending the interest

One of your members of Parliament is dead. I here have sent down my man post to let you know that I would stand to be chosen either this or the ensuing parliament. Pray let me know what interest you can make and if you think fit I will come down presently and stand ... Pray see about and make what friends you can.

Sir James Ashe to John Snow, 1698[1]

Mr Adams, If either Sir Roger Mostyn or Sir George Warburton, one or both of them, stand for Cheshire as Parliament men I would have you take especial care all my interest appears for them, letting me know the names of each particular person (if such there be) who do not comply with this my reasonable desire. Pray be very careful and stirring herein.

Lord Cholmondeley, 1701[2]

We have seen that the period from the outbreak of the Civil War to the fall of the Protectorate represented a watershed for the estate steward and his role. After the Restoration absenteeism among landowners increased markedly, and one reason for this was increased attendance at Parliament which now became more fully a permanent institution rather than an event. Charles II ruled continuously without Parliament for four years and his brother for three but these were the exceptions which prove the rule. The history of the preceding twenty years had taught landowners that Parliament was a potentially powerful and certainly a potentially dangerous institution, and one well worth seeking membership of, at least for a member of one's family or for a close friend, if not for oneself. Similarly peers were more diligent in their attendance at the upper House, and perceived advantages in having the lower House dominated by men they considered sympathetic and trustworthy, preferably dependants, members of their personal web of patronage and 'interest'. The Royalist great landowners, which included most noble families extant in 1642, had suffered heavily during the Civil Wars and its aftermath: their estates sequestrated, their forests and properties pillaged, their castles slighted,

---

[1] 10 May 1698, Radnor 490/909. Snow was steward of the manor of Downton, near Salisbury, of which Ashe was lord farmer under the Bishop of Winchester.
[2] Cholmondeley to Adams, 20 November 1701, Cholmondeley DCH/L/49.

their military significance largely extinguished. Yet after 1660 they embarked on a road which led to the extraordinary hegemony we associate with the eighteenth-century Whig ascendancy, during which an elaborate mansion, the country seat, was a far more potent focus of local authority and influence than their ancestors' now crumbling castles had been in the early seventeenth century.[3] One reason for this remarkable resurgence over a period of no more than two or three generations was the landlords' determined struggle for supremacy in borough and county elections. As a consequence of that struggle many stewards found they had another duty to discharge in which they would regularly speak as their masters' surrogate: they became election agents.

The new role derived partly from the landowners' increased interest in Parliament and elections to it, partly to the fact that Parliaments were more frequent, indeed almost constant for much of the later Stuart period, but most importantly because in many constituencies and especially in the boroughs, parliamentary elections became real contests. Before the Civil War contests in elections for the knights of the shire hardly ever occasioned a formal poll of the freeholders, and even in the boroughs such contests were rare.[4] Any voters who turned up on election day were simply an affably boisterous rabble who cheered when the names of just two candidates for the two places were read out by the sheriff at county elections or the mayor at borough elections.[5] Following this vociferous but politically meaningless cheer, technically known as 'the shout', the returning officer declared the candidates 'elected by universal acclaim' and everybody set about putting away the food and drink the candidates had furnished. As Kishlansky points out, before the Civil War members of Parliament were not 'elected', they were 'selected': for the counties usually by meetings of the country gentry; for the boroughs by aldermen, mayors or bailiffs. The selection was determined by various criteria: the family or personal status and standing of the candidates, elite influence, notions of 'Buggins' turn', or a desire to strike a balance between two important local families. This process led to the appearance of two aspirants for two seats, and no contest and therefore no poll. Obviously in many constituencies others hankered for a parliamentary seat but they were persuaded to withdraw before the

---

[3] A striking example of this change of habitat was the abandonment by the second Marquess of Worcester, subsequently (1682) first Duke of Beaufort, of the slighted Raglan Castle in favour of the comforts of Badminton. His successors allowed their stewards to quarry the vast ruins of Raglan Castle for the rebuilding of estate farm buildings. Horatia Durant, *Raglan Castle* (Gwent, 1980), 85.

[4] Recent research by Derek Hirst and Mark Kishlansky has shown that in from 80 per cent to 95 per cent of constituencies in elections to Parliament prior to 1640 the voters had no opportunity to cast a vote because no contest was held. Hirst and Kishlansky.

[5] Each English county and all but seven of the 215 English parliamentary boroughs were represented in the House by two members each.

election. The chief reason for withdrawal was the dread of the public humiliation for themselves and their families implicit in a defeat. Also they feared to make dangerous enemies and to offend valued friends if they imposed a genuine contest on their local community. Those who persuaded superfluous candidates to withdraw were concerned to avoid a contest which might tear apart the fabric of elite governance within a county, destroy old friendships, shamefully divide members of the same family and dangerously divide neighbouring families. With such social evils to fear little wonder that landowners preferred selection to election. Moreover contests led to a poll and in a poll commoners counted as weightily as their superiors. Lord Maynard declared he would attend no more contests where, as he put it, 'fellows without shirts challenge as good a voice as mine'. His attitude is hardly surprising. An election in which the meanest freeholder carried as much weight as the worthiest gentleman violated all the social assumptions which governed the local community.[6] Occasionally the system broke down and a contest occurred, dividing family from family, friend from friend, poisoning the life of a county community sometimes for years but such disasters only occurred after the failure of strenuous efforts to avoid them.

The crisis of 1640 polarised the conflict between 'court' and 'country' candidates and their supporters and as a result contests occurred in about 40 per cent of English constituencies. This remarkable development presaged what was to come after 1660 when contested elections in counties became more frequent while in boroughs they became commonplace. We must not exaggerate the rapidity or universality of the change. Even in boroughs contests were very far from universal and most gentlemen still considered them undesirable. In 1681 Sir Thomas Thynne, subsequently Lord Weymouth, asked his steward to mobilise support for Sir Thomas Vernon for Shropshire but the steward found that Vernon made no 'pretence at all to it that I could hear of. There was a private election amongst the gentlemen of the county. They elected' [he means selected] 'Mr Corbet and Mr Lucen Gower [sic].' Two gentlemen had thought to combine their interest to oppose Leveson-Gower and set up one of themselves in his place 'but finding themselves too weak did desist'. This letter could have been written half a century earlier.[7] In 1679, that year of violent party controversy, B. D. Henning in *The Commons 1660–1690* states that only 17 out of 52 counties and 84 out of 215 boroughs went to a poll.[8] However, Henning's figures may be rather too weighted against change for not even this magnificent compilation can always be relied on to detect a contest. For

---

[6] Kishlansky, 61.
[7] Samuel Peers to Sir Thomas Thynne, 11 March 1681, Thynne xx, fo. 219.
[8] *Commons 1660–1690*, vol. 1, 106.

example, it states that in the election for 1685 Lord Sherard and John Verney were elected for Leicestershire unopposed.[9] In fact in that election Leicestershire witnessed a classic example of the transition from 'selection' to 'election by view' to 'election by poll'. As an agent of the Earl of Huntingdon put it in his old-fashioned way: 'There was no persons talked of amongst us for knights but the Lord Sherard and Mr Vaney [*sic*] and for these the Lord Lieutenant, his deputies, the justices and gentlemen appeared.'[10] A classic selection, in fact. However, as Huntingdon's steward's report discloses, that was not the end of the story. When on the appointed day the supporters of John Verney and Lord Sherard marched to Leicester Fields, they found themselves confronted by Sir Edward Abney and a Mr Whalley and their respective supporters. (Abney represented what his opponents chose to refer to as the 'fanatick party', although Verney himself had the support of many Whigs.) Whalley's support was so modest he hastily withdrew his candidature, asking his supporters to join those of Verney and Sherard. However, most of them joined the forces of Abney. 'Viewing' the respective forces the sheriff declared Verney had two votes for every one for either Sherard or Abney. Abney would have yielded Verney the first vote but this Sherard would only accept if Abney withdrew altogether, which Abney refused to do. Sherard then demanded a poll. This was held the following week and took three days to accomplish, 'Mr Verney carried it above 800 votes and my Lord Sherard not many less.'[11]

The increased demand for parliamentary seats, the perception of control of seats as a mark of a major landlord's prestige and status, together with the increasing domination of English political life by party politics, ensured that contests such as occurred for Leicestershire would become commonplace events (although they were always more common in boroughs than counties), and especially during the reigns of William and Mary and Anne when there were more elections held than in any period before or since.[12] For a landowner to exert on the result of such contests an influence commensurate with his standing, wealth and local influence, it was not

---

[9] *Commons 1660–1690*, vol. 1, 296. And also incorrectly that Sir Edward Abney contested the borough of Leicester. He had indeed intended to but the mayor frustrated him by calling the election unexpectedly early before he could announce is candidacy and Sir Henry Beaumont and Thomas Babington did not face a poll.

[10] Archdeacon John Gery, 20 March 1685, Hastings HA3975.

[11] Gervas Jaquis, steward at Ashby de la Zouch, to Huntingdon, 28 March, HA7744. According to Verney's report to Lord Huntingdon of 27 March (HA12967) he himself polled 3,489, Sherard 2,643 and Abney 1,178. For the elections for the county and for Leicester generally see letters from Jaquis, Archdeacon John Gery, Lawrence Carter (Huntingdon's lawyer in Leicester), Verney, Abney, Thomas Ludlan (Mayor of Leicester) and Sir Henry Beaumont to the Earl of Huntingdon throughout March 1685, Hastings HA7742, 7743, 8414, 1248, 8415, 3975, 4, 1249, 3976, 12967, 658 and 7744.

[12] J. H. Plumb, *The Growth of Political Stability in England 1675–1725* (London, 1969), 11.

enough for him to turn up at the preliminary meeting with his friends and
such other gentlemen who would follow his lead. He had to play his part
not in a selection but in an election – that is, he had to organise his political
interest to vote as he voted. If he or a member of his family was a candidate
he had to solicit the support of other gentlemen and make sure that they
and their 'interests' voted for him. Since Maynard's 'shirtless men' were
going to have an opportunity to vote steps must be taken to ensure that
enough of them voted as the landowner wished. If the seat was a borough
then he had to negotiate the hazardous waters of borough politics for
which pilots with local knowledge were essential. The governing elite
needed agents in the country to tend these political concerns just as they
needed agents to tend their estates. It is hardly surprising that they tended
to employ the same men in both functions. Local attorneys, local clergymen, tradesmen or a substantial urban tenant might all work for the landlord's political interest, particularly in the boroughs, but the main burden
of managing the interest between elections and mobilising it at the poll
inevitably fell on the shoulders of the estate steward.

Before the Civil War stewards had played some role in elections. Stewards with absentee masters informed them about possible candidacies,
about the deliberations at the country gentry meeting or in the council
chambers of the local borough. They carried letters to local gentlemen
announcing their master's candidature and seeking their support.[13]
However, with the gradual but persistent shift from selections to elections
the functions of the steward became more complex, and he increasingly
began to fulfil the role of an election agent. This made his duties much
more onerous and difficult, and they were made no easier by the fact that
while the local political situation might have changed to one of frequent
contests, their masters' assumptions, attitudes and beliefs about parliamentary elections had not always kept up with the changing situation. Certainly their perceptions often changed more slowly when they changed at
all. Many masters, and no doubt many stewards also, still perceived the
objects of the game to be personal prestige, family prestige, influence and
authority, both locally and at the centre. Not even the gradual emergence
of party politics during the last decades of the Stuart era could change this.
The landowners' dread of losing status or of diminishing their own or their
families' reputation remained as strong as ever. Twenty-five years after the
Restoration the dowager Viscountess Cholmondeley could write to her
son's steward of her son's possible candidacy for knight of the shire: 'I am
not for it unless he were very sure to carry it which I doubt would be diffi-

---

[13] Kishlansky observes that it would be 'more than anachronistic' to describe them as
election agents and he is certainly correct. Kishlansky, 82.

cult.'[14] This encapsulates the old notion 'only stand if you are sure of winning'.

This fear of the consequences of failure extended not merely to candidates and their immediate families. Landowners considered they would be damaged in their influence and prestige if the candidate they backed lost the election. As the second Viscount Cholmondeley succinctly put it as late as 1701: 'be very stirring to do [Sir George Warburton] the best service you can ... since if I once appear for him the credit or discredit will in some measure come to me as he succeeds or fails'.[15] Twenty years before, in the course of an unhappy election for loyal supporters of Charles II's government, Lord Cholmondeley's father had been stirred by similar anxieties, as the instructions he sent to his steward clearly show. Cholmondeley recognised that the political situation in Cheshire was unfavourable to the court party, and assumed in his old-fashioned way that this might persuade one of the Tory candidates, whom he favoured, to withdraw disheartened at the preliminary meeting of the county gentry. If that occurred his steward must switch the Cholmondeley interest's votes to the least objectionable Whig candidate. 'I would not be understood a forward fool that shows his teeth and cannot bite' he observes and clearly he considered the way to avoid being reputed a toothless dog was to switch his support to the opposing party rather than discredit his political authority and influence by having a candidate win without his help – nay worse, win in spite of his declared opposition. Indeed if Cholmondeley had realised quite how hopeless the cause of the court party was in Cheshire he would probably have instructed his steward to hold the Cholmondeley interest aloof from the election entirely, a course actually adopted by his son in 1704. As it was Cholmondeley distanced himself from the election somewhat, instructing his steward only to promise to meet the election expenses of the Cholmondeley interest if the other gentlemen at the preliminary meeting announced that they intended to pay the expenses of their interests. Cholmondeley also instructed his steward to march his interest to the polls with the voteless rack tenants intermingled with the enfranchised leasehold tenants in the hope that the deceptively inflated numbers might deter the Whig candidates from facing a poll.[16] Such a nostalgic but unrealistic resort to the practices of earlier days cannot have made his steward's role any easier.

[14] 'Let me know what your judgment is' she asks the steward anxiously. Viscountess Cholmondeley to William Adams, 7 March 1685, Cholmondeley, DCH/K/3/6. 'You will do well to be vigorous for I would be very loath to be baffled' wrote one candidate anxiously to his agent. Sir Joseph Ashe to John Snow, at Downton, Wilts, 1 February 1679, Radnor 490/909.
[15] Cholmondeley to Adams, 28 November 1701, Cholmondeley DCH/L/49.
[16] 'If you bring the rackers with the leasers the one will not be discerned from the other till they come to polling upon oath.' Cholmondeley to Adams, 12 February 1681, DCH/K/3/4.

The stewards' difficulties as political representatives of their masters were rendered much worse, however, by an anachronistic assumption which was shared by all landowners, however up-to-date their political awareness might be. Landowners expected that enfranchised tenants and neighbours would loyally follow their lead at election contests as their forebears had formerly expected their tenants to follow their lead in war. If parliamentary elections had become unavoidable contests then voters must be led as their forefathers had been led to musters and battlefields in sterner days. Even the reports of their stewards sometimes tend to have a military flavour:

I went to Leicester accompanied with about three score horse of your honour's tenants and friends besides very many that were on foot ... and at Leicester town end we all joined my Lord Beaumont ... and many more gentlemen ... being then about 500 horse besides foot and so we marched through Leicester crying for Verney and Sherard ... We drew up in Leicester Fields being about a thousand horse and many hundreds of foot.

It sounds more like the preparation for a battle in 1644 than an election of two county members in 1685.[17]

It was not just that the landowners assumed that the unquestioning obedience of the simple was their natural right, the natural expression of their social superiority. If landowners were to assert and preserve their political hegemony they must control the poll. Before the Civil War, since polls were rare, most landowners had never tested their assumption that those whom they considered members of their interest, particularly their tenants, would obediently vote as they directed. In the changed circumstances of elections after 1660 the stewards had to try to make the new realities match the old assumptions. They found it hard going. A substantial element of the lord's political 'interest' was the leasehold tenants who might indeed follow the leadership of their landlord in cheerful obedience and vote as he voted. Then again they might not. This was particularly true if their master wavered in his decision, appearing first to favour one candidate and then changing his mind. John Mainewaring found himself grappling with such a problem at Tamworth in 1690, reporting to Lord Weymouth that he is repulsed everywhere and that the 'modestest answer I meet with is that though your lordship be pleased to change your mind so often, they will not'.[18] The point was, however, that while the voters might appear to support their lord's choice, they would not

---

17 Gervas Jaquis, steward at Ashby de la Zouch, to the Earl of Huntingdon, 21 March 1685, Hastings HA7743.
18 Mainewaring to Weymouth, 17 February 1690, Thynne xxiv, fo. 144. Not all the answers were so 'modest'. 'It is not fit for me to tell your lordship what they say to it' Mainewaring tactfully reported.

do so blindly and tended to appear most obedient in those boroughs where they had no particular view of their own. Once they were engaged for a candidate, however, a belated command from their lord was likely to be ignored. However, since the lord was convinced that his vote and his tenants' votes were one he felt outraged when the tenants' behaviour demonstrated that they did not share this conviction. When their tenants refused to march loyally into the polling booths, they believed such disloyal refusals should be punished at the first opportunity. Lord Cholmondeley's order to his steward in 1681 expressed this succinctly: 'Be diligent to take notice who of either my tenants or friends shuffle in this service that I may set a mark upon them for time to come.'[19] He was furious when he discovered that a distant kinsman had not only shamefully changed sides during the campaign but in addition had had the temerity to try to persuade Cholmondeley's tenants in Nantwich to do the same. The language Cholmondeley uses to report this outrage is significant, describing the offender as 'labouring ... to draw off my tenants and neighbours ... to give their votes from the gentlemen to whom I have given them, a thing so treacherous and base that I did not think he had so little of a gentleman in him'.[20] Cholmondeley is describing a process which we would simply call 'canvassing', which demonstrates that we are still a long way from a modern election. However, Cholmondeley's choice of words is significant: 'to give their votes from the gentlemen *to whom I have given them*' shows that he perceived the votes of his tenants as a package which he should be able to bestow at will. The stewards themselves were sometimes assumed to possess an interest over packets of votes which they could marshal – or, if their masters so decide, set free. Thus in 1677 the Earl of Huntingdon, learning that a candidate he would have supported had declined to stand for Leicester, decided to play no part in the election. He promptly wrote to his chief steward for his Leicestershire estates: '[I] do leave you ... to your own discretion whether to assign your friends to any person *or else to leave them to their liberty.*'[21]

A few years later the second Viscount Cholmondeley delivered some classic expressions of the landlord's right to control the votes of his tenants and clients. In 1701 he instructed his steward that if either Sir Roger Mostyn or Sir George Warburton stood for Cheshire he must take care that all his master's interest 'appeared for them'. Moreover, the steward must inform

---

[19] Cholmondeley to Adams, 22 February 1681, Cholmondeley DCH/K/3/4.
[20] Cholmondeley to Adams, 24 February 1681, DCH/K/3/4. The prospect of parts of a landlord's interest 'changing its mind' always aroused outraged fury. In Yorkshire in 1679 Sir John Kaye was appalled by 'the perfidiousness of persons who promised me their interests under their hands' but subsequently reneged. 'What an age are we in when honour and honesty are laid aside by persons of good rank'. Quoted in Kishlansky, 20.
[21] My emphasis. Huntingdon to Archdeacon John Gery, 8 January 1677, Hastings HA5930.

his master of any '(if such there be)' who failed to comply with Cholmondeley's 'reasonable desire'. Adams must be very 'careful and stirring' in the
business. This archetypal assertion of landlord hegemony was weakened by
his peevish letters of five weeks later complaining that he hears a considerable interest is made among his tenants against the candidates he has
ordered them to support, adding 'you may if you think it convenient
intimate that all who appear on my account shall hereafter have their
expenses allowed them'.[22] Implied threats to the recalcitrant have been
replaced by the tentative offer of recompense for the obedient. However,
what must be the ultimate expression of the notion of lord and tenants as
forming an indivisible whole for polling purposes comes from a letter
concerning the election of 1704. Here Cholmondeley was estranged from
the candidates he had formerly favoured for reasons of personal pique, and
was miffed that the Cheshire gentry had not consulted him about the
election. As a result he felt he must hold aloof or appear ridiculous which
would weaken his political interest for the future. He writes revealingly: 'I
therefore at present have no thoughts of appearing at this election myself,
or any of my tenants'[23] and indeed orders his steward to pass the word to
his understewards 'to keep my tenants from appearing at the election'.
Thus even during the reign of Queen Anne, when elections were hotly
contested party affairs, a landowner like Cholmondeley still perceived
elections as local contests of personal influence and power; elections were
still contests in which a mere personal estrangement from a candidate might
make a landlord withdraw from the election; and finally, and most important of all, if the lord did not choose to vote he expected his tenants not to
vote either. One could hardly have a more succinct expression of a landlord's notion of the role of his interest than that if he did not choose to take
part in an election he assumed the members of his interest would also
decline to do so. However, Lord Cholmondeley's tenants and dependants
often failed to demonstrate that loyal obedience which he assumed he could
expect, and Cholmondeley's outraged disappointment was shared by many
other landlords.

The steward who also served as political agent had a complex mesh of
functions when a new Parliament was to be summoned: most of these
related to the conduct of the election, knowing the voters, keeping or
winning their loyalty; frustrating the opposition; constantly reporting to his
absent master, and offering advice well seasoned with local knowledge.
However, far and away the most important single duty of the steward as
political agent was to tend his master's interest, to nurture it, to seek to

[22] Cholmondeley to Adams, 20 November, and late December 1701, Cholmondeley
DCH/L/49, and see epigraph to this chapter.
[23] Cholmondeley to Adams, 16 January 1704, DCH/L/42. My emphasis.

enlarge it, to keep it loyal and, when a new Parliament was summoned, mobilise it on his master's behalf. We must, therefore, understand this curious, rather amorphous phenomenon always known as 'the interest'. The political interest a lord was deemed to command was as much a potent symbol of his status as his elaborate country seat. However, the interest was much more amorphous than something constructed of brick and stone and marble. It was subjective, a matter of assumption rather than an objective reality. This is a truth landlords were not always willing to accept, and their unwillingness to do so did not make the stewards' labours any easier. Although spoken of as if it were a unity, almost an impersonal force, it was decidedly composed of individual human beings. First and foremost, obviously, were the lord's tenants. In elections for knights of the shire the franchise since the Act of 1430 had included all of landed society, members of the House of Lords excepted, down to the level of freeholders holding property worth forty shillings a year. The sum of forty shillings may have denoted substance in 1430 but after the drastic inflation of the succeeding two centuries it was a puerile qualification. Moreover, the definition of voters for knights as forty-shilling freeholders is misleading for not only freeholders were potential voters in county elections. Many leaseholders were accorded the status of freeholder. Sir Edward Coke asserted that even copyholders who held an estate for life in their farms could be deemed freeholders, and while most legal authorities would not have followed him so far they certainly agreed that men who held lands on lease for more than one life were freeholders for electoral purposes.[24] 'I have taken order to secure the votes of all your lordship's *leasehold tenants* and have endeavoured to get the votes of *your freeholders* in these parts' reports William Adams to his master in 1681.[25]

In the boroughs the franchise varied widely. Some boroughs had large electorates which comprised payers of municipal taxes (known as 'scot and lot' men), freemen, and sometimes people who lived quite outside the community but had some connection with it (usually possession of at least one burgage tenement) and occasionally even women as the widows of holders of substantial urban property. All these amounted potentially to several hundred voters. However, in other boroughs the franchise was confined to the town council, and might amount to no more than two dozen voters or even less.[26] In some boroughs there had been no contests

---

[24] Hirst, 34.

[25] Adams to Cholmondeley, 5 February 1681, DCH/K/3/3, my emphasis. The wording of the report shows that leasehold tenants were – at least on the face of it – more amenable to the steward's directions than the freeholders.

[26] In 1669 a steward reported to his mistress that her servants had been searching the records at Tamworth 'and find that the elections before the late troubles were made solely by the 24 magistrates [that is, councillors] ... without any of the commonalty [*sic*]' which they

within living memory so that it was not always known who were entitled to vote, while in others the king had revoked the charter under a writ of *quo warranto* and had issued a new one which had changed it from a wide to a narrow franchise. If the king in question was Charles I and the Long Parliament or Cromwell had overturned his charter it was not easy for the steward to discover for his master how the franchise stood in 1661. In general, boroughs tended to assert ancient rights, although the aldermen who had the vote under the narrowest of franchises were not always as enthusiastic to do so as were those townsmen who had been disenfranchised by time and bad memories or by royal policy. Lord Latimer wrote to his father, probably in 1688, that Buckingham had formerly chosen members 'by the populace' (that is, scot and lot men) who would certainly vote for him, but the mayor would not return him 'upon such a choice for that would lessen the power of the aldermen' – not to mention the mayor's own power, Latimer might have added.[27]

As for the gentlemen who increasingly stood for boroughs, displacing the men of lesser rank who had stood in earlier centuries, and the landowners who claimed to possess a political interest in the borough, their attitude to the franchise sometimes coincided, sometimes it did not. Both were for the franchise which was likeliest to do them good rather than for a franchise which would be fair or just or more in line with ancient tradition. Candidates would simply see the short-term interest: if the magistrates were for them then it would be better if the scot and lot men were not allowed to vote; if the magistrates' support was doubtful, it would be better to have the scot and lot men included, and grin and bear the cost of lavishly treating them to food and drink. 'The commonality will adhere to you *if you think fit to adventure on that way*' wrote the Reverend S. Langley of Tamworth to John Swynfen, adding that 'if Mr Thin [*sic*] would remain firm to have an election of the burgesses at large' it would strengthen Swynfen's interest (for the other seat) 'but I fear he is altered therein'.[28] Local landowners would tend to take the long view, favouring a broad electorate if that would increase the size and therefore the significance of their political interest within the borough. Certainly landowners were very interested in the number of those among their tenants and dependants who were qualified to vote both in the county and the boroughs. In 1681 Lord Cholmondeley

hoped 'to bring it to again and then my Lord Clifford is certain of election'. George Crowther, steward at Drayton manor, to the Duchess of Somerset, *Bath*, vol. 4, 265. So far as women were concerned Coke considered that women might technically possess a legal right to vote but believed firmly that they should never exercise it in reality.

27 BL Add. Ms 28,087, 'Letters Concerning Buckingham Elections 1673–1688'.

28 My emphasis. Swynfen, a well-known Member of Parliament, was himself the estate steward of Lord Paget of Beaudesert. 'Mr Thin' was Thomas Thynne, the future first Viscount Weymouth. BL Add. Ms 29,910, fos. 86–7, Swynfen Papers.

mourned the fact that some had persuaded his predecessor to grant rack leases which were only from year to year and did not qualify their holders to be voters, thereby diminishing the Cholmondeley interest in county elections.[29]

However, there were more than just tenants among the components of the interest. In 1690 a parliamentary candidate asked Cholmondeley's steward to 'write effectually to my lord's tenants and *dependants of all sorts*'.[30] Lord Fitzwilliam's perception of what elements composed his interest at Peterborough shows what 'dependants of all sorts' might include. Although Fitzwilliam had been an MP for Peterborough in younger days and was always a Whig he did not think of himself as a committed party supporter in Peterborough elections, perceiving himself as favouring friends and acquaintances over 'strangers'.[31] When his friend Wortley Montagu appeared to be at risk there in the election of 1700 he was prompt to order his agent to mobilise his interest, and in his instructions spelt out just who he considered to be its members. Fitzwilliam had obtained from Wortley Montagu a list of the scot and lot men marked so as to show who were for Montagu and who against. Writes Fitzwilliam to his agent:

I took this enclosed note of the names of some of my friends that I wonder have not promised their votes for Mr Wortley [*sic*], as Bates and Mr Willis, my saddler and plumber ... William Briers that rents my rushes, Thomas Stamford that brings up my coals ... the Andrews, both brothers, that buys my bark; Mr Pendleton's nephew; and Robert Fearey the carrier ... Howson my brazier; John Deborough one of my masons, and Seth Meekes my old friend. Pray speak to every one of these to give one vote for Mr Wortley or I shall take it unkindly of them.[32]

So for Fitzwilliam the tanners who were customers for his bark, the brazier who mended his kitchen utensils, the plumber who leaded his roofs and repaired Milton's pipes and waterspouts, the carrier who transported his belongings from London to the country and brought venison and other country produce to London, the waterman whose lighters moved his coals from King's Lynn to Milton, the leather workers who made his saddles and harness, the man who bought his rushes once a year and a mason occasionally employed on the fabric of his mansion, were all deemed to be part

---

[29] Cholmondeley to Adams, 22 February 1681, Cholmondeley, DCH/K/3/4.

[30] My emphasis. Richard Levinge to Adams, 16 February 1690, Cholmondeley DCH/M/27

[31] 'I declare I am for Mr Wortley and Mr St John ... and for Mr Dolbin I have not the good fortune to be known to him, and being a stranger to him I shall sooner be for my acquaintances and good neighbours than him.' Fitzwilliam to Guybon, 26 November 1700, Fitzwilliam F(M)C 1152; *Fitzwilliam Correspondence*, Letter 163.

[32] Jeremiah Pendleton was Fitzwilliam's chaplain and incumbent of two Fitzwilliam livings. The nephew was not directly a receiver of Fitzwilliam's bounty, although as a close relative of the Fitzwilliam 'family' he might have been qualified to receive it. Fitzwilliam to Guybon, 26 November 1700, F(M)C 1152; *Fitzwilliam Correspondence*, Letter 163.

of his legitimate electoral interest. It was not confined to his tenants. Customers and tradesmen were part of the circle of influence, patronage and dependence which constituted an interest, and this could be further extended by economic pressure upon debtors. Guybon, the agent, was to compare a list of qualified voters with his master's timber accounts and to tick those voters who owed Fitzwilliam money so that he would know who would be susceptible to pressure.[33] Fitzwilliam was to summarise succinctly whom he perceived as part of his legitimate interest in a later letter, writing: '[I] shall take it ill if any that works for me and takes my money or that owes me any money will not vote for my friends.'[34] However, Fitzwilliam added a further dimension to his interest by targeting debtors at one remove, suggesting that if Guybon knows of any tenants who have an influence over any of the voters 'pray let them all be for Mr Wortley, and surely many of the inhabitants of Peterborough owe my tenants money either for corn, malt or one thing and another'. Even when his steward was to carry a message of condolence to an old friend on the death of his wife ('a better woman could not live than she was') he must at the same time 'let him know that his waterman, Stamford, is against Mr Wortley'.[35]

Thanks to the reports of their stewards, landowners must have been aware that their tenants and other dependants were not feudally bound, unthinkingly obedient political retainers, however much they tended to refer to them as if they were, and however much they sent instructions which implied that they were. These stewards' reports, sometimes bluntly explicit, sometimes tactfully implicit, demonstrated that the interest, especially in the boroughs, had to be cultivated, tended, flattered, cajoled and, at the last, when polling day dawned, bribed. They could not simply be commanded. Even in the era of Sir Robert Walpole Nottinghamshire voters could assert that it was 'oppression and arbitrary for landlords to compel them to vote contrary to their inclination and takes away their liberty allowed to them as subjects of having a free vote in the choice of members of parliament'.[36] Some landlords, outraged at what they deemed to be insubordination, disloyalty, even treachery, preferred menaces to

---

[33] The possibilities for electoral influence of the debtor–creditor relationship were well recognised then and later: an attempt to influence a tenant through a friendly neighbouring landlord failed on one occasion because the tenant 'had borrowed money of a high flyer [i.e. Whig] to purchase his freehold who awes him to vote [for] Willoughby and Levintz'. Thomas Smith to Sir George Savile, 10 March 1722, Savile DDSR/211/227/22.

[34] 5 December 1700, Fitzwilliam F(M)C 1154; *Fitzwilliam Correspondence*, Letter 165.

[35] Fitzwilliam to Guybon, 26 November 1700, F(M)C 1152; *Fitzwilliam Correspondence*, Letter 163.

[36] Thomas Smith at Rufford to Sir George Savile, 26 February 1722. He continued: 'Never considering that argument holds good in the high side as well as the low, but speak as they're governed by inclination and treats of ale without weighing any rhetoric or obligations.' Savile DDSR/211/227/23.

diplomacy. One last vestige of military authority survived in landowner hands: control of the county militia, service in which was unpopular but could be compelled. In 1679 the Earl of Manchester sought to exploit this ancient source of political muscle on behalf of the Tory candidate for Huntingdonshire, Robert Apreece. Manchester as lord lieutenant sent for the deputy lieutenants and justices, some of whom were officers in the county militia, treated them at his house, Kimbolton Castle, and they all 'agreed for Apreece'. To effect this the militia was summoned twice, the second time a week before the election, and Apreece 'exercised' the militia. Meanwhile, militia freeholders were examined by their officers and those who declared for Apreece were discharged, those opposed were threatened to be continued on duty. Moreover, militia service was visited on those freeholders who were opposed to Apreece, some being summoned who had never served in person in their lives, including chief constables and men 'of good estate'. Those who refused to serve were fined but were told they would be discharged the fines and of militia duty for life if they agreed to vote for Apreece. Other men of military age were threatened with being pressed for service in France the next spring if they did not, and if that proved ineffective Manchester's local agents carried these threats to their wives so that 'their cries might do the work'. Meanwhile 'whole towns' (that is, villages) allegedly opposed to Apreece were threatened with increased militia contributions. It must be admitted that the evidence for this 'reign of terror' comes from a decidedly partial source, the election petition of Apreece's opponent in the by-election, Sir John Bernard.[37] Apreece was elected and the House of Commons Committee of Privileges rejected Bernard's petition. Nevertheless this military authority, if limited in scope, and possibly not exercised as brutally as Bernard alleged, was real enough and could have been employed in the way described. Moreover, if Apreece is to be believed, Bernard was as capable of using menaces as anyone, for he was alleged to have entered Huntingdon on polling day accompanied by 3,000 to 4,000 horse and foot mainly from neighbouring counties, who, when they saw the election going against their candidate, threatened to make the streets run with blood. However, 'nobody was killed, which, according to Sir Nicholas Carew, was unusual in this tumultuous constituency'.[38] Violence and menaces could take bizarre forms. Nearly thirty years later it was alleged that election menaces accomplished the death of the Alderman of Malmesbury (that is, the mayor) who was returning officer at elections and committed to Lord Wharton's interest.

---

[37] For Bernard's allegations see the copy of his petition in the Manchester Papers in the Huntingdonshire CRO, M16/C/23, 'Bundle of papers re property of Robert Bernard, Serjeant at Law, in Hunts'.
[38] *Commons 1660–1690*, vol. 1, 273.

A group of Wharton's opponents surrounded the house where the alderman lay gravely ill, leaped on the roof, yelled the house was on fire, and
even invaded the house and fired muskets up the chimneys. Hayes survived
this traumatic experience by only a few days.[39]

In general, however, threats, menaces and random violence could
accomplish little and stewards, who often knew their regions better than
their masters, preferred more diplomatic methods. Good stewards were in
fact very aware of the prejudices and interests of potential voters. Sir
Thomas Thynne had a certain interest in the borough of Lichfield,
although it was not as significant as his strong political interest in neighbouring Tamworth. His agent, Captain Morgan Powell, chief steward of
his manor of Drayton, mayor of Tamworth and the archetypal steward as
political agent, kept a wary eye on Lichfield as part of his duties and was
alarmed when he discovered that his master's wilful employment of a
Quaker butcher was upsetting his rivals among the Lichfield butcher frater-
nity. They were part of the Thynne interest or would be if well treated.
Powell warned his master that while it was true that the Lichfield men did
not complain to Thynne about this 'unkindness' they could whisper it at
large, 'and shall you but seriously consider the kindness of that city doubtless thirty shillings will not part you from them'.[40] Powell knew that some
boroughs were inhabited by decidedly independent-minded householders
who were not prepared to be politically deferential to country gentlemen of
whom they disapproved. Lichfield was a good example of this. In July 1688
John Mainewaring, Powell's successor as steward of Drayton and chief
political agent at Tamworth, reported that the predominantly Whig town
had blatantly celebrated the release of the seven bishops by lighting bonfires in the streets. A group of Tory gentlemen with drawn swords had tried
to disperse one group of revellers and a brawl followed during which the
gentry had to retreat back into their tavern. However, they carried with
them a captured reveller and at sword's point compelled him on his knees
to drink the king's health which he said he did very willingly and then
called for more wine so that he could drink the health of the bishops.
Despite threats to run him through for his impudent Whiggery the man
was quickly released when the mob, discovering their loss, began to pull
the tavern down to get at him. The following day some thirty of the mob
were haled before a magistrate who threatened them with imprisonment if
they did not stand surety for each other's good behaviour. This they flatly
refused to do and their defiance was followed by a humiliating backdown

[39] Francis Goodenough of Sherston to Sir Richard Holford, 30 December 1702, Holford.
[40] Powell to Thynne, 14 February 1680, Thynne xxviii, fo. 4. The thirty shillings was the
financial advantage Thynne might gain by patronising the cheaper Quaker over the dearer
Anglican butchers.

by the establishment with the men allowed to go free without surety or penalty.[41]

Clearly men like this were not to be led by the nose by country gentlemen or by peers, whether or not they were their landlords. Indeed the fact of a voter being a tenant could work to a landlord's disadvantage for if landlords had long memories so had tenants. One of Weymouth's tenants steadfastly refused to vote for a Weymouth candidate 'because' as the steward frustratedly reported, 'you raised his rent from £2 to £4'. Two leading members of the interest were sent to reason with him but in vain, finding him 'the resolutest fellow in the world'.[42] There were a lot of very resolute fellows entrenched in English boroughs as many landlords and stewards discovered every time a Parliament was summoned. The steward's job was to do his best to win their support using persuasion or threats or patronage or, finally, outright bribery. Tending the interest was, in fact, a continuous process which occupied the good steward between elections as well as during them. Even if an election was not even on the horizon it was the steward's duty to cultivate the friendship of men of influence in the locality, particularly men who commanded an interest of their own. They might be local gentlemen who owned houses in the borough, or who had tenants capable of voting for the knights of the shire, or they might be townsmen with considerable influence within their community. As we have seen, one way to do this was to judiciously distribute venison, a haunch here, a forequarter there. Sometimes a steward would exploit venison more widely by inviting the voters most likely to be loyal to the interest to feast on a buck from the landowner's park. In the summer of 1688 with much talk that James II would call an election in the autumn the borough of Tamworth saw a tense struggle between the Jacobite mayor (Lord Weymouth's former steward, Powell, now dismissed), and John Mainewaring, Weymouth's new chief steward and political agent there. Struggling to hold his master's interest together in the face of a powerful foe backed by the royal government, Mainewaring decided to hold a dinner for the interest and anybody else who might be persuaded to vote for a Weymouth candidate for which his master would supply a fat buck and two dozen bottles of wine. Despite threats from the mayor sixty brave souls turned up to drink Weymouth's health. At the dinner's climax Mainewaring proposed the health of Mr Howe, Member for Tamworth in the Parliament of 1685, and Weymouth's favoured candidate. Those present, having

---

[41] Mainewaring to Thynne, 23 June 1688, Thynne xxviii, fo. 221. Ironically Powell, who was the staunchly Jacobite mayor of Tamworth, and who had been dismissed from Thynne's service earlier in the year, was then ordering the Bellman to go about Tamworth forbidding bonfires – an order the townsmen cheerfully disobeyed. Same to same, 7 July 1688, xxviii, fo. 223.

[42] Mainewaring to Weymouth, 25 September 1688, Thynne xxviii, fo. 235.

consumed Weymouth's venison and drunk Weymouth's claret, assured the steward they were ready to swallow Weymouth's candidate also. The way they expressed this readiness is significant for they did not declare that Mr Howe was of their political persuasion, nor that he was a member of a party to which they owed some allegiance, nor that he was a member who would support policies in the Commons of which they approved, nor even that he had been a satisfactory member in 1685. Rather they 'avowed that by the great favours they constantly received from [Lord Weymouth] they were highly obliged to serve him in whatever way lay in their power'.[43] England might have been moving into party politics by 1688 but it was not doing so all at once and party politics was still largely a sport for the governing elite, like stag hunting or whist.

Recognising, however reluctantly, that their stewards could not simply command in their name the loyalty of the local voters the landlords tried to help in various ways. Some like Weymouth feasted their interest on venison and wine. Other landlords would supply arguments which the agent could employ to convince wavering voters. Lord Fitzwilliam once told his steward that he should point out to a recalcitrant voter the steps the parliamentary Member had taken to get locally billeted troops paid their arrears to the great advantage of such Peterborough tradesmen as the voter himself.[44] In 1681 Sir Thomas Thynne sent down persuasive arguments to be employed on voters committed to the adverse party, and these were used with all the eloquence that a Welsh steward could muster, but to no avail: 'should an angel come from Heaven 'tis all one, they will not believe', reported Powell in disgust.[45] Sometimes the persuasion was a shade more aggressive than simply political argument, as when John Mainewaring reported that he had been 'several times with old Wilcox and spent money in the house and at his son's house' and had warned them how angry Weymouth would be if they voted against his interest, and reminded them what a small rent they paid and (with sinister significance) 'of the shortness of the lease' but he feared it was all to no purpose.[46]

The most helpful action the master could take was to exercise patronage, using the word very broadly, on behalf of beneficiaries nominated by his steward. There was no more vital (and often no more frustrating) aspect of tending the interest than that which involved the steward's efforts to obtain through his master favours and places for the faithful – favours ranging

---

[43] Mainewaring to Weymouth, 17 September 1688, Thynne xxviii, fo. 231. It will be appreciated that this was an election which never occurred, for it was overtaken by revolution.

[44] Fitzwilliam to Guybon, 13 January 1698, Fitzwilliam F(M)C 1027, *Fitzwilliam Correspondence*, Letter 47.

[45] Powell to Thynne, 5 January 1681, Thynne xxviii, fo. 7.

[46] Mainewaring to Weymouth, 25 September 1688, Thynne xxviii, fo. 235.

from the removal of a bastardy order by a friendly magistrate to a curacy for a merchant's brother to a position in the Excise (one of the most valued places of all) for a voter who might otherwise be lured away. 'You will see what humours' among the voters 'we have had to deal with' observed William Gilpin after a hard fought election at Carlisle but then hinted to his master that if he could do 'some little thing' it might be means to preserve his interest 'for the future inviolable'. Their adversaries' constant refrain had been 'Mr Musgrave prefers his friends.'[47]

There were many such ways to voters' hearts. It was the steward's task to discover the appropriate way to secure particular voters, especially influential voters who could persuade others by word or example. John Browne, agent for Sir Henry Johnson, sought out Aldeburgh freemen along the Suffolk coast. He found more than a score living at Southwold, all mariners, and also that a Mr Postle had great influence on them. Mr Postle's son-in-law was building a small ship of 150 tons and Browne urged his master to pay for a one-eighth share in the vessel for 'it will wonderfully encourage those men'.[48] By Queen Anne's reign, with politics and government more solidly party based, there was a tendency for 'to the victor the spoils', with landlords of the victorious party better able to reward the loyal and punish turncoats. However, the point is that while voters could be persuaded to follow their landlord there was usually a price: the relationship was symbiotic, not one of mindless deference, and the steward must labour to meet that price.

If the agent's duties were often onerous between elections they became positively frenzied during the election itself. It was the responsibility of the absentee landlord to let his agent know as quickly as possible that a Parliament was to be dissolved, and that the writs were on their way to the sheriff, but it was the agent's duty to discover when the sheriff would call the county election and when the mayors would call the borough elections, and not be caught unprepared. This was not always easy. If the sheriff was of the adverse party he might conceal when (and sometimes even where) the election was to be held in the hope of rushing it through before other candidates could muster their forces.[49] If his master was a candidate the steward would provide him with lists of men to be written to, and have the

[47] Gilpin to Sir John Lowther of Whitehaven, 21 November 1695, *Lowther Correspondence*, 251. By 'prefers' Gilpin meant 'sought preferment for'.

[48] BL Add. Ms 22,248, no. 7 Johnson Papers, Browne to Johnson, 8 July 1698. Earlier in his career Johnson had bought himself a firm political power base in Aldborough by financing the rebuilding of the fishing fleet after a destructive storm.

[49] For a classic 'shuffle' of this type see Sir John Lowther of Lowther's complaint of 1695 about the Sheriff of Cumberland, Sir John Ballantyne who 'not only denied to issue out his precept but refused to tell my Cousin Aglionby when he would.' *Lowther Correspondence*, 443.

letters delivered. He would even indicate who should receive a letter in his master's handwriting and who could be delivered merely a copy. James Lowther and his steward, William Gilpin, when campaigning for Westmorland in Queen Anne's reign, used this method, Lowther being especially anxious that nobody should accidentally get two copies which he deemed to be as bad or worse than not receiving a copy at all. The agent would also indicate those members of the interest who should receive a grateful letter from the master acknowledging their efforts on his behalf. As Thomas Carleton wrote to James Grahme of Levens Hall: 'Always in your letters take notice of Mr Lambe, Mr Banks, Mr Robinson, Mr Atkinson, etc. It pleases them.'[50]

While borough voters were conveniently bunched and so could be contacted personally by the agent, the agents would still have letters sent which they could show or read aloud to waverers in order to bolster their loyalty or show to influential borough voters to encourage them to use their influence on others. Letters, however, could never be sufficient in themselves: it was the constant presence and indefatigable diplomacy and attention to detail of the agent and his assistant managers which secured and maintained an interest. Indeed some members had grasped that even when an election had been successfully concluded much could be done to massage the interest against the next occasion it would be needed, for who could tell how soon it would be necessary to call on the voters again? By the century's end there are signs that gentlemen are aware that they must sometimes stoop to conquer. Following Edward Nicholas's successful poll at Shaftesbury in January 1701 some voters observed that they did not expect to see him until the next time he needed to make use of them. Hearing this, on the day following the poll Nicholas took the highly unusual step of visiting on foot every householder who had voted for him and thanked them personally. His father's steward, who served as his election agent, accompanied him and reported to his employer that this had caused a sensation. It was unprecedented at Shaftesbury, and the voters 'took it very kindly from him'. He had several of the town's chief citizens walk with him from house to house. Some of the voters were embarrassed to see a gentleman so 'demean himself' and repeatedly told him they did not expect it, but the steward shrewdly observed 'this and more must be done in such a borough as ours'.[51]

Before the election the agent had regularly sought firm commitments to vote as his master wished, not mere expressions of good will, and the news that the writs were out meant that the agent's efforts would soon be put to the test. Now it was time to mobilise the voters. Within twenty years of the

---

[50] Hopkinson, 200.
[51] Greene to Sir Edward Nicholas, 15 January 1701, Nicholas 76/27.

Restoration this had become a sophisticated exercise. In 1681 Morgan Powell at Tamworth supplied Sir Thomas Thynne with a list of scot and lot men coded to indicate who would give both their votes as directed, who would vote for Thynne but would not yet promise to vote for his running mate, and who would definitely 'split the ticket' between Thynne and his chief opponent.[52] At Carlisle in 1695 the agents of Sir John Lowther of Whitehaven (whose son was a candidate) and of Lord Carlisle (on behalf of Carlisle's brother), finding the Musgrave agents menacingly active, searched the corporation records to get an exact list of all living freemen, many of whom lived dispersed about the countryside, and assigned each one (as Lowther's steward reported) 'to the particular care of one or another of our managers who are to use their interest with them and to guard them from contrary impressions'. There were also a score or so of men about to become freemen. Most of these were secured for the Lowther interest, but any who refused to commit themselves found their 'freedom' mysteriously delayed until after the election.[53]

Promises alone were not enough. Voters had to be led to the poll. Prominent men of the interest would set out for the poll in the company of their tenants and kinsmen and other dependants, but once again the bulk of the work fell on the shoulders of the agent. In 1710 James Spedding, James Lowther's steward at Whitehaven, set out for Carlisle with sundry under managers of the interest and the principal Whitehaven freeholders, where they met William Gilpin, his late father's former steward and still a Lowther electoral agent, who had gathered up other Lowther voters, and so they rode to the poll near Penrith.[54] All mounted, wearing Lowther favours, the formidable appearance of this body would, it was hoped, discourage opponents and encourage wavering voters to join them. Political agents could be masters of theatre as well as of dusty poll lists. Once the agent got his voters to the town he could not relax. The taverns were full of thirsty voters and the agent must see that their thirst was quenched. Similarly with borough voters. For days and nights before the poll certain taverns would have been keeping open house for the voters of this or that interest. In 1721 Thomas Smith, steward at Rufford, anxiously reported to a master who had been neglecting his duty to his favoured county candidates that Lord Harley's stewards were busy treating in neighbouring townships and people there were grumbling very much 'that all other places have been treated and yet you order them nothing and ... that other people of neighbouring towns jeer at them ... at markets and places of public

---

[52] Powell to Thynne, 12 February 1681, Thynne xxviii, fos. 21–2. List follows fo. 25.
[53] Gilpin to Lowther, 7 and 17 September 1695, *Lowther Correspondence*, Letters 232 and 239.
[54] Hopkinson, 208.

meeting'.[55] This was somewhat after our period but it was no different
during it. Men whose fathers had fought the king at Naseby and Marston
Moor did not surrender rights at a lordly nod. 'I believe we are sure of the
best of the town ... but the rest are biased by ale. Without that nothing can
be done' reported John Mainewaring mournfully to Lord Weymouth in
1690.[56] Landowners were always hopeful that electoral expenses could be
kept down but their stewards knew that they would complain bitterly if
parsimony led to a lost election. 'I think if you can keep off treating them at
dinner until the day of the election t'will be advisable' observes Sir Joseph
Ashe thriftily 'but treating them with beer will be little charge, but therein I
refer myself to your discretion.'[57]

Often ale was not enough. Bribes, thinly disguised, appeared. One
alehouse keeper explained his vote by saying that whilst one (unsuccessful)
agent had certainly bought drink in his house Mr Orfeur had paid him a
guinea for a pint of beer. Thomas Carleton, steward to the Earl of Thanet,
peering disapprovingly down from the battlements of Appleby Castle in
1702, reported that Lord Wharton's stewards would buy five-shillings'
worth of goods at a tavern but leave ten shillings, and so on pro rata 'and in
my opinion the overplus ... is corruption and punishable and makes all
void'.[58] Parliament had indeed sought to curb bribery by curbing election
expenses prior to the election of 1698 and certainly many stewards were
anxiously scrutinising the activities of their own people that year as well as
keeping a wary eye on those of their opponents as the reports of William
Gilpin to Lowther of Whitehaven make clear.[59] In December 1700 a Dorset
agent observed that while Parliament 'took good care to prevent expenses
in elections' only his master's candidate son could tell how beneficial this
had been. While the agent did not doubt the efficacy of the Act he clearly
felt some anxiety about the loyalty of the voters who were 'a sort of people
that are not to be depended on.' After the election's successful outcome,
however, he remarked complacently that 'master ... can say that few
members ... have so clean hands as to bribery as himself'. His belief that
Parliament's attempt to curb bribery would make all careful in the future
('for I find the censure of the House falls not only on the principals but their

---

[55] To Sir George Savile 22 February 1722. Savile DDSR/211/227/23. In fact Savile's favoured
Tory candidates, Lord Howe and Sir Robert Sutton defeated their Whig challengers but
only after such a prodigiously expensive contest for both sides that both resolved to
compromise in future 'rather than face another'. *Commons 1715–1754*, vol. 1, 299.

[56] Mainewaring to Thynne, 8 February 1690, Thynne xxviii, fo. 266.

[57] Ashe to Snow, 3 February 1681, Radnor 490/909.

[58] Hopkinson, 191.

[59] *Lowther Correspondence*, 367 and see references to the election of 1698; also Hopkinson,
191. Parliament had legislated that after the 'teste' of the writ of summons, or the issuing
out of the writ, no candidate was to provide entertainment for any voter, or to promise to
do so.

agents and friends') was to prove naively optimistic. After the next election in 1701 he admitted that his master's son had felt little benefit from the act. His father would find him after three weeks' hard campaigning 'not a bit wasted in the flesh but considerably in the pocket', although nothing had been done (that is, spent) which could possibly have been avoided.[60]

When the poll was held a high degree of organisation was needed, and indeed was widely perfected. By 1722, somewhat beyond the period considered here but the methods were perfected during it, James Lowther's steward could march voters into the polling hall in blocks of fifty, who were then followed by blocks of fifty of his opponent's voters. It takes organisation and much massaging of the electorate to be able to send blocks of fifty voters into a hall, confident that they will all vote as you wish.[61] At the same time the agent had to be alert to see that the opposition were not sneaking into the poll men who were unqualified to vote – a particularly onerous task in boroughs, but hours spent earlier scrutinising poor levies to see who paid scot and lot, or freeman records to see who was qualified paid large dividends. At the same time agents would not merely check to see who honoured his voting commitment and who reneged, but also who discreetly left the town on the day of the poll without voting. This was a halfway house between open defiance and obedience to the lord's wishes. It was favoured by Lord Fitzwilliam who ordered his agent to inform those he could not persuade to vote for Fitzwilliam candidates that he would 'take it as kindly of them if they contrived business to go out of town' and so not vote at all, 'but of their going out of town that day they must acquaint no man with – nor their wives'.[62]

Finally when the election was over the agent had to be quick to gather evidence which would be halpful if their opponents challenged the result in the Commons' Committee of Privileges. Should such a challenge come he would conduct witnesses and documentary evidence to London to help his master fight the case. In 1710 Joseph Relfe, long-suffering agent at Cockermouth Castle of the Duke of Somerset, had to bring a host of witnesses to London. He visited London twice, was absent from home a total of five months and expended £37 on board and lodging for himself and his horses.[63] This was a bad time for any steward election agent and it could have a horrid outcome: the election might be declared void which meant he had to start all over again.

[60] This was at the Shaftesbury, Dorset, election referred to above. Greene to Sir Edward Nicholas, letters for 2 December 1700, 15 January and 11 March 1701, Nicholas 76/24, 27, 29.
[61] Hopkinson, 211.
[62] Fitzwilliam to Guybon, 2 January 1701, Fitzwilliam F(M)C 1158, *Fitzwilliam Correspondence*, Letter 169.
[63] Hopkinson, 218.

Such then was the steward who served as an election agent in later Stuart elections: a man of all work, bearer of burdens, orator, tireless horseman, wheedler, cajoler, doomed to many frustrations, the diplomatic gifts of a Talleyrand and the patience of Job would have been no extravagant qualifications for his tasks. Rarely appreciated by their masters at their full worth, many suffered exhaustion, bitterness and despair. Elias Ashmole's agent at Lichfield was so frustrated by his master's endless procrastinations, induced by a determination to make no decision until the astrological portents were favourable, that finally he fell into a frenzy and died raving – an example hopefully as rare as it was extreme.[64] What was the impact of these men? Whatever their individual disappointments, whatever inadequacies for this task some stewards may have displayed, as a group their efforts were probably salutary. They made it possible for the governing elite to adjust to the changed political circumstances without chaos or public violence. By their 'treating', by bribes and by distribution of patronage they worked with some success to make a practical reality of their masters' fantasies of having their interest as a disciplined regiment of voters that could be swung this way or that as the landowners ordered. Within this hierarchical society, at least during the reigns of William and Mary and Anne, about 20 per cent of adult males were qualified to vote, a higher potential participation in the political process than was to be encountered before the later years of Disraeli and Gladstone. The skilled efforts of the steward election agents may have made this odd situation acceptable to the governing elite who would surely otherwise have closed ranks to end it. Certainly anyone who wishes to understand how the machinery of English society in the later seventeenth century was made to work in a way which was at least tolerable to all above the ranks of the indigent should remember these men, mediating at the interface between governors and governed.

[64] This was at Lichfield in 1658; *Commons 1660–1690*, vol. 2, 384.

8

The almoner

Christmas now drawing near I would have you give to the several towns as formerly.

Lord Fitzwilliam of Milton, 1697[1]

they answer your lordship always remembered them after an election and if you were put in mind of their poor condition and the severity of their masters, would not forget them now. Indeed their poverty pleads their excuse. Everything (especially for the belly) is extravagantly dear, and the markets rise every day and all manner of trade is dead. Cloth which is the chief manufacture of that town does not go off so that little is made and ... the weavers ... and shearmen are ready to starve. Its much worse with them than common wandering beggars. The latter if they miss at one door will have it at another, whereas the former ... cannot make their wants known, and many of them have great families to maintain ... I doubt not but your lordship will be pleased to pardon my presumption to mention them, since there are more than two hundred families, which I have a list of, that are in want in that town.

John Mainewaring, from Tamworth, 1711[2]

John Mainewaring's letter reminds us that from the point of view of the modern historian stewards were valuable witnesses of social processes, social conditions and social change because of their tendency to report on all aspects of local life including times of dearth, communal plagues, individual illnesses, climatic disasters, the numbers and condition of the poor. They were also, no matter how unconsciously, agents of social adjustment. It was one of the steward's duties to make effective his lord's charitable impulses and one of his activities to prompt those impulses by pointing out those who deserved to benefit from them. In an age in which there was no safety net provided by a welfare state beyond the grudging provisions of the poor laws they were mediators who supervised the flow of charity, patronage and other forms of assistance. Some of the charitable

---

[1] To Francis Guybon, 16 December 1697, Fitzwilliam F(M)C 1025; *Fitzwilliam Correspondence*, Letter 45 and note.

[2] To Lord Weymouth, reporting on the poor Tamworth tradesmen, 15 January 1711, Thynne xxviii, fo. 363.

payments were to particular individuals, others to the poor of the manor in general.

The payments to individuals often took the form of 'pensions', usually paid quarterly, the recipients of which were usually former servants, household or estate. Not long after commencing his stewardship Thomas Tickell found his master's old nurse recommended to his care. 'She lives at Braconthwaite, enquire how, and supply her yearly with forty or fifty shillings according to her need.' With that odd reluctance to use the names of females so characteristic of the seventeenth-century male, Lowther omitted to supply her name but Tickell tracked her down, paid her ten shillings and told her to call on him quarterly for the same amount.[3] Similarly Lady Cholmondeley through her page ordered her husband's steward to pay Elizabeth Wickstead five shillings at Lady Day. 'If any of my lady's poor pensioners are dead she would have you enquire of such old widows or other women as you think fit to make up the same number.' As a subsequent letter made clear 'Bess' Wickstead was to have a pension of 'a crown a quarter'.[4] Five years earlier Mrs Wickstead had been very significantly helped when Adams was instructed to ask an understeward to seek out 'an honest man' who would take her son, for Lady Cholmondeley would pay £8 'to bind him 'prentice'.[5] Sometimes the steward would jog his master's arm about these individual payments: 'Your lordship was wont to give 40s at Christmas to Mrs Atwood. I believe she wants it now as much as ever.'[6] Sometimes the landowner would order the steward to spy out or to suggest suitable individual beneficiaries, as when James Lowther asked his steward whether it would be 'a proper charity' to give £5 among four or five poor clergymen that were 'men of worth' and had 'very mean livings', and if Gilpin approved this he was to suggest who the beneficiaries should be and detail their incomes. In the same letter Lowther pointed out that in London every great parish had a charity designed to clothe and educate poor children and afterwards bind them to trade. This was financed by subscription and there were about 4,000 or 5,000 poor children taken care

---

[3] 'Your nurse with great thankfulness and many prayers acknowledges your goodness.' Lowther to Tickell, 18 September, Tickell to Lowther 5 October 1666, Lonsdale D/Lons/ W2/1/1.

[4] Jonadeb Colley to William Adams, 9 March 1686, Cholmondeley DCH/K/3/6. Two years later there are payments to Nan Rogers ('who used to weed in the garden at Chomley [*sic*]' as she is later described, and a Malpas widow, Amy Press (8s 8d), which are probably quarterly pensions. Since they were women likely to be unknown to the steward she directs him to pass it on through the Cholmondeley housekeeper, and he must pay five shillings each to John Weaver's wife and Ann Turner by the same medium. Elizabeth Lady Cholmondeley to Adams, 13 April 1688, DCH/K/3/1.

[5] Lady Cholmondeley to Adams, 30 December 1680, DCH/K/3/4. The letter simply says 'Wickstead' so possibly the father was meant.

[6] Thomas Allen, steward at Longleat, to Lord Weymouth, 28 December 1689; Thynne xxiv, fo. 115.

of about London in this way. He would be happy to join in such a subscription if such a design would be acceptable to Whitehaven which, by implication, his steward must discover.[7]

As with individuals so with groups of poor, particularly at Christmas. If a landowner decided to make regular Christmas gifts to the poor the steward would be charged with its distribution. The recipients were usually tenants or present or former servants but could be simply inhabitants of a village parts of which belonged to the estate. In October 1707 James Lowther directed his steward to set £5 aside to distribute among poor and sick families between then and Christmas. A month later he observed that because poor people were 'sufferers by my not living in the country' he wished forty-shillings' worth of bread in sixpenny loaves to be distributed on Christmas Eve at 'the Pay House', one loaf 'to every poor body belonging to the collieries that has any child or old parent to provide for besides themselves', and any overplus should be given to poor families but not to single persons who only had to provide for themselves. Their names were to be set down beforehand so that there would be 'no wrangling at the place'.[8] Even the chief steward of a nobleman with many estate servants under him had a general and often a detailed oversight of such matters. Lady Cholmondeley gave to the poor of the manor and of the town of Malpas every year, and, as with her 'pensioners', tended to specialise in women, usually aged and poor, but sometimes widowed with large families to bring up. The payments were in theory made at Christmas but the letter authorising the payments was often written too late for Christmas Day or even for the New Year. When that happened the poor had to wait. At his first Yule Tide in the service of the Cholmondeleys, William Adams received specific instructions to pay 'out of my money' a shilling each to Nan Rogers and Amy Press (two of her 'pensioners') and £5 to the Malpas vicar who was to dispose of it as she had earlier ordered. Understanding her husband was unwilling that 'dole' (here a distribution of food to the poor on the estate) be given that Christmas as it used to be, Adams must 'give them instead two shilling a piece in money'. The housekeeper at Cholmondeley had a list of names of those who were to receive it. The following year Adams sent his mistress a list of beneficiaries for her to confirm. She put a cross against certain names who were not to receive it, along with those she knew to have died, and added three others in their place. The steward himself had a part to play in the choice for if he heard of two others who were very poor he might add them, making up thirty beneficiaries. She wished him to give two shillings apiece as he had before. Charity was tempered with practicality. Adams must order an old cottage pulled down

[7] James Lowther to William Gilpin, 6 November 1707, Lonsdale D/Lons/W2/1/140.
[8] Lowther to Gilpin, 7 October, 6 November 1707, Lonsdale D/Lons/W2/1/140.

which 'old Margaret Eatton lived in by the gate at Chomley [*sic*] . . . or else some beggarly brood' would get into it.

In 1683 she is annoyed that her agents in Malpas, presumably the rector and curate, had not given her 'notice in time' (that is, reminded her before Christmas) but instructs Adams to pay them £5 and hopes Adams has paid the dole at Cholmondeley as usual, although she wishes a list of the beneficiaries for she intends it only 'for them that are very poor'. Three months later she is dissatisfied with the list; some are not poor enough, others are not on it who need the charity much more.[9] After a few years Lady Cholmondeley relaxed her anxious supervision, and sent for no more lists. In 1684 she simply told her steward to distribute as usual and to replace any that were dead with others that were deserving 'but let them be aged or have a charge of children'. In 1685 she simply repeated the reminder and in 1686 left it to her page to pass on the reminder.[10] While Lady Cholmondeley may have thought of her commands as 'reminders', to ensure that Adams had carried out a regular Christmas distribution, in truth Adams saw them as formal authorisations because he would never give out the dole without them. 'Several of the poor have been at Cholmondeley expecting their Christmas dole but I could do nothing in it until I had your ladyship's orders' wrote Adams in a reminder of his own, and this after he had distributed her charity every year's end for nine years. Lord Fitzwilliam similarly distributed to the poor of the towns in which substantial parts of his estates were located, but year after year he sent his authorisation and if it was slow in coming he would receive a reminder from his steward as Christmas approached. The instruction once arrived ('Christmas now drawing near I would have you give to the several towns as formerly'), Francis Guybon promptly paid sixpence each to forty poor of Castor, to twelve of Ailsworth, to thirty-two of Helpston, to six of Etton and to one at Northborough, all villages in which his master was a substantial landlord. Similarly Lady Fitzwilliam instructed him to give twenty shillings to the poor at Marholm at December 1704 and left it to the steward to do 'as he thought fit' about what she used to distribute to the poor in the years when she lived at Milton – probably a reference to food and fuel.[11]

---

[9] Lady Cholmondeley to Adams, 25 December 1679, Cholmondeley DCH/K/3/1 (see also her postscript to her husband's letter of 30 December 1680, K/3/4), 24 December 1681, DCH/L/25, 29 December 1683, 1 March 1684, K/3/6; Lady Cholmondeley to Mrs. Ann Harding, 16 January 1683, DCH/M/25.

[10] Jonadeb Colley to Adams, 25 December 1686, Cholmondeley DCH/K/3/7.

[11] Fitzwilliam to Guybon, 16 December 1697, Fitzwilliam F(M)C 1025; Fitzwilliam Accounts: 'Accounts of Disbursments 1684–1700'; *Fitzwilliam Correspondence*, Letter 45 and note. See postscript to Fitzwilliam's letter, 14 December 1704, F(M)C 1369; *Fitzwilliam Correspondence*, Letter 354.

A local crisis, or even one of wider scope, could enlist the services of the steward as almoner. In 1689, at the time of the Irish Rebellion, Lady Cholmondeley directed Adams to pay the vicar of Malpas £10 to distribute among Irish refugees who were billeted there, and the following year he was directed (since he was compelled to visit Shrewsbury), to call on the refugee Bishop of Cloyne there and to pay him three guineas 'and his lady one'. During the same crisis Sir John Lowther charged Thomas Tickell at Whitehaven with the responsibility of distributing to Irish Protestant refugees the funds supplied for their relief by the government because, together with the manor court, Lowther's stewards were the only local government the town had. Whitehaven was a major port of entry for refugees because of the Whitehaven–Dublin collier fleet.[12]

On occasion, though the lord would always decide the scale of the bounty, the form it took might be decided by the steward. 'I yesterday distributed your gift to the poor in money not in beef ... 'tis too dear for poor people', reports Thomas Greene in 1698. Two years later he had found a butcher who would sell him beef at twopence a pound so he reverted to the beef his master had originally intended. The poor had become so numerous that he found the distribution a deal of trouble and told them they could only expect the gift once in two years. Over the years it had already cost Sir John Nicholas fully £400 and he warned them they must all be careful they did not abuse so good a master. (He had in mind the regular depredations committed on his master's woods.)[13] This constant awareness of his master's interest was characteristic of the steward as almoner. On another occasion when a serious fire had destroyed many houses in Gillingham, Dorset, and a fund was raised to help the homeless, Greene was one of the commissioners charged with administering the relief funds. He also had £20 contributed by his master to distribute. However, it irked him sorely that Nicholas money was passing to poor people whose almshouses had burned down when he was well aware that the regular administrators of the houses had funds in their control which should be applied to them first, and he protested about this, although he did not stem the flow of his master's charity. He also made sure that every recipient of his master's money knew from whom it derived, for those who bestowed local charity could enhance their local influence, something which all stewards' were anxious to do on their master's behalf.[14]

This watchful care over their masters' purses was heightened by the fear

---

[12] Jonadeb Colley to Adams, 27 April 1689, 31 May 1690, DCH/K/3/8; *Lowther Correspondence*, xxxv.

[13] 'Sir, ... if the prayers of the poor are prevalent you are to expect health and long life.' Greene to Nicholas, 5 June 1700; see also 30 May 1698, Nicholas 76/13, 75/7.

[14] See above Chapter 7.

of establishing dangerous precedents which might in time assume the force of law. In 1687 a deputation from the overseers of the poor of Lichfield called at Drayton Basset manor and demanded what they termed 'Smith's gift' from the steward, Captain Powell. This donation from Lord Weymouth to the poor of Lichfield he seems to have 'inherited' from the time of the Earl of Essex's ownership of the manor. (The manor had come to Weymouth through his wife from her grandmother who was Essex's widow.) In 1690 and perhaps in previous years it amounted to £18 and even in 1690 Powell's successor found the Lichfield bailiffs reluctant to supply a receipt because they believed the money was theirs by right from an old charitable bequest from a benefactor named Smith rather than simply the result of Weymouth's generosity. However, at this confrontation in 1685 Powell was instantly on guard against the danger of the estate being saddled with a permanent charge whether his master wished it or not, and sent them away empty handed, insisting that his master was under no obligation or debt to Lichfield, and that anything he gave the town or its poor simply came from 'his bounty and kindness to that city'. Reporting all this to his master Powell observed that he had long considered the matter since the deputation and 'as the case stands, you pay it of your own charity to the poor. I know your lordship understands my mind: charity is near to chancery.' Probably he meant that charity, once established as a right rather than a bounty, could be as interminable and as expensive as a chancery suit.[15] Later Powell visited Lichfield and disputed the matter of the 'gift' with the town clerk, Rawlins, long a loyal member of the Thynne political interest, in which Rawlins strongly argued against Lord Weymouth 'in chancery' and Powell 'as strong in common law' for him. That is, Rawlins adduced natural justice and equity on the side of the town's claim while Powell fought on behalf of his master's liberty to pay or not pay at will on the line of strict construction of the law. 'The arguments were too large for this paper' he reported 'but I told him they would e'er long claim a buck every season for their feast as a custom!' Thus it was 'convenient' that they should have the donation refused for that summer, 'they having the impudence to send for it'.[16]

However, if stewards could be alert to spare their master's purse from fixed charges and dangerous precedents, they could also be alert to the danger that a failure of generosity on his part might lead to ill consequences for his political interest. This, of course, was particularly true where

[15] Or less probably that charity was a matter of equity and justice rather than a matter of strict legal obligation.

[16] I am indebted to my colleague Wilfrid Prest for the suggested interpretations of Powell's words. Powell to Weymouth, 18 and 30 October, 14 November 1685, Thynne xxviii, fos. 112v, 116v, 119v. For the suggested origin of the 'gift', see reference in John Mainewaring to Weymouth, 17 March 1690, xxviii, 278v.

landowners were substantial landlords within parliamentary boroughs. The steward's role in nursing his master's political interest has been considered at length. Suffice it to say that within boroughs charity was rarely entirely disinterested among those who maintained a political interest and stewards would be alarmed if a rival should appear to be more generous, more sympathetic to the problems of the borough than his master. On the other hand, the local inhabitants would be more aggressive in their requests for charity than in boroughs where no serious rival existed. In 1711 John Mainewaring discovered whenever he went into Tamworth from Lord Weymouth's neighbouring manor of Drayton Bassett that he was always surrounded by poor townsmen whom he could not persuade that he did not have £20 to distribute among them. Their conviction was due to the action of Lord Ferrers, a nobleman determined to attain a strong interest in the town, who had distributed £20, 'chiefly amongst the housekeepers that have votes'. In vain did Mainewaring assure the impoverished weavers who clustered about him that Weymouth's charity was 'very extensive in other respects and in their own town', but they insisted that Weymouth always remembered the poor after an election, and if only his master was 'put in mind of their poor condition and the severity of their masters [he] would not forget them now'. Mainewaring admitted that their poverty 'pleads their excuse', everything 'especially for the belly' was extravagantly dear, prices rose every market and trade for the town's industries was dead. Weymouth had a long-running political relationship with Tamworth, having been elected burgess himself in both elections of 1679 and returned in an unresolved double return in 1681 and had played a major role in support of 'sound churchmen' since his elevation to the peerage in December 1682. His steward knew that Weymouth would not wish to appear less generous to the inhabitants of Tamworth, where even poor householders might be on the lists of local taxpayers and therefore enfranchised, than some potent rival with an open purse.

Two years earlier Mainewaring had persuaded Weymouth to 'restore' Tamworth's Spinning School, after an alleged philanthropist and former parliamentary candidate, Guy, had abandoned its support. The school 'taught poor children spinning and winding jersey and also in their learning and catechisms whereby they are not only kept from begging and worse but made fit for servants and to get their livelihood' as the bailiffs of Tamworth gratefully explained to their benefactor whom 'the whole town ought to gratefully acknowledge [for] your great charity'. It appears that Weymouth would be supplying about £13 or £14 a year which furnished the girls with materials, with a new gown each year, and covered the loss of spoiled wool before they were properly trained. In transmitting this letter of thanks Mainewaring smugly observed that the townsfolk seemed able to 'distinguish aright' between Weymouth's charity and that of the backsliding Guy which they now saw was 'only for his own interest', as he had not only cancelled his support for the school but also £10 he annually distributed through the vicar and £20 he distributed to the poor at Christmas.[17]

Stewards often put into effect quite substantial examples of their masters' benevolence, such as almshouses, hospitals and schools, and we must not cynically suppose that these only occurred in parliamentary boroughs. Sir John Lowther contributed substantially to the cost of building a church in Whitehaven, and his successive stewards Thomas Tickell and William Gilpin were closely involved in establishing the church as an institution in the town and having a clergyman appointed to it.[18] Lord Weymouth built a church at Minsterley which still stands much as he completed it, a rare example of a completely new church erected in the reign of James II, and once again the church's progress can be followed in the correspondence of the local steward. Although a Mr Taylor was responsible for the design and overall supervision of its construction on a basis of regular visits, Samuel Peers was responsible for providing timber from the estate, supervising the making of bricks, the hauling of rubble for the foundations from the already ruinous Caus Castle, the labour contributions of the tenants and the day-to-day oversight of the building.[19]

In 1707 Weymouth endowed and built a free grammar school at Warminster, a market town governed by his manor court, perhaps following the example set by his brother-in-law, Lord Lonsdale, who had done the same at Lowther late in the preceding century. He in turn may have been influenced by the example of his cousin Sir John Lowther who had built a school at his town of Whitehaven in 1694. This had been long planned and his steward, William Gilpin, was closely involved not merely with supervising its erection but in choosing a site, then rejecting it in favour of another better suited to his master's intention; discussing whether the building should be set back from the street with wings coming forward to form a forecourt; whether the main body of the building should be built first and the 'wings' later; or, if Lowther had decided to forgo the wings, whether it had better be built flush with the street. The foundations were laid in

---

[17] 'Above all' Guy had sent home a boy that he had formerly taken into a hospital in London despite the fact that the boy's father had constantly voted for him. This suggested that Guy 'would trouble them no more' as a parliamentary candidate, Mainewaring observed in his letter of 12 February 1709, enclosing letters from Charles Parker and Daniel Road. 3 February 1709, Thynne xxviii, fos. 355, 357.

[18] The project was delayed for years by the outbreak of the Irish Rebellion and the war with France, and did not come to fruition until 1693. For the difficulty of appointing a clergyman in the face of the town's factionalism see below Chapter 9; and *Lowther Correspondence, passim*.

[19] See Peers to Weymouth, 2 March, 28 April, 25 May, 26 June, 13 July, 1 August, 15 September 1688, Thynne xxiii, fos. 294, 338, 364, 377, xxiv, fos. 7, 15, 27.

March 1694 under the steward's watchful eye. He assured his master that he would ensure the building cost no more than the £100 Lowther had allocated which obliged him to 'consult convenience rather than ornament' and 'retrench the balcony' and substitute a stone stair 'on the backside rather than the covered staircase' originally planned. Even when no political interest was at issue no conscientious steward would allow the beneficiaries to forget who was their benefactor: 'Only, methinks though it should exceed a little, I would have the great door adorned with a handsome architrave and (instead of a frieze) a compartment for some suitable inscription to be a remembrance of your beneficence (for I find some people naturally troubled with bad memories).' The whole would be surmounted, of course, by a cornice and pediment bearing his master's coat of arms.[20]

These were large and long-running benevolences to supervise, but all stewards were confronted with a variety of day-to-day social problems. They were in a position to intercede with their master for relief for needy tenants in arrears with their rent, on behalf of bereaved widows with young children who would be homeless if they were turned off their farm, with urban tradesmen whose debts in hard times threatened to deprive them of the tools of trade without which they could not hope to gain a livelihood and on all manors at one time or another with the problem of the aged, particularly their difficulty in keeping a roof over their heads when they were too old to work. Since all such sufferers knew that the steward could prove a potent spokesman on their behalf they were not slow to seek his help. Most stewards, starkly confronted by these problems, were usually willing to intercede on their behalf, and appear often to have done so without any formal approach from the distressed.

When a tenant farmer died in arrear of rent to his landlord the steward could have a complex mesh of functions to discharge. For example, when in 1680 a tenant named Pearson on Lord Fitzwilliam's Norfolk estate died £70 in his landlord's debt, the first duty of the steward, Arthur King, was to secure the deceased tenant's goods by getting letters of administration for his master over them as security for the debt. This was to forestall any other creditors who might be about to pounce. The lord's interest having been protected, the widow and her children could be considered. King persuaded the widow's brother to settle the debt within nine months and in return King permitted the widow and her family to occupy the farmhouse and 8

---

[20] *Lowther Correspondence*, Letter 99. For the full story of the school's planning, construction and development, *Lowther Correspondence, passim.* Seven years earlier Lowther had donated a library building to St Bees School and had sent a consignment of books to stock it. His steward, who represented his master on the Board of Governors, oversaw this capital grant. See Lowther–Tickell correspondence for 1687 and particularly 9 July, 18 October and 5 November, D/Lons/W2/1/22.

acres of land until the debt was settled, meanwhile enjoying her own goods 'on loan' from Fitzwilliam. Other creditors were helpless to seize her goods because technically they were her landlord's. She would be restored to full ownership when the arrear was settled. [21]

At times one can only marvel at the closely detailed and sustained concern shown by many stewards, themselves gentlemen, financially secure and unlikely ever to experience first hand the terrors of indigence. A case in Tamworth illustrates this perfectly. William Heath, a tradesman-tenant of Lord Weymouth's worked one winter day until candlelight, then went in to sit by the fire where he suddenly fell dead. He was much in his landlord's debt for rent and the only possessions of real value in his house were the tools of his trade, which John Mainewaring seized along with the contents of the house to secure the debt. (Whilst it is not stated Heath was almost certainly a blacksmith.) He left 'a poor old widow behind him who must be kept by the town' unless Mrs Heath's son, Gibbins, by an earlier marriage took her in. However, while Gibbins could well afford to do this he was 'an ill natured man' and had much resented his mother's second marriage. The son had taken Heath's house and the widow was currently living in a room attached to her husband's workshop and indeed she could remain there but then the shop would be hard to rent at a worthwhile rent. Mrs Heath hoped to have her husband's possessions, at least those of the household, which would be as much hers as his, and if Weymouth granted this her son might take her in so as to acquire them himself at her death. By February Mainewaring still lacks orders about Mrs Heath who was still hoping to have the goods and tools restored. Meanwhile Mainewaring had seized seven sheep of old Heath's then in a neighbour's hands, and offered the son the household goods in exchange for giving his mother a home, but he too awaited Weymouth's decision. Since the files among the tools would soon rust with disuse the matter was urgent. Weymouth thus prompted must have decided generously for Mainewaring now offered Gibbins goods, tools and sheep to take his mother. Gibbins, however, insisted on Weymouth letting him have the house she now lived in for her life also which Mainewaring thought too much, so, exercising the judgment of Solomon between the interests of the master and the widow, he sold sheep and tools for his master's arrear, let the woman have her household goods back and let her keep the house on a small rent, all the more readily because he had heard she had a little money at interest which neither her late husband nor her son had ever been allowed to know about. As a result Weymouth got some of his rent back, the widow kept her home and household goods and

[21] As King reported to Fitzwilliam, by his scheme 'your lordship's kindness will redown [*sic*] to her own profit and so secure her from the rest of her enemies'. 21 December 1680, Fitzwilliam F(M)C 467.

was not compelled to live with a mean-spirited son, and she did not become a charge on the parish. All this took three months to accomplish but the steward could congratulate himself on a job well done.[22]

Mainewaring was not permitted to rest on his laurels for the next month he had to seize the goods of a small tenant farmer, Peter Porter, whose rent was a year and a half in arrears and had other debts for which his creditors were 'ready to fall on him', so that Mainewaring had dared wait no longer. It was true that the stock seized would cover the arrear, but Porter had three young motherless children to care for. The house and land he could continue to hold that year. This sounds like a bare report but probably it was intended as a hint for Weymouth to do something for his tenant. Certainly in a subsequent letter Mainewaring reports that Porter begs him 'to acquaint your lordship with his condition and hopes your lordship will consider him a little.' The steward supported this plea because he knew he was very poor, and careful enquiry among Porter's neighbours had established that he had patently had a hard bargain for he had money in hand when he took the farm and had always been 'a very good husband'. His only mistake was 'that he bought his stock at first very dear from his father'.[23]

The activities of Mainewaring in Tamworth and at Drayton Bassett manor were in no way unusual or uncharacteristic. The steward was always a 'broker', a 'mediator', in the anthropological meanings of those terms, and it was inevitable that the central core of his mediations should be tenant concerns. Some of these mediations on behalf of landlord benevolence might seem trivial to the modern eye but they did not appear so to those concerned. Typically an eighteenth-century steward seeks leave from one of England's richest landowners for the tenant of his rabbit warren to burn bracken upon it to protect his sheep from 'mildew' and that he might thereby earn thirty or forty shillings, adding solicitously 'he stands in need of all helps'.[24] Two generations earlier Charles Agard had been equally solicitous for the needy among the tenants of his master and kinsman, the Earl of Dorset, intervening on behalf of widows, aged farmers and indigent husbandmen. As a result a heriot is waived for a widow, an elderly tenant in poor health is permitted to let his ploughing to somebody who is not his kindred, whilst the right to pay the 'old' rent rather than the much costlier 'new' rent actually due, originally granted by Dorset's mother, is continued to an aged tenant in good standing. When some poor cottagers are threatened with losing their vital common grazing to a more powerful neighbour,

---

[22] Mainewaring to Weymouth, 11 December 1689, 5 February and 17 March 1690, Thynne xxviii, fos. 257, 265, 278.
[23] 28 April, 3 May 1690, Thynne xxviii, fos. 284v, 287v.
[24] Thomas Smith to Sir George Savile, 3 July 1717, Savile DDSR/211/227/77.

Agard mobilises Dorset on their behalf.[25] Of course, as we shall observe in the following chapter, in all their relations with tenants stewards must seek to promote the harmony and well-being of the estate and an estate was not simply composed of lands and buildings and forests and deer parks. An estate was people, almost all of them tenants. If these people were not sustained, or at least 'carried' in bad times by their landlord they might not be there to pay their rent in good times. Moreover, they were liable to become a burden on the poor rate, thereby dragging down those of their neighbours who were still afloat. It was in the interests of both lord and steward as well as the tenants that prosperity or at least 'well-being' should be promoted and hard times and indigence combated. The letters stewards wrote to their masters make one of the best sources for the year-by-year incidence of hard times, dearths, stagnations of trade, or perilous price rises in vital foodstuffs, for it was an area in which their vigilance must be unceasing and their reports timely and detailed.

This concern for the welfare of the people of the estate and the steward's role as agent of his lord's benevolence might extend to health as well as poverty. Any student of medicine or illness in seventeenth-century England cannot afford to ignore stewards' correspondence. Not only did they report on outbreaks of such scourges as smallpox and 'agues and fevers' but they reported on the illnesses of individual tenants and servants or neighbours, both gentle and simple. Many masters took a close interest in such illnesses, particularly when they knew the patient concerned, and were quick to send down advice culled from London doctors of repute, and also London medicines. It also worked in reverse: Lord Fitzwilliam ordered his steward to posthaste to Peterborough to discover what medicaments the son of a local innkeeper had received when he had suffered from the 'gripes' because the boy, now a page in Fitzwilliam's London household, was suffering from them again.[26] When Lord Cholmondeley's maltster, Thomas Basford, was finally driven insane by excessive drinking and made frequent attempts to kill himself, his lord and lady both exerted themselves on his behalf, trying to find him secure accommodation among his own family, then bringing him to London at considerable cost and difficulty for not just confinement but also treatment over several months in Bedlam. They finally returned him to the country, warning that if he resumed his drinking he would be as bad as ever.[27] No less concern was manifested when Francis Guybon

---

[25] Agard to Dorset, (no day) June 1653, 23 May, 23 November, 12 December 1655; Charles to Francis Agard, Dorset's receiver, 2 December 1668, Sackville U269/C63 and C64/26.

[26] Fitzwilliam to Guybon, 11 November 1697, Fitzwilliam F(M)C 1020; *Fitzwilliam Correspondence*, Letter 40.

[27] This lengthy saga, in which the moving spirits were the chief steward, William Adams, in the country and, after her husband's death, Lady Cholmondeley in London, can be followed in the steward's correspondence for 1680 and 1682, particularly Adams c. 29

reported that the former chief gardener at Milton, Joseph Chamberláine, aged about eighty-five, had gone blind. Fitzwilliam immediately sought the advice of London experts, and later instructed his steward to enquire if Chamberlaine had gone blind suddenly for then there was hope of cure, but if gradually there was none. Meanwhile Chamberlaine must have every care. The steward must make sure that his acquaintance regularly visited him which was a great comfort to someone so afflicted. His family might neglect him now that he could be of no further service to them. Guybon must ensure that they did not, indeed ensure that they were kind to him for he had been 'a great pains taker' on his family's behalf. Meanwhile he must report on his condition by every post.[28]

The deep concern about illness, particularly where breadwinners were concerned, was partly due to the fear of the poverty and deprivation which would be inflicted on a widow with young children and the fact that they would then become a burden on the rest of the community, including other hard-pressed tenants. Prevention was better than cure. The tenants must be kept alive to prevent the social problems which would surely follow their deaths. Therefore, stewards must be sure that everything was done to combat an illness and that no tenant died from the insufficient care of those about him. When Tom Freeman falls ill Francis Guybon must advise his wife not to neglect him for 'her and her children's welfare depend on his life' but a physician must be sent for and the apothecary must provide good cordials 'suitable for his distemper'. The concern for widows with children was no less. When a valued female tenant and neighbour suffers a fall from her horse the steward is deputed to pass on metropolitan medical advice as to treatment: she must be bled, should take *balsamum locatelli* for possible internal injuries, while 'seare' (waxed) cloth must be applied to her back and foot. If she is in the least danger Guybon must send for a physician and in any event must take care of her for her children were very young and 'want sober heads to direct them'. When another tenant's wife dies leaving young children the steward is mobilised to protect the parish from the expense of their care. The father must work to support his children, not idle away his time, or Fitzwilliam would consider him 'an idle fellow' and have him pressed for a soldier so that he might bring no greater charge on the parish. His eight-year-old son could accompany him to the fields, the older women of the parish could look after the younger children, the youngest

May, Edward Cholmondeley 4 and 10 August, Adams 14 August 1680, Hugh Beheathland 14 September, Lady Cholmondeley 17 October, 9 November 1682, respectively Cholmondeley DCH/K/3/3, K/3/1, K/3/2, K3/3, K/3/4, L/25.

28 Fitzwilliam, 12, 14 and 28 November 1702, Fitzwilliam F(M)C 1240, 1241, 1243; *Fitzwilliam Correspondence*, Letters 243, 244, 246. Remarkably, by the following year Chamberlaine had recovered enough sight to be able to travel about on his own and was still a tenant for some of Fitzwilliam's hayfields. *Fitzwilliam Correspondence*, Letter 265.

being 'dry nursed'. In fact the steward was able to report that the bereaved husband was 'laborious' and that the children were to be brought up by relatives at little or no expense to the poor rate.[29]

As with the ill, so with the bereaved, for even here the surrogate lord had his part to play. When the same neighbouring tenant suffers the loss of her married daughter the steward must visit her frequently to 'comfort her up' and to do whatever he can 'to put off her melancholy'. When the lord's chaplain, Jeremiah Pendleton, dies the steward must be 'very obliging and kind to the poor widow and fatherless, and countenance her' all he can. However, a steward must not in such a situation be so obliging that he forgot either his master's interests or to be diplomatic in suggesting in which ways his master might express his benevolence or he might earn a sharp rebuke. 'I am not to be told by you or anyone how far I am to extend my kindness to her and hers' wrote Fitzwilliam indignantly a few months later. 'I know best my own intentions and shall take my own time.' Mrs Pendleton's sheep must leave the property and she and her family must move from Milton for he and his wife were 'advanced in years and become sickly and must not be disturbed by the noise of children'.[30] However, the aged steward's suggestions prevailed in fact if not in policy, the widow, her sheep and her children remained at Milton, not least because its absentee owner remained firmly in London.

There were many ways in which the steward could find himself involved in questions of social policy, charity, aid, and general benevolence, always as his lord's surrogate, and always reporting regularly on what had been done in his name.

---

[29] 4 April 1700, 20 February 1706, 10 and Guybon 14 June 1708, F(M)C 1121, 1459, 1671, 1672; *Fitzwilliam Correspondence*, Letters 133, 418, 572, 573.

[30] Fitzwilliam, 18 June 1698, 2 August 1704, 8 March 1705, Fitzwilliam F(M)C 1044, 1342A, 1382; *Fitzwilliam Correspondence*, Letters 63, 333, 366. For their anguished reactions to the tenant's daughter's illness and death, Letters 59–62.

9

Filling the pulpit

Parson Roberts ... is either dead or past recovery so that you must speedily resolve whom to present ... Several have come to me within a few days to procure my letter to you which I have refused, and in regard I heard one Mr B. of the Wheme ... intends to wait upon you on his son's behalf I take the boldness to give you this caution that I am informed both are inclined to tippling and withall very quarrelsome, not becoming his coat.

Thomas Hawkes to Sir Thomas Thynne, 1680[1]

Really Mr Jackson is a very good plain preacher, in my opinion, as any minister I do know of his age, but yet for all it will be a very hard matter to give some people in the parish content for they are heady and high minded and lifted up in the imaginations of their own hearts.

John Drew to Sir Richard Holford, 1703[2]

On most estates of any size the lord held one or more advowsons, the right to appoint ministers of religion to the local parish churches.[3] These were important elements in the cornucopia of patronage which a lord might control for such positions were eagerly sought, and the lord was likely to be approached by many hopeful candidates even where the stipend and revenues of the local church were meagre. Thomas Tickell, desperately seeking a parish for his son-in-law, an impecunious physician with a large family who had sought financial independence by taking holy orders, actually considered paying Sir George Fletcher of Hutton £100 merely for the right to fill Asby rectory the next time it became vacant.[4] When the

---

[1] 10 February 1680, from Stretton, Shropshire, Thynne xx, fo. 388.
[2] Drew to Sir Richard Holford, 20 December 1703, Holford. Sir Richard, a Master in Chancery whose permanent residence lay in Lincoln's Inn Fields, was lord of the manors of Westonbyrt, Gloucestershire, and Avebury, Wiltshire.
[3] For the technicalities of qualification and ordination into the Stuart ministry, see John H. Pruett, *The Parish Clergy under the Later Stuarts* (Chicago, 1978), 31 ff.
[4] As he confided to his master, Sir John Lowther of Whitehaven. However, Lowther counselled caution: while the purchase might be of use to Dr Wilson 'if the incumbent be old and that the doctor can wait, the price seems high and if the doctor should die I know not whether you will make your money of it again so know not what well to advise'. The scheme was abandoned. Tickell to Lowther and Lowther's reply, 15 January and 1 February 1687, Lonsdale D/Lons/W2/1/22.

parish of Westonbyrt, Gloucestershire, fell vacant in December 1702 a local agent reported to the lord of the manor that 'the priests do flock to Westonbyrt to enquire the truth of this [vacancy] by couples as the fowls did to Noah's ark', although here the benefice, if not rich, was worth £50 a year.[5] Where the church's revenues were low the lord often increased the stipend from his own pocket, as Sir John Lowther did at St Bees, or tried to combine the position with another within his gift as the same landlord did with the church at Distington, seeking a minister who was also a mathematical scholar who could teach in Lowther's school at Whitehaven and thereby foster the navigational skills of future master mariners.[6]

The churches on the estate were as much a part of the steward's responsibilities as his master's lay properties. He had a complex web of duties towards them. Firstly, when a minister had died or retired from the benefice the steward had to ensure that services were conducted every Sunday until a new minister could be appointed. Reported one Norfolk steward: 'I have got all the livings supplied by Mr Creamer of Gyle Grimston who preaches [one sermon] on Sunday at Castle Rising and another at Royden, which gives very good content to both parishes until the [new minister] can come down'.[7] When Lord Fitzwilliam's chaplain died in 1704 he held two livings, Marholm and Etton, which his master was in no hurry to fill.[8] He was, however, determined that there should be no interruption in preaching and wrote to his steward that he hoped he took care that 'the cures' of Marholm and Etton were 'performed', asking who Guybon had found to preach there, and reminding him that they must be paid.[9] Secondly, while the lord might himself find a replacement minister of whom he approved and appoint him, the steward was, as so often, a conduit to his master's patronage. Sometimes he would take the initiative and approach his master on behalf of a candidate. Thomas Smith, perceiving that his master, Sir George Savile, would soon lack a chaplain, hastened to frustrate one man's candidature and urged the qualifications of a candidate he approved better. While the minister at Worksop had several

---

[5] Continuing in this avian vein he reported three days later that 'the parsons do flock toward Westonbyrt as the eagles do towards Heaven'. Drew to Holford, 9 December 1702, Holford. Drew was not a true steward but an agent who fulfilled at least one of a steward's roles: feeding his master intelligence about his manor.

[6] 'According to the instance of Mr Norwood who by inhabiting a few years at the Bermudas raised the place from a very low condition to the best navigators of the world'. Lowther to Sir Daniel Fleming, Fleming 4464, 4267.

[7] Thomas Wilkinson, steward of Castle Rising to Thomas Matthew, servant of Lady Diana Fielding of Ashdown, Surrey, 10 February 1707, Howard, 663, 349x1.

[8] 'When I come into the country I shall inform myself what young ministers there are that deserve my kindness. I shall not dispose of them to boys.' Fitzwilliam to Guybon, 26 August 1704, Fitzwilliam F(M)C 1342A; *Fitzwilliam Correspondence*, Letter 333.

[9] Fitzwilliam to Guybon, 5 September 1704, Fitzwilliam F(M)C 1344.

times approached him on behalf of his brother, 'a very young man', he knew, he said, that Savile's mother desired a minister 'of more years'. Again he feared the young man was a Tory. He had inspected him and while he was 'loath to say anything,' Smith was persuaded 'you would not like nor he would not like'. After this death blow he urged the qualifications of the schoolmaster at Worksop, admitting he suffered from the 'unapprovable objection' that he was not a university scholar, but the Archbishop of York had admitted him to orders and he 'proves a fine reader and preacher, and is a mighty good honest man' who could take the chaplaincy, fill a vacant curacy at Wellow and would be suitable for Savile's other advowson at Walsby when it fell vacant.[10]

Sometimes the landlord would take the initiative and canvass the steward's opinion. 'Send me word who you most approve for Etton living, and likewise Marholm, for I intend to part them' Fitzwilliam directed.[11] It was in no way an unusual request from a lord to his steward in such circumstances. Recognising this, men who had the ear of the steward, either because they were understewards or other estate servants, or because they were closely linked to the lord's local political interest and known for their loyalty, were quick to apply to him on behalf of friends or relatives, or simply because they knew of a suitable candidate. After a paragraph of forthright advice on the parliamentary candidature of the Duke of Devonshire's heir, Robert Revell applies to the duke's chief steward for the parsonage of Heath for his younger brother. The incumbent, Twigg, 'as I was last night informed by a special messenger from a particular friend' was 'past recovery'. Others were already 'making interest' for it.[12] It was usual for the vultures to gather before the incumbent of a living was even dead, let alone buried. News of a clergyman's illness spread rapidly through his region and aroused intense interest and speculation. Sometimes a chief steward whose charge was a great and dispersed estate with many advowsons and therefore the possibility of frequent vacancies, would seek the help of distant understewards. In 1698 James Whildon dropped such a hint to an understeward, then visiting Chatsworth, about a vacancy near Retford, and the subordinate lost no time in discreetly casting his net. He was soon approached by a man not long graduated from Cambridge, who was serving as a curate and combining this with arduous journeys to Chesterfield to preach, and who would gladly accept a benefice worth only £20 a

---

[10] Smith to Savile, 7 March 1720. However Savile would need to guarantee him £26 a year or it would not be worth his while to come for 'his gets now I fancy are more by teaching school, drawing, writing, and preaching.' Savile DDSR/211/217/47.

[11] 31 August 1704, Fitzwilliam F(M)C 1343; *Fitzwilliam Correspondence*, Letter 334. Marholm and Etton are neighbouring livings in the Soke of Peterborough.

[12] 'In this you will lay a perpetual obligation on my mother'. Revell to Whildon, 3 April 1702; Devonshire E.cxvii.

year.[13] It is possible that some stewards were occasionally allowed to make presentations themselves, a very valuable perquisite, although the person appointed would have had to be approved by the real patron and be a man who would be sure to support his political interest. Certainly the steward at Castle Rising was told an earlier steward had enjoyed such a privilege, and had received £30 from a grateful recipient of his patronage. However, when he applied for the same favour for himself he received a dusty answer from his mistress, and retired discomfited.[14] On the other hand, when Thomas Tickell sought the living of Egremont for his eldest son he told his master he was prepared to offer the Countess of Northumberland's chief steward, Clark, £50 for the presentation, and subsequently a whole year's revenue. Clark appears to have had the patronage in his gift for Tickell's application was successful.[15] In general rights of presentation were greatly prized and jealously guarded.

Stewards could be called on to advise in matters more fundamental than the choice of a candidate. Since clergymen were often appointed young and sometimes remained in the same benefice over a long life, the interval between presentations could encompass the lives of successive lords, and a patron could find himself on the death of an elderly parson possessed of a right which, so far as its technicalities were concerned, he did not know how to exercise. The steward would then find himself offering advice as to the procedure to be followed. When Thomas Smith at Rufford discovered that a neighbouring minister was seeking possession of the curacy at Wellow, a living of £11 a year which Smith was sure lay in his master's gift, he hastened not only to urge his master to assert his right but wrote out a specimen of the certificate so that the inexperienced Sir George Savile would know exactly what should be sent down.[16] When an elderly clergyman died at Castle Rising the steward obediently ransacked the old man's papers in search of his presentation, but he knew it would be in vain for, as he reported, such a document was always left with the bishop. He advised that his mistress's man of business should consult 'Sir Simon Degg's book *The Parson's Councellor*' for a precedent. Usually, he observed, the patron

---

13 Thomas Smith to Whildon, 28 January 1698; Devonshire E.cxxx.2.

14 'If my asking the presentation has offended her ladyship I am heartily sorry. I had never thought of it had I not been put upon it by a very good friend who told me it was usual for the steward to have it, and that Mr Cusand had £30 of Mr Thorne when he came to North Wootton living.' Thomas Wilkinson to Thomas Mathew, 10 February 1707; for his request see 8 January 1707, Howard 790/3, 349x3; 663, 349x1.

15 Tickell to Lowther, 4 and 30 December 1672, Londsdale D/Lons/W2/1/7.

16 'This may certify the most Reverend Father in God William Lord Archbishop of York that the curacy of Wellow in the county of Nottingham and diocese of York is now void. The nomination of a curate thereto being in my predecessors at Rufford I recommend Mr John Justice, BA, to the said curacy and all its rights and appurtenances, witness my hand, this day of May 1719, G. S.' Savile DDSR/211/217/57.

of the living sent a presentation to the bishop of the diocese who then sent out his orders for the induction. Any bishop would do, but the bishop of the diocese was 'most proper'. Apparently Lady Diana Fielding disliked the notion of the Bishop of Norwich granting an induction to 'her' clergyman, so her steward consulted one of her other clergymen, who confirmed the steward's view that there was no other way of getting a man into a living than by way of presentation, whilst induction by the bishop did not give him any power over a clergyman in Lady Diana Fielding's 'peculiar'. However, landlords who feared the influence of the bishop, real or fancied, over 'their' clergyman could avoid the local bishop by obtaining an induction in London from the Archbishop of Canterbury and his Registrar, and any local clergyman could carry out the induction itself.[17] Clearly landlords as patrons of livings perceived the beneficiaries of their patronage as 'their men', wearers of an invisible livery, and distrusted any external authority which might have a claim on their allegiance even as they would have resented any outside assertion of authority over their household servants.

Probably it was this attitude which made landlords who welcomed the steward's advice about a candidate quick to resent advice, or even simple expressions of preference, from the congregation to whom the successful candidate would minister. When Lord Fitzwilliam learned that a candidate for the vacancy at Marholm had gained 'a good opinion among the inhabitants there', and that they intended to petition Fitzwilliam on his behalf, Fitzwilliam coldly instructed his steward: 'Pray let them not give themselves that trouble, for I am as good a judge as they are of preaching, and will be satisfied myself who is fit to preach before me.'[18] This may seem a decidedly self-centred response, especially from a landlord who did not visit his estates for years at a time, and from one who was usually exceptionally considerate of the concerns of his tenants and neighbours, and took a keen interest in their welfare. However, it simply underlines the lord of the manor's perception of a minister whom he had appointed to a benefice as 'his man'. The minister owed him an allegiance which the patron was not prepared to share with a congregation of his tenants and neighbours. It was perfectly proper for the steward, who was unquestionably 'his man', to offer his master advice. Offering his master advice on local matters was a crucial aspect of his duties. Moreover, men with some claim on the lord either as servants, as friends, or as respectable neighbours could seek patronage for themselves or for others. Thomas Hawkes, chief steward of the Shropshire estates of Thomas Thynne, first Lord Weymouth, who had refused to further the solicitations of others for a vacant living,

[17] Howard, 663, 349x1.
[18] 31 August 1704, Fitzwilliam F(M)C 1343; *Fitzwilliam Correspondence*, Letter 334.

nevertheless ventured to present his wife's humble request for 'a cousin german of hers who is a civil honest man, but no great scholar, but is a man (I can assure you) of a good life'.[19] Congregations, on the other hand, should discreetly and respectfully await their master's decision on their behalf.

Since congregations in post-Civil War England were not invariably discreet, respectful and compliant, the patron's jealousy of anything which might diminish his rights and authority gave the steward some difficulties. He must mediate between his master's determination to maintain his right to appoint a minister of his choice and the determination of the congregation not to be arbitrarily saddled with a minister whom they disliked or who was an unknown alternative for someone they did like. With some congregations and with many masters this was a task which might have defeated the diplomatic skill of a Talleyrand. It was not only at Westonbyrt that the parishioners were 'heady and high minded and lifted up in the imaginations of their own hearts'.[20] When Thomas Tickell sought to have his master's brother-in-law, Richard Lamplugh of Ribton, present Tickell's son to Lamplugh's advowson of Bridekirk the local congregation made it clear to Lamplugh that they wanted no part of him. Lamplugh, alarmed, informed Sir John Lowther that the parish was much incensed against young Tickell and intended to petition the bishop against him. He asked Lowther to see if he could persuade the bishop to present him, and Lamplugh 'would lapse it', for otherwise 'I should lose myself for ever amongst my neighbours.'[21] The petition was sent, to the elder Tickell's 'grief, disappointment and expectation'.[22] It was signed by 117 parishioners, 'by which you will see what malice there is in that parish'. (In fact it revealed that the congregation had no illusions about Tickell's worldly, tavern-haunting son.) However, Tickell senior's gaze was concerned less about the 'malice' than about the £40 a year additional income his son would receive if successfully inducted, and he begged his master to obtain a dispensation for his son who would then 'gradually proceed to the possession notwithstanding the opposition'.[23] On this occasion Tickell prevailed,

---

[19] However, he somewhat distanced himself from the application, writing: 'I cannot refuse her to write on his behalf but submit to what you shall ... order.' 10 February 1680, Thynne xx, fo. 388.

[20] See epigraph and footnote 2 above.

[21] See Lowther to Tickell, 6 March 1680 enclosing a copy of Lamplugh's letter dated 23 February, Lonsdale D/Lons/W2/1/15.

[22] Tickell to Lowther, 29 March 1680, Lonsdale D/Lons/W2/1/15.

[23] Tickell to Lowther, 1 April 1680, Lonsdale D/Lons/W2/1/15. Twenty substantial freeholders among the congregation even petitioned Lowther, protesting at his obtaining a dispensation for Tickell, pointing out that Lamplugh had promised not to impose a man they disliked, and they disliked Tickell because of the unsuitable company he kept. Freeholders could not be ignored since Lowther was their Member of Parliament. Lowther

but when a few years later he sought to get his son-in-law appointed as curate at Egremont in succession to his eldest son, who as a pluralist had held it with Bridekirk, the stiff-necked congregation put up a fierce resistance which seems to have been successful in the long term. On the first Sunday the local smith nailed up the doors of the church to prevent the minister entering, while on the second when he entered the pulpit to preach the congregation fled the building. On the third they shut up the church again and petitioned the Duke of Somerset and the Bishop of Chester against the unwanted minister.[24]

Of course, the Bridekirk and Egremont cases were not typical of a steward's role because here a steward was advancing the cause of his own family in manors which were not part of his master's estate. More typically a steward charged with filling one of his master's pulpits, and finding the congregation hostile, would not blindly assert the patron's authority even though he was his salaried servant. There were dangers in simply telling the congregation that it was the lord's will and they must accept it. He was more than simply a broadcaster of his master's views and decisions. Rather this was one of the many circumstances in which it was the steward's function to try to maintain that harmony which was in the best interests of the estate as a whole, and thereby of the master who was its current lord. Nothing was more likely to promote disharmony and warring factions in a community than a dispute about a minister between the congregation and the lord who filled the benefice, and few controversies were harder for the steward to calm. Moreover, if the steward's first duty was to his lord, he often lived in the community concerned and naturally wished to be on good terms with his neighbours. Indeed on such an issue he was likely to share his neighbours' views. In any event the steward had to be capable of influencing the local community on his lord's behalf as a part of his responsibility for maintaining the 'interest' of the landlord. Alienating the flock by simply forcing an unwelcome shepherd upon it might seriously compromise the steward's effectiveness. For these reasons stewards sometimes sound more committed to the congregation than to their master.

John Peck found himself in this mediating role between a determined congregation and a master with contrary views in 1653 and the embarrassment

---

adopted the traditional expedient of all politicians caught in such a trap: he lied. He replied that he wished he had known their wishes earlier, but the very day he received their letter 'the Great Seal finished all'. He had, of course, known of their opposition all along and had chosen to ignore it. Lowther to Tickell with copies, 12 and 24 April 1680, Lonsdale D/Lons/W2/1/15.

24 Tickell's hope that 'such men of honour will not stoop to hear the solicitation of a pillory man fermented with this gross plebeian opposition not agreeable to the government' appears to have been vain, at least in the long run. Tickell to Lowther, 8, 16 and 23 November 1686, Lonsdale D/Lons/W2/1/21.

he felt can be deduced from the very text of his letter for the reader has to grope for its sense among some remarkably confused syntax. Dodleston, a village 5 miles south west of Chester and the resting place of James I's Lord Keeper Egerton, had a provisional minister who was much liked by the congregation but the presenter, Sir John Trevor of Trevalyn, did not wish to confirm him because of bad reports he had heard about him. Rather he seems to have favoured an alternative candidate of whom the congregation disapproved. Perhaps as a means of wearing down the congregation's resolve, Trevor was demanding that the congregation should certify by troublesome and expensive affidavits that their candidate was a suitable man. The parishioners resented this, and especially, as Peck put it, the imputation that their 'discretions' were distrusted, as if they would permit a minister to come among them unless they were well satisfied of 'his ability, life and conversation'. Peck pleads that the congregation judge their candidate Whittingham to be a good scholar and an excellent preacher and 'as for my opinion of him, I heartily wish that you had his fellow at your chapel at the Rossite'. He encloses a letter from the traduced minister in which he answers the charges brought against him. Trevor's next move was to reveal to the leading members of the congregation the precise accusations made against their favourite, and in response the steward tried to persuade his master to allow the accusations to be answered before two or three justices locally so as to avoid the heavy expense of having the parties heard in London. While the upshot is uncertain the obduracy of the congregation and the role of the steward as advocate in their cause is clear.[25]

Sir John Lowther had no illusions about the capacity for obduracy of his Whitehaven tenants. Having got a new church built at public expense, although he was the chief subscriber, he was not about to arbitrarily force a clergyman on a congregation whose pew subscriptions would be the chief component of the minister's stipend. On the other hand, although the church was a new creation in a community which had scarcely existed at the beginning of the century, and there was no ancient right in the lord of the manor (as there was at the nearby parish church of St Bees), Lowther had no intention of completely surrendering the choice of minister into the hands of the congregation, which, at best, was faction-ridden. His solution was to give the subscribers to pews a right to select and submit to him the names of two candidates, the final choice being his. The stormy aftermath

[25] Peck to Trevor, 8 and 19 March 1653, Trevor D/G/3276. The presentation up to the Civil War (and after the Restoration) was in the gift of the Dean and Chapter of Chester. Trevor may have temporarily acquired it for his services to Parliament. The 'chapel at the Rossite' (*sic*) refers to the village of Rossett on the outskirts of which Trevalyn Hall still stands. The church there is no more than a bowshot from the Hall so that Peck was referring to Trevor's local place of worship.

of this apparently statesmanlike compromise can be traced in the increasingly anguished letters of his chief steward and his steward of collieries, themselves bitterly divided, as low church and high church and crypto-dissenters contended over candidates. In the end while it would be going much too far to say that the steward composed all differences, an impossible task even if he had not been too much identified with one of the factions, he at least contrived to achieve the election of a minister who in the short term was satisfactory to himself, his master and the more substantial members of the congregation, and in the long term proved a satisfactory minister for Whitehaven's Anglicans over many years.[26]

The determination of landlords to protect their right to advowsons was never more manifest than when they were under the threat of a rival claimant, something which occurred more often than might be expected. As we have seen, landed estates did not march across the English landscape in discrete clearly defined portions like the fenced patchwork of a nineteenth-century field system but were jumbled in an almost inextricable confusion, with two or more lords of manors owning parts of the same villages, parts of wastes, owning rights in the same open fields, common pastures, common meadows. In such a situation it was not unusual for a lord of the manor to find when a living became vacant some other local landowner claiming that it was his turn to nominate the incumbent of the living. It might be thought that such disputes would be a matter for lawyers rather than stewards, but in fact it was the steward who would be mobilised first, scrabbling among deeds and jointures and settlements in draughty muniment towers in search of the evidence which, hopefully, would prove his master's title to the advowson. The lawyer would only be brought into action when evidences had been gathered, and even then, only when a suit seemed inevitable, or at least so likely that a legal opinion was needed about the strength of the case and the likely outcome of a court action. In manors where such a dangerous possibility existed and where the current incumbent was not yet dead, but only seriously ill, the steward would be warned that he must keep a careful watch over the situation. The landlord might even send down a signed 'presentment' with the beneficiary's name left blank but with secret instructions about possible candidates. All this speed and secrecy was inspired by the need to present a new incumbent quickly and have him in the benefice as early as possible after the death of his predecessor so as to thwart the rival landowner with a *fait accompli*. As

---

[26] The struggle can be traced in the letters for 1693–4 in *Lowther Correspondence*, and in R. Hopkinson, 'The Appointment of the First Minister of St Nicholas's Church, Whitehaven', *CWAAST*, vol. 72 (1972), which is too brief to provide a satisfactory analysis of the affair. For a much fuller analysis see Churches, 'Lowther and Whitehaven', 226–37.

a steward realistically observed: ''tis said that possession in these cases is so strong that 'tis hardly possible to move the party possest'.[27]

In the spring of 1676 a messenger brought word to Archdeacon Gery of Swepston, Leicestershire, that the minister at Stoney Stanton was either dead or dying and the archdeacon, who combined his spiritual duties with the chief stewardship of the Earl of Huntingdon's Leicestershire estates, hastened to the village at once. However, he did not go there, as we might innocently suppose, to comfort the dying and hearten the minister's family. He does not appear to have so much as entered the rectory. His purpose was to find out whether the minister lived and whether or when he was likely to die, as also to spy out any possible challenge to his lord's right of presentation from close questioning of the neighbours. From them he learned that the minister could not live long but that a man who had bought part of a small estate in the neighbourhood was claiming that he had acquired the right of presentation with his purchase, and indeed had passed that right to a local gentleman named Captain Brent. However, Gery believed they had little confidence in their title for it was offered to Brent for only five guineas. He observed that his journey might not 'prove fruitless' if he had 'spoiled their market' for he had 'as your lordship's servant talked very roundly, wondering how any one durst set up a title in opposition to your lordship's and how vigorous your honour would be in defending your right though it was to the spending of many hundred pounds', adding that it had been 'several years in your honourable family'. However, he warned his master he was not satisfied that enough had been done, perceiving there was 'another title on foot', that 'possession would prove a sure card', and that the opposing claimants might get to the bishop earlier than Huntingdon's clerk and pre-empt the presentation. Later correspondence makes it clear that at least one hopeful presenter (and perhaps Gery also) had bribed household servants of the dying minister to bring them the vital news. This ended unsatisfactorily for Huntingdon's rivals because, when the rector lapsed into a coma and his wife ran about the house crying that her husband was no more, she immediately found herself mysteriously without staff as the suborned servants vanished to pass the news and claim their reward. Unhappily for their paymasters the rector returned to life, at least for a few more days. This was embarrassing for Gery who, by the time he received the second report, had obtained a presentation from his master dated the day of the supposed death. However, he said he could scrape off the offending date and fill in a new one when genuine tidings arrived and

---

[27] Thomas Smith to Madam Savile (mother of Sir George), 1 February 1720, Savile DDSR/ 211/217/52. In the already-quoted letter from Thomas Hawkes to Thomas Thynne about the imminent decease of Parson Baker the steward emphasised the need for haste because 'of the Longdons who formerly contended for the presentation'. Thynne xx, fo. 388.

pointed out that Huntingdon could console himself with the reflection that the rival claimant was in a much more embarrassing pickle. Although the rival claimant had beaten Gery to the Bishop of Oxford and obtained a presentation, it would be void automatically since the rector was alive when it was granted. Indeed the apparent deception would greatly offend the bishop. In the end Huntingdon prevailed and seems to have presented either Gery or some one very close to him to the living.[28] No more than a month after these excitements a minister named Purefroy agreed to resign a living to which Huntingdon considered he had the right of presentation in favour of a protégé of Huntingdon's named Smart, on condition that the profits of the cure should continue to Purefroy while he lived. Unhappily for this scheme a much more dangerous rival than Captain Brent set up a rival claim: the Crown. If Smart went ahead and the Crown triumphed he would have to fulfil his part of the bargain even though he had not achieved the presentation, and although Huntingdon assured him he would assist him all he could in the contest with the Crown, later evidence suggests that Smart withdrew and the Crown probably triumphed over the earl.[29]

There were other aspects to the problem of contested presentations, as a Cheshire steward found. Shortly before his own death the first Lord Cholmondeley learned of the serious illness of Mr Bridges, Vicar of Malpas. Cholmondeley sent Adams a 'blank' but signed presentation, and told him to secretly approach a clergyman in Chester named Wright to discover if he was willing to take the benefice.[30] Cholmondeley's suspicion that somebody would assert a right to a turn was well founded, for a local landowner, Sir William Drake, was soon discovered to be entering the lists. Ironically Bridges, although mortally ill, outlived Cholmondeley, but this merely meant that the situation was still more complicated for the steward, for the new Lord Cholmondeley was abroad on the Grand Tour and until he could return to London the widowed Viscountess Cholmondeley and Adams must together act in his name. The thought of allowing Drake to exercise his turn and spare themselves trouble, expense and anxiety appears never to have crossed their minds, which was as well because once the young peer had grasped the situation, which was while he was still abroad, he showed himself even more resolute than his father to defend his right.

---

[28] In May Gery sent 60 strike of oats to Ashby de la Zouch Castle for Huntingdon, asking the local steward to keep secret that it was a gift; by July a further 20 strike had arrived. For the correspondence between Huntingdon and Gery on this advowson of 18 March, 4, 5 and 22 April 1676, see Hastings HA3960, 5920, 5922.

[29] Huntingdon to Gery, 4 May 1676, Hastings HA5923.

[30] 'I desire you'll not fail in case Mr Bridges should die to enter a caveat to prevent any from surprising me with presenting in my turn ... Carry this affair with all the secrecy imaginable that there be no wind thereof.' Cholmondeley to Adams, 29 April 1680, Cholmondeley DCH/K/3/1.

His father had seemed anxious to maintain his right only on the cheap, for he expected the Cholmondeley candidate to stand the legal costs of any suit brought by the rival patron, with the clear implication that a candidate who would not shoulder the financial burden was no satisfactory candidate at all.[31] The son was more wholeheartedly committed, writing that he would meet all charges in defending his right and Adams was to be 'very careful in the business'. John Wybunbury a Chester lawyer in the Cholmondeley interest was mobilised to do this, but his entry into the lists in no way absolved the steward from responsibility. His master, his master's mother and his master's secretary all continued to urge him to be very 'careful' (that is, painstaking) in the matter.[32]

At Westonbyrt Sir Richard Holford found himself in the infuriating position of being challenged by an eighteen-year-old youth of humble birth ('bred to husbandry and a small estate') who had been set on to this impudence by a candidate for the living, a Mr Lancelot Stevens.[33] Brandishing a dubious document from the reign of Edward III, Stevens and his lawyer ('a very expert and dextrous man in matters of difficulty' as Holford described him with admirable restraint) sought to show that the humble Minchin family were entitled to a presentation every fourth vacancy. Since the estate had twice fallen in to the Crown through attainder since the date of their only documentary proof and since they could offer no proof, even if they had such a right, that this was a 'fourth turn' the Chancellor of Gloucester had no difficulty in finding for the lord of the manor.[34] The story rather illustrates the thirst for livings among seekers of patronage (Stevens was not yet even in holy orders) than the contests of landlords, but only the confused and confusing divisions within manors made such a contest possible.

In general landowners used stewards in matters like this, as in so many others, where one would expect a lawyer to be employed from the first,

---

[31] 'I pitch on Mr Richard Wright ... or if he refuse it and [refuse] to be at the charge of the suit if any arise, then Mr Taylor ... *if he will undertake to be at the charge.*' (my emphasis) *ibid.*

[32] See letters from Lord Cholmondeley, Hugh Beheathland, John Wybunbury and so on, to Adams during January, September and October 1682, Cholmondeley DCH/3/4, L/25, M/25. There could be a very practical reason for a landlord getting 'his' man into a living. The clergyman would be unlikely to demand tithe of his patron's properties, as a steward shrewdly pointed out to his master's mother. Thomas Smith to Madam Savile, 1 February 1720, Savile DDSR/211/217/52.

[33] 'The man who married the boy's mother is a plain, honest, harmless, laborious man that knows little but in his own way, and hath been, I believe, imposed on.' Holford to the Chancellor of Gloucester diocese, Dr Richard Parsons, 27 January 1703, Holford. Stevens was alleged to be the ringleader in the outrage committed at Malmesbury during an election campaign which was claimed to have occasioned the death of the mayor, see above Chapter 7, footnote 39.

[34] See Holford's correspondence for 20, 24 February, 6 March 1703, Holford.

probably because they never trusted their lawyers as wholeheartedly as they trusted their stewards. The stewards were their servants, their loyalty to their master's interests total. A good steward would always strive to mediate so as to avoid a lawsuit in order to save the estate expense.[35] Landowners and stewards alike considered lawyers to be slippery fellows, only serving for a fee with expensive suits much in their interest. Moreover it was the duty of the steward to defend the estate against attack, and poachers were not the only type of predator to be guarded against. A challenge to the right to present to a living, however it was couched, was simply an attempted encroachment, and it was the steward's function to do all he could to frustrate it. It is their role as defenders of the lord's manor and his other rights in it which must now be considered.

[35] For a Yorkshire advowson dispute which ended unsuccessfully in court, see the letters of William Elmsall to Sir George Savile for 4 November 1717, 20 January, 2 February, 3, 17, 23 March 1718, Savile DDSR/211/2.

⤚ 10 ⤙

The constable: defending the manor

As I should very unwillingly see your privileges lost, so on the other hand be as unwilling to put you upon an unnecessary suit.

Samuel Peers, 1680[1]

You all know my master is a peer of this realm, and that the House of Lords is now sitting. If you disturb me in the possession of the Market House or the setting out standings or gathering the toll, I will presently send me up to make oath of it, upon which his lordship will immediately send the sergeant-at-arms to fetch you up to answer it at the bar of the Lords' House.

John Mainewaring to the rebellious tradesmen of Ross-on-Wye, 1693[2]

The steward of a seventeenth-century estate was a man perpetually on guard. He occupied the role of 'constable', not in the sense of a village constable but in the mediaeval sense of a man set in authority to hold a castle, a fiefdom or a baronial estate on behalf of his lord against all enemies. The era of the later Stuarts was mercifully more peaceful than the age of Simon de Montfort but there was still a constabulary role for the steward to play. The bulk of crime in the English provinces in the seventeenth century consisted of crimes against property, and as the largest and most conspicuous possessors of property the landlords were obvious, and indeed vulnerable, targets. With the public law enforcement outside the courts largely confined to such ancient instruments as the village constable and the 'hue and cry', it was up to the property owner to defend his own property and institute investigations of crimes against it, and the steward as the man on the spot, the man with local knowledge, was the obvious person to carry them out. The stewards had to be aware of crime on their estates even when those crimes were not directed against their masters' property, firstly because it was they who summoned the disciplinary court of the manor, even if a lawyer, feed for the occasion, presided. Secondly, because on many estates the lord had the right of 'felons goods', that is, the possessions of a convicted criminal were forfeit to him rather than to the

---

[1] Peers to Thomas Thynne, 27 August 1680, Thynne xxi, fo. 72.
[2] As reported to Lord Weymouth, 2 December 1693, Thynne xxviii, fos. 293–6.

186

Crown, as on a minority of estates were the possessions of someone adjudged to be a suicide. Where such crimes had been committed, even if they had not been committed against his master's property, the steward had an obvious duty to find evidence to secure a conviction against the guilty, as well as the duty of upholding his master's manorial right to the felon's goods should it be challenged by Crown officers. When the Sheriff of Flintshire seized the goods of a man now fled who was accused of being an accessory to murder, the steward of Sir John Trevor was quick to ask his master if felon's goods was one of the privileges he enjoyed as lord of the manor. If it was the steward would assert it on his behalf.[3] Frauds or thefts by tenants, frauds or thefts by estate or household servants or servants in husbandry, seizing of debtors' goods to prevent their being spirited out of the lord's reach, defending the lord's feudal rights and obligations and dues (especially the vexed right to heriot), warding of trespassers and encroachers, chasing runaway tenants and employees, ejecting squatters, defending the lord's forests, hedges, furzes, underbrush and peat mosses against the depredations of a fuel-hungry populace, and, perhaps most onerous of all, defending the lord's deer parks and fish ponds against the assaults not merely of hungry tenants but of well-organised poaching gangs, all formed part of the steward's constabulary role.[4] He was there to defend the estate whatever form the assault might take.

As guardian of the manor, or manors, which composed the estate the steward had to be particularly alert to crimes and misdemeanours within the lord's rural household. Although the chief household would be maintained in London, or wherever the lord permanently resided, there was often a considerable household permanently at the country seat consisting of gardeners, grooms, gamekeepers, gatekeepers, cooks, housekeepers, dairymaids and laundrymaids on whom, as his master's surrogate, the steward was obliged to keep a watchful eye. Various varieties of theft were, of course, the felony most commonly encountered. In seeking to prevent such offences or in tracking down offenders, the steward often appears in the unlikely role of detective. Whether the offences were trivial or more elaborately organised assaults on his master's property, the steward's reports of his investigations provide vivid glimpses of life in seventeenth-century society. Francis White, steward to Lady North, seems to have been beset by petty crime, both from within the household and from the

---

3 'There liveth in Marford ... one Panscrosse that is fled away as accessory to the murder of John ap Progar and the sheriff of Flintshire hath seized his goods. Now I would be glad to be speedily satisfied from you as being lord of the manor whether the goods belong to you or him, for I should be very sorry you should either lose benefit or privilege if I could help it.' John Peck to Trevor, 24 November 1652, Trevor D/G/3276.
4 The defence of the forests is considered in the following chapter.

tenants.[5] On an autumn day in 1667 whilst 'in my perambulations' (as he put it in his report to Lady North) he met one 'Goody Norman' crossing a field carrying a pitcher of milk. She claimed to have bought it in the village but White, deeply suspicious, persisted in his interrogation until finally the woman fell to her knees and confessed she had obtained it from Lady North's dairy. The following day White met another countrywoman, 'Goody Coat', also carrying a pitcher of milk, who 'resolutely' told him it was 'a folly to lie' and that she had obtained it at the home farm. These discoveries, combined with his suspicions that the dairymaid was supplying local people with 'cut meats', persuaded him, as he rather quaintly put it, that the dairymaid was 'no good Christian'. However, he did not confront the culprit, explaining to his mistress that this would only make her 'the more crafty to deceive, having used this trade, as I am informed, many years'. White was clearly a steward on a modest scale. A steward of greater status would have confronted the dairymaid immediately, but White seems to have been fearful of the impact of local opinion or perhaps the wrath of the dairymaid herself, for he suggests, somewhat timorously, that 'your ladyship may please to be silent in this as to the informer', merely recommending that his mistress should find a replacement for what was in this period a responsible position.[6]

Gardeners on country estates were a frequent source of trouble to stewards, who tended to keep a wary eye on them. Although they were under the direct authority of the steward as his master's surrogate, like all household and estate servants, gardeners tended to be an independent-minded breed, proud of their expertise and able to gain the ear of their master because of the master's keen interest in his gardens. On the other hand their independence and their charge of orchards and kitchen gardens gave them opportunities to sell produce and pocket the proceeds without their master's consent, while Lord Cholmondeley's chief gardener even had the impudence to charge visitors admission to his master's garden for his personal profit. Mr White had his problems with a gardener whom he did not like for 'several sly tricks' that he had, one being his refusing to eat his breakfast with the rest of the servants preferring to take it 'in his chamber with Abraham Elline', an under-gardener he strongly suspected of stealing from his mistress. Elline he intended to sack, but the gardener was beyond his reach without the backing of his mistress.[7] Sometimes the gardener's offences were so blatant and so much directed against the estate and his employer that a resolute steward would act without direct orders from his

[5] Lady North was the wife of Dudley, fourth Baron North. The manor was Kirtling, Cambridgeshire.
[6] White to Lady North, 20, 29 October 1667, North C.10, fos. 23, 26.
[7] White to Lady North, 7 November 1667, North C.10, fo. 29.

master. One of the responsibilities of a steward was to curb drunkenness among the household and estate servants and, where necessary, suppress local illicit alehouses. Finding shortly after his appointment in the late summer of 1658 that Longleat was afflicted with a lazy, drunken gardener and that other servants were patronising an illicit ale seller, William Thynne raided the house of one Gratwood at a time when the Longleat gardener, coachman and 'horserider' were 'in the middle of their mirth'. The following day Gratwood came to beg forgiveness and that Thynne would not take the matter before a justice but steadfastly refused to give a £40 bond that he would never sell ale again and would never entertain Sir James Thynne's servants there again (which was the steward's prime concern), simply offering a bare promise. Assuring his master that he would prosecute Gratwood as far as the law allowed, Thynne had him before a justice in Warminster. However, to Thynne's fury, while the coachman confessed his sins and testified 'honestly' the gardener, determined to resist the steward's authority to the last, 'like a very rogue' denied ever having been at Gratwood's before that occasion, ever having paid for drink there or ever having seen anyone else purchase drink there. Indeed at first he refused to be sworn at all until threatened with remand to the sessions or to be sent to gaol. The testimony of two witnesses to the fact, both present 'at one time', was necessary to a successful prosecution which, as Thynne grimly remarked, 'somebody had put into the knave's head'. However, unknown to the gardener Thynne had two other witnesses to produce who confirmed the offence and Gratwood was convicted of keeping an illicit alehouse. Nothing would persuade the gardener to change his testimony however, and, as Thynne indignantly reported, 'the company that were present admired the rogue's villainy that against his master he should take part with a knave, and in so high a nature that rather than he would speak against his master's enemy he would hazard the ruin of his own soul'. Thynne assured Sir James that such a man was most unfit to be a member of his family for if he would go so far to ally himself with a knave against his master in so small a matter he would do much worse if it ever lay in his power. The steward trusted, therefore, that his master would back him in his intention to sack the gardener and meanwhile Thynne would ensure the gardens did not suffer until he could be replaced.[8]

Not for the last time the experiences of William Thynne illustrate the degree to which a steward could be isolated, as a gentle among simples, when it came to maintaining discipline and protecting his master's interests and indeed his property, even though as steward he was clad in considerable authority and could enlist the help of local justices. On this occasion

---

[8] William Thynne to Sir James Thynne, 4 and 11 October 1658, Thynne ix, fos. 49–51.

he triumphed, but, like other stewards, he was not always to do so. It is also significant that it took a crime of this magnitude – betraying his master to save his master's 'enemy', as Thynne rather melodramatically termed it, to justify the steward in sacking a gardener, a senior member of the estate servants, without his master's direct order. The steward was his master's surrogate but only up to a point and had to tread warily where the issue concerned another member of his lord's family.

The steward as constable did not only have to defend his master's physical estate, he also had to defend the rights which were attached to it. They were, after all, as much part of the assets of the estate as were its mills, its warrens, its forests, ponds, rivers and game parks and its farms. If they were allowed to decay through lack of enforcement the tenants would claim that the custom of the manor did not include them, or that since they had fallen into desuetude they were no longer enforceable. Since this would mean a loss of income, however irregular its incidence, the estate would decline in value which, as we have already seen, was a nightmare possibility which haunted the minds of many landlords, particularly during the second half of the seventeenth century.[9] Had the tenants who lived on the estate been contentedly submissive and accepting of immemorial traditions the stewards' task would have been easy enough. In fact, for many stewards, and particularly those who defended estates which included urban tenants, defending their lords' rights was an unending and thankless struggle and it needed a stubborn man of great persistence but also with exceptional skills at managing men to emerge victorious. For more than a quarter of a century Thomas Tickell was embroiled with the tenants, traders, merchants, mariners, coal leaders and colliers of his master's port-town of Whitehaven. Mills were set up in opposition to his master's windmills which tenants readily patronised. Visiting ships and ships which belonged to the port and often were owned by tenants cast ballast illegally in his master's harbour. (Needless to say, if Tickell found it difficult to assert his master's harbour rights over tenant shipowners it was harder still to assert them over visitors. One Liverpudlian mariner he challenged over ballast casting 'did publicly affront me by his scurrilous language, tendering me the salutation of his posteriors and bidding the Devil take both your person and mine.'[10]) Leading tenants asserted that the town's weekly market belonged to the townsfolk who had established the market under the Protectorate during Lowther's minority and resisted any of Sir John's claim that the market had

---

[9] See above Chapter 4.
[10] He added wistfully: 'If I had been any way qualified in the Custom House I could then have humbled him in that way.' It would be an effective way to 'quickly quell the insolence of such rude fellows'. 18 August 1666, D/Lons/W2/1/1.

been established by members of his family and refused to pay market tolls. A dispute with a recalcitrant tenant led to a riot in the manorial court which led to its closure for five years. Tickell's successor, William Gilpin, despite being a professional lawyer, fared no better although his ordeal was not quite as prolonged and he was a younger man. Inspired by memories of the time when the manor was under sequestration, and their landlord was a helpless infant, there were other rights that these strong-willed tenants were prepared to challenge, which are considered below.[11]

Thomas Tickell was not the only steward to find that town tenants were likely to challenge the lord's authority and to resist any assertion of his rights. John Mainewaring found the same entrenched resistance at Ross-on-Wye in 1693, and again it involved the lord's assertion of rights over the market and the Market House. The episode is instructive because it is one of those shafts of light striking a particular place at a particular time which can illuminate the workings of seventeenth-century society. Here it gives some indication of how a skilled manager of men could frustrate the combined and determined and certainly far more numerous townsmen even though he utterly lacked the sanctions and backing of modern institutions of law enforcement. In the later seventeenth century the power of the landlord had usually to be asserted in ways which were less harsh, more subtle, certainly more adroit than those that would have served during the first forty years of the century if it was to be done successfully. It was the steward, as man on the spot, who normally had to mobilise such skills, the lord giving directions from afar or simply expressing his wishes and leaving it to the steward to devise the means to achieve unpopular ends.

The manorial lord of Ross-on-Wye was the first Viscount Weymouth. Ross then had, as it still has, a market building, then known as the Market House, consisting of an arcaded area on the ground floor supporting on its pillars a substantial room above. Certain inhabitants of Ross claimed the Market House was theirs because they had held ancient cottages which once stood on its site. On that basis they claimed the right to let 'standings', stalls built of boards on trestles, to stallholders on market and fair days and to collect the market toll. The chief claimant was a man called Hill. Other inhabitants claimed the right to set up standings in the street outside their houses which they also rented to stallholders who were usually country people bringing in market produce. Lord Weymouth asserted that the Market House was his, that the land outside the houses was simply part of

---

[11] Tickell's long, dispiriting and exhausting battle has been vividly reconstructed by Dr Christine Churches (Churches, 'Lowther and Whitehaven'). The chief source for the struggle is the Lowther–Tickell correspondence; and various court cases preserved in the Lowther legal papers and in the PRO. For Gilpin's experiences see *Lowther Correspondence, passim.*

the manor and the right to set up stalls and rent them out was therefore his, and he had indeed let his right to do this to a group of Quakers led by one Sparry. On the other hand the inhabitants of Ross were on the spot, Lord Weymouth was either in distant London or remote Longleat. The Quakers feared they could not withstand the hostility of the inhabitants on their own and were greatly relieved when on 2 November John Mainewaring, one of Weymouth's principal stewards, rode into Ross to assert his master's claim and offered to supervise the next day what would be the first letting of the standings since the lease. He seems to have employed a mixture of bluff, of threats, of 'dividing to rule', of a sort of street theatre and sheer nerve.

Confronting Hill and the claimants to the Market House on the street, watched by the excited inhabitants, Mainewaring insisted on his master's right to the building, pointing out no rent had been paid for fifty years for the land beneath it and so it was forfeited to the lord. Hill, for the tenants, replied that he would either be paid rent for his land or take the benefit of the market toll and the rents of the stalls. Mainewaring insisted he was there at his master's order to take possession of the Market House, to collect the toll and the rents for the stalls which he intended to set out, removing any stalls illegally set up in opposition. Hill declared defiantly that he would set up stalls and receive money for them and the other townsmen cried out that they would do the same. Mainewaring was facing a mutiny of the inhabitants of Ross which he had no force majeure to quell, no police force to appeal to. His response was to warn them that they were running into a great deal of danger, remarking that they all knew his master was a peer of the realm and that the House of Lords was sitting. If they 'disturbed' Mainewaring in taking possession of the market building or in setting out standings or in gathering the market toll he would immediately swear to an affidavit of it and send it up to the House, at which Lord Weymouth would send down the sergeant-at-arms to bring the offenders before the bar of the House 'to answer it'. At this Hill made a tactical error, for without consulting his supporters he swore that he cared not where he answered it and that he would put out his standings. Spotting a possible chink Mainewaring promptly drove in the wedge, for, telling Hill ironically that he thought him the 'fittest man to answer it' and that he desired nothing more than to see him at the bar of the House, he observed that he hoped the rest would prefer to wait and see how Hill 'fared' and then act accordingly. At this the crowd quietly and no doubt thoughtfully dispersed, although Hill still asserted he would put out his standings.

It was now time to gain possession of the Market House. Since the man with the key refused to bring it Mainewaring got John Kirle, Ross's famous philanthropic citizen to send for the key and the two men entered the building, climbed to the upper room where Mainewaring solemnly took

possession of the structure in Weymouth's name. When leaving the building Kirle tried to courteously usher Mainewaring out but the steward, very
conscious of the watching crowd, ostentatiously waved Kirle ahead, to
demonstrate theatrically that he was showing Kirle off his master's
premises rather than Kirle showing him off premises belonging to townsmen. Before dawn the next day Mainewaring helped the Quakers to set up
stalls, beginning underneath the Market House. The townsmen hearing the
bustle emerged and set up stalls in the streets but none dared to set up in the
Market House itself for Hill, their champion, did not appear. Mainewaring
challenged their stalls, asking whether they would pay rent for the privilege.
They said they had ever put up stalls in right of their houses and hoped to
do so still. Mainewaring insisted that they could not occupy the lord's
ground rent free and when they refused either to pay or remove their
standings Mainewaring had them taken down, which none resisted. The
country people entering Ross with their produce peacefully paid market toll
and their stall rents to Mainewaring.[12]

So at Ross the rights of the lord were upheld over the counter-claims of
the tenants. The records surviving do not permit us to say whether the
victory was permanent. After Mainewaring left Ross he reported that the
townsmen had been quiet while he was there but had threatened the
Quakers with 'what they would do when I was gone, and give out they will
all join together to dispute the Market House with your lordship' (that is, in
a law suit). Mainewaring meanwhile did what he could, setting a local
Thynne agent to watch over matters and recommending that 'a course must
be taken with [any troublemakers] to afright the rest'. However, no matter
what the long-term result may have been, in the short term at least
Mainewaring had triumphed on behalf of his master.

Defending the lord's rights from challengers could be a vexing and
frustrating part of a steward's duties, not least because challenges to the
jurisdiction of the lord's courts were often difficult to defeat in law. One of
the least sought and most evaded duties in the seventeenth century was that
of village constable. It was the function of the manorial court, rather than
the lord himself, to choose a constable (or constables). At Whitehaven the
constable was chosen by the court jury, but in fact the office moved around
the town street by street, each street having the duty of furnishing that
functionary in turn, and within streets there was a recognised system of
'turns' among the householders. Since the chosen householder from the
street whose turn it was might also be a mariner and much absent on
voyages to Ireland or even Virginia, it was common for such an appointee

---

[12] 'Their great champion, Hill, never showed his face in the town all day long' Mainewaring
caustically reported. For all above Mainewaring to Weymouth, 2 December 1693;
Thynne xxviii, fos. 293–6.

to pay a substitute to fill the position.[13] This system seems to have worked reasonably amicably, perhaps all the more because the system of paid substitutes mitigated against the nuisance of selection. In rural areas things did not always pass so quietly and it was common for a man chosen constable to be taken before a local justice to swear to serve the following year and enter bond for a penalty which he would forfeit if he failed to perform his duty, or if he refused to take the oath. In Minsterley, Shropshire, a community whose manor court was Thomas Thynne's, there were two constables and to reduce the burden on Minsterley itself in 1677 and 1679 one of the two constables was chosen from the householders of the hamlets of Upper and Nether Heath close by. The Heaths were assessed with Minsterley for taxation, 'watched and warded' with Minsterley and were considered to come under Thynne's suzerainty. In 1680 another householder from Upper Heath was selected but he refused to take the oath, declaring the Heaths were no part of Minsterley, and went instead to the court of a neighbouring manor, and there took the oath to serve as their constable. Samuel Peers, Thynne's steward, indignantly imposed the fine of forty shillings and seized the man's horse, which he as promptly replevined. After much consultation with Shrewsbury lawyers it was decided to appoint another Upper Heath man constable and if he refused, have him up at the next quarter sessions, meanwhile taking care to fee the best two local lawyers so that their services would be denied the appointee and his Upper Heath friends. The new appointee did refuse to take the oath, and indeed his neighbours at the Heaths now refused even to do watch and ward with Minsterley, all claiming they were no part of the town. Thomas Hawkes, steward at Church Stretton, complacently assured his master that the lawyers who acted as stewards of courts at Thynne's manors of Minsterley and Stretton gave the charge at the sessions and managed all sessions business, turn about, so Thynne would 'have them both for your friends'. However, at the sessions the justices refused to decide the case as being simply a matter of fact (whether the lord's rights extended to the Heaths or not) and left it to Thynne to try his luck at common law. Hawkes pointed out to his master that if he could not demonstrate from his 'writings' that he held such suzerainty he would 'never do any good in this case'. The long-term result is again unclear but certainly it is unlikely that any Upper Heath householder obediently served as constable for Minsterley.[14]

Another area of the lords' rights which stewards had to be constantly

---

[13] I am indebted to Dr Churches and her knowledge of the operations of the St Bees–Whitehaven manorial court for this information; see also Lonsdale D/Lons/W, Whitehaven Court Book.

[14] Peers to Thynne, 6 and 27 August, 22 October 1680, 1 and 28 January, 6 May 1681; Hawkes to Thynne, 28 October 1680, 14 January 1681; Thynne xx, fos. 71, 72, 85, 87, 128, 146, 161, 272.

alert to defend were incidences and dues which had survived since the feudal era. It might perhaps be thought that by the second half of the seventeenth century such dues as heriots, felons' and suicides' goods (where they were in the right of the lord rather than the Crown), deodands for deaths by accident and so on, boon days, reek hens, Christmas geese or other similar gifts, might be little regarded by landowners. In fact they were seen as of great significance and never more so than on manors where many tenants were still paying 'old rents' for copyhold farms rather than rack or half rack rents or leases for a specified period of years. They were a significant portion of the manor's income and not to be lightly set aside. Of course, once again the technical right to some of these feudal incidences could prove hard to enforce in reality. This was particularly true of the right to a suicide's goods. When a John Ribton fell to his death from Bransty Rocks near Whitehaven the steward refused to accept a heriot because there was 'some cause to suspect a *felo de se*' which would have enabled him to seize the whole estate. However, although he told the coroner and his jury of his suspicions and instructed them to 'enquire diligently' into the cause of death, the jury were 'induced to find it accidental' by such circumstances as his leaving his hat on the rocks, and the fact that the rocks just there were 'deceitful' and 'crumbling'. The same week a boy was killed by the wheel of a horse mill and, as the steward reported, if the jury were to find the mill going (and he believed they could 'not well avoid it') the 'horse and mill will be deodand'. However, no subsequent letter mentions this affair, and there is no trace of such a forfeiture or a financial composition in the steward's accounts which suggests the jury may have found against the lord, as juries had a great tendency to do.[15] A more extreme Cumbrian case involved a man who had deliberately wounded himself in the throat and died of it three days later, but once again the steward was frustrated by the jury which obstinately insisted he had not died of the wound, but of a fever (occasioned by it) and that although he had recovered his sense before he died, he had been mad when he committed the act. Most remarkable of all was a Cumbrian case in which a man hanged himself but the jury insisted on bringing in a verdict of accidental death, the rope, they declared, having caught around his throat![16] Significantly, perhaps, when Joseph Relfe, described as 'gent.,

---

[15] Another possibility is that Lowther, whose replies do not survive for this period, simply instructed his steward not to seek to enforce the right. The mill was owned by Thomas Addison, once an obdurate enemy of Lowther's but more recently a partner with him in a mill-stone quarry and a fellow resident of London. For both accidents see Gilpin to Lowther 20 September 1693, *Lowther Correspondence*, Letter 56.

[16] See the case of John Atkinson of Longwath, Inquests 1696, Leconfield D/Lec/CRI/5 (no. 3). See also the case of the woman who drowned herself (accidentally the jury insisted) in a washtub, 1696, D/Lec/CRI/3. I am indebted to Dr Churches for these examples. For a

coroner of their graces the Duke and Duchess of Somerset' who was the chief steward of their West Cumberland estates, presided over the court, the jury respectfully found that a John Dixon, 'being moved and seduced by the devil' had 'hanged or strangled himself upon a tree' with a leather strap 'wilfully and feloniously'.[17]

Sometimes the tenants would seek to evade the landowner's right by avoiding a coroner's jury altogether and it would then be the steward's role to insist on a coronial enquiry. On Christmas Eve 1708 John Ord, Weymouth's steward at Longleat, learned that a wagon returning from Warminster to Norton Davenant in Corsley parish had overturned and one of the passengers had suffered a broken leg, which turned to gangrene of which within a few days he died. The victim was buried that day, the locals 'pretending he having made a will and died as t'were a natural death there was not any need of a coroner's inquest'. Ord had then sent for Wiltshire's only coroner, one Axford of Devizes, who eventually summoned a jury at Corsley. The witnesses swore to the accident, that it was dark, and that the wagon was moving and agreed 'in their consciences' that the broken leg caused his death. They would not say whether the deceased was thrown out, fell out or leaped out of the wagon, although one witness said that the deceased had told him subsequently that he jumped to save himself and that if he had kept his feet in the wagon he would have suffered no more injury than the others. The coroner stated the point was crucial because if he jumped then he and not the wagon was responsible for his own death and thus the wagon and the five horses would not be deodand. Alarmed, Ord told the coroner that it was surely his business and the jury's simply to determine the fact and not to trouble themselves with the 'construction of law arising from that fact'. The coroner accepted this and told the jury that the statement of the deceased had no legal force, there was no valid evidence that he jumped from the wagon but rather a 'violent presumption which the law allows of as good proof' that since the rest fell from the wagon so did he. The jury was made of sterner stuff than the coroner, however, and brought in a verdict that, being apprehensive of the wagon's overturning, the deceased had leaped out 'whereby he broke his leg and thereby died'. Ord was not to be so easily defeated, however, and turned to what law books Longleat's library could furnish, examining many cases of men falling from mills, boats, carts 'or the like' but could find no parallel case of a man who jumped. He suggested that Weymouth might consult counsel in London while he tried his master's lawyers locally but the matter seems to have been allowed to die.[18]

Despite any setbacks from recalcitrant tenant jurymen, stewards and lawyers were not only quick to assert 'ancient' rights, they were quick to see the possibility of attaching more rights to an estate. When a Cheshire lawyer, John Wybunbury, heard a rumour at Chester assizes that his client Lord Cholmondeley had obtained a patent for the hundred of Nantwich he was quick to point out that Cholmondeley should 'be sure to get the word "deodand" into the new patent' which would be very advantageous in the future.[19] Similarly a steward might learn of a right claimed by a neighbouring estate which would be equally advantageous to his lord's estate could it only be established by a close scrutiny of estate records or the marshalling of the collective wisdom of the 'ancient men' among his tenants and neighbours. In 1717 the Duke of Portland at Welbeck successfully asserted over the protests of nearby Worksop that Welbeck had an exemption which prevented a servant who had worked there long enough to 'gain a settlement' from remaining there as a charge on Welbeck, and sent him to Worksop as his last 'legal' place of residence to be a charge on their poor rate. This coup was enviously observed by Thomas Smith, Sir George Savile's steward at Rufford, who was quick to alert his master that Rufford might be able to assert the same privilege, which would be 'a very great ease and an advantage', although he feared that Rufford's 'formerly receiving such' might be asserted as a precedent against it. Smith spoke for many stewards and landowners too when he concluded wistfully: ''tis great pity such a privilege should ever be lost' and hoped his master's 'writings and management' could 'rectify the error'.

The question of which community was responsible for poor people, or even for 'incomers' who were not indigent but might become so in the future, was a great source of contention in the seventeenth century and it was the duty of the steward to protect his master's villages and townships from attempts by neighbouring communities to unload their poor onto them. Of course, if the steward could work the trick in reverse so much the better. In 1689–90 John Chaunler, Lord Weymouth's recently appointed steward of Kempsford, Gloucestershire, had a hard but successful struggle to prevent the squire of neighbouring Fairford and his agents from 'settling' a young, indigent couple at Kempsford. The man had moved to Kempsford and signed a year's agreement for his labour to a widow on a farm there. He left behind in Fairford a girl who a month or so after 'charged him with a

---

[18] Ord to Weymouth, 7 February 1709, Thynne xxv, fo. 476. Ord's next three weekly letters have survived and make no reference to the matter, and since Weymouth was a notably charitable landowner he probably instructed his steward to drop it.

[19] Wynbunbury to Cholmondeley, 18 August 1680, Cholmondeley DCH/L/50.

great belly' and he quickly married her. She remained in Fairford but the steward there, knowing the couple were very poor and that she would certainly produce still more babies in time, tried to have her forcibly removed to Kempsford to join her husband. The labourer assured Chaunler that he was prepared to swear that, on learning of the girl's pregnancy, he had renegotiated his employment with the widow to working for weekly wages and that his wife had washed his clothes at Fairford throughout his stay in Kempsford. Chaunler, finding the widow 'but cold' to this claim in the evidence she would give, strongly encouraged her fear of travelling to the sessions to testify for fear of an outbreak of smallpox, and in the event, lacking her evidence, despite twice appealing the sessions, the Fairford men were baffled.[20]

Stewards could be in a difficult position when it came to heriots. Their masters took the right very seriously, and were far from seing it as a feudal survival of little practical importance – as may be deduced from the fact that it was not to be abolished until the prime ministership of Sir Robert Peel. Lord Cholmondeley was deeply suspicious when his steward mentioned a heriot, expressed in general terms as being due for a particular farm for he felt sure the farm was out of lease. His father would never have renewed the lease to a man who had been a sequestrator and 'a knave who ever hated' the Cholmondeley family. If the man or his heir had a lease he felt sure it must be fraudulent, and the more so because he had seen a hundred of his father's leases and not one of them mentioned a heriot 'in general terms but it was best goods or so much in money'. This shows the care that was taken in drawing that 'modern' instrument, the lease for lives, to specify a heriot, and in unambiguous terms. Similarly, when years later this Lord Cholmondeley's successor was extremely anxious to persuade a substantial tenant to take a particular lease he was prepared to accept several demands much in the tenant's favour, but to his request for the waiving of heriot he replied indignantly that he could not understand such a request.[21]

The tenants saw heriots from a very different perspective as a much resented feudal due, and even among those who had no intention of resisting it or of seeking to defraud their landlord, it could prove a ruinous imposition which might have (from the landlord's viewpoint) the unappeal-

---

[20] The Fairford agents tried strenuously to subpoena her but could never find her, no doubt because of Chaunler's skill in concealing her. He had already asked his master to send her a 'protection' to assure her safety from the malice of the baffled Fairford squire. Chaunler to Weymouth, 28 December 1689, 11 and 22 January, 10 May 1690, Thynne xxiv, fos. 113, 123, 213, 272.

[21] First Viscount Cholmondeley of Kells to William Adams, 2 February 1680; Michael Laroche (for second Viscount Cholmondeley) to Adams, 22 February 1700, Cholmondeley DCH/K/3/1 and 14 respectively.

ing consequence of reducing tenants' heirs to indigency and thus have them become another burden on the poor rate or at best make it more difficult for them to pay their rent. However, although these ill consequences could be avoided by waiving the heriot, or at least setting it at a derisory payment charitably to assist a poor widow, landlords and stewards usually insisted on asserting the right to a heriot for fear of it falling into desuetude, or of a precedent being unscrupulously asserted in the future. A steward might be anxious to be helpful to a female tenant recently widowed, yet fear the consequences of the precedent because a nearby tenant, whose estate was well able to sustain a heriot, was considered to be terminally ill.[22] Many tenants paid their heriot in cash or forfeited their best beast on the death of their father or husband without cavil. Others, however, tenaciously and ingeniously sought to evade it, or even to protect their heirs against its incidence before their deaths. Some tenants were even prepared to frustrate their landlord after their deaths by ensuring that when they died there would be no best beast, or indeed any goods of value, on the property at their deaths for the steward to seize. 'Old Mr Clayton is at last dead who I believe was near a 100 years old. He took care I should have nothing that was good for a heriot' bitterly remarked one landowner.[23] This may not always have worked. Finding that a deceased tenant had no stock of any kind or indeed any considerable 'dead' goods either, an understeward wrote to his chief steward to discover whether it would not be possible to seize a heriot from the man who had actually enjoyed the estate and only allowed the nominal tenant 'keeping' there.[24] Most evaders were, of course, the heirs of the deceased tenant. One method was to appear to comply but defraud the landlord of the best beast. Stewards had to be alert to this trick, and when they discovered it tended to seize what they considered the best beast (even though it might be claimed that it had not been the property of the deceased) and then leave it to the heirs to brave the expense and doubtful issue of a recourse to law.[25]

One steward found himself in difficulties because of what had seemed at

[22] Roger Kenrick reported to his master in 1668 that a widow had been left in difficulties by her husband's death and if he took her best beast, a cow, the family would not be able to make the rent, 'yet something must be done because the next neighbour ... Widow Madox, is like to die ... who is well able to give a heriot'. To Sir John Trevor, 4 July 1668, Trevor D/G/3278.

[23] Dowager Viscountess Cholmondeley to William Adams, 7 August 1686, Cholmondeley DCH K/3/7.

[24] The correspondence does not reveal the result of this enquiry but it is likely a heriot, or payment in lieu, was demanded of the occupier. Peter Wever to William Adams, 27 November 1682, Cholmondeley DCH/L/48.

[25] 'They have set apart two little beasts for heriots ... there are four better cows upon the land and I do believe they will swear the two little ones to be the deceased's and none else' reported Thomas Hawkes, asking whether he should seize the best and 'let them take what course they will'. Hawkes to Thomas Thynne, 5 June 1675, Thynne xx, fo. 242.

the time an ingenious solution to this problem: he had loaned the widow of a poor tenant the best beast which had been forfeited as a heriot at her husband's death so that she could sustain a living. When she died and he went to reclaim the heriot, no beast was to be found, and it is clear that the woman's son, whom the steward had tactfully left alone for six days after his mother's death, was trying to cheat the landowner of what had really been the landlowner's property for some months.[26] Certainly stewards often sought to mediate to relieve the situation of widows, and certainly many widows sought such mediation. 'I shall forthwith repair to John Matthew's widow for the heriot but (as it is usual) they hope your honour will deal kindly with them' writes Charles Agard, dropping a typical hint. In fact, the lease did not specify what the heriot should be, leaving it in general terms so that Agard asks his master how he wishes to 'deal with the widow', the emphasis on 'widow' being probably deliberate.[27] Kindness could take more than one form. Stewards often persuaded their master to sell back to the heirs a prized beast (or simply take payment in lieu), as when Samuel Peers assured his master that the heirs of a dead tenant would pay a good price for the best ox so as not to 'part' a good working pair.[28] Sometimes it was the landowner himself who took the benevolent initiative, as when Sir John Trevor ordered his steward to let a son pay a modest sum in lieu of a heriot, and also to let him have his father's lands 'at pleasure' along with the lands the son already leased so long as this did not harm the widow whom he would be loath to turn out.[29]

Tenants in their resistance to heriots were not only ingenious and resolute, they were also prepared to combine and to pool their resources for a resort to law. This could be a very worrying development for those landlords whose assertion of the legal basis of their 'rights' tended to be based on assumptions rather than known facts. Sir John Lowther of Whitehaven was embarrassed to discover that his St Bees-Whitehaven tenants claimed that by custom of the manors of West Cumberland heriots were not due unless the heir to the farm was the deceased tenant's widow.[30] If this might be difficult for the tenants to prove it was also difficult for the lord to disprove and he set his steward and lawyers ransacking his muniments and discreetly consulting neighbouring landlords about the customs of their manors. He did not at first simply assert his right for fear

---

[26] Samuel Wood to Sir John Trevor, 20 July 1639, Trevor D/G/3275.
[27] Charles Agard to the Earl of Dorset, 9 August, 21 September 1655, Sackville U269/C63.
[28] Peers to Thomas Thynne, 3 March 1673, Thynne xx, fo. 146.
[29] Sir John Trevor to Thomas Crewe, 14 January 1635, Trevor D/G/3273.
[30] When a widower tenant died Tickell marked a beast for heriot at which several neighbouring tenants came and declared that no heriot was due without a widow 'and for ought I yet perceive will rather encourage a ... suit than suffer us to have it'. Tickell to Lowther, 16 December 1672, Lonsdale D/Lons/W2/1/7.

the tenants would take him to court, where the jurors would probably be tenants themselves, and where he might be defeated. This cautious policy was supported by his steward who, after consulting both Lowther's brother-in-law and his stepfather, found that while the former was resolute on the ground that tenants held as he put it 'by heriot service', the latter, older and more experienced, insisted that heriot was only a manorial custom, and the custom was only to pay where a widow survived the husband. As a result Tickell feared the outcome of a trial. When finally Lowther decided to take this dangerous course, his steward remained pessimistic and fearful of the outcome, and those fears may have infected his master for at the last moment the suit was 'let fall until further fortified with precedents', as Lowther put it.[31]

Where there was no dispute about the heriot's legality his steward could be very aggressive, in word at least if not in deed. Learning from a local squire that Sir George Middleton, a Westmorland landowner, had seized a coach in London as a heriot, 'a "dead" good and legally done as it proved at the trial' Tickell suggested that a dead tenant's ship might be seized since he had left no 'quick' goods.[32] Such an extravagant suggestion was probably the fruit of much frustration and anger at the successful defiance by tenants of what Thomas Tickell saw as his master's rights, and his own failure to defend them successfully. Certainly the right to heriot presented stewards with one of the most difficult and onerous of their duties as defender of the estate. At times they were confronted by tenants determined to cheat their master of his rights, at others by co-operative heirs who might be ruined by their compliance unless the steweard could persuade his master to be generous.

Encroachers on the estate were a problem of a different order, an assault mercifully rare but which had to be stoutly resisted. As we have already seen it was the steward's function, when acting in his ambassadorial role, to seek to prevent disputes with neighbouring landowners over boundaries.[33] That is, he should always seek to achieve a harmonious conclusion and not involve his master in lawsuits in which the issue invariably would be doubtful and the expense damnable, whatever the result. Naturally such peaceful courses were not always successful. Perambulations, however careful and thorough, could lead to friction with a neighbouring steward

---

[31] Tickell to Lowther, 19 May, Lowther to Tickell, 22 July 1673, Lonsdale D/Lons/W2/1/8. See also a thorough discussion of this dispute in Churches, 'Lowther and Whitehaven', 57–60.

[32] This remarkable suggestion came to nothing, not least because the tenant shipowner only owned shares in ships, not whole ships, a common practice, and a landlord could not seize a share of something as a heriot. Tickell to Lowther, 18 March 1672, Lonsdale D/Lons/W2/1/7.

[33] See Chapter 6 above.

who feared that the perambulators might be about to encroach on his lord's
lands. Whilst considering the possibility of diverting the course of a beck
running into Whitehaven harbour, William Gilpin uneasily observed that if
the beck was considered a boundary between Whitehaven and Bransty it
might bring the Duke of Somerset down on them. Shortly after he last
perambulated the bounds Joseph Relfe, steward of the Duke's West Cumberland estates, had come 'with open mouth upon' him, (presumably
abusing him for allegedly overstepping the Duke's boundary).[34] Where a
dispute involved a powerful neighbour a steward must proceed with
caution, since he could not tackle a nobleman or even a wealthy gentleman
without his master's full support. The first step a steward took, therefore,
was to check that his master wished to pursue the matter or had not perhaps
permitted his neighbour to make the encroachment for some reason of his
own. When John Warren at Milcott, Warwickshire, found that some men
had cut ditches across the Earl of Middlesex's land in order to divert the
flooded Avon to relieve some levy breaks on Lord Windsor's neighbouring
estate, he arrested the men but first checked that Windsor had not obtained
Middlesex's permission before proceeding further.[35]

Trespasses were often more serious in their implications, threatening
permanently to deprive the estate of some part of its 'ancient' lands.
Valuable tracts of ground might be claimed by a neighbouring landowner,
or by some of his tenants as part of their grazing. The steward would then
be faced with the task of gathering evidence both verbal and written. The
second kind might perhaps be left to the lord's lawyers, particularly if the
lord's documents were held in town or on some distant headquarters
manor, but the verbal evidence must be gathered by the steward. At a time
when there were no local public institutions in which plans and maps could
be consulted which would clearly show the boundaries of properties, and in
the absence of proper surveys of the various estates of which England was
largely composed, the steward had to rely on ancient landmarks, boundary
stones, posts, ditches and so on. Since these, where they existed at all, were
often overgrown, or concealed by forests or underbrush, he had to rely on
the evidence of local men with long memories, the 'ancient men' so often
referred to in stewards' correspondence, who might be able to point them
out and show the steward just where the boundary had always been deemed

---

[34] Gilpin to Lowther 24 August 1697, *Lowther Correspondence*, Letter 396.
[35] John Warren to Robert Pennocke (Middlesex's receiver and man-of-business in London),
19 July 1676, Sackville U269/C125/26. Similarly when Thomas Hawkes discovered that a
local gentleman called Ireland, currently the High Sheriff of Shropshire, was taking in a
field on the Long Mynd for ploughing he cautiously made no other move than to advise his
master to consult his father, Sir Henry Frederick Thynne, what settlement he and Ireland
might have negotiated about the bounds of the commons on Long Mynd. Hawkes to
Thomas Thynne, 26 July 1673, Thynne xx, fo. 112.

to run. These men possessed this knowledge because of the custom of walking the bounds of the manor at regular intervals, clearing marks, instructing the young in where they lay and what they signified and generally refreshing and extending the collective memory.[36] The final part of the steward's duties came when all attempts at a negotiated settlement had broken down and the matter must go either to the arbitration of a brace of local gentlemen (or professional lawyers) chosen by the contenders, or, most vexatious and expensive and therefore most dreaded, to a law suit. He must then find oral and written evidence for his lord's lawyer and advise as to the best way of proceeding to settle the dispute. In the end, if the affair went badly it was often his uncomfortable duty to send the painful tidings to his distant master.

A classic example of a steward's progress through these various stages has been furnished us by Thomas Smith at Rufford Abbey in 1717. The villagers of Bilsthorpe, supported by their landlord, Sir Bryan Broughton, were asserting that the boundary line between Rufford and Bilsthorpe ran along the Nottingham road, which, if established, would have cut off a chunk of woodland and pasture from Rufford and its tenants. Lacking documentary proof or precise maps Smith sought the oral evidence of 'ancient men'. The first witness Smith consulted, who lived close to the disputed area, provided cold comfort. He asserted that the perambulations of the boundaries in Lord Halifax's time and in Sir George Savile's time had both proceeded along different and therefore conflicting boundary lines. In fact Smith lacked really 'ancient men' because those who had lived through most of the previous century were dead, and those who constituted the last of the 'old stock' gave 'but a weak account'. Smith even considered the risky course of consulting the former steward at Bilsthorpe, one Birch, who was alleged to be disaffected from Broughton. (Either Smith decided not to do so or found Birch useless for his purpose.) Finally Smith found a county coroner, John Gray of Wellow, who seemed the perfect witness. Born in 1663, he had perambulated the bounds of Rufford, on which estate he had been brought up from a boy, at every biannual perambulation since the age of ten. Moreover, his father, John Gray senior, born in 1626, had attended every perambulation since his boyhood until shortly before his death in 1700. Gray the elder and other 'ancient knowing neighbours' had taught Gray the younger all the marks, and he had attained such a knowledge of the Rufford boundaries that in places where marks had been covered by heath, and 'the whole body of the perambulation' had been 'at a stand',

---

[36] For a useful discussion of the boundary problem (albeit with respect to parishes, not estates) and the custom of perambulation or 'beating bounds' on Rogation Day, see Maurice Beresford, *History on the Ground* (Gloucester, 1984), Chapter 2: 'A Journey Along Boundaries'.

young Gray had often guided the perambulators to the concealed marks. Gray had resolved boundary disputes in the past in Rufford's favour.

Perhaps he did so on this occasion for the dispute disappears from a correspondence which is far from complete. However, it revived in 1720 with the arrest of a Rufford tenant at Broughton's warrant, presumably for some form of 'trespass' on the disputed ground. The assizes were drawing nearer and Smith, to avoid an uncertain and expensive court case, urged his master to have the matter put to local arbitration. Smith firmly believed that local gentlemen without professional knowledge of the law would be more likely to settle the matter finally and speedily than skilled lawyers, although he recognised that if Broughton chose for his side a lawyer or a local gentleman who practised law then Savile must do no less. Despite his advice the case went to a law suit which dragged on until March 1721, and in which Savile was unsuccessful. In this affair a steward was defeated in a long-drawn-out defence of the estate. The loss of land was trivial but the legal expense (as Smith had always feared) proved damnable.[37]

[37] Smith to Savile, 6 June, 6 July 1717; 2 and 9 January, 1 February, 12 March, 2 April, 7 May 1720, 20 March 1721, Savile DDSR 211/227.

11

The constable: defending the forests

I wish the tenants do not conceal other trees blown down in their grounds and so make use of the wood themselves. You should send some young body to ride into every ground about Etton and Woodcraft to inspect, and for Milton and Marholm you may ride into them yourself.

Lord Fitzwilliam to Francis Guybon, 1707[1]

I am under great concern and differences with several gentlemen who send their servants into Sir George's manors who destroy both his game and fish notoriously. His honour's charge was great to me on that account so that I must think myself more obliged to observe it than connive at the best of them, in so much we are all at ears in prosecutions.

William Elmsall, 1712[2]

As constable the steward appears largely in a defensive role as the guardian of the manor, however aggressive he may have seemed at times toward those who appeared to threaten it. The same could be said of his role as guardian of his lord's woods and forests and the deer and other game which might inhabit them. As we have seen, a steward could be specifically allocated the duties of a wood-reeve, but in fact whether their letters of attorney or statements of duties actually mentioned them, all stewards in their constable role were guardians of their masters' woods and forests. Few of their duties were more exhausting, demanding and indeed ceaseless than their struggles to protect their lords' estates from the depredations of woodthieves.[3] It was a lonely struggle in which the stewards had few friends other than neighbouring landowners faced with the same problem, and in which there was inadequate assistance from the law. During the first half of the seventeenth century stewards were handicapped by the fact that timber stealing had not yet been defined as the statutory crime of larceny but rather was punished in manorial courts under the heading of 'committing waste',

---

[1] Fitzwilliam F(M)C 1617; *Fitzwilliam Correspondence*, Letter 541.
[2] Elmsall to Madame Savile, 6 July 1712, Savile DDSR 211/2.
[3] The significance of underwoods to the poor and the efforts of landowners to check their depredations is considered in Keith Thomas, *Man and the Natural World* (London, 1983), Chapter 5.

a term which included unlicensed cutting of furzes on heathland or pillaging hedgerows. A late Elizabethan statute against 'lewd persons' committing 'misdemeanours' by entering on private ground to lop trees, spoil underwoods and so on, and which prescribed payment of compensation to the landlord or whipping of the indigent seems to have been of little effect, and certainly did not define it as larceny. In 1664 a new statute replaced it designed to discourage 'unlawful cutting or stealing or spoiling of wood and underwood' and destroying 'young timber trees' by not only exacting compensation to the landowner, but fining the convicted ten shillings to the poor, and if they failed to make these payments they were either to be whipped or spend not more than a month in the house of correction.[4] This legislation, however, was probably less easy to enforce than its framers hoped and certainly stewards seem to have had little success at suppressing wood stealing outside the manorial courts. Even here there were problems for to combat the landlord's powers tenants would sometimes band together to set up alleged ancient rights to gather fallen wood. The rights might be fictitious but this was difficult to prove and the device enabled tenants to successfully defy or at least evade the court's authority. Many were not fictitious, having their origins in mediaeval rights to timber for house repair (housebote), for making farming implements (ploughbote) and for fuel (firebote). Moreover, on some manors tenants had a right to the underwoods whilst the lord had an exclusive right to the timber.[5] However, many rights had been lost in the past or deliberately challenged and eroded by landlords anxious to preserve their timber in a more populous and forest-depleted era.[6] Husbandmen, perhaps belonging to a neighbouring manor, sometimes challenged a steward's authority by asserting that particular ground or common land was no part of his lord's lands, and that they had a right to gather furzes or other fuel, whereas the lord or his servants did not. A furze 'war' might break out on such debatable land,

[4] *Statutes at Large*, 15th Chas. II, 1665. For a second offence a month at hard labour was mandatory and for a third the offender was to be deemed 'an incorrigible rogue'. A reliable informer was no longer necessary (as under the Elizabethan statute), houses and land could be searched and persons bearing timber could be arrested and interrogated simply on suspicion.
[5] This was true, for example, on the manors of the Richmond and Marquess fees in Westmorland; see C. E. Searle, 'Custom, Class Conflict and Agrarian Capitalism: the Cumbrian Customary Economy in the Eighteenth Century', *Past and Present*, vol. 110 (February 1986), 127.
[6] For discussion of fictitious claims see Roger B. Manning, *Village Revolts, Social Protest and Popular Disturbances in England 1509–1650* (Oxford 1988), 270. For a description of a fiercely contested claim to a mediaeval right as late as the nineteenth century see R. W. Bushaway '"Grovely, Grovely, Grovely and all Grovely!" Custom, Crime and Conflict in the English Woodland', *History Today*, vol. 31 (May 1981). For a more general discussion see also Bushaway, *By Rite: Custom, Ceremony and Community in England 1700–1880* (London, 1982), Chapter 6: 'Crime, Custom and Popular Legitimacy'.

with the steward cutting furze bundles and scattering them about (to assert his lord's right) and his opponents threatening to set fire to the lord's cart and the furzes in it if the steward sent men to carry away furzes in the future.[7] However, this reference to neighbours serves to remind us that the steward who defended his lord's woods, copses and hedges had more to fear from outsiders than from the manor's tenants. Whatever ancient rights the tenants might have to gather winter fuel, outsiders had none, but were a constant threat, particularly where the countryside was reasonably thickly populated, or where the manor was located near to a country town. Woodthieves were a universal problem which all stewards had to grapple with whether their estates were small or large, whether or not they had forests or game parks to defend, whether or not the tenants still asserted ancient rights.

Within the limits relating to underwoods referred to above, all wood on an estate was the lord's, whether timber trees or underwood, whether in forests or copses or free standing on the margins of their tenants' fields; so were all hedgerows and fences. The fact that such individual trees or copses or woods might stand on farm leased to a tenant for lives, or by copyhold, made no difference. Save for some improbable and highly unusual exception in a particular lease, all tenancy agreements provided that no tenant could cut down trees, even if they were dead, or remove fallen trees, whether long blown down or knocked over by some recent storm, or even cut furzes or take peat from the lord's wastes, without the lord's permission. (It was a peculiarity of some church land leases that the clerical landlord could not exploit timber on such land without the consent of the tenant, but this in no way empowered such a tenant to exploit the timber without the permission of the landlord.[8]) So far as timber trees were concerned this permission was hardly ever likely to be given except where a tenant needed timber to repair farm buildings or to replace or repair fences, and then the landlord would benefit from the timber's use himself, or where the tenant was purchasing specific timber or fuel for an agreed price.

All this may seem straightforward enough. The problem the stewards faced was that all simples in the English countryside were possessed of a very natural hunger for firewood. All landlords were possessed of an equally natural desire to prevent their estates being denuded of all natural vegetation. Moreover, the timber on an estate, whether isolated trees or standing in woods and copses, was one of its most valuable assets. This

[7] William Thynne to Sir James Thynne, 4 October 1658, Thynne ix, fo. 74.
[8] See Lord Guildford's letters to Francis White, 6 and 17 January 1682, respectively North C.7 fos. 31–2, C.5, fo. 99. Guildford leased the manor of Wroxton, Oxfordshire from Trinity College, Oxford, where the same rule applied, Guildford remarking 'it is usual in church leases where the landlord cannot fell without the tenant's consent for the tenant to have half the money for which the timber is sold'.

conflict of interest led to a perpetual tug-of-war which absentee landlords with idle or elderly stewards, rather too fond of a quiet life, were bound to lose more often than they won. If stewards were inactive a manor could be denuded indeed. On one estate which had formerly been 'well planted with timber and wood' there was scarce a tree to be found big enough to make a gatepost.[9] Thomas Greene, steward at Gillingham for Sir John Nicholas, was only one of hundreds of stewards perpetually seeking ways to protect his master's woods from shivering cottagers. He even took the opportunity of a charitable distribution of meat to tell the poor of Gillingham that they should be careful not to abuse so good a benefactor, and any that abused his master's woods or trees must never expect this gift again.[10] However, Greene, like many other stewards, found that it was not the inhabitants of his rural manor but the folk of a neighbouring town who represented the biggest threat to his master's woods. The poor of a town, with no way to warm themselves at a fire save by plundering neighbouring woods and hedges, were a constant threat in winter and active even in summer because of the need for fuel for cooking. Greene reported in March 1699 that he had cut down two coppices, for if he had not the poor of Shaftesbury 'would have done it for us'. (Similarly Francis White had recommended in the winter of 1667 that 'Parsonage Wood' should be felled and sold because it was 'daily cut and spoiled and the longer it stands the worse it proves'.[11]) A local justice living on the other side of Shaftesbury claimed the poor had cut near £1,000 worth of faggots from his trees (though Greene considered this estimate 'too extravagant'). Meanwhile Greene was paying a man twenty shillings a year to protect one of his master's woods, and recommended that another man should be paid as much to maintain the fences and to repair them when cattle broke through into the wood before woodstealers used the gaps to make mischief. He had recently been at great charge and trouble to mend the fences by planting brambles and thorns.[12] Francis White reported to Lord North that he had let some grounds for a period of less than a year – a very unusual decision – rather than keep them in hand until Lady Day 'for all people break and steal away the fences and prey upon us as if a landlord

---

[9] Robert Britiffe to Dacre Barrett, concerning Horsford manor, Norfolk, 25 November 1701, Barrett-Lennard D/DL/C3/24. The newly appointed bailiff of the manor had told the same story four years earlier, observing that he would only lease farms in future for copyholders took no care to preserve the estate. All agreed there had been great quantities of timber formerly but now there was not enough to repair the manor house. Robert Caudell to James Sloane, 26 October 1697, Barrett-Lennard D/DL/C4/1.

[10] Greene to Nicholas, 5 June 1700, Nicholas 76/13.

[11] White to Lord North, 12 February 1667, North C.4, fo. 129.

[12] These measures were all to protect a wood of about 400 young oaks. 4 March 1699, Nicholas 76/3.

were a common enemy'.[13] Let a storm blow and estate servants would soon after be galloping around the estate to note what trees were down and to set men to rescue them from the plundering habits of the tenants on whose land they had fallen.[14] After a storm in which his steward had reported the loss of only one tree Lord Fitzwilliam hoped that the tenants were not concealing other trees falling on their grounds and making use of the timber themselves. Guybon must send some young man to ride into every ground on Fitzwilliam's more distant manors while the steward himself should inspect the nearer manors.[15]

Some thefts amounted to more than filching firewood. Timber was a major industry on great estates. Often the timber was felled and then sawn into boards on site and this was a time when the timber was peculiarly vulnerable as the local woodthieves would wait until the boards had been sawn and then come in the night to make away with them. Lord Weymouth's steward, having had four windfall trees cut up into boards, hastened the sawn timber to the safety of the Minsterley manor barn, because he knew that once the timber was 'merchantable' thefts would begin. 'There is not a thiefisher country in the kingdom' he bitterly explained.[16] His predecessor, Hawkes, had the same experience a generation earlier. Thomas Thynne, as he then was, was heavily exploiting his Shropshire woods but once the timber was down Hawkes found their neighbours and even the workmen were stealing it. He had made searches, found stolen wood and his colleague, Samuel Peers the Minsterley steward, was to launch prosecutions against the offenders, although on what charge and in what court we do not learn. However, even such a case as this may have been heard in the manorial court rather than at the sessions, on a charge of committing waste rather than larceny. Indeed as late as 1677 a steward could urge his lord to call the manorial court at the next Lady Day so as to curb the destruction of timber by presenting and fining offenders.[17]

Some stewards found it necessary to steel their master to apply the rigour of the law to woodthieves, especially those who cut down trees, and at least

---

[13] Three days after one tenant quit his farm 'there was not so much as a hedge stake left'. White to Lady North, December 1667, North C.10, fo. 33.

[14] 'Ride into every ground of my estate and set down in a paper what trees are down ... and let them be valued and sold to the best chapman' directed Lord Fitzwilliam after the famous 'Great Storm' of 26–7 November 1703. Fitzwilliam, 2 December 1703, F(M)C 1289; *Fitzwilliam Correspondence*, Letter 294.

[15] Fitzwilliam, 18 December 1707, F(M)C 1633; *Fitzwilliam Correspondence*, Letter 541.

[16] Meaning by 'country' the county of Shropshire; Mainewaring to Weymouth, 13 December 1703, Thynne xxviii, fo. 324.

[17] He pointed out that the costs, chiefly a twenty-shilling fee to the attorney who would keep the court, would be covered by the presentments. H. Carter, steward at Paulers Purvey (near Towcester), Northamptonshire, to the Earl of Middlesex, 18 March 1677, Sackville U269/C127.

make them pay for the timber they carried off. On one occasion William Thynne warned his master not to excuse a woodthief who had cut down trees, but who was very humble now that he was 'sued for them'. Sir James should not 'excuse him' but rather 'let him pay for them'.[18] Many stewards found themselves challenged by tenant offenders who were trying to play off the steward against his master by claiming that they had a right to cut down a tree, either because (as they asserted) their lease permitted it, or because they alleged that the lord had given them the tree for repairs to their farm buildings. William Thynne found himself baffled by such a tenant in 1659, who had cut down a magnificent elm tree ('I know none like it in the country') who had the boldness to put forward both these excuses at once, although one might have thought them mutually exclusive.[19] Later in the century stewards were able to invoke harsher penalties than a manorial court and a manorial court jury, composed no doubt of enthusiastic woodstealers, could or would impose. In 1698 Thomas Greene found the justices at the sessions very 'hearty' in convicting two stealers of wood from his master's estate, one was to be whipped or to pay five shillings to the local overseers of the poor, the other's penalty if any, was not mentioned, but both had their convictions recorded and their next conviction 'sends them to the House of Correction for a month'. Indeed the justices assured Greene they would inflict the 'extreme penalty of the law' if he desired it.[20]

There could be various grounds for either mercy or prosecution in individual cases and it was for the steward to be alert to these possibilities, even if the justifications for prosecution or forgiveness might seem a trifle odd to our eyes. In January 1704 a man called Bell was seen stealing wood. The steward obtained a warrant for his arrest from his brother-in-law who was a justice but the young man 'absconded from his family', while his father had been to beg the lord's pardon, offering to enter bond that his son would never more offend and had pleaded 'as something of merit that his son gives his vote in elections as your lordship disposes'.[21] In contrast, discovering that a tenant had cut down three trees on his farm, Thomas Allen at Longleat asked Lord Weymouth whether he or the carpenter who cut them up should be sued, remarking that the offender had told a tax assessor's wife that her husband was a 'forsworn rascal' for rating Weymouth so low.[22] Thus one woodthief might be thought to deserve mercy because he was a loyal voter in his master's interest at parliamentary

[18] William Thynne to Sir James Thynne, 2 May 1659, Thynne ix, fo. 113v.
[19] William Thynne 21 March 1659, Thynne ix, fo. 104.
[20] 5 December 1698, Nicholas, 75/17.
[21] Thomas Newton to the Earl of Northampton 13 January 1704, Northampton (Warwickshire).
[22] 7 April 1690, Thynne xxiv, fo. 197.

elections, whereas mercy should be withheld from another because he had criticised the tax assessors for under-assessing his master for the land tax.

Of equal concern to masters and stewards was the protection of the estate from poachers, whether poachers of rabbits, hares or game birds, robbers of rivers and fishponds, or, most serious of all, deer stealers. Few aspects of life around a great estate can prove more revealing about the mechanisms and workings of seventeenth-century society than the problems faced and the experiences encountered by stewards in combating this type of assault on property. Poachers came in all kinds of guises. The popular view of the poacher as a humble cottager or farm labourer, desperate to feed his family, and so succumbing to the temptation to bring home one of his wealthy neighbour's pheasants or rabbits for his wife's empty cookpot has little relevance to the problems of seventeenth-century stewards. Had such humble pawns been all they had to contend with they would have thought themselves fortunate indeed. Such men existed but the stewards tended either to wink at their activities or to intervene to persuade their masters to treat those who had been caught and convicted with leniency and to mediate between them and their masters in order that penalties should fall less heavily upon them. As late as 1717 when resistance to poachers was supposed to be stiffening, and at a time when Rufford Park was sorely beleaguered by poaching gangs, Thomas Smith sought to persuade his master that one convicted poacher who had only been fined forty shillings as an act of clemency by Sir George Savile, should be given extended time to pay even that modest fine on the grounds that he was not worth 'forty pence'.[23] These were the small fry and even they had their different varieties, which did not exclude schoolboys, particularly when it came to taking fish from the lord's stretches of a river. As Thomas Hopkins drily reported from Drayton Bassett manor in the spring of 1680, those Tam-worth anglers who fished his master's river included some schoolboys 'who at taking jacks are masters of art'. His comment reminds us that poachers were not necessarily villagers. Provincial towns were so small that at haying the scents of the mowing fields could be smelled from the very centre of their marketplaces. So could the possibilities for sport and profit provided by neighbouring estates. A tenant of the same manor, who had filled a pond with eels taken from mill-dams for miles about, had a breach made in his dam deliberately to plunder its stock and as the steward mournfully reported the robbers were probably from Tamworth and 'I fear will scarce be found out'.[24]

23 Smith to Savile, 4 February 1717, Savile DDSR 211/227/82.
24 William Hopkins to Sir Thomas Thynne, 19 April 1680, Thynne xx, fo. 436; John Mainewaring to Thynne (now Lord Weymouth), 27 December 1693, xxviii, fo. 307.

Probably most troublesome, and certainly potentially the most embarrassing, species of poacher was the neighbouring gentleman with a passion for shooting or fishing and with no inhibitions about where he gratified it. Here the steward was in a dilemma. It was his role to maintain good relations with his master's neighbours if only as part of the task of massaging his master's political interest. Having such a man brought before a local justice would scarcely help this important duty, particularly as the action was likely to offend a wider circle of the culprit's family and friends. Stewards were conscious of the fact that the gentlemen of a county had ways of making their displeasure felt. One steward expressed the hope that his master would protect him from the annoyance of having local offices imposed upon him, which (he claimed) was a favoured way of avenging some alleged offence among the county gentlemen.[25] Then again these poachers, if pests, were, after all, gentlemen. A gentleman did not lightly drag another gentleman before a local justice – who in any event was himself likely to be a friend or neighbour of the accused. Finally, such men were likely to be at least acquaintances of the steward himself, men of the same rank when they were not of higher rank.

One inglorious but practical way a steward might keep on good terms with such neighbours and spare himself embarrassment was simply to look the other way. Unhappily stewards had enemies who were only too happy to report such dereliction of his constabulary duties to his master, and stern rebukes accompanied by embarrassingly explicit directives were certain to follow. 'I am beholding to other people' for information about poaching, grumbles Lord Fitzwilliam in 1707, 'and not to you who ought to inform me of all these poachers but you connive too much at all people who trespass upon my royalties.' That these poachers were gentle rather than simples is clear from Fitzwilliam's catalogue of them: 'Mr Richardson the petty canon and parson of Eye', 'a minister's son' belonging to John Drydon of Chesterton's household, his father the minister was as great a huntsman as the son was a shooter and both lay 'much in my woods'. Another poacher, 'Holmes the warrener', a Fitzwilliam tenant, was a substantial yeoman rather than a gentleman, but in Fitzwilliam's eyes a 'very rascal and will say anything to pleasure his neighbour rather than be true to me', but his real complaint was that while 'all the country took notice of his shooting pheasants and plundering my woods … you are passive and say nothing to him … you suffer all people to do what they will'.[26] Other stewards grasped the nettle and preferred to sacrifice local

---

[25] Hawkes to Thomas Thynne, 21 October 1673, Thynne xx, fo. 124. The circumstances which aroused this anxiety are discussed in the following chapter.
[26] Fitzwilliam to Guybon, 27 March, 4 September 1707, F(M)C 1569, 1608; *Fitzwilliam Correspondence*, Letters 494, 524.

harmony than see damage to their master's estate, one remarking grimly that he was 'under great concern and differences' with several local gentlemen who sent their servants into his master's manors where they destroyed 'both his game and fish notoriously'. However, his master's 'charge was great to me on that account' so that he thought himself 'more obliged to observe it than connive at the best of them'. As a result they were 'all at ears in prosecutions'.[27] In general, however, perhaps the most significant element revealed by the activities of the gentlemen poachers is the odd lack of solidarity among the elite. It is a phenomenon which we shall see reappear in the battles against the most worrying of all the poachers: those who did it for profit rather than for sport or to fill hungry bellies.

The former were primarily deer stealers although they often plundered fishponds and rivers on a large scale. For those stewards who had charge of extensive deer parks they were probably the most worrying problem with which their constabulary role involved them. Beneath the apparent calm, even torpor, of rural life there lay concealed a vein of criminality which was much more organised than the petty thefts which might occasionally plague any estate or village. Venison was highly prized and butchers in London or in such county towns as Oxford or Bristol or Nottingham would pay substantial sums to obtain it. Lord Fitzwilliam occasionally complained to his steward that he could buy better venison in London than his estate could provide (implying that his deer were ill cared for or had been poached). However, the fact that London butchers had venison hanging in their shops for Lord Fitzwilliam to buy reminds us that some landowners kept deer for profitable sale and since a poached deer appears the same and tastes as good as one legitimately sold (at least if it has not been run down by dogs) the legitimate venison provided cover for a clandestine trade.[28] Similarly fishmongers were happy to furnish a market for carp, pike and eels which appeared at their back doors after dark, and would refrain from embarrassing questions about their provenance. Indeed they would hardly need to make such enquiries since often they were the instigators of their netting. William Thynne at Longleat discovered that a man called Cut Phillips of Mere, Somerset, had bought so much poached venison from

---

[27] William Elmsall to Madam Savile, mother of Sir George Savile, 6 July 1712, Savile DDSR 211/2.

[28] Lord Weymouth, through his London agent, John Tayldor, informed his head keeper, Crowther, at Drayton Bassett manor that he would 'dispark' his deer park if it could not be turned to profit. Much 'mortified', Crowther, who considered venison could be sold more profitably in the country than 'hazarded' to London, sent up two bucks to try the market. Tayldor reported that although he sold them 'well enough' the town was so empty and venison so cheap, with porters hawking it about the streets at very low rates, that he had postponed sending for more until the market improved. Tayldor to Weymouth, 4, 9 and 25 August 1687, Thynne xxix, fos. 90, 92, 94.

Longleat Park that the market price had been depressed to only twelve shillings a carcase, although Phillips had sold one buck in Oxford for £5. Much to Thynne's indignation he discovered also that at a time when he had been assured by the keepers that there was not a buck fit to send to his master, a very fine buck had been killed and profitably sold clandestinely. The poachers, it appears, felt they could not spare Sir James any of his own venison.

It is clear, of course, that poaching on this scale could only be carried on with at least the connivance if not the full participation of those who had been set to protect the deer: the keepers. The vein of criminality crossed the park pale, suborning keepers and gatekeepers along the way. In general it would appear that keepers tended to fall into one or other of four categories: those who actually organised poaching; those who were simply participants in poaching organised from outside 'the pale', or at least connived at it in exchange for a share in the profits; those who refused to participate but failed to reveal the poachers' activities to their master; and those who were too stupid to realise what was going on. The last were probably the type of keeper least likely to be encountered. The steward was a busy man, with multifarious duties and responsibilities to discharge. He could not be everywhere, he was compelled to delegate and to whom should he delegate the preservation of his master's park if not the keepers who were employed to protect it? Nothing was more calculated to enrage both steward and lord than the discovery that members of the lord's own family were involved in a conspiracy against his estate. To counter this situation the steward, once alerted, needed a bulldog's persistence and a bloodhound's nose.

The experiences of William Thynne, who appears to have possessed both, are illuminating. In the winter of 1659, learning from a keeper called Pearse that he had found evidence that a deer had been killed by crossbow and that he suspected a man called Roe, who, although not an estate servant, was the son of a Longleat gatekeeper, Thynne assembled three keepers for a descent on Roe's house. However, suspecting the other keepers of complicity he did not reveal why they were going there until they arrived at Roe's cottage, where he sternly told them they were to search for 'the fruit of their neglect or knaveries'. Although Roe was absent, carrying venison to a customer Thynne suspected, plain evidence of poaching was found, including crossbows, nets, the head of a freshly killed doe, and a hound 'unfit for him to keep' which Thynne had destroyed. Thynne had the house watched and Roe was seized at his return, carried before a magistrate and imprisoned. Meanwhile Thynne's interrogations of the keepers finally revealed that Pearse had known of the poaching all along but claimed he had refused to take part and had even threatened from time to time to betray it if they did not desist, that another keeper Heyter was a confederate of Roe in the enterprise from the beginning, and that a third keeper, Fry, had refused bribes of a share and held aloof but had not reported the attempt to suborn him. To all of this Roe simply replied that Pearse had tempted him into poaching, and that Fry was a poacher himself who had supplied him with rabbits. Thynne, who suspected that Pearse had originally been a confederate but had become alienated from his accomplices by not getting a proper share, indignantly described his investigation as a discovery of 'roguery' by keepers and others 'related to your house' worse than had ever been in any other place. His short acquaintance with the county had already persuaded him that the 'ordinariest sort of people' were 'the worst of men', but he had held a better opinion of his master's servants. 'They having thus failed me I shall trust no more to any' he grimly concluded.[29]

It was one thing to investigate poaching successfully and even to make an arrest of the poachers. Unhappily for the stewards involved, this rarely proved the end of the matter. From the point of view of the landowner the laws were feeble, and law enforcement was feebler even at the level of the courts. The poachers were resolute and well aware of the weakness of the laws, which they were apt to exploit, and many were capable of violence and intimidation against their equals (who might otherwise be tempted to testify against them), and even toward their superiors and victims if they considered their investigations posed a serious threat. In this respect one large-scale fish poacher over-reached himself for he lay in wait to ambush and shoot a steward, Captain Morgan Powell of Lord Weymouth's manor of Drayton Bassett, and having failed in this was heard to vow to accomplish Powell's death. However, hearing that Powell was threatening to have him remanded from the sessions to the assizes, his nerve broke and he came to Powell to confess his sins and in exchange for betraying his accomplices and the place of concealment of their nets, and undertaking to abandon his poaching, Powell promised 'to pass his offence by'.[30] The significance of the story is, however, that although the man was one of his master's 'grand trespassers', as Powell put it, and had actually planned to murder the steward, he suffered no penalty at law. The steward was content simply to know the culprit's accomplices, seize their nets and obtain a promise of good behaviour. The objective was to break up the gang and stop its depredations not to achieve convictions in court or exact punishment for past misdeeds.

Convictions were difficult to obtain because the onus of proof was heavily on the plaintiff. The justices could not convict on hearsay evidence.

[29] William Thynne to Sir James Thynne, 20 and 21 February 1659, Thynne ix, fos. 91–3.
[30] Powell to Weymouth, 11 January 1686, Thynne xxviii, fo. 122.

The steward must produce two witnesses to the fact, and in poaching cases that almost inevitably meant that the steward had to obtain confessions from two accomplices who were prepared to inform on the ringleaders in order to achieve a lighter penalty or, and this was more likely, no penalty at all. If the ringleader had been captured, strenuous efforts would be made to get him to name his accomplices with offers of lighter penalties or at least to bail him from an uncomfortable, often unhealthy imprisonment prior to the hearing of the case. Unhappily stewards suffered a double disadvantage: the simples, whether poachers or not, demonstrated what a later age would define as 'class solidarity' and the gentles, who included the justices themselves, often did not for reasons which are examined below. Moreover, all simples were inhibited by fear of reprisals even when they were prepared to betray secrets to the stewards. Thus Captain Powell in October 1685 had to report disconsolately that while two informers had actually witnessed two poachers, including a young man called Smart, shooting pigeons the previous winter, he could not persuade them to swear to it in court because they feared that Smart's father, who was very thick with a local justice, would swear against them in revenge. Meanwhile the steward raided their houses and seized two or three guns and 'divers little purse nets' which Powell believed to be for taking hares. Here was a skirmish won no doubt but no conviction had been achieved. So bold were poachers and so little in awe of the processes of the law that, as the steward of Lord Wharton informed Sir John Lowther's steward on one occasion, the deer stealers had been active in Wharton's park even while they were on remand to appear at the next sessions for past forays. The steward, Hugh Wharton, was urging that Lowther, who was a justice, should be particularly severe with them or Lord Wharton's game would be quite destroyed.[31] This awareness of the law's weakness encouraged imprisoned poachers to resist the temptations of betraying their comrades. William Thynne found the arch-poacher Roe resolutely silent, apart from impudently declaring that he had been 'a knave to [Sir James] already and will not be a knave to more of his friends by confessing them', a response Thynne must have found peculiarly aggravating.[32] With the poacher-keeper Heyter Thynne was no more successful, although he refrained from dismissing him for some time in the vain hope that this deceptive appearance of forgiveness would move him to confess.

William Thynne's experiences with the Longleat poachers, and his

[31] Hugh Wharton to William Atkinson, steward of Lowther, 3 January 1681, Lonsdale D/Lons/L, Agents Letters 1/4.

[32] William Thynne to Sir James Thynne, 28 February 1659, Thynne ix, fo. 95. On an earlier occasion another poacher incarcerated as a consequence of Thynne's vigilance had sworn he would lie in prison for the rest of his life before he would betray his accomplices. Thynne ix, fo. 66.

problems in successfully prosecuting them, occurred at the very beginning of the period here considered. By happy chance a similar episode shortly after its close provides an apt comparison. Interestingly, it proves a comparison with little contrast for the underlying similarities are more striking than the differences of detail. In the early eighteenth century Sir George Savile's great Nottinghamshire estate based on his mansion and park at Rufford was an obvious target for poachers. As chief steward, Thomas Smith had the duty of defending it, investigating crimes committed against it and of doing all he could to bring about a successful prosecution of offenders. Contemplating his efforts in 1717, it is soon clear that he faced similar problems to his Longleat equivalent nearly sixty years earlier. Sir George Savile, in addition to his deer, had fish ponds which poaching gangs were prepared to drain to get at the fish. At least twice Savile had a dam cut in the period 1715–17 in order to steal the carp from the artificial ponds the dams created. In February 1717 discovering that Savile's 'little stew pond' had been robbed, Smith rode with a band of estate servants to a village well known to be a haunt of poachers. They had a mixed reception as they began searching the houses, one of the suspects' wives 'exceeded the scolds of Billinsgate' (*sic*) and bestowed blows on the keeper's man. The searches were all fruitless, but within a few weeks Smith and other estate servants had a very clear picture of the poaching gang responsible. The leader of the gang was a man called Widdison, who chiefly operated with two accomplices, Beesly and Alwood. Widdison seems to have occupied the same place in Smith's nightmares which Richard Roe had occupied in William Thynne's two generations earlier. Four months after the stew-pond robbery Widdison was in gaol serving a three-month sentence for poaching in the fishponds of John Digby of Mansfield Woodhouse, a neighbouring estate. A year earlier he had been convicted of poaching deer in Savile's park but Savile had reprieved him from gaol on condition of good behaviour, an act of clemency both Savile and his steward bitterly regretted because of his subsequent crimes. These they had good reason to believe included breaking dams and stealing fish on at least two occasions, including the stew-pond incident of the previous February. Both Savile and Smith believed that for the better preservation of the estate Widdison must be kept in gaol for as long as possible and certainly for at least a year after the expiration of his three-month sentence. There were two possible ways to accomplish this: prove against him his more recent crimes, or have him gaoled for the crime for which he had already been convicted a year earlier but which he had been 'forgiven'. Smith as steward had three functions: the first was to carry out an investigation of Widdison's suspected crimes which hopefully would lead to a successful prosecution; secondly, to use all the influence which the prestige of his position as his master's surrogate could furnish on the local magistrates to ensure their full co-operation; and finally, if the investigation failed, to advise his distant master whether or not to revive the old conviction.

For the investigation, like Thynne in 1659, Smith used 'information received'. He took his informer, one Lynly, to Justice Digby, and Lynly answered freely all the questions Digby and Smith put to him, but unfortunately for Savile's cause could not 'lay anything to Widdison's charge' that he had himself witnessed. His evidence was hearsay, derived from one of Widdison's accomplices, Alwood, who had told Lynly that he, Widdison and Beesly had eighteen months earlier sold a man a horseload of venison from Rufford Park, killing four bucks to make up the load, and had killed two or three other bucks for themselves.[33] At about the same time Alwood was also involved with the same confederates and others in an attempt to cut one of Savile's dams. However, Lynly assured them that although Alwood knew all about the poaching-ring's activities he would never be persuaded to confess anything. Smith decided to have Alwood hunted down and brought before Digby at the earliest opportunity. Meanwhile Smith, as a result of his cordial discussions with Digby, felt able to assure his master that the justice 'continues desirous to discover and punish these rogues'. A week later Smith visited Widdison and Beesly in gaol and questioned them for some hours but they proved 'close' and would confess to nothing.[34] Both denied selling horseloads of deer, breaking dams or the latest robbery of the stew pond, and Beesly denied ever confessing to Justice Digby that he had once killed a deer in Rufford Park. While at the gaol Smith confirmed the gloomy fact that, since Widdison and Beesly were there because of their conviction for robbing Justice Digby's fish pond, 'which in the rigour is but three months' imprisonment with security for good behaviour', they would be out in five weeks, and would then be very hard to retake. In his desperation Smith actually suggested to Widdison that he might prefer to approach Sir George direct (in order to confess) and offered him Savile's address which Widdison 'seemed pleased with and took the directions in writing'.

Needless to say, nothing came of this optimistic suggestion but Savile himself favoured sending Widdison to gaol for the offence he had 'forgiven' a year earlier. Smith consulted Digby about this, tracking him down at a stag hunt with the Marquis of Granby and Lord Lexington, and the two men conferred on horseback but Digby did not recommend the option of renouncing a 'forgiveness' once given. As Smith sadly advised his master, to

---

[33] An Alwood was later arrested but acquitted for lack of evidence. He was almost certainly the same man.

[34] Bilsthorpe is a village 2 or 3 miles to the south of Rufford, and part of the Lumley (Earl of Scarborough) estates.

imprison Widdison now for the old offence would 'ring through the country strangely' for, although the mercy was conditional on his good behaviour, the country people would not consider that. Moreover, it would 'beget so much ill blood in him and his crew as to make me fear they would study revenge to your dwellings, etc.' He apologised for his 'timorousness' but said he could not help it when he considered that 'such rogues had no check but dare do anything of mischief whenever opportunity admits'. Smith's anxieties may seem exaggerated but country houses were notoriously vulnerable to fire in ordinary circumstances and so were peculiarly vulnerable to arsonists. Moreover, some poachers were aggressive enough to attack the dwellings of their victims with little or no provocation at all. Lord Weymouth leased several rabbit warrens to various tenants, all of whom regretted they had ever taken them because Warminster men poached them day and night. Three of them came into a warren leased by one Morley in broad daylight and when Morley tried to stop them they threatened him with a gun. They came the following day with a larger band which encountered Morley's wife and their leader tried to kill a little dog she had with her, and that night the gang returned and attacked Morley's house, trying to lift the door off its hinges with their staves, and breaking in the windows in their efforts to get at the warrener. Not surprisingly Morley was one of the warreners who had no intention of renewing his lease.[35]

It is not the aggressiveness of the poachers which is so surprising, nor their tendency to stick together in the face of the investigations of their victims, but rather the inability of the landowning class to unite to suppress them. There appears to be a complex web of reasons for this. For example, Digby, a justice, a landowner himself who had been a victim of Widdison's poaching, had promised to do all he could to secure Widdison's further imprisonment at the sessions if any proof could be obtained against him. Far from doing so a year or so later, as Smith discovered to his great indignation, Digby had appointed Widdison as a forest keeper which seems to have been some sort of public employment, possibly in the royal forests. As a result he was trespassing in Savile's forests again, although this time under the excuse that he was ensuring that none shot or abused his straying red deer. He did not himself carry a gun but his boon companions did, and had shot pheasants and other small game. One of them was the steward of Sir Brian Broughton's Lincolnshire estates, which suggests that stewards could not even trust their fellow stewards. Certainly they could not rely on their neighbours because Sir Brian Broughton was typical of many landowners in that he was prepared to protect his tenants against prosecutions for poaching (Widdison was his tenant), and all landowners tended to

---

[35] Thomas Allen, Longleat, to Lord Weymouth, 16 December 1687, Thynne xxiv, fo. 106.

protect members of their household and their estate servants. They might rebuke or fine or even beat servants who committed such offences, they might dismiss them from their service, but they would not allow outside authorities to interfere between 'master and man' if they could possibly avoid it. Captain Powell uttered a classic expression of this view when he reproved a landowner for opening suit against some of Lord Weymouth's tenants to eject them from some land they were occupying, observing that it was not 'convenient' Weymouth's tenants should be sued without his consent. The complainant promptly stopped all proceedings for that term.[36]

Since the landowners were also members of the local bench of justices, getting convictions could be very difficult even when the person charged was not a member of their household, for he was unlikely to have acted alone and they might be aware or at least suspect that members of their household were involved with him.[37] If he was convicted, and especially if he was sentenced to a year in gaol, he might betray these accomplices to his advantage and their employers' embarrassment. Some justices were liable to other fears. They were susceptible to the pressures of public opinion even from the simples and they feared to convict if the hard evidence appeared at all flimsy in case they were sued for damages in the civil court by the men they had sentenced. This situation had plagued William Thynne in 1659. He had hoped to put the arch-poacher Roe in gaol where the rigour of confinement might persuade him to confess and reveal his accomplices. However, although the magistrate imposed a heavy fine of £15, he was only held in an inn overnight for the next morning friends 'from around Hornisham' appeared and effected his release by providing five substantial guarantees that the fine would be paid within two months. Justice Rideout excused this leniency on the grounds that his conviction and sentence of Roe were on mere 'supposition' and a favour to Sir James, there being no witnesses to the actual poaching, and feared he would have been sued by his prisoner if he had not released him. Significantly, on an earlier occasion, Thynne had mourned the death of a local justice called Ash, observing to Sir James: 'I doubt we shall want him. Other of the justices may be as willing to serve you as he yet not so bold to punish a knave.'[38]

This description of the problems faced by stewards in defending their

---

[36] Powell to Weymouth, 19 June 1680, Thynne xxviii, fo. 13.
[37] Smith suspected that this consideration had influenced the actions of a Justice Beacher in the Widdison case.
[38] Thynne had seized the greyhound of a Warminster man which he suspected had been used to run down a deer at Longleat park, but he had had the man examined before Justice Melecott without avail. If it had been before Justice Ash 'I do believe he would have convicted him upon such evidence I brought against him for stealing a deer'. William to Sir James Thynne, 14 February 1659, Thynne ix, fo. 89.

bailiwicks against poachers of all types demonstrates that there were severe limitations on the hegemony of a landlord even if he was a wealthy nobleman. That vulnerable target, the great estate, could only be protected within the law, and the law was often more helpful to poachers than to their prosecutors. That was certainly not the law's intent but the requirements of proof made confession or turning state's evidence by at least one of the poachers essential for a conviction, for hearsay evidence alone would not convict. Solidarity amongst the simples when in confrontation with the gentle is once more in evidence, and it is clear that public opinion was a force to which the steward was sensitive. Breaking the unwritten code of landlord behaviour, the taking back a clemency once offered, would have a serious impact here, as well as being likely to provoke a violent reaction on the part of the poachers which the lack of modern law enforcement institutions made a very real menace. Better lose a few deer and carp without redress than see the mansion or even its outbuildings in flames. More significantly it was an important function of the steward to promote harmony, or pursue policies likely to further it rather than dangerously erode it, and to maintain 'friendship' and goodwill among his master's neighbours whatever their social rank, so that his master's interest in the county should be at least as well preserved as his deer park and his forest walks. Where the master owned a deer park, extensive fishing rights to lease or game-infested moors the steward had to steer his craft between dangerous shoals here, and it took a man of considerable judgment, experience and local reputation to fulfil his constabulary duties effectively and simultaneously keep on good terms with his master's neighbours.

12

Exploiting the estate

To me [the ropeworks] seems to be a thing that might ... be made to turn to account if right managed, and in time much more, and that so long as the stock is sufficient to carry it on (without advancing more money unless upon an adventure to Riga which is very proper to be considered) we should not give it over.

William Gilpin, 1697[1]

The complexity of large or at least substantial estates ensured that stewards could never be mere rent collectors, negotiators of leases and seekers of tenants because their masters' estates yielded more forms of income than those which derived from tenancies and leases. Many of these other sources of income required the supervision of a man with a keen nose for business, capable of handling substantial business transactions which were often complex and demanding. Occasionally one encounters stewards, like William Gilpin at Whitehaven, who were quick to perceive potential assets and eager to exploit them on their master's behalf. In brief, some estates were well served when they were placed in the charge of a man of enterprise, a man with entrepreneurial skills. This type of steward was needed on a greater proportion of estates than might be supposed. The industrial emphasis which Sir John Lowther's coalmines gave to his estate at St Bees-Whitehaven was certainly unusual, but it was not unusual for some estate income to derive from mining royalties in regions which were rich in coal, lead, tin or copper, or for some income to derive from quarries for slate, stone and millstones. Most estates contained one or more flour mills, whether wind or water driven, and fulling mills were common enough in regions producing textiles. Of all the assets on an estate which a lord could profitably exploit, however, none was more common, and scarcely any more rewarding, than its trees.

There can have been few stewards who at one time or another did not find themselves involved in the sale of forest products. Timber for building and shipbuilding, wood for fuel, bark for tanning, were all sold profitably decade after decade. Some woods had yielded profitable 'harvests' for

[1] To Sir John Lowther, 22 December 1697, *Lowther Correspondence*, Letter 428.

centuries under careful management, using the well-tried techniques of lopping, coppicing, and replanting, both natural and contrived.[2] There would have been few if any estates in which sales of woods did not represent a valuable portion of the income during certain years. The Cholmondeley estate accounts reveal that in the year 1686 Lord Cholmondeley's woods earned a total of £566, which would represent about 10 per cent of the gross yield of the estate, and this figure was probably incomplete since not only would it only reflect wood paid for, not all wood sold, but the understewards who were responsible for the collections of different areas of the estate did not always keep accounts in which wood sales could be plainly distinguished.[3] Moreover, the estate accounts were by their nature incomplete, since they only recorded sums of money passing through the hands of the stewards and understewards which was not necessarily the total income of the Cholmondeley estate. For example, they did not record payments made directly to Cholmondeley in London by timber merchants, shipwrights or the Navy Board.[4] The importance which landowners attached to woods and their profits can be detected from the eagerness with which they demanded that wood accounts be sent up separately from the general account, and the detail they often demanded in the stewards' reports. Cholmondeley complained on one occasion at the lack of an account which showed such details as the date the account began, the number of trees felled, the girth of each tree, what money each tree had yielded or to what particular uses they had been put.[5]

Now while a landowner might employ a forester to develop this valuable asset and keepers to help the steward to defend it from fuel-hungry tenants and outside woodthieves, it was the steward who bore the responsibility for turning the woods to profit. It was a more onerous duty than might be supposed. It involved lengthy negotiation with competing purchasers, all the more prolonged and frustrating because no decision could be taken and no agreement sealed which the distant master had not first approved. For

[2] For the history of this rural activity see Oliver Rackham's *The History of the Countryside* (London, 1986, 1990), and his *Trees and Woodland in the British Landscape* (London, 1976, 1983).

[3] A failing which was still irritating the timber's owner in 1703. 'I do find by Mr Brescie that he jumbles two accounts together, that of the wood money ... and the other that Mr Vernon charged him with ... in short I can make neither head nor tail of what he says', and he charged his chief steward to keep the wood account according to a previously prescribed method. Lord Cholmondeley to Adams, 24 October 1703, Cholmondeley DCH/L/42.

[4] Cholmondeley received £50 from Robert Driver, a Lambeth shipwright, during 1700, and above £460 from sales to the navy, but neither figure appears in the accounts for that or the following year. See Cholmondeley DCH/Estate Accounts.

[5] Cholmondeley to Adams, 11 December 1703, Cholmondeley DCH/L/42. Similarly Fitzwilliam wrote to his steward: 'I have no wood books neither for the last winter nor the winter before. Pray let them be writ out for me.' To Guybon, 4 November 1697, Fitzwilliam F(M)C 1019; *Fitzwilliam Correspondence*, Letter 39.

stewards only recently appointed it could prove especially nerve-wracking, particularly if the steward found himself dealing with competing gentlemen who had ways of making their resentment felt should a valuable timber contract be awarded to a competitor. Such fears could make the choice of a buyer rather more complicated than simply selling to the customer who offered the highest price. Early in his service with Thomas Thynne, the future Lord Weymouth, Thomas Hawkes at Stretton begged his master to conclude his timber bargain himself with a potential buyer named Foley, rather than leave the matter to Hawkes. By this means, Hawkes rather timorously argued, he would escape 'censure' if things went wrong subsequently. In fact his nervousness was due to the fact that an influential neighbour, Sir Richard Corbett, had 'sent' to him to recommend two potential purchasers, Mr Walker and Colonel 'Screvin'. They were deeply involved in the timber trade but would not pay as favourable a rate as Foley. However, if he ignored Corbett's urgings they would 'sting at' him for 'bringing in Mr Foley to take the meat off their trenchers', and although they would not be 'palpable in it yet it is possible as well as common in our country [Shropshire] to work such revenges privately by clapping offices upon those that displease them'. Finally, he could not conclude an affair of such importance without the help of the steward at neighbouring Minsterley, Richard Clayton, who was ill and could not come to assist. To sweeten the pill Hawkes had arranged for a lawyer named Powell, who lived near Temple Bar, to seek useful insights from a friend heavily involved in the trade who would furnish information useful to Thynne when he negotiated his bargain with Foley.[6]

When timber was to be felled and sold there were significant decisions to be made. Should a lower price be accepted from a more reliable paymaster, or a higher price from one who was notoriously slow? Should a bargain be struck with one timber merchant which, although less profitable to the landowner in the short term, might help sustain him and prevent his being bought out by local competitors? If these competitors succeeded in engrossing the trade they might be able to dictate terms to the landowner in the long term. On one occasion Thomas Hawkes discovered that the local rivals of Foley, the timber merchant and iron master, were negotiating to buy out all his interests in Shropshire because they anticipated that he was about to sign a major contract for Thynne's woods. He hastened to warn his master that this takeover appeared to depend on Foley's bargain with

---

[6] Hawkes concluded that he would negotiate the contract if Thynne insisted on it, so long as he had the help of Clayton or some other experienced man, and would strike as good a bargain as he could, 'with the proviso that you shall excuse me from what offices shall be imposed on me on that account for I fear nothing else'. Thomas Hawkes, 21 October 1673, Thynne xx, fo. 124.

him so it was vital that Thynne 'played his cards rightly'. He should persuade Foley not to conclude the sale to his rivals of all his Shropshire timber and ironworking concerns, and certainly not before he had bought and carried off Thynne's timber, for after the takeover there would only be poor prices offered if Foley's chief rival, Walker, engrossed the trade.[7]

Stewards also had to investigate and then advise their masters whether timber merchants should be dealt with at all or whether it would be better to deal directly with the real consumers: shipbuilders, the navy, etc., for timber, and the local tanners for bark. In theory cutting out the middle man should be more profitable because the consumer was accustomed to paying a high price to the middleman for timber which the merchant had bought cheaply from the landowners. However, such buyers bought only to fill their needs, not in great bulk, so that such direct selling would involve many sales in small parcels. The merchants usually bought in one or more large sales, perhaps under a contract for felling to be carried out over several years, with a guaranteed quantity to be taken at a fixed price. Moreover, they were more reliable and certainly speedier paymasters than the tradesmen who could rarely pay for their raw materials until they had sold their products. Thomas Hawkes noted that he had been correct to insist on holding Foley to his articles when that timber merchant seemed eager for Hawkes to deal directly with one of Foley's customers, because while the customer offered sixteen shillings a cord he also saw that the customer would only buy the very best timber, leaving much timber behind. By his agreement Foley had to take all that was felled at the agreed price.[8] The advantages of selling to a large timber merchant could be very tempting (particularly to the steward one might think), but there was naturally a considerable fall in price if the buyer shouldered all the labour and expense of extracting the timber.

Early in 1701 Lord Cholmondeley, who had suffered greatly from his dealings both with a Lambeth shipwright and with the navy for his Cheshire timber, found himself confronted by a remarkable offer from a considerable timber merchant named Howard. Howard would measure the trees and choose those trunks and branches which could provide timber 8 inches square. He would pay down up to £500 and his price for the timber was at a rate of £2 a load of 50 square feet a load (that is, a ton). He would fell, square, and carry away all his timber at his own expense. The Lambeth shipwright, Driver, who introduced the merchant to Cholmondeley, assured William Adams, Cholmondeley's steward, that the price in the

---

7 Hawkes, 30 September 1674, Thynne xx, fo. 190.
8 Hawkes, 21 April 1675, Thynne xx, fo. 227. For much enlightening discussion of these various problems see Hawkes, 18 December 1673, 17 April, 23 May, 30 September 1674, 22 February, 4 March 1675, Thynne xx, fos. 133, 156, 162, 190, 210.

circumstances was too high, particularly as he was promising to take £1,500 to £2,000 worth and that Cholmondeley could never hope to find such a 'chapman' again. It is revealing of the steward's significance in such estate business that Howard would not even come to view the timber unless Adams as chief steward was prepared to recommend the bargain to his master, and Cholmondeley would not close the bargain in any event until he had received the advice of his steward (reinforced by that of his cousin Cholmondeley at Vale Royal).[9] The negotiations continued during 1701. The price offered may have seemed low to Cholmondeley because Driver had agreed to pay £3 4s a load for his timber, but that had been felled, cut into thwarts and planks, and transported to Chester all at Cholmondeley's expense.

There was one customer landowners were prepared to deal directly with simply because this customer bought in hugh quantities with a thirst for timber which seemed unquenchable. This was the navy. However, there could be drawbacks even to this customer, in spite of the potential profits, and certainly dealing with the navy did not make the task of selling his lord's timber less arduous for a steward. Firstly, there was no bargain to be made with the navy akin to that offered by Howard the timber merchant. While the navy might supply a 'purchaser' who actually supervised the felling, the costs of paying the timber-getters' wages was born by the seller. When Lord Weymouth was selling timber on a large scale to the navy in 1704 chief steward Thomas Mainewaring found himself carrying £50 or more a week from Drayton manor in Staffordshire to Weymouth's woods about Caus and Minsterley in Shropshire to pay the forty-two sawyers ('21 pairs') who were felling and shaping the timber into planks under the indefatigable directions of Williamson, the navy 'purchaser'. The landowner also had to arrange the carriage of the timber to the nearest port from which it could be shipped to a navy yard either by calling on his tenants to provide teams for the work (free labour and 'gift carrying' under the terms of their leases) or pay for outsiders. This could furnish the steward with many problems since estates were not usually conveniently located close to a port. (Sir John Lowther of Whitehaven had the port but lacked the forests. What timber he had was consumed by his mines.) However, transport was a general problem and will be considered more fully shortly.

The chief headache in selling to the navy was that no payment could be

---

[9] 'His proposals are so very low that I dare say nothing to him till I have consulted with my Cousin Cholmondeley and you', so Adams must ride over to his cousin at Vale Royal to discuss the offer, and then send some draft proposals to his master showing the lowest rate Cholmondeley should take. Cholmondeley, 1 February 1701, Robert Driver, same date, Cholmondeley DCH/K/3/4; Robert Driver to Adams, 1 February 1701, DCH/L/49.

received by the hungry landowner until the wood had been shipped on a vessel dispatched by the navy and no timber would be so shipped until it had first been inspected by a naval surveyor, who would reject all plank or other timber he deemed unfit for the navy's use. This placed a heavy burden of responsibility on the steward's shoulders. He would be anxious that his master did not meet the cost of moving timber from the estate to the port only to have it expensively rejected on its arrival, and so would try to have the surveyor inspect it as early in the journey from forest to port as possible. John Mainewaring soon realised that there was no hope of getting the surveyor to the rear of the Long Mynd, but was determined that his master should not risk having timber rejected on the wharf at Bristol. As a compromise he succeeded in having the surveyor come to Shrewsbury where the timber was to be shipped to Bristol on Severn rivercraft.[10] When the surveyor arrived not only had the steward to be there, he had to provide labourers who would bring out the plank for inspection. He must also ensure that he matched whatever favours other timber sellers extended to the surveyor. In 1704 Mainewaring made careful enquiries to find what another steward did on such occasions and discovered that he met all the surveyor's expenses, even though, as Mainewaring put it, 'he comes upon the Queen's account and is allowed all manner of charges' but the other steward's careful generosity 'makes him very easy with him I find'. There was also the delicate question of whether to slip him a gratuity and how much ('I suppose it can not be less than five guineas').[11] All this, gratuity and all, seems straightforward enough, although involving much hard riding and consumption of time for a steward who was based in Staffordshire, not Shropshire. However, the problem was not always so straightforward, as William Adams and his master had discovered a few years earlier. It was a difficult piece of organisation in an era predating telegraph or telephone to assemble at one place a steward from a rural estate, a consignment of timber (possibly from a distant part of the estate or even a distant branch of it), the ship freighted by the navy and a surveyor who would travel to the port from Plymouth overland. The surveyor might not turn up for weeks, even months at a time, leaving the timber dangerously exposed at the port. William Adams' experiences with Thomas Netherton between November 1700 and May 1701 moved his choleric master to vow that he would never supply the navy again. 'When you have got a note upon the Navy Office for the money for that timber you may assure that spark [Netherton] from me that the pitiful usage I have received

---

[10] 'Mr Williamson thinks the surveyor will not refuse anything he sends. If your lordship can be secure in that point it will be a great one gained.' Mainewaring, 8 March 1704, Thynne xx, fo. 334.

[11] Mainewaring, 2 September 1704, Thynne xx, fo. 349.

shall be a sufficient warning for the future not to deal with them at any rate whatsoever.' As to a gratuity Cholmondeley would not allow him sixpence though it 'was to keep him from starving'.[12]

Whether for the public or private sale, large contracts involved heavy labour for a steward. When John Mainewaring was organising his master's naval contract the sheer scale of the enterprise made heavy demands upon his time and organising ability. Since not all the timber would prove suitable for the navy there would be a very substantial amount of saleable timber to market outside the contract, together with a considerable volume of cord wood, that is, branches and twigs. Williamson, the naval purchaser, wanted the timber to remain in the wood until the following year to season, but Mainewaring was very conscious of the dangers of theft and other damage which would be a loss to his master whilst it remained on his master's ground and insisted on getting it to Shrewsbury the same summer. It was often part of the steward's duties to oversee the felling, usually carried out by workmen operating on behalf of the purchaser who were always liable to steal some of the wood themselves if not supervised, which again was a loss which the vendor would bear.[13] He also had to visit the woods with the purchaser or his agents and carefully mark the trees which were to form part of the contract that year, and where timber was being sold by the square foot to measure and establish how many square feet each tree contained. It was necessary to establish which trees bore merchantable bark and which did not. Moreover, it was necessary to ensure that the tree felling did not damage other trees which formed no part of the contract. Indeed, on occasion secondary contracts had to be entered into with other buyers to fell less valuable parts of the woods which would otherwise impede the main felling and be damaged by it. All such activity usually took many arduous journeys on horseback and much difficulty in arranging such meetings with the customer and his representatives who often lived miles from the steward. He had also to arrange for the presence of other estate servants who might themselves live a distance away but who could help with selecting and marking the trees and with estimating their timber content, and who could also act as witnesses to what was agreed. Finally,

---

[12] To Adams, 8 May 1701, Cholmondeley DCH/L/28. When he discovered that although Netherton's excuse for tardiness was that there was not enough timber for him to come and inspect, he left 20 tons behind because the vessel was not large enough to remove all at once, he was moved to one of his more explosive outbursts. He had complained to the Admiralty and if Netherton was not sacked he was resolved to petition the Commons against him that 'they might know what sort of rascals are employed in the King's service thus to discourage gentlemen from finding the navy with timber'. 22 May 1701, DCH/L/28.

[13] 'I go constantly once a week thither and conceive neighbours and workmen are too apt to steal the wood.' Hawkes, 7 May 1675, Thynne xx, fo. 238.

the steward, rather than the buyer, was often saddled with the responsibility of arranging for the carriage of the timber either directly to the timber merchant's yard or to some port of embarkation on the nearest river or on the coast.

Reporting that he had sent his master's timber down to Tewkesbury by the Severn from Shrewsbury, Samuel Peers observed that he had encountered a 'great deal of trouble in getting it to Shrewsbury for our country is gone very weak for carriages'.[14] Almost thirty years later, with the same forests fulfilling the substantial naval contract already referred to, John Mainewaring was deeply engaged in finding carriage to Shrewsbury for most of the timber before the harvest, and for the remainder before Michaelmas. The first date was significant because the steward hoped to mobilise his master's tenants to employ their teams in this labour in fulfilment of the boon days specified in their leases, and later in the summer the tenants would need their teams to bring in their harvest. As for Michaelmas, that date heralded the onset of autumn rains and, as he reported, 'when the roads grow dirty they cannot pass with it, especially the tenants whose teams are weak, and outcomers will not carry under 9s or 10s a ton'. With Mainewaring based in Staffordshire in 1704, affairs at Minsterley and Stretton in Shropshire were managed by the understewards who had replaced Peers, now retired, and Hawkes who had recently died. Mainewaring would not trust these inexperienced newcomers to oversee such a work as this and therefore arranged to be at Minsterley at midsummer to 'forward the work'. He feared the tenants could not carry such a quantity and so he would be compelled to hire outsiders who must only carry on summer roads because of the expense. Boggy roads meant half loads which made for expensive carriage for such heavy building materials as stone and timber.[15] Getting the tenants' teams organised proved no bargain, for he found only four teams on the manor capable of carrying such loads, and it was only with great difficulty that he could get them to act, for the tenants 'are a parcel of drones and hate work they are not used to'. Mercifully the steward did not have to oversee the timber's loading at Bristol, which would be accomplished by others, but he had to make sure his master appreciated the problems involved so that he could send appropriate instructions to his Bristol agents. It took the 'trowmen' who transported the timber via the Severn to Bristol three weeks there and back, so that either timber must be warehoused in Bristol or the ship must wait

---

[14] Peers, 31 August 1675, Thynne xx, fo. 258.
[15] Mainewaring to Weymouth, 12 June 1704, Thynne xxviii, fo. 339. 'If there has fallen as much rain in the country as we have had here there will be no carting of stone ... as yet unless you would have half loads which is not in my interest.' Lord Fitzwilliam to Guybon, 28 April 1698; Fitzwilliam F(M)C 1038; *Fitzwilliam Correspondence*, Letter 57.

several weeks for its lading to be completed, and both alternatives would be 'chargeable'.[16]

It is not surprising, therefore, that stewards often contemplated the duty of selling large quantities of timber with aversion, often pleaded total ignorance and incapacity for carrying it out, or even demanded that their salary be augmented to compensate. Samuel Peers simply observed that 'for my part it is a thing I want judgment in' but Thomas Hawkes, perhaps bolstered by his status as a close kinsman of his master, went much further. Observing that his salary was so inconsiderable that if the miles he rode each week on behalf of his master were computed it 'would scarcely yield me the ordinary wages of a very butcher's boy, being ordinarily a penny a mile' so unless his master would allow him £20 a year for the 'wood service' both for the time past and the future Thynne must seek someone else, 'for under I am resolved I will not take'. Only very strong feelings could have induced such an outburst from a steward to his master in this period.[17]

As has been mentioned, stewards often had responsibilities which involved minerals and quarrying. Most landowners preferred to pursue the safe if only moderately remunerative road of leases and royalties rather than investing themselves. It is clear from the mere handful of letters which have survived of the correspondence of William Cock of Redruth to Lady Arundel of Trerice, that investment in copper mines in the early modern period was a risky business. Both Cock and his mistress had invested in a mine which, on the evidence of these letters (haphazardly surviving over a period of fourteen years), rarely yielded much ore and when it did the sale (considering the investment as a whole) did not repay the cost of extraction. The current Lord Arundel, however, who was son or stepson to Lady Arundel and at odds with her, received substantial profit from the mine because as the landowner he received a proportion of the ore as a royalty without risking any investment himself.[18] Stewards like Thomas Hawkes at Church Stretton or Samuel Peers at Minsterley, managing estates for Thomas Thynne which extended into opposite sides of the ore-bearing Long Mynd in Shropshire, would encourage prospectors to seek for minerals on their master's land and regularly report to him on their activities, knowing that success would bring him one-sixth or one-seventh of the ore. Even that great mining magnate James Lowther was prepared to lease the lead mines on his Westmorland manor of Hartsop on a royalty basis.[19]

---

[16] A 'trow' was a type of sailing vessel used on the Severn. Mainewaring, 24 June 1704, Thynne xxviii, fo. 341v.

[17] Peers, 1 February 1675; Hawkes, 12 January 1676, Thynne xx, fos. 204, 269.

[18] See Cock's letters of 11 February, 4 November 1706, 10 April 1707, 1 April, 19 August 1708, 13 December 1710, 16 August 1716, Galway (Arundel) 12,322.

[19] 'Two Cumberland men ... and two Derbyshire men ... have made ... a proposal of taking my leadmines at Hartsop and either allowing me every 8th or 9th bing of ore, or else

Similarly Sir Daniel Fleming of Rydal Hall earned royalties for copper mines in the ore-rich Coniston district. Although Fleming was a stay-at-home landlord, these were negotiated for him by his steward, Thomas Banks, because Fleming's manors were widely scattered across Westmorland and Cumberland.

Compared with the labour of harvesting his master's timber a steward would find leasing quarries and negotiating mining royalties a light task, although even this could involve spending a considerable time on horseback travelling over bad roads in all weathers to remote corners of his master's estates. For the steward whose master was an active participant in mines on a large scale, and even more where his master was the sole owner, the labour could be so considerable that it was more than one man could cope with. In these circumstances a colliery steward would be appointed who might well have other interests and sources of income but whose duty to the landowner was solely managing the collieries and marketing their harvest. Nevertheless, since an estate steward's responsibilities embraced every aspect of the estate, no matter what other servants might be employed, he would have a general oversight of the mines and be expected to report on their progress and the prospects of profit, and offer detailed advice about future operations. Thomas Tickell at Whitehaven was a particularly good example of this kind of steward. Tickell's master believed that two heads (and pairs of eyes) were better than one and expected his steward to enter the mines, discuss every detail with the colliery manager, and provide him with his own reports and opinions quite independently of the man ostensibly employed for that purpose. Moreover, it was twenty years after Tickell's appointment as estate steward before Lowther finally found a man really capable of discharging the full responsibilities of a colliery steward (and even he turned out untrustworthy in the end and was much in Lowther's debt when he was finally dismissed by Lowther's son and successor). This meant that the estate steward had to do much of the work which was really the business of another and in the interregnums between colliery stewards he had to do it all.

During the period of Tickell's stewardship the Lowther mines expanded from a series of small 'bear mouths' and primitive shafts of little depth, to one of deep mines drained by expensive levels. Indeed, such was the scale of the operations that after Lowther's death his son James would startle the region by installing a 'fire engine' (that is, an early atmospheric steam engine) to pump out the mines, a very expensive capital investment. The chief but far from the sole supplier of coal to Dublin from his port of

working them for wages. The latter is hardly worth mentioning but I would be glad to know your opinion of the former.' James Lowther to William Gilpin, 12 September 1706, D/Lons/W2/1/39.

Whitehaven (of which he was the sole ground landlord), Lowther depended on Tickell and his successor Gilpin as well as his longest-serving colliery steward, John Gale, for guidance as to where to sink shafts and drive new levels and adits and where to try to make purchases of adjoining lands or at least the right to extract the coal under them. As Lowther once remarked to Tickell, who was worried by the responsibilities he bore and wished his master present to judge matters for himself: 'were I there I could only direct according to advice given me upon the place'.[20] This of course would always have been Lowther's reply to any suggestion that he could not expect successfully to establish, expand and manage a large-scale coal industry from a residence 300 miles away. In fact, his stewards made it possible for him to found a business which was to make his son one of the wealthiest men in England.

They did not succeed in doing this without Thomas Tickell shouldering a heavy burden. Lowther's increasing dominance in coal extraction aroused the fears of the shipowners of Whitehaven who believed that a Lowther monopoly would bring higher prices to Lowther and lower profits to themselves. Local colliery owners were often able to undercut Lowther's prices because their small-scale operations were inexpensive to operate, or to dispute the boundaries of his underground workings or to connive at sabotage (a form of warfare which the steward himself adopted in retaliation). Lowther's answer was always to seek to buy out competitors although this was never easy, sometimes impossible and involved his stewards in lengthy and often tortuous negotiations.[21] Not only did the stewards have to negotiate the purchase they had to estimate the value of the coal stock in the ground, discuss with the mine foreman the usefulness of the purchase in obstructing the drainage levels of neighbouring mines, or in facilitating the drainage of their own, or its possibilities as a beachhead in a particular locality in which further coal-bearing lands might be acquired. They then had the difficult task of determining a reasonable price, although often if Lowther decided he must have the ground he had to pay unreasonable prices for it.[22] The estate steward was not permitted to leave even the decision making about developments underground entirely to the colliery steward, but must report to his master and offer advice about such weighty matters as the inclination of 'dykes' (breaks in the seam of coal), how best to relocate a vanished seam, where to make exploratory bores and how to interpret their often confusing messages. While it was the colliery steward's

[20] Lowther to Tickell, 16 July 1678, Lonsdale D/Lons/W2/1/13.
[21] See also above Chapter 6.
[22] 'The Case of Sir John Lowther, Bart.' in Lonsdale D/Lons/W, Whitehaven, various papers, item 10; Lowther, 14 January 1679; Tickell, 15 January 1680, Lonsdale D/Lons/W2/1/14, and 15; Gilpin, 25 November 1695, *Lowther Correspondence*, Letter 259. In general see Churches, 'Lowther and Whitehaven', Chapter 2.

responsibility to ensure that the coal, once extracted, flowed efficiently from mine to harbour to supply the collier fleet, it was the estate steward's duty to keep a watchful eye on this vital link and step in if any incompetence or unforeseen situation should threaten it. The coal 'leaders', mostly operating with packhorses, were independent contractors not employees and it was important to see that a sufficient stock of horses was maintained in the neighbourhood, that the leaders carried the coal as cheaply as possible, yet not so cheaply that they melted away to the service of rival employers or to other coal-bearing regions.

Thomas Tickell had acquired some experience of mine management when he was associated with his uncle, Richard Tickell, who was in partnership with London merchants in the Earl of Northumberland's Vale of Newlands lead mines during the Protectorate. This must have stood him in good stead throughout his twenty-five years' service at Whitehaven, but especially during the years from 1678 to 1682 when he acted as colliery steward virtually unaided. It was Tickell who persuaded Lowther to send a local miner, Richard Scott, to learn the Yorkshire miners' methods and later had Lowther place him in charge of the workings underground. He also helped to arrange the importation of expert Newcastle miners to his master's pits. William Gilpin, a professional lawyer with no mining experience, could not match Tickell's skills or experience. Moreover, he was confronted by a colliery steward, John Gale, who was unrelentingly hostile to him because Gale had desired the appointment for his eldest son who had acted as estate steward for some months after Tickell's death. On the other hand, Gale was an able man of great experience so there appeared to be less need for an estate steward with mining knowledge. If Lowther insisted on detailed advice about matters underground Gilpin simply relied on the reports of Richard Scott, although he was prepared to make uncomfortable and even dangerous visits to the coal face in response to his master's urgings. His chief merit lay in his capacity for clear-sighted analysis of particular problems, which was reflected in his sage advice on the best strategy to overcome an alarming shortage of labour in 1696, or in his untangling of the legal complexities in a purchase of land and a colliery where a prior mortgage had been 'industriously concealed'.[23]

Probably Gilpin's greatest attribute in his master's eyes was his enthusiastic and ingenious promotion of various entrepreneurial activities in Whitehaven of the kind his master longed to see established there. Lowther was not particularly interested in founding new trading or manufacturing ventures for his own profit but rather for the impact they might have on his

[23] I am indebted to Dr Churches for guiding me through these intricacies. Churches' 'Lowther and Whitehaven' explores in depth Lowther's relationship with Whitehaven through the medium of his stewards.

town's growth, and also in the hope of reducing poverty by promoting industry and thereby reducing the burden of the poor rate. With these desirable objects in mind he was prepared to invest a little money to encourage a new venture, and to back his steward's entrepreneurial schemes by obtaining technical information in London. For example, Gilpin discovered that his master's mines were rich in marcasites from which copperas, used in dyeing, could be obtained. He 'brought home about two ton, made a little bed, and in half a year's time had a liquor so strong that with an easy boiling' could have great quantities of copperas. The greatest copperas works in England was at Deptford and Lowther sent him a plan of the works there and a volume of the *Philosophical Transactions* which described the process. Gilpin also sent his master specimens of iron ore and alum stone, laboured to further the production of stockings, textiles and earthenware, even importing an expert with the resonant name of Wedgwood from Burslem in what would later be called the Potteries. He also sought much detailed information about earthenware and china from his master to which Lowther apparently sent detailed answers.[24] Gilpin's initiatives often had no long-term success, but they demonstrate the range of a steward's possible functions on a highly complex estate like that of St Bees-Whitehaven.

One further role must be considered: Lowther's stewards managed their master's involvement in shipping ventures. Lowther owned a one-eighth share in a Virginia ship the *Resolution*, and therefore was an occasional importer of tobacco. However, he acquired an interest in the Scandinavian trade and later in the Baltic trade to Russia as a consequence of his steward Tickell persuading him to become a partner in one of the Whitehaven ropemaking companies.[25] (With an entrepreneurial ruthlessness worthy of a robber baron, Tickell planned to ruin a rival ropewalk by sinking a small coal shaft in the middle of their long ropewalk, but this was promptly vetoed by his master.[26]) Late in his career as an absentee landlord, partly inspired by a desire to encourage trade between his port and the Baltic, partly by the needs of the ropery, Lowther accepted Gilpin's suggestion that he should invest in ventures to import hemp, flax, tar, spars, etc. In December 1697 Gilpin observed that a voyage to Riga on Russia's Baltic coast was 'very proper to be considered'. Lowther agreed to take a share in such a voyage, and from then on the steward became a bustling entrepreneur indeed as he investigated the problems and possibilities of such a

[24] For Gilpin's very full correspondence on these and other entrepreneurial initiatives see *Lowther Correspondence, passim*.
[25] Tickell paid £41 9s 2d for Lowther's one-eighth share of the ropery on 2 April 1680, D/Lons/W Estate Accounts 1666–85, fo. 103.
[26] Tickell, 14 July, Lowther 27 July 1680, D/Lons/W2/1/15.

voyage. He dispatched his merchant brother to Newcastle to obtain intelligence from venturers there. He asked his master to discover if they needed to take their freedom from the Eastland Company as the Newcastle men did. He discussed with him whether to hire a factor at Riga or to send a supercargo on the ship who would gain experience useful in future voyages. He peered over the maps and books devoted to navigation in his master's library at Flatt Hall and tried to determine whether it would be better to carry tobacco direct to Riga or, as another Whitehaven venture was doing, carry tobacco to Holland to exchange for bills to carry from there to Riga. He had heard a gloomy prediction that anything taken to Riga for sale would cost six months waiting for payment during which the ship would probably be frozen in and miss her return. Meanwhile, in response to his many queries, Lowther sent a series of notes on the Russia trade obtained from an Eastland merchant.[27] Certainly the picture we have of Gilpin is of a busy bustling man, thoroughly relishing his entrepreneurial role, a role of which Lowther thoroughly approved and, despite his frailty and ill health, bestirred himself to support.

[27] See *Lowther Correspondence*, Appendix H. Lowther vetoed the supercargo although 'the master must be a man of good judgment'. Exports could be salt, lead, smith's coal, coarse woollen and grindstones, but the chief resource was to be dollars. The ship should bring flax, hemp always and clapboard if they could find a good market for cask. *Lowther Correspondence*, Letter 475.

The clerk of works

As I compute what the workmanship will come to when the manner of finishing it is laid down, it will certainly prevent uneasiness in your lordship when you are sure the workmen cannot wrong you. And it will save me a great deal of trouble in looking after them, for I shall take care to descibe the method in such a manner in the contract . . . that they shall want no further instructions till the work is finished.

Daniel Eaton to Lord Cardigan, 1727[1]

The era of the later Stuarts was a period of massive rebuilding or extending of mansions, stables and gardens. Tudor houses, no matter how charming to modern eyes, were characterised by low ceilings, inconveniently large dining halls, gargantuan staircases leading too often to draughty, unappealing passageways, and cluttered mullioned windows which were ill-suited to revealing increasingly elaborate gardens and grounds. Such houses were replaced by mansions on a grander scale, high ceilinged, lit by large sash windows, equipped with dining rooms which were designed to seat the family and their guests in some degree of intimacy and privacy, despite their grandeur, rather than the whole household as in earlier centuries. Architects like Wren, Hawksmoor, Vanbrugh and Talman and their less famous competitors laboured to meet the demands of noblemen and the greater gentry for elaborate seats which would not merely house them in greater comfort but also symbolise and indeed assert their wealth and their status in the county hierarchy. Some did not completely rebuild but nevertheless 'modernised' their houses or enlarged them or modified them in a variety of ways. Lord Cholmondeley chose not to demolish the old 'black and white' manor house of his ancestors but rather to clad it in new exterior walls of neo-classical design, whilst greatly modifying the interior rooms. Sir John Lowther both in the 1680s and 1690s extensively remodelled Flatt Hall, his Whitehaven residence, even though he once remarked that it could never be 'made into a seat'. His cousin celebrated his elevation to the peerage by pulling down much of the old fortified manor house at Lowther and replacing it with a pedimented, pilastered handsome mansion of three

---

[1] 3 December 1727, *Eaton Letters*, Letter 149.

storeys. Lord Weymouth scarcely needed to do much rebuilding at Longleat, although even here there were substantial modifications, but seems to have embarked on extensive remodelling at his sixteenth-century mansion at Kempsford, which in its day was reputed the largest country house in Gloucestershire. Lord Fitzwilliam rejected Talman's offer to raze Milton to the ground and build him a new mansion for £3,000, but later he had elaborate stabling constructed which still survives and besides pulling down the old gatehouse to the height of the first storey had several rooms constructed with varying levels of decoration. Although his chaplain, Pendleton, played some part in this in general Fitzwilliam's steward was his link with the builder, Robert Wright of Castor, and required to supervise and report on the work.[2]

This era of transformation for the country seat has been much studied and has evinced an extensive literature.[3] However, the role of the estate steward in this activity seems to have attracted little attention. This is surprising because it was an important one. Where mansions and their supporting stables and offices were either being rebuilt or greatly modified the steward usually served as 'clerk of works'. His local knowledge of the estate and of the surrounding region with their resources of timber and stone, builders and craftsmen, were all considered essential to the successful prosecution of the project. Moreover, he was not simply the man on the spot and therefore handily placed to supervise the work, he was a member of his master's 'family'. He was therefore deemed trustworthy. Architects, builders, master craftsmen in wood and stone, were mere employees. They were not family and as such needed close and suspicious supervision. No master could be convinced that they would do the work properly without such supervision, and indeed most masters found that builders and tradesmen could scarcely be persuaded to work continuously with it. When in 1688 William Talman inspected Milton House with a view to reporting to Lord Fitzwilliam about the possibilities of remodelling or rebuilding the old Tudor mansion, his guide was the Reverend Jeremiah Pendleton, his lordship's chaplain. Pendleton was a trusted member of Fitzwilliam's household and over the years reported to him on a number of issues of importance to his master or to the estate. When he did so he was acting as a surrogate steward, the tasks having been delegated to him by the official

---

[2] For Robert Wright, a building surveyor and master craftsman to the Peterborough diocese, see Howard Colvin, *A Biographical Dictionary of British Architects 1600–1840* (London, 1978). For Fitzwilliam and Guybon's experiences with him, see *Fitzwilliam Correspondence, passim*. The stable's architect was John Sturges not William Talman, despite a family tradition to the contrary.

[3] For the significance of the noble 'seat' both practically and symbolically see Lawrence Stone and Jeanne Fawtier Stone, *An Open Elite? England 1540–1880* (Oxford, 1984). See also Mark Girouard, *Life in the English Country House* (New Haven, 1978).

steward, Francis Guybon (thankfully one would think) or directly by his master. Not surprisingly Pendleton addressed Talman a number of searching questions and was decisively snubbed for his pains, reporting that he 'found him very shy of discovering his mind all along and told me that enquiry after these things did not belong to my province'. Talman could not have been more wrong, and his inability to see the surrogate steward beneath the clerical 'cloth' could have cost him dear for it may partly explain why nothing came of his offer to replace Milton with a more splendid mansion.[4]

There was another aspect of the steward's duties which tended to ensure the office of clerk of works would rest on his shoulders. The steward was his master's purse bearer for he received his master's rural income before the master did, and so must bear the responsibility of paying the workmen – not paying them too slowly so that they abandoned the task for better paymasters elsewhere, nor too quickly so that they were tempted to leave work ill finished and run off to other projects. William Thynne at Longleat sought to hold a family of recalcitrant plumbers to their work by keeping them short of money, though this ploy met with some opposition from these 'very knaves ... never to be more employed' and was not totally successful in preventing them from running off to other jobs.[5] Seventy years later that admirable eighteenth-century steward, Daniel Eaton, found himself in the mortifying position of having over-credulously paid a brickmaker his money 'as fast as he earned it' only to find him abscond and leave his own workmen unpaid.[6]

Stewards with their heavy and diverse workload were not always enthusiastic about being saddled with a duty which at best was onerous and at worst was bound to involve them in much blame and criticism from their masters. It was apparently when William Atkinson complained of the lack of anyone specifically appointed to supervise the workmen then rebuilding Lowther Hall that his master pointed out that Atkinson himself was the only person who could furnish him with 'punctual', that is, reliable, reports of the progress of the work and so was the only person he could rely on to

---

[4] For Talman's visit see Reverend Jeremiah Pendleton to Fitzwilliam, 14 August, 11 September 1688, Fitzwilliam F(M)C 651B, 651A. Talman was no more tactful in his scornful estimate of the house, stating that the existing front was 'not worth gaining an avenue to so as to have a sight of it before one comes at it'. Ironically this 'front' is the only scrap of the mansion Talman inspected to survive the rebuilding of the mid eighteenth century, and still stands as a remarkable example of the Elizabethan mansion at its best and as a permanent reflection on Talman's judgment.

[5] To Sir James Thynne, 16 May, 6 June 1659, Thynne ix, fos. 117, 120. When Sir John Lowther complained of his builder's dilatoriness, he expressed the hope he had not already been paid. Lowther, 29 June 1678, Lonsdale/D/Lons/W2/1/13.

[6] He would never have done it but for the 'good character' of the man supplied by Lord Gower's footman and butler. Eaton to Cardigan, 25 April 1727, *Eaton Letters*, Letter 132.

maintain 'any life' in it.[7] Certainly serving as a clerk of works was onèrous and largely thankless, and occasionally the steward would enlist the help of others. As we have seen Francis Guybon was glad to delegate such duties to his master's chaplain, and William Blathwayt's steward in Gloucestershire was no doubt happy that the task of supervising the construction of Dyrham Court had been placed in the hands of the incumbent of Dyrham Church which stands adjacent to the mansion. Not only was it onerous, it inevitably attracted to the steward a great deal of criticism and complaint which was often the fault of men over whom he had little control. Even a cursory glance at the archives of some stewards will reveal the problems encountered in co-ordinating the skills and activities of builders and glaziers, stonemasons and carpenters, slaters and brickmakers. He had to direct them and mediate between them and constantly report to his absent master. Those readers who have had some experience of building would note at once that the stewards faced problems which are not unknown to twentieth-century clients: plumbers would arrive and then disappear with the work barely begun – or not arrive at all. Builders supposedly solely committed to their master's project would prove to be heavily engaged for other clients and could not be relied on to attend to business or even to keep their workmen continuously employed on the project. Thomas Tickell's letters concerning the work going on at Flatt Hall and detailing the frequent absences of the master builder, William Thackeray, at other commissions call a roll of Cumbrian manorhouses: Drawdykes Castle, Newbiggin Hall, Ribton Hall, Muncaster Castle and Lowther Hall among them. Such derelictions tended to be blamed on the steward and Tickell was admonished to call Thackeray to a proper sense of duty. Since Tickell was well aware of Thackeray's great local reputation and of the demand for his services, he probably ignored this command. In any event builders had deaf ears for such calls. Taking on more work than the builder could well handle was not the only cause of delay. The English climate can be unkind to building projects. Heavy rains would make roads impassable, or at least greatly increase transport costs because carters could only bring half loads through the muddy ways. Work must be shut down through winter's snows and frosts, unless the fabric was up and roofed. Even then damp weather could delay painting or plastering, sometimes for weeks. High summer saw • the onset of harvest strip the project of much of its labour force. A worse time would not have been for that work' reports Charles Agard in a typical letter, 'but that was not to be foreseen nor any remedy but patience.' Unfortunately patience was a quality few masters demonstrated when involved in such projects.

---

[7] See epigraph to Chapter 3 above.

The steward's problems began well before the project got under way. Where the materials were to come from his master's estate it was his responsibility to extract them, mobilising and paying the workmen who felled and sawed timber or who quarried stone, cut slates, burned lime, dug clay or made bricks. Where the materials came from outside the estate it was his role to decide from what source they should be obtained, and what price should be paid for them, although, of course, his master would have to approve the various bargains and he would have advice from the builder. William Thynne at Longleat sought local advice on the type of stone and timber to be used and its price but, dissatisfied, decided to ride to Bristol to choose for himself, finding there was 'no trusting to these country workmen'.[8] Thomas Pope at Kempsford marked out suitable trees, but delayed stone carting until the weather eased and the ways improved.[9] At timber-starved Whitehaven Thomas Tickell had no suitable trees to mark and so sent master builder Thackeray to Ireland to seek better trees for Flatt Hall.[10] John White, steward to Lord Gower, calculated that he needed to fell 120 oaks for building, 20 more to furnish lathes and 2 further large oaks for window sashes, and only needed precise measurements from his master to begin sawing.[11] Slightly beyond the period considered here Daniel Eaton, steward to Lord Cardigan, carefully calculated that rebuilding Little Deene would require 400 feet of boards for the floor, 450 feet of finest deal to build the staircase. The stone would come from a quarry within the lordship, as would the slate, and bricks could be made from clay dug from the park.[12] Running short of materials and delays in supplying more brought frequent complaints from impatient masters. Perhaps with some prescience Francis Guybon stored a supply of cut planks in a fish pond at Milton to prevent deterioration so that they would be ready for the next project his master conceived.[13]

If goods needed to be purchased elsewhere the steward had to plan and co-ordinate the organisation of labour and packhorses, wagons or oxteams to bring them in. The expense of this often irritated their masters. The cost of slate carting appeared 'extravagant and ridiculous' to Lord Cholmondeley, who grumbled that carters never yet let him 'have anything at common rates as other people have'. Hoping to cut costs elsewhere to compensate he instructed his steward to enquire the price of Sir John Wynn's slates, hoping for a present of some to help save costs, but the

---

[8] To Sir James Thynne, 7 and 28 February 1659, Thynne ix, fos. 59, 87.
[9] To Thomas Thynne, 20 June 1673, Thynne xx, fo. 104.
[10] He found them too dear and returned empty handed. Tickell to Lowther, 3 October 1676, Lonsdale/D/Lons/W2/1/11.
[11] White, 26 March 1701, Leveson-Gower D868/9/55.
[12] Eaton to Cardigan, 25 April 1727, *Eaton Letters*, Letter 132.
[13] Guybon to Fitzwilliam, 19 May 1695, Fitzwilliam F(M)C 931.

steward must do it tactfully so that he would not think Cholmondeley either designed or expected such a favour.[14] Where possible the tenants' plough teams were mobilised to bring heavy loads, as part of the labour they owed their landlord under the terms of their tenancies, although this expedient was not always available and could involve various problems even when it was. Thomas Tickell, defeated in Ireland by the dearness of timber there, imported it from Norway, ships from Whitehaven sailing there each spring to bring timber for pit props. The slate to roof Flatt Hall was brought from Loweswater, his master having first considered and then rejected Welsh slate on the grounds that he shrank from 'new experiments'. 'Our slaters I doubt can neither lay it on, nor mend it, and to depend on foreigners will not be well.' Tickell mobilised more than a hundred people from neighbouring manors to bring 283 loads of slate.[15]

These steward clerks of works had not only to supervise the work once it began, they had to prepare detailed estimates of costs beforehand. Edward Lawrence was to write in 1727 that a steward should 'endeavour to make himself master of the true prices of all sorts of work ... that he be not imposed on, or obliged to watch the day workmen, which commonly proves the most chargeable method'.[16] He had workers in husbandry in mind, but the dictum was equally pertinent to builders, craftsmen and other workmen. Lord Cholmondeley regularly complained about what he considered excessive builders' quotations and admonished his steward to measure and remeasure in an effort to extract the lowest possible price. Even then success did not always satisfy his distant master, for once when he supplied an estimate for joinery work Cholmondeley was gripped by the opposite anxiety, London cabinet-makers having assured him that at so low a price the work could not be done 'to perfection'. In fact his steward did have some expert assistance when it came to reconstructing Cholmondeley Hall. Cholmondeley retained Robert Jones, a building surveyor, to provide advice and make periodic inspections of the site. Jones provided Adams with meticulous instructions on how to measure the work as a prelude to bargaining with the workmen, and on what working conditions they would expect. Nevertheless, despite such elaborate preparation the steward bore the responsibility and the arrival of his accounts in London would invariably bring recriminations: Adams had made 'such loose articles' with the carpenter ('a sharp spark' in his master's eyes) 'as brings me into ten thousand inconveniencies and disputes with such fellows'. Moreover Adams had allowed too much new material to be ordered so that the old might well be smuggled away for the builder's own use. Adams

[14] Cholmondeley to Adams, 9 May and 4 April 1704, Cholmondeley DCH/K/3/16.
[15] Lowther, 13 September, Tickell 13 November 1676, Lonsdale/D/Lons/W2/1/11.
[16] Edward Lawrence, *The Duty of a Steward to His Lord* (London, 1727).

sometimes bargained for 'day work' which his master's suspicious eyes perceived as a 'gross cheat', instead of 'by the great', a requirement which Adams could not always insist on.[17] What masters wanted was what that paragon among eighteenth-century stewards, Daniel Eaton, promised to supply. He promised that once his lord had determined the way in which a project had to be carried out he would compute its cost and contract with the workmen at that price, which would relieve his master of 'uneasiness' that the workmen might be cheating him. Moreover, the contract Eaton set down would specify how the work was to be carried out so that they would not need further instructions as they executed it.[18] Whether this counsel of perfection was fully realised in reality is more doubtful, but it certainly summarises what were believed to be the advantages of piecework formally contracted rather than employing workmen paid by the day.

As the building proceeded orders and counter-orders flowed out from London, invariably accompanied by criticisms of the steward's capacity to understand instructions or to relay them accurately to the workmen. Sir John Lowther ordered his steward to repeat in his letters whatever he directed and then 'I shall know if you apprehend me aright', one of his dictums being 'a message is never known to be right taken without repeating it again to the giver'.[19] Despite such doubts masters persisted in relaying all instructions to the workmen through their stewards, in part no doubt because some of the craftsmen and tradesmen engaged were illiterate. Francis Guybon claimed to have read his master's instructions 'over and over' to the carpenter.[20]

A very important reason why stewards stood as intermediaries between a London-dwelling master and the local craftsmen was the master's desire to have his mansion built, ornamented and furnished with the latest fashions. In this way the steward often found himself acting as a 'mediator' between metropolitan culture and the provinces. At Cholmondeley the windows were to be constructed in the style of those in Lord Cholmondeley's London house and London fashion was also to be followed in the design of the wainscotting. Cholmondeley had first referred to sash windows when his steward was supervising the building of a new greenhouse in 1689,

---

[17] 'By the great' meant at a fixed price for the task. The advantage for the client was obvious, so long as the workmen did not skimp the work in order to finish it more quickly. For Cholmondeley references see Laroche to Adams, 7 October 1707; Jones to Adams 26 February 1702; Measom to Adams, 2 May 1706; Cholmondeley to Adams 19 November 1706; 5 February 1709, 22 November 1707, 25 December 1711, 9 December 1707; 4 April 1704; respectively DCH/K/3/21, L/47, L/29, K/3/20, K/3/22, K/3/21, M/28, K/3/21, K/3/16.

[18] Eaton to Cardigan, 3 December 1727, *Eaton Letters*, Letter 149 and see epigraph to this chapter.

[19] Lowther, 21 July 1677, 21 January 1682, Lonsdale/D/Lons/W2/1/12 and 17.

[20] Guybon to Fitzwilliam, 16 July 1695, Fitzwilliam F(M)C 937.

remarking that it seemed unnecessary to go to the expense of sending up a plan, preferring to leave it to the joiner's expertise. He may well have misjudged the man's knowledge, or indeed that of his steward, for in May 1690 he instructed Adams to send the measurements to London so that they could be made there if the man could not successfully construct them in the country. Sir John Lowther, during the second phase of rebuilding at Flatt Hall, considered installing sash windows instead of the existing casements and wrote of sending down a pattern of a sash window 'which is very proper for streets or such sides of a house as are not too exposed'. A month later he instructed his steward to have the lower part of the window sill thick enough to serve as a seat within the window, a method which had become fashionable in London. Finally the glass in the windows must be cut in the manner used in the first rebuilding twenty years earlier 'which if you observe well is a little different from the usual cut in the country, a little larger than usual there'.[21] Similarly in the first phase he had instructed Tickell that single doors were now more fashionable than double, and sent mouldings in wood to be copied exactly for the chimney pieces. He also sent two marble chimney pieces by sea and drafts of panelling, rails and moulding 'so as country workmen cannot mistake', followed by patterns of window shutters and chimneys.[22] Even humble housing for domestic poultry could be influenced by London practice, for Francis Guybon was instructed to delay the completion of the new henhouse floors until his master came into the country 'for the experienced women here differ in opinion from yours in the country. It would be too long to write their several sentiments.'[23] On the other hand, stewards were apt to relay to their masters news of fashions or at least desirable practices which they had observed within their own or neighbouring counties, as when Tickell recommended level walks and hewn steps for the Flatt in the style of 'Sir Richard Bradstone's house in Lancashire'. Stewards indeed were often urged to visit other country seats to spy out their arrangements, although this usually involved gardening, orcharding and horticulture, an area of their responsibilities considered more fully below.

Of course, stewards were not only clerk of works to their masters' mansions and their outbuildings. Usually they were charged with supervising

21 Cholmondeley to Adams, 15 July 1710; 24 March 1709; Cholmondeley to Adams, 2 May 1689, Laroche to Adams, 6 May 1690; respectively Cholmondeley DCH/K/3/24, L/47, K/3/8, M/27. Lowther to Gilpin, 8 March, 23 April 1698; *Lowther Correspondence*, Letters 477 and 507.
22 Lowther, 21 November 1676, 16 January 1677, 2 April, 19 November 1678, 10 July, 31 December 1681, 4 March 1682; respectively Lonsdale/D/Lons/W2/1/11, 11, 12, 12, 16, 16, 17. The first building phase is discussed in some detail in Blake Tyson, 'The Work of William Thackeray and James Swingler at Flatt Hall (Whitehaven Castle) and other Cumbrian Buildings 1676–1684', *Ancient Monument Society Transactions*, 28, 1984.
23 Fitzwilliam, 26 August 1697, *Fitzwilliam Letters*, Letter 29.

the building, rebuilding and major repair of all buildings on the estate, whether it be a new quay for Whitehaven harbour or school for Whitehaven town, a new church for Minsterley, or a row of almshouses built as an act of benevolence by their lord.[24] In the ordinary course of events this chiefly involved the homes and barns of tenants. Again they were liable to much criticism and to encounter a barrage of anxious letters from their lord. If they kept the farms in repair they were liable to be charged with extravagance. If the farms fell into ruin they were charged with neglect. If the lord considered it was the fault of the tenant who should, by the terms of his tenancy keep the house and buildings in repair, the steward was still blamed for allowing the tenant's negligence to flourish unchecked. Thus Francis Guybon was blamed for repairing some cottages at his master's expense when, in his master's eyes, there could be no necessity for it because the old tenants still lived in them and were 'obliged to maintain and uphold'. He should have been consulted before the money was spent. On an earlier occasion Fitzwilliam is indignant that a barn has been allowed to fall into disrepair when prompt expenditure of a modest sum and some timber on it would have held it up for years. 'The roof might have stood many years if the walls had been repaired' he grumbles, 'but nothing is mended if I am not there to look after things.'[25]

Where the complete rebuilding of an estate house was involved, the steward's clerk-of-works duties were more demanding and still more so when the task at hand was such a semi-public work as the rebuilding of a fallen bridge. When Lolham Bridge on Lord Fitzwilliam's estate at Maxey fell in March 1706 the steward went straight to view the bridge before reporting the accident to his master, and quickly obtained rough quotations from a stonemason who would not turn an arch in stone under £25, he finding stone and lime, and from a carpenter, who would do it for £4 if Fitzwilliam provided all materials. He then reported to his master pointing out that while the bridge had been temporarily repaired, if it fell Fitzwilliam would be liable to a fine three times larger than rebuilding the bridge would cost. 'Go the cheapest way we can it will cost £10.' Fitzwilliam ordered the work to go ahead, dismissing the cost of stone on the ground that a stone bridge would outlast three of timber, and the work's progress can be followed in the steward's correspondence, although he delegated much of the supervision to an understeward who lived closer at hand.[26]

---

[24] The steward's role in such public-spirited building has been discussed above in Chapter 8.
[25] To Francis Guybon, 25 March 1697, Fitzwilliam F(M)C 987; *Fitzwilliam Correspondence*, Letter 11.
[26] Guybon, 14 March 1706, Fitzwilliam F(M)C 1464; *Fitzwilliam Correspondence*, Letter 421; there are regular references to the progress of the work during 1706.

The steward was not simply responsible for buildings and semi-public works. He was also responsible for gardens, parks and grounds. If the second half of the seventeenth century was a great age of building, it was also a great age of gardening. Landowners planted trees and flowering bushes, many of them exotic importations.[27] They established elaborate kitchen gardens, orchards, espaliered fruits such as pears, peaches and vines, and had greenhouses erected. Some noblemen were inspired by the example of their neighbours to build orangeries, others aviaries, while all tended to commission elaborate combinations of canals or ornamental ponds with fountains and other hydraulic wonders, complete with suspended garden houses and statuary, together with elaborate formal topiary gardens. Of the latter, one of the last survivors is the well-known topiary garden at Levens Hall, Westmorland, which was laid out by a French gardener for Colonel James Grahme, Master of the Horse to James II. Lord Gower's steward, George Plaxton, personally designed an ornamental fish pond with a long canal for his master – 'all done for under £40 or else blame my judgment'.[28] Lord Cholmondeley commissioned very elaborate garden hydraulics, and Adams found himself directing the enlargement of a spring to provide a sufficient flow of water, estimating the cost of piping water to the fountain in the Little Yew Garden, unpacking thirteen boxes from two wagons laden with pieces of fountain equipment and decoration and collecting and sending to the nearest seashore to collect shells for a proposed grotto. Adams and the specialist plumber spent many hours adjusting the hydraulics to make the water flow to the various fountains, sphinxes, cupids and dolphins, meanwhile receiving the familiar torrent of abuse at the slowness or ineptness of the work. It was all very onerous, as was constructing his master's orangery which had been inspired by Cholmondeley's witnessing the arrival of a consignment of a hundred oranges at Lord Ferrer's London home, all grown in his orangery. Nothing would do but Adams must post off to Ferrer's mansion to view this prodigy for himself so that he would know how to build a similar one at Cholmondeley with sash windows and Dutch stoves.[29] Similarly he had to visit Ferrer's house again when, with a growing menagerie of bantams, pheasants, canaries and blue turkeys arriving at Cholmondeley, he had to learn how they were to be fed, and above all, housed in an appropriate aviary.[30]

[27] The enthusiasm for planting trees and developing gardens in this period and later is considered at length by Keith Thomas, *Man and the Natural World* (London, 1983), Chapter 5: 'Trees and Flowers'.

[28] Plaxton to Gower, 8 February 1696, Leveson–Gower, D593 Add./4/2.

[29] Cholmondeley to Adams, 28 April 1688, 2 May 1689, 17 May 1690, 7 and 16 January 1696 respectively Cholmondeley DCH/K/3/8, M/27, K/3/10.

[30] Laroche to Adams 15 February 1705, Robert Jones to Laroche (detailing the type of wire mesh which would be needed) 14 January 1706, Cholmondeley DCH/K/3/18, DCH/L/47.

Thomas Tickell long resisted his master's wish to have the mount at the Flatt levelled because he knew it would be expensive, labour intensive and, worst of all, that he would have to supervise the work personally. His resistance was a prolonged rearguard action and indeed some of the mount remained in his successor's time.[31]

Just how onerous the clerk-of-works duties about the gardens could be can be judged from a set of instructions Philip Swale, steward of Aske, received from Lord Wharton in February 1685. February might seem a quiet month for gardening affairs in the Yorkshire dales. It would not have seemed quiet to Swale who found himself charged with the following: cutting away part of a hedge to permit a drive to descend less steeply, plant a new quick-set hedge beside the altered route, and grub up a further stretch of hedge no longer needed. He must consider the advisability of building bridges, or erecting a causeway, across two low-lying parts of the route, estimating their proportions and cost. He was to discover the cost of improving other ways delineated on a map of the locality his master sent him. He was to provide estimates for making ornamentations for the mouldings around the Great Court. If not too late in the season Swale was to begin planting quick sets immediately and to begin levelling ground for a new orchard for which fruit trees would be dispatched in due course. Meanwhile he was to demolish some 'old tattered' walls and fences, enlarge the 'broad close' and 'make it lie fair before the house'. He was to hunt out the plans of the coping and scroll work for the forecourt walls, send a copy to London with estimates of cost, and suggest a scheme for sloping the way from the upper to the lower courts without using stairs so that coaches and horses might pass through. *En passant* his master foreshadowed further plans for continuing a hedge from the plantation through the broad close to form 'a fair lane' between the close and the new orchard's wall, and of making a 'graceful going out from the great gate of the court' to the 'walk of four rows of trees'. Lord Wharton, who personally issued these instructions, had the grace to recognise that he was making substantial demands on his servant, remarking apologetically that he realised 'a better time might sooner have been pitched on to do these things' but since he had already done so much to 'ornament that seat' about the 'ways, plantations and courts' he wished to finish 'these outward parts' which might encourage those that came after him to make further additions about the stables at least, if not the house itself. Subsequent letters reiterated these instructions, sought further plans, proposed amendments to what had been decided and issued new directions for the design of wall copings, decorative pillars and

---

[31] See letters of 18 October 1684, 29 September, 10 October 1685, 5 April 1686, 8 October 1690, Lowther–Tickell Correspondence, D/Lons/W2/1/19–21, 25; Gilpin to Lowther, 26 February 1696, *Lowther Correspondence*, Letter 271.

many general repairs, although perhaps because he recognised the burdens he was laying on his steward's shoulders, he asked Swale to engage a surveyor to carry out all estimates of cost.[32]

The role of the stewards in this period when all England's gentlemen seemed set on transforming their gardens inevitably makes their correspondence a magnificent source for the historian of the garden. Of course they had, indeed badly needed, much expert advice and assistance. The great London nurserymen, George London and Henry Wise, established a very considerable business (on the site of the Victoria and Albert Museum) which not only supplied plants and trees as far as Sir John Lowther's remote Flatt Hall, but also provided advice, plans and even gardeners whose services were sometimes 'leased' to their clients with these well-trained experts remaining in the employ of the London firm. This access to professional advice meant that when William Adams at Cholmondeley took delivery of 100 orange trees or Thomas Tickell at Whitehaven found himself saddled with a large quantity of stone-fruit trees, they were also furnished with technical advice about where and when to plant them. Thus Adams was instructed by his master, who had consulted experts, to put them in the type of basket normally used by maids to carry coal, but filled with good mould. At Michaelmas he was to set them in boxes, baskets and all, for the baskets would rot away about the roots to the benefit of the trees.[33] Similarly when Sir John Trevor directed Thomas Crewe to transplant some elms at Trevalyn Hall, he advised him to do it a fortnight after All Hallows, and to take them up with large roots, to 'head' them and to dig 'great holes' for them and surround the planted trees with earth and dung. Some of the instructions appear rather quaint to modern eyes, as when Lord Fitzwilliam instructed Francis Guybon to tell the gardener that when he planted certain seeds his master had sent down he must first soak them in order to 'plump them a little' and then, in order that they might remember which was which, plant a cleft stick with the name of the seed on a small piece of paper and 'let that stick be stuck down at the head of the bed' so that they could see which flourished best and save its seed for the coming year.[34] The instructions could hardly have been more detailed.

It might be thought that with all this expertise available there would be little or no role for the steward and he could thankfully abandon his

---

[32] Lord Wharton to Philip Swale, 19 February, 13 and 17 March, 10 June, 4 July 1685, reproduced in M. Y. Ashcroft, ed., *Documents Relating to the Estates of Lord Wharton in the Sixteenth and Seventeenth Centuries*, North Yorkshire County Record Office Pubs., 36 (April 1984).

[33] 'This I am advised is the best way', Cholmondeley to Adams, 20 March 1688, Cholmondeley DCH/K/3/8.

[34] To Guybon, 7 and 20 February 1706, Fitzwilliam F(M)C 1456, 1459; *Fitzwilliam Correspondence*, Letters 416, 418. For Trevor, Trevor to Crewe, no date but 1635, D/G/3273/25.

master's gardens to other hands. On the contrary, the arrival of foreign gardeners, often French, simply made his life more difficult. The ultimate responsibility for overseeing all this digging and hewing, constructing, collecting and planting, was the steward's however many gardeners his master employed, however many experts turned up to direct matters, even if these included Mr London or Mr Wise themselves. Stewards could often leave day-to-day direction to the builder who had contracted to carry out major works like canals or aviaries, greenhouses or grottoes, but the overall supervision and the final responsibility for the fulfilment of their masters' projects was theirs alone. The gardeners often needed as much supervision and tight control as the builders and tradesmen temporarily employed. Lord Cholmondeley, no psychologist, sent a French gardener to Cholmondeley and with blithe naivety told his steward that he expected neither this new man nor the present gardener should 'pretend either to be master over the other, but let each do his several works as I shall give directions'. This situation, which gravely disturbed the jealously guarded hierarchy of the household, was further complicated by the fact that the Frenchman brought a 'servant' with him who might, if the Frenchman proved satisfactory, be put in the place of the English gardener's deputy, who was his brother. It was not long before his lordship was forced to conclude that his gardens would never be in order while he had 'two who pretend to be master, especially when one is French and the other English'. Meanwhile the unfortunate steward was the butt of complaints by both men, each complaining that he favoured the other. A few years later Cholmondeley tersely denied responsibility for his gardener's death by 'a melancholy' induced by the conviction that his master intended to displace him in favour of a gardener sent by George London. A further four years later George London himself was complaining that his man was treated as a 'cypher' by the undergardener, who behaved as if he was really the gardener![35] In general gardeners were a stiff-necked breed, and a frequent source of trouble to the steward, insubordinate, often bibulous and sometimes dishonest. William Kirle complained on one occasion to Sir George Savile that his 'covetous, drunken, peevish, gluttonous gardener' had dismissed all the workmen that had 'either honesty or industry', employing men of his own choosing, and that he had agisted cattle for his own profit in the kitchen garden and the bowling green. Since many gardeners were allowed to sell surplus produce to augment their wages – which helped to keep wages down – it was difficult at times for stewards to monitor what was dishonest and what was not. Moreover, gardeners were adept at playing off lord against steward. Significantly Kirle, a respected steward, felt he had to excuse himself for

[35] Cholmondeley to Adams, 25 February, 10 and 29 March, 28 April, 28 May 1688, Cholmondeley DCH/K/3/8; 12 May 1691, 26 August 1695, DCH/K/3/9.

making these complaints, admitting that his master had complained often of his being 'too choleric' which made him 'almost Spanish' in discharging his duty for fear Savile should dismiss a truthful account as one exaggerated by anger.[36]

Certainly this was a great age of interest in horticultural and botanical science, with the stewards helping their masters to grace their grounds with exotic, imported fruits, bushes and trees. The quantities involved were often very substantial and the variety of species remarkable. William Adams received orange trees, jasmins, figs, cuttings of Bon Chrétien pears, tuberoses, vines, cherries, apricots, plums, peaches, bay trees, pomegranates, a mastic tree, a balm-of-Gilead, and in 1699 4,000 hornbeams, 340 alders and 1,470 yews, the last three species destined for Lord Cholmondeley's 'wilderness'.[37] Some stewards closely involved themselves in expanding their master's woods. Lowther's steward, William Gilpin, seized the opportunities provided by his master's port of Whitehaven, with its trade with Virginia and Scandinavia and the Baltic, to import seeds and engage in experimental plantations. In September 1697 he was hoping that the embargo on sailings from Virginia, imposed in fear of French naval and privateering threats to the tobacco fleet, would have kept the fleet there until it was the season to acquire seeds. He had sent to Norway unsuccessfully but was employing a Dane, now resident in the port and 'labouring to make an acquaintance'. He had several times sown fir seed, but only the variety from Norway 'comes up'. He also prompted his master to send seeds from London and asked him to send him 'Mr Evelyn's *Sylva*' if he did not need his copy there, which Lowther duly sent along with some other horticultural texts a month or so later.[38]

Gardens, of course, were not merely for show, nor simply there to impress visitors by the richness or variety of their blooms or the elaboration or ingenuity of their waterworks. A large area was normally devoted to kitchen gardens and not all their produce was consumed in the mansion.

---

[36] Kirle to Savile, 22 May 1661; Savile DDSR 221/94/19. Forty years earlier Sir Richard Saltonstall's steward had similarly complained that the gardener agisted his horses in the garden in part of which he had planted hemp for his own profit. William Warde at Chipping Warden to Sir Richard Saltonstall III, 24 June 1620, North C7/136. For stewards' measures against gardeners' deviant behaviour, see above Chapter 10.

[37] Cholmondeley to Adams, 10 March 1688, 21 December 1689, 24 February, 24 June 1693, Downes to Cholmondeley 22 January 1699, respectively Cholmondeley DCH/K/3/8, M/27, K/3/10, K/3/13.

[38] Gilpin to Lowther, 1 September 1697, *Lowther Correspondence*, Letter 398; see also Letters 323, 358, 362, 412. In the same spirit in 1693 Lord Cholmondeley sent Adams a copy of 'the book of gardening of Monsieur Quentenan' to lend to his chief gardener, Holdford. Cholmondeley DCH/K/3/10. A Lowther notebook used between 1696 and 1698 listed the varieties of seeds and nuts which might be collected in Virginia, D/Lons/W1/46.

Absentee landlords who lived most of their lives in London found the capital expensive. One way to reduce the heavy expense was to draw on their estates as much as was practicable for foodstuffs. It might be thought such purveyance was most common and most varied from estates in the Home Counties, the Midlands and East Anglia because of the shorter distances involved, but stewards at least as far away as Lord Cholmondeley's Cheshire estates employed wagoners and packhorse carriers to transmit a rich variety of garden produce together with game (rabbits, hares, pheasants, pigeons, woodcock, snipe and, of course, venison) and poultry, geese especially, massive cheeses and various cooked meats prepared by the mansion's housekeeper: chines of beef, potted meats, game pies, together with vast jars of honey from the estate's bees and boxes of fruit and vegetables. 'My wife desires you would send two flitches of bacon by the first opportunity for it will be very dear here against Lent' Cholmondeley writes, a typical request.[39] On other occasions his steward supplied beer and cider, corn, brawn, cooked and potted fowl, partridges, turkeys, venison, woodcocks and even candles. Some stewards laboured to supply delicacies which were peculiar to their region. Remote Westmorland supplied Sir Christopher Musgrave with vast char pies, the chars specially caught at the steward's prompting in Lake Windermere and Coniston Water, their only English source. Char pies, considered a great delicacy in London, were used by gentlemen resident there not merely for their own sustenance but to win the favour of influential friends. They were huge pastry containers of baked fish seasoned with herbs and spices, weighing from thirty to sixty pounds. Musgrave's steward, Jeffrey Beck, had to mobilise relatives in Westmorland to employ men to catch the fish and women to bake and prepare the pies, but, as he wrote to them, 'let the charge be what it will so they be big enough, soon done and good fish'.[40] Those landowners with deer parks drew heavily on their estates for venison. The letters of Lord Fitzwilliam are packed with calls for venison and detailed instructions on how the deer must be killed, how it must be packed and to which carrier it must be entrusted, and what weather conditions would permit it to be dispatched at all.[41]

In these ways objectives both practical and related to conspicuous consumption conspired to ensure that the steward was kept busy as both a clerk of works and supervisor of household servants and gardeners whenever his master was in London, abroad or resident on one of his other estates.

[39] Cholmondeley to Adams 10 January 1681, Cholmondeley DCH/K/3/4.
[40] Letter undated but about 1710. Musgrave D/Mus/A1/2.
[41] *Fitzwilliam Correspondence*, passim.

14

Master and man

who ought we to trust to but our children and our stewards, and if they will be
unfaithful, the lord reward them according to their merit.

Lord Fitzwilliam of Milton, 1705[1]

Lord Fitzwilliam's observation reflects the curious position of the seventeenth-century estate steward in his relationship with his master. It was a
relationship quite different from that of the late-eighteenth-century steward
who was evolving into the salaried land agent so characteristic of the
nineteenth century.[2] Stewards were salaried servants but they were also
members of the lord's household, his family, a contemporary usage which
still retained deep significance. A familial relationship existed between
masters and servants in noble and gentry households throughout the
seventeenth century, a persistent late-mediaeval survival that was to perish
during the eighteenth century.[3] In this familial situation masters and
servants were surrogate kin, which helps to explain how servants were
treated both when they were treated badly and when they were treated well.
It also helps to explain how servants, including stewards, perceived their
masters, how they reacted to them and their expectations from them. This
status of surrogate kin applied both to servants who were simples and
servants who were gentles. The latter embraced such senior household
servants as chaplains, secretaries, receivers, and particularly the stewards,
for the latter, although often living distant from their lord's household,
were very much part of it. As we have seen a steward was usually a
gentleman, sometimes a landowner in his own right, and often written to as
a much respected, even beloved, friend. Yet he was also a retainer, a
servant, a member of the family, and his place in the family helped to make
this friendly relationship possible. Stewards were greatly trusted partly

---

[1] To Francis Guybon, 5 July 1705, Fitzwilliam F(M)C 1404; *Fitzwilliam Correspondence*,
Letter 380.
[2] See especially Eric Richard's 'The Land Agent' in G. E. Mingay, ed., *The Victorian
Countryside* (London, 1981). For a brief summary of the careers, rewards of agents and the
relationship of agent and employer see Beckett, *Aristocracy in England*, 139–56.
[3] Throughout this chapter the word family is used in the wider sense of household.

because they were family and partly because they were gentles not simples. However, both qualifications were necessary to attract this trust and of the two it was the surrogate kin relationship which was the more important. Whilst a gentleman was more likely to be trusted than a 'clown' (to employ the first Lord Cholmondeley's old-fashioned term) gentility alone was not enough. Lawyers were gentlemen but it would have been a remarkably trusting lord who would trust his lawyer as far as he would trust his estate steward. Lawyers were not members of the family, not surrogate kin, unless like William Gilpin at Whitehaven they happened to be professional lawyers who were employed as stewards. Lawyers were independent. They had other clients whose interests might conflict. Indeed, while it might seem an economically enticing arrangement for a landowner to have a lawyer as his steward, the fact that such a steward would be permitted to practise his profession during his spare time could itself bring problems. In 1697 Sir John Lowther's colliery steward, John Gale, warned his master that Gilpin's fierce advocacy for one side in a case of a disputed inheritance, which had bitterly divided the Whitehaven community, could prove damaging to Lowther's interests there.[4] Nevertheless this problem could be solved by a speedy intervention by the master. A lawyer-steward might from time to time have several clients but he had only one lord, and the lord's interests were paramount.[5] Because of the nature of the lawyer's profession, with its successive client relationships, a lord could not trust lawyers outside the household invariably to further the lord's 'interest', to commit themselves to extending his network of patronage and influence, as he could trust such members of his family as his estate steward, receiver, chaplain or secretary.

The difference in attitude to and relationship with stewards and lawyers is well exemplified by Lord Fitzwilliam's relationship with Francis Guybon, very much a member of his family, and his lawyer, Roger Pemberton of Peterborough. Pemberton is a particularly good example and worth observing in a little more detail just because he had an unusually close relationship with Fitzwilliam which transcended that ordinarily linking lawyer and client. His mother was a very old and close friend of the Fitzwilliams, and

---

[4] 'I could heartily wish and humbly pray you would give some cautions to Mr Gilpin's proceedings, whose implacableness to Collins relick [*sic*] may hurry him on to ... a rash or unadvised thing ... Mr Gilpin has been lampooned and libelled very scurrilously ... nor does he suffer alone in those satires' (that is, they attacked Lowther also). Gale to Lowther, 2 May 1697, *Lowther Correspondence*, Letter 360.

[5] In the very professional environment of the nineteenth century, agricultural experts universally condemned the practice of employing lawyers as stewards, but this was for quite different reasons. The latter included their neglect of the estate as they pursued their private practice, but more importantly, their ignorance of farming methods. Beckett, *Aristocracy in England*, 146. Professor Beckett's chief reference, William Marshall's *The Review and Abstract of the County Reports to the Board of Agriculture*, is dated 1818.

Pemberton would always dine with them when he visited London. When he was struck down with an 'apoplectic fit' in 1707 Fitzwilliam and his son visited him daily, saw him 'cupped', and ensured that he had the same treatment which had successfully restored Fitzwilliam from the same condition four years earlier. Throughout his illness Fitzwilliam sent regular reports via his steward to Pemberton's mother and his wife.[6] Again when Pemberton was ill at Peterborough Fitzwilliam received regular reports on his health and sought the best medical advice obtainable in London on his behalf. Yet Fitzwilliam did not trust Pemberton as he would have trusted his steward. It was Pemberton he suspected of not doing his utmost to calm a dispute because lawyers were 'willing to have lawsuits go on, it being for their profit'.[7] Nor was his distrust without foundation. At a time when Fitzwilliam and his son were labouring to have a former servant appointed bailiff of Peterborough they found that Pemberton, whose influence was vital, would not exert himself on their candidate's behalf. His son had written two letters to Pemberton who had 'never had the manners to answer him. He is a knave and expects a bribe and values no man's friendship. This will certainly be remembered.'[8]

Such behaviour, however much it might enrage a landowner client, would never take him completely by surprise, but such a dereliction by a steward would seem as appalling and as unnatural as if it were by a son. A dissatisfied landowner could sack a lawyer and hire another. As we have already seen, no matter how furious a landowner was with his steward, however much he might threaten to place his affairs in other hands, as Lord Cholmondeley so often did, the steward was hardly ever replaced. He bobbed up and down on the waves of his master's wrath until the storm blew itself out. It was probably as rare for a lord to sack his steward as it was for him to disinherit his eldest son. No matter how vigorous the rebuke, no matter how volcanic the rage, no matter how dissatisfied the lord might be from time to time, no matter how increasingly convinced he might become that his steward was getting too old for the duties involved, he was no more likely to turn him away than he would be to disown a member of his real family.

I believe that this status of surrogate kin helps to explain the otherwise

---

[6] Fitzwilliam to Guybon, 20 and 27 February, 6, 13 and 20 March 1707, F(M)C 1563, 1564, 1566A, 1567B, 1568; *Fitzwilliam Correspondence*, Letters 488, 489, 490, 492, 493.

[7] Fitzwilliam to Guybon, 3 April 1701, F(M)C 1165; *Fitzwilliam Correspondence*, Letter 177. See above, Chapter 6, p. 110.

[8] Fitzwilliam to Guybon, 18 March 1708, F(M)C 1653; *Fitzwilliam Correspondence*, Letter 558. The 'betrayal' was remembered. Six months later Fitzwilliam learned that Mrs Pemberton, 'a bold confident sort of woman', had a mind to have Fitzwilliam's calash bring her from Oxford to Peterborough and Guybon was promptly ordered to deny any such request. 'I shall not forget his carriage in the business of the Peterborough bailiff.' Same to same, 2 September 1708, F(M)C 1691; *Fitzwilliam Correspondence* Letter 590.

mysterious reluctance of greatly trusted servants to act on their own responsibility. In that patriarchal structure neither sons nor stewards, wives nor housekeepers, took decisions without consulting the patriarchal head of the household. To do so would derogate from his God-given right to govern. Certainly seventeenth-century stewards constantly behaved as if they were afraid to use their initiative. 'I am very unwilling to do anything until I hear from your honour': Thomas Barnham's disclaimer encapsulates the characteristic attitude.[9] Constantly they besought their masters for direct orders, for decisions, for permission to take actions which were clearly necessary and often dangerous to delay. Richard Pollard assured the Countess of Bath early in our period that he would always let her know his intentions before acting, and he certainly kept his promise, for in April 1642 we find him refusing to pasture a neighbour's horse without her husband's written permission although the neighbour had already secured a verbal permission for himself. In 1675 Thomas Hawkes at Stretton would not even pay the servants' wages until he heard from his master, an inhibition which would have been common to most stewards. This inhibition reflected the wishes of their masters. After more than thirty years as chief steward at Cholmondeley William Adams could receive a letter from his master's secretary reminding him not to pay 'one farthing' of Cholmondeley's money 'without a particular order' from his master.[10] Thomas Massey would not negotiate with the local tax assessors until he had first heard from Lord Cardigan, which was probably a wise decision for when Francis Guybon, hard pressed by the Taxation Commissioners for his county, agreed to pay Fitzwilliam's poll tax there rather than in London he was much blamed by his master. Even then he had sought his master's permission but the letter arrived too late.[11] Masters were distant and because of that often not well able to make decisions which had been better left to the men on the spot, and when the fastest thing on land was a galloping horse delays were inevitable and might prove damaging. Thomas Smith at Rufford would not destroy a dog, Jemmy, which was a proven sheep-worrier until he had his master's leave.[12] The matter was often trivial, merely routine. It made no difference. The early-eighteenth-century steward who pursued his master with letters across Europe for permission to fell a particular tree for timber to fabricate a desperately needed haywain

---

[9] Thomas Barnham to Richard Barrett, 2 October 1662, Barrett-Lennard D/DL C2/19.
[10] Laroche to Adams, 13 September 1712, Cholmondeley DCH/M/28.
[11] Pollard to Rachel, Countess of Bath, 8 April 1642; to Henry, fifth Earl of Bath, 22 April 1642, Sackville C276; Hawkes to Sir Thomas Thynne, 22 February 1675, Thynne xx, fo. 210; Laroche to Adams, 13 September 1712, Cholmondeley DCH/M/28; Massey to Cardigan, Brudenell of Dene I.xiv. 40 Northamptonshire CRO; Guybon to Fitzwilliam, 19 February and 24 April 1695, Fitzwilliam F(M)C 924, 930.
[12] Thomas Smith to Sir George Savile, 1 August 1722, Savile DDSR 211/227/11.

was an exaggerated but not an untypical example.[13] Occasionally a master would complain because his steward had caused an unfortunate delay by waiting to obtain his direction or consent, but such complaints were rare and usually received with astonishment. Samuel Peers, so chided, protested that his master's rebuke was a 'surprizall' (*sic*) for he did not think it was a fault to seek his lord's opinion.[14] Francis Guybon had to endure a blistering rebuke when his master found he had evicted a tenant and taken a farm in hand, all without his permission. As Fitzwilliam subsequently explained, he was not angry at the eviction but at not being informed about it, 'for I supposed it was but reasonable since the estate is mine that I should be acquainted with all transactions upon it and have my opinion before anything is done. This had been but good manners in you.'[15] This is a classic expression of the lord's point of view and the stewards were all aware that although their responsibilities were boundless and their local power formidable they were nothing without their master's authority. Indeed, one steward complained that the locals treated him with disdain and as 'a very Turk' unless he had his master's signature for they would trust to nothing less.[16]

Sometimes certain stewards were privileged to act without authority: John Mainewaring once apologetically informed Lord Weymouth that he had not obeyed his instructions concerning the elections at Tamworth and had acted on his own initiative (thereby averting a disaster although he was much too tactful to say so). John Peck once went contrary to his lord's commands regarding a leasing agreement because he felt that he could strike a deal much more to his lord's advantage.[17] We have seen that Sir John Lowther of Whitehaven was prepared to let Thomas Tickell conclude bargains for the purchase of much desired properties without waiting to consult him where time was of the essence and the amount did not exceed £200 or £300.[18] In general, however, these were marked exceptions to a firm rule of conduct. Although the steward would find tenants for land, purchasers for timber or minerals, contractors for building or fencing, mill-

---

[13] P. Roebuck, 'Absentee Landownership in the Late Seventeenth and Early Eighteenth Centuries: a Neglected Factor in English Agrarian History', *AHR*, vol. 21 (1973), 4 and note.

[14] Peers to Sir Thomas Thynne, 1 February 1675, Thynne xx, fo. 204. Similarly Lady Cholmondeley was annoyed when an understeward, Manning, failed to pay some bills without an express order. Lady Cholmondeley to William Adams, 26 April 1683, DCH/L/25. In fact Adams, as we have seen in Chapter 8 above, would not even pay his mistress's regular Christmas dole without her direct order year by year.

[15] Fitzwilliam to Guybon, 5 June 1707, F(M)C 1584; *Fitzwilliam Correspondence*, Letter 506.

[16] John Peck to Sir John Trevor, 8 February 1650, Trevor D/G/3276.

[17] Mainewaring to Weymouth, 17 February 1690, and see above Chapter 7. Jasper Peck to Sir John Trevor, 18 February 1671, Trevor D/G/3277.

[18] See above Chapter 6, note 64.

stones for his master's mills and millwrights to install them, grooms for his
stables and footmen for his household, cook-maids for his service when in
the country or to send to town, he would decide or complete nothing
without a direct written command or agreement from his master. This is the
more noticeable because it is so different from the behaviour of land agents
during the nineteenth century who, as Professor Richards has demonstrated, ran estates, made all day-to-day decisions, framed long-term policies and took initiatives as a matter of course. Their masters tended to be
remote rentiers who took little or no interest in detail so long as the income
was sustained, or better still, increased.[19] However, the explanation is
simple. While the masters of the agents were only employers, the stewards'
masters were patriarchs, and in a patriarchy there can be only one decision
maker.

If stewards hesitated to act without instruction they were not slow to
offer advice because this was a most important part of their duties. We have
seen stewards on numerous occasions in the preceding chapters offer advice
on a very wide range of topics, from ploughing agreements to the terms of
leases, from the suitability of potential tenants to the defence of manorial
customs, from the desirability of a possible land purchase to the suitability
of a recipient of the lord's beneficence, from the best way to exploit a new
coal seam to the best way to engage in a voyage to Riga. Where advice was
not volunteered lords were quick to demand it, and they did not complain if
the advice they received was lengthy and detailed. Rather they were likely
to complain bitterly if it was not. Since, as Lowther wrote, landlords saw
'with others' eyes', the flow of advice was as necessary as the flow of
intelligence. Indeed, from conscientious stewards the flow of intelligence
was so sustained, detailed and frequent that a lord must often have needed
his steward's advice to make sense of all the information he received. Some
advice, however, shows the familial relationship in which stewards and
masters were involved. For Captain Morgan Powell to warn Lord Weymouth against keeping Roman Catholics among his servants, as rumour
suggested he did, was advice going far beyond the functions of a mere
employee, however high his status in the household. Considering the scope
of the advice he was prepared to offer it is not surprising that ten days later
he warned his master not to leave his steward's letters lying about where
others might read them.[20] William Swynfen was prepared to offer Lord
Paget advice about family matters, including his grandchildren's education.
The latter was somewhat testily received, prompting Swynfen to respond
that his advice had always been welcome in the past, and to persist with the

[19] Richards, 'The Land Agent', 439–55.
[20] Powell to Sir Thomas Thynne (subsequently Viscount Weymouth) 15 and 25 June 1681,
Thynne xxviii, fos. 54, 57.

same advice, arguing that its only aim was to further the honour of Lord Paget's 'house'. We find Swynfen advising the sixth Lord Paget what payments he should make as a godfather to a midwife and a nurse, informing him what the baron's father had paid in the same circumstances, and on another occasion warning his master that the baron's brother and his wife both needed his master's urgent advice to save them from financial ruin. He also advised Paget about the possible marriages of his sons and daughters, suggesting that Paget was not in such dire financial straits as he appeared to think, and that he could afford to pursue negotiations concerning some likely candidates. This advice was not warmly welcomed, Paget responding that he did not wish to impoverish himself for his children when he could easily delay a year or so. Nevertheless, even when advice was contrary to the lord's own designs, stewards were not usually rebuked for sending it. Paget's comment to Swynfen in 1670 that his advice had been kindly taken even though the opinion expressed was very different from his own was a typical rejoinder.[21] Some advice seems remarkably personal, not to say impertinent, as when Mr Plaxton recommends his master not to 'game at the chocolate house on a Sunday' and to 'serve God truly' who was 'so wonderfully kind' to him. However, Plaxton was a clergyman, and as such may have felt he had a responsibility for his master's soul as well as his estate, particularly as Sir John Gower was barely nineteen.[22]

The familial relationship is nowhere emphasised more emphatically than in the field of marriage negotiations. Stewards were employed to investigate and even negotiate on behalf of their masters both for marriage partners for the lord's own children and occasionally for more distant relatives or even friends.[23] The last category might occasion surprise but it must be remembered that lords employed stewards as extensions of themselves, the steward doing anything and everything that the lord would have done himself had he been in the country. Matchmaking was a business which in careless, indiscreet hands could cause great harm, embarrassing elite families, derogating the personal honour and esteem of a potential groom and adversely affecting the marriageability of a potential bride. Nevertheless, lords considered their stewards particularly well suited for this delicate and highly confidential matter. They were after all the trusted repositories of many confidences and were accustomed to protecting the concerns of their lord and his family from prying eyes. Lord Huntingdon employed his clerical 'over-steward', Archdeacon Gery, to convey a letter from an

---

[21] Paget to Swynfen, 10 May 1670; see also for grandchildren 23 July 1673; for marriage negotiations Paget to Swynfen May 1670, for godfather payments Swynfen to Paget, 3 November 1679; variously Paget D603/K/2/4, K/2/2, K/3/2, K/3/4.

[22] Plaxton to Sir John Gower, 8 February 1696, Leveson-Gower D593/P/13/9.

[23] Huntingdon to Gery, 23 April 1683, Hastings HA6006.

unnamed friend to a lady containing overtures of marriage, but to be
delivered very secretly for although it contained 'infinite respects and
submissions' yet 'all matters of gallantry being subjects of mirth and
diversion' Huntingdon's friend 'would not undergo other censure than that
of the fair lady'. Similarly when the question of a match arose for the 'fair
lady's' brother, while Huntingdon arranged for young Mr Dixie to view a
prospective bride in London, it was Gery who had to visit Sir Beaumont
Dixie in the country and negotiate the matter (for naturally the son would
not consider choosing a wife without his father's approval).[24] Stewards
were assiduous at pursuing both negotiations and enquiries. Morgan
Powell was heavily involved in investigating the accomplishments and
fortune of a young lady ('no education wanting', 'the best of masters' had
attended her, the fortune itself 'of no small account'), a possible match for
Lord Weymouth's son Henry, and even urged his master not to drag his
heels but to let his intentions be known if he wanted to seriously pursue the
match.[25] Sometimes the lord would place the steward in the more delicate
position of urging his master's heir to honour his father's wishes. Thomas
Greene, although he claimed to be timorous about meddling in business of
this nature, wrote several letters to John Nicholas on behalf of his father,
urging the desirability of marriage upon him. Indeed, he informed the
anxious father that he feared his pressing the matter too far had not so
much inclined his son to it as encouraged him to think up arguments
against it. Here no precise match appears to have been in view, for the
steward consoles his master by assuring him he will not be negligent in
enquiring after a 'person such as you like and such as master may have no
exceptions against'.[26]

The familial relationship does not simply manifest itself in the degree of
trust reposed in the steward's discretion. It appears in the very tone of the
correspondence of the lord and of the members of the lord's immediate
family, and in their concern for the steward's welfare. Francis Guybon was
not visited by his master or indeed any members of his family for years at a
time, but the Fitzwilliams' affection for him grew no less. Fitzwilliam's
surviving sons and daughter, who had all spent much time at Milton in his
care when juveniles but scarcely ever visited their country seat later, wrote

---

[24] The data which Huntingdon furnished his emissary was appropriately precise: the
parentage and lineage of the lady, that she would have £1,000 at her marriage plus near
£400 a year, that £2,000 must be settled on Mr Dixie at marriage, with £400 a year for
present maintenance, with a jointure of £800. Huntingdon to Gery, 6 June 1683, HA6023.
Gery's negotiations between Huntingdon (acting apparently for both young Mr Dixie and
the girl's family) and Sir Beaumont dragged on for months.

[25] Powell to Lord Weymouth, 28 May 1687; see also same to same 2 and 23 July, Thynne,
xxviii, fos. 180, 184v, 186.

[26] Greene to Sir John Nicholas, 4 and 22 February 1699, Nicholas 75/22, 23.

to him and even reproached him when he did not regularly write to them. Anna, Fitzwilliam's daughter, wrote in 1690 that while friendship was commonly only apparent when the parties were close at hand, she believed their friendship was as strong at a distance. Indeed it must have been. In 1708 her father passed on a request from his daughter for a letter. She was by then several years married and away from home, and it is doubtful if she had seen the ageing steward more than once or twice during the intervening eighteen years. As we have seen, Guybon presided over the obsequies of Fitzwilliam's eldest son at Marholm Church, a ceremony at which he was undoubtedly perceived, and was intended to be perceived, by all the gentry there as the family representative, no member of the actual family being present.[27]

When a steward fell ill the lord might be expected to have a self-interested concern that no harm should come to a servant it would be difficult to replace. However, it is clear that the anxiety is often much more personal, reflecting a very real concern for the safety of a family member. This was all the more true where the steward was elderly and therefore more likely to succumb to fevers and agues which a younger man might throw off. Certainly any Guybon illness brought great perturbation to the Fitzwilliam household in London and a torrent of advice and questions. On one of his visits to Islington Fields, where he was wont to ride out hoping to encounter countrymen from his neighbourhood who would be bringing up sheep and cattle, Fitzwilliam discovered by chance that his steward had been ill for a week. He promptly chided him for not getting somebody to write on his behalf to pass on the bad news. 'My wife was so afflicted for fear you might be dead that we could not pacify her, and had we not received your letter would certainly have been at Milton tomorrow to see you.' A few weeks later Fitzwilliam advised that he must always be accompanied when he went abroad so that he could be helped on and off his horse and he must not attend the manorial courts if this might endanger his health.[28] On another occasion Lady Fitzwilliam sent word that Guybon must have a nurse sleep 'on a pallet' in his chamber at night so that he would not need to get up for anything, while his master recommended he keep his chamber a week for fear his ague should return. In the last winter of Guybon's life his master observes anxiously: 'By no means stir abroad this terrible cold weather but keep warm at home. I had rather want money than you should endanger yourself.'[29]

---

[27] See above Chapter 6.

[28] 'If God lets me live to come down we will contrive to ease you of so much riding about.' Fitzwilliam, 28 September, 19 October 1704, F(M)C 1351; 1357; *Fitzwilliam Correspondence*, Letters 339, 343. (See also 5 October, Letter 341: 'I am glad you recover more and more but sorry you venture out so soon for fear of a relapse', and 12 October, Letter 342.)

[29] Fitzwilliam to Guybon, 8 February 1705, 13 January 1709, F(M)C 1378, 1720; *Fitzwilliam Correspondence*, Letters 362, 613.

This anxiety about the health of an old servant was not confined to stewards and was not peculiar to the Fitzwilliams. It crops up frequently in references to members of households in any long run of letters from lord to steward or to other family members.[30] It was simply a symptom of the familial relationship which household members had with their lord. Moreover, it extended through them to their own close kin. In 1642 the Earl and Countess of Bath turned aside from a journey to visit the wife of their steward, William Lynne, for she had prematurely given birth to a dead infant.[31] In a similar spirit Thomas Thynne's wife sent advice and 'recipes' to Thomas Hawkes whose daughter was terminally ill with consumption. We have already observed that the relationship was sufficiently familial for stewards to be able to call upon their masters for patronage not only for themselves but for their sons and daughters and even their brothers or nephews.[32] In 1719 we find Thomas Smith at Rufford writing to thank Sir George Savile and Madam Savile, his mother, for their care and trouble over Smith's son who had run away with a girl of no fortune. It is an instance typical of many. Often the master or his lady would stand as godparents to the steward's children, as Samuel Peers requested of Lord Weymouth in 1687 or as Lowther or his daughter, Jane, volunteered to do for the Gilpins' expected child in 1697 (which of them would actually stand would depend on the baby's gender).[33]

If symptoms of affection and closeness between lord and steward simply reflect the fact that stewards were family rather than salaried employees, the same could be said for the reactions of a master to his steward's failings or derelictions of duty. The reaction often contains pronounced feelings of deep hurt that the steward should have let him down, while the steward, if he considered himself innocent of any wrongdoing, would be equally hurt that his lord believed him guilty of such a betrayal. Betrayal it would certainly be if the accusation was well founded, just as it would have been if a close relative, especially a son or daughter, was so unnatural as to betray his father's trust. Once again the interchange is redolent of patriarchalism and indeed paternalism. Of course some masters were in no hurry to believe ill of their stewards, even when confronted by bad reports (often malicious) from others. Sir John Trevor assured Thomas Crewe in 1631 that he

---

[30] Several examples could be adduced from the Cholmondeley Papers, for example.
[31] Lynne to Lady Bath, 4 June 1642, Sackville C277.
[32] See above Chapter 2.
[33] Though gratified at the offer Gilpin was in fact embarrassed because his wife (who was of a dissenting background) preferred the private office conducted in the home rather than the full public ceremony in church which limited the function of the person representing Lowther merely to pronouncing the name and Gilpin feared that 'inconsiderate people' might deem this a lack of respect to his master. *Lowther Correspondence*, Letter 427; Peers to Weymouth, 13 September 1687, Thynne xxiii, fo. 204.

believed none of the ill reports he had received about his activities and indeed thanked him for all the care he took in his business.[34] On the whole, however, lords, like fathers, were quick to chide and slow to bless. The second Viscount Cholmondeley directed a stream of abuse and accusation at his chief steward, William Adams, or at his subordinates, for more than thirty years. Only too typical was Cholmondeley's suggestion in 1710 that it was time his steward, in view of his great age and the uncertainty of life, should put all his papers in order so that he should not die with the reputation of an unjust and negligent steward, which might cast aspersions upon Cholmondeley as an ignorant and negligent master. Anyone who has studied the remarkably clear and detailed sets of accounts Adams kept during his stewardship could only marvel that his master should offer such a gratuitous insult.[35] What Adams replied to this near continuous stream of criticism is unknown for few of his letters survive but his defences must have had some effect for, despite many threats, Adams was never dismissed, and a household officer confided on one occasion that his lordship's anger had been somewhat abated by the receipt of Adams's last letter.[36] Cholmondeley was simply an extreme case. All stewards, even one in so close a relationship as Francis Guybon with Lord Fitzwilliam or John Mainewaring or Thomas Hawkes with Lord Weymouth, could expect to encounter their lord's wrath at some time in their careers. All were ready to defend themselves in tones of reproachful dismay that their lord should ever imagine them capable of the disloyalty which would be implied even by carelessness or negligence, let alone dishonesty. As Richard Pollard told Rachel, Countess of Bath, at a very difficult time for the estate in his charge:

I hope what I have done shall not give you cause of discontent, but if I have done amiss herein it is the error of my judgment and not my want of any good affection to serve your honour were it to the effusion of the last drop of blood that warms my veins.[37]

In conclusion there was one aspect of a steward's responsibilities which introduced a rather more modern and certainly less familial note into the relationship of master and man. This was the steward's accounts. One can detect in the attitude toward accounts a hint of a different relationship, of one more appropriate to a salaried employee than to a member of the household in the neo-feudal sense, particularly when we contemplate two sets of anxieties which accounts tended to raise. The lord worried that his steward might die in his debt, or might not keep proper accounts which would lead to complications and loss after his death or departure. These

[34] Trevor to Crewe, 2 February 1631, Trevor D/G/3273.
[35] Cholmondeley to Adams, 6 June 1710, Cholmondeley DCH/K/3/24.
[36] Jonadeb Colley to Adams, 1692, Cholmondeley DCH/K/3/10.
[37] 24 July 1644, Sackville C276.

anxieties arose, not unreasonably, from the fact that large sums of money passed through the steward's hands, and often lay within his grasp for months at a time. When in residence at Levens Hall, Colonel James Grahme kept accounts of his own, presumably as a check on the reliability of his steward's accounts. (When absent he tended to write separately on the same subject to several stewards and understewards, presumably to check the veracity of the reports he was receiving, so he may have been a preternaturally suspicious master.[38]) The steward in turn was always eager for his lord to agree, sign and discharge past accounts for fear that after the steward's death claims might be made against his estate, to the detriment of his widow or offspring, which he would not be around to dispute. The stewards' letters often contained repeated requests for accounts to be 'agreed' so that such anxieties would be allayed. When Thomas Hawkes found himself ceasing to be the steward of Sir Henry Frederick Thynne and becoming the steward of his son, Thomas Thynne, as a result of the transfer of Shropshire properties from father to son, he bitterly complained to the son about his former master's endlessly delaying a final settlement of accounts:

I can call Heaven and earth to witness that I never got directly or indirectly the worth of one penny by any concern of . . . his, and therefore it is strange that he will hold me so in suspense about a discharge of what is just . . . if such tediousness as this will be the reward of all my pains and trouble taken for him it will utterly spoil a bailiff of me.[39]

It was not the last such plea his master was to receive. In 1687, Thynne, by then Lord Weymouth, had a letter from Morgan Powell at Drayton Bassett 'earnestly desiring' that as he sent his accounts half yearly to Weymouth so his master would discharge them half yearly. God had created 'great and small mortals'. He had not the least fear but that Weymouth would do him and all men right, but he dreaded the thought of enemies and was unwilling to be left to their mercy 'from which God deliver me and mine'. If Weymouth objected to anything in the accounts he had only to let Powell know and he would satisfy his master about it within the week.[40] Less dramatically emotional and therefore more typical is the simple observation of William Thynne to Sir James Thynne in 1659 that it 'would be very much to the content' of his mind if Gould, Sir James's lawyer, would audit his accounts often so that they could be passed.

---

[38] J. V. Beckett, 'The Finances of a Former Jacobite: James Grahme of Levens Hall', *CWAAST*, new ser., 85 (1985), 134.

[39] Hawkes to Thomas Thynne, 30 September 1674. Thynne xx, fo. 190.

[40] Powell to Weymouth, 11 April 1687, Thynne xxviii, fo. 168v. This was written when relations between master and man were descending from bad to worse, and were in part perhaps a reaction to an acidulated thrust from his master the year before: 'your own accounts are your greatest accusers'. Weymouth to Powell, 16 May 1686, xxviii, fo. 138.

The lord's reaction to his own fears was to try to secure himself from an unjust servant by a bond, backed by 'sufficient' sureties, which would guarantee him against financial loss. William Adams had signed such a bond on entering the service of the first Viscount Cholmondeley in 1679. When his master died in 1682 his successor sent down a request for a new bond 'that you may be accountable for what money you have or may have in case you should die, etc.' That was in January 1683. This bond Adams neglected to supply, so in February 1684 Cholmondeley, when sending down his power of attorney, informed Adams bluntly that he had instructed the messenger not to surrender this document until Adams delivered him the signed bond.[41] The trouble with bonds was that they were only as good as the sureties who signed them. Lowther's too much involved colliery steward Thomas Jackson had signed a bond for £1,000 but his master's difficulties in getting his own money back over several years following Jackson's departure from Lowther's service in disgrace shows the severe limitations of such a security. Such sureties might seem men of substance at the time of signing but were often found to be men of straw, if indeed still alive, when the bond became enforceable years later.[42] Certainly the provision of a bond by both stewards and understewards to their employers was increasingly a routine measure by the beginning of the eighteenth century. When Fitzwilliam reported to Guybon that one John Catlin of Maxey had written wishing to serve under his chief steward, the first comment Fitzwilliam offered was that Catlin claimed to have a promise from 'some sufficient neighbours that will be bound with him for his truth and honesty'.[43] Sometimes these bonds could give a steward anxiety. William Elmsall after five years in Sir George Savile's service as steward of his Yorkshire estates, began to wonder if he would be liable for any bills stolen by highwaymen. He confided his fears to his master when they were returning from a day's stag hunting at Rufford and Savile enquired what was done on other Yorkshire estates. Elmsall told him most stewards operated under a simple letter of attorney and had no liability for any losses the estate might suffer under their stewardship. Some had undertaken responsibility for loss, such as a Mr Rhodes of Flockton, steward there to Mr Wortley. However, Rhodes received a salary of £150, a huge salary for caring for an estate which only yielded £2,000 a year in rents, and this induced him to take the risk. Elmsall, caring for a much more

---

[41] Hugh Beheathland to Adams, 20 January 1683, Cholmondeley to Adams, 27 February 1684, Cholmondeley DCH/K/3/4.

[42] Thomas Tickell found that Jackson's chief surety was by then bankrupt. However, the bond itself left much to be desired since whoever drew it had required the steward to 'well account' but not 'well pay'! Tickell to Lowther, 7 December 1674, Lonsdale D/Lons/W2/1/9.

[43] Catlin was eventually given the position. Fitzwilliam, 13 April 1704, F(M)C 1321; *Fitzwilliam Correspondence*, Letter 313.

valuable estate with a salary of only £62, could not run such a hazard.[44] All this anxiety about liability and accounts and risks to the steward's family and posterity or to the master's coffers seems to take us far from the relationship based on good lordship which we have explored above. It is a symptom of the gradual but significant change in the relationship between steward and master from family member to mere salaried employee which lay ahead later in the eighteenth and during the nineteenth centuries.

Finally, it has been demonstrated continuously throughout the foregoing narrative that seventeenth-century stewards could be required to discharge a very diverse array of duties and functions and responsibilities. How onerous was it for them? Were some stewards driven into retirement by the rigorous demands made on them? Certainly stewards did not pursue a sedentary occupation. A conscientious steward would be frequently and long on horseback, not simply riding about the estate but visiting nearby market towns and the county town for quarter sessions and assizes. John Mainewaring commented to Lord Weymouth that 'indeed your lordship's business lies so wide that all the time I have is little enough to do it in'. John Warren wistfully hoped that the Earl of Middlesex would not 'put more on' him than he could do. Morgan Powell assured Lord Weymouth that far from being idle all the trouble he went through on his master's behalf had impaired his health. All the business Thomas Smith was involved in, including the haying and the wood felling, required such constant super-vision, that he declared he could not possibly finish the previous year's accounts although if he had some help, he hinted, he might finish them in the fortnight.[45] Thomas Tickell's duties were certainly strenuous. Not only could he be found scrambling up the sides of beached ships in his master's port, a dry harbour at low tide, he was also required to penetrate to the depths of his master's coal mines to report on their condition, progress and prospects. For some who combined their stewardship with agricultural pursuits of their own it could prove too heavy a burden, even when their responsibility was for a quite modest estate, so that they begged to be relieved from their burdensome posts. Lord Fitzwilliam was a considerate employer by the standards of the time but successive stewards of his Norfolk manors threw up their employment. John Farthing found he could not serve any longer, complaining that even at £40 a year he would be a great loser, besides loss of time and 'slight' of clothes and horses. 'But he that intends to do honestly between your lordship and your tenants and *all*

[44] Elmsall to Savile, 21 January 1716, Savile DDSR.211/2.
[45] Mainewaring to Weymouth, 7 June 1693, Thynne xxviii, fo. 310v; Warren to Middlesex, 30 September 1674, Sackville C125/11; Powell to Weymouth, 18 February 1686 Thynne xxviii, fo. 158; Smith to Sir George Savile, 9 July 1718, Savile DDSR 211/227/70.

your other affairs must be both a good fellow and a good husband.'[46]
Although Farthing here seems concerned with financial loss, it is clear from
his repeated requests for replacement that the demands of what should have
been the quite modest stewardship of two manors made such inroads on his
time that his own farm was neglected, and this aspect of the burden is still
more clearly emphasised by his successor, Arthur King, who also repeatedly
begged to be replaced.

Nevertheless for the vast majority of stewards the financial rewards, the
access to patronage and above all the psychic rewards which derived from
being the surrogate of a great man exerted a gravitational force which held
the steward in his master's orbit. Although the stewards shone by a
reflected light they all, large and small, glittered in their places in the
firmament of provincial society.

[46] My emphasis. Farthing to Fitzwilliam, 24 July 1677, Fitzwilliam F(M)C 435.

A NOTE ON THE MANUSCRIPT SOURCES

The chief source for the foregoing study is stewards' correspondence, whether 'in' or 'out', supplemented by various enclosures to correspondence which might consist of isolated accounts, letters received by the steward from other correspondents, copies of negotiated agreements for the lord's approval and so on, and also runs of estate accounts. Naturally the correspondence tends to suffer from the fact that only one side of the correspondence has survived, either the lord's letters (or letters from his secretary or receiver in London) or those from the steward to the lord. The correspondence of William Adams, chief steward to first and second Viscounts Cholmondeley, to the first dowager Viscountess Cholmondeley and the second Viscount's younger brother, General George Cholmondeley (subsequently the second earl) amounts to more than 3,000 letters. However, this is a collection of in-letters for only thirty-seven of Adams' own letters to his successive masters between 1679 and 1715 have survived, about 1 per cent of the collection. Fortunately, the correspondence is supplemented by Adams' meticulously kept accounts for much of that period. Lord Fitzwilliam's surviving estate archives include a useful run of 136 letters from his steward at Milton, Francis Guybon, from 1678 to 1696, with only 14 of his master's replies surviving, and none dated earlier than 1694. From 1697 historians are then confronted with a run of 536 of Fitzwilliam's letters to Guybon from 1697 to 1709 with only 50 of Guybon's replies. (It is this part of the archive which the writer recently jointly edited for the Northamptonshire Record Society.) Very few of the letters to his stewards of Sir Thomas Thynne, first Viscount Weymouth, have survived (although many of his family and political letters have been more fortunate), but a substantial number of his stewards' letters from various branches of that great estate are still at Longleat. Similarly Sir John Lowther of Whitehaven's letters to William Gilpin between 1693 and 1698 have not survived save for about 50 from 1698 and a few drafts from earlier years, whereas Gilpin's letters from his appointment to the beginning of 1698 are virtually complete but they have failed to survive from about the time that his master's letters begin their run, while the steward of Lowther's cousin, the first Lord Lonsdale, William Atkinson, is only represented by in-letters and only a small proportion of those. It is the accidental circumstance that Thomas Tickell, Lowther of Whitehaven's steward from 1666 to his death in 1692, almost invariably drafted his replies on the back of his master's letters (or on odd sheets of papers inserted within them) and then carefully kept Lowther's letters tied up in bundles, which has provided us with the immensely valuable resource of an almost complete set of steward's and master's letters covering a quarter of a century. Such archives for the seventeenth century must be very rare. Certainly I have not discovered another to compare with it. I have listed the collections consulted below, giving a rough indication of the size and length of the runs of correspondence together with the names of the stewards chiefly involved, in the hope that this may prove useful to other labourers in the vineyard who wish to garner from them the social history data in which they are so rich.

MARQUESS OF CHOLMONDELEY ARCHIVES

The estate correspondence here is chiefly but not entirely that of William Adams, the chief steward for the period 1679–1715, and includes among its more than 3,000 letters, 57 letters from Robert the first viscount (1679–81), 546 from Hugh the second viscount (1679–1715), together with 611 from Cholmondeley's long-serving secretary Michael Laroche (1688–1701, 1704–15), 24 from his sister (Lady Egerton), at least 100 from his brother George (1679–1715) and 145 from Elizabeth, Hugh's mother (together with 128 from Jonadeb Colley, her page, mainly written on her behalf), chiefly from her husband's death in 1681 to her own death in 1691 because Adams was steward of her jointure estate. The remainder of the letters are chiefly from members of Cholmondeley's London household, from his various lawyers both in London and Cheshire and from the understewards who were in charge of various parts of the estate in Cheshire, Shropshire and Somersetshire, together with many other estate servants, tradesmen, neighbours, timber purchasers and so on. All, together with Adams's accounts for 1681–94, 1698–1711, are held in the Cheshire RO.

EARL OF LONSDALE ARCHIVES

These include the correspondence of Sir John Lowther of Whitehaven with Thomas Tickell (1666–92), 1,793 letters together with some enclosures, and William Gilpin (1693–8), 331 letters, and John Gale, colliery steward (1692–8), 147 letters; also of William Atkinson, steward successively to Sir John Lowther of Lowther (*obit.* 1675) and his grandson, Sir John Lowther, first Viscount Lonsdale (1663–96), 91 letters. There are excellent sets of accounts for the Lowther of Whitehaven and Lowther of Lowther estates. Among the Lonsdale papers are also some stray letters of Thomas Carleton, steward at Appleby to the Earl of Thanet (1704–15), 17 letters, and a beautifully written set of accounts for 1711 of Thanet's Cumbrian estates. All held at Cumbria RO (Carlisle).

MARQUESS OF BATH ARCHIVES

The archives at Longleat much of which have been issued on microfilm contain stewards' letters from different estates including Kempsford, Gloucestershire, 1673–1709 (John Coelinge, Thomas Pope, John Chaunler), 163 letters; Minsterley, Shropshire, 1672–88 (Richard Clayton, Samuel Peers), 65 letters; Stretton, Shropshire, 1672–93 (Thomas Hawkes), 83 letters; Drayton Bassett and Tamworth, Staffordshire–Warwickshire, 1677–1711 (Morgan Powell, William Hopkins, John Mainewaring), 234 letters; Longleat, Wiltshire, 1658–70, 1683–90, 1709 (William Thynne, Thomas Allen, John Ord), 49 letters, London properties 1684–90 (James Tayldor), 69 letters. There are a number of stewards' letters relating to Drayton prior to its acquisition by Thomas Thynne in the Seymour Papers. These have also been issued on microfilm and can be traced also in Historical MSS Commission Reports, Marquess of Bath, 58, vol. 4, *Seymour Papers 1532–1680.*

FITZWILLIAM OF MILTON ARCHIVES

The correspondence of the steward at Milton, 1678–1709 (Francis Guybon) and of the stewards of the Norfolk estates, 1677–1703 (John Farthing, Arthur King, Edmond Beales), approximately 1,100 letters. There are useful sets of accounts, some for the Norfolk properties but chiefly those of Guybon at Milton. All held in the Northamptonshire RO.

SAVILE PAPERS

Estate correspondence of successive Sir George Saviles during the seventeenth and early eighteenth centuries, including the first Marquess of Halifax, from Rufford Abbey, Nottinghamshire, and various estates in the West Riding of Yorkshire, 1609–1731 (W. Vernon, Robert Turner, Captain Thomas Lister, Thomas Smith, William Elmsall), 581 letters, together with Elmsall's abstracts of accounts 1713–30, and 'Memoranda of Actions to be Taken' 1712, 1721–31. All held in the Nottinghamshire RO.

HASTINGS, EARLS OF HUNTINGDON ARCHIVES

Held at the Huntington Library, California, but now available on microfilm, this collection contains the correspondence of Gervas Jacquis (for 1659–88) and the Reverend John Gery (or Geary) (1675–96) concerning the seventh earl's Leicestershire estates, political interests, patronage links and so on, amounting to 154 and 187 letters respectively. There is a wealth of correspondence also concerning the earl's Irish estates not consulted by this writer.

TREVOR OF GLYNDE AND TREVALYN ARCHIVES

There are useful runs of correspondence of the estates of Sir John Trevor II (1596–1673) in Flintshire and Denbighshire, 1630–73 (Thomas Crewe 1630–9, Samuel Wood 1638–48, John Peck 1649–55, Jasper Peck 1665–73, Roger Kenrick 1667–74), approximately 400 letters. Held in the Clwyd RO (Hawarden).

SACKVILLE OF KNOLE PAPERS

There are runs of correspondence of stewards in Sussex, Warwickshire, Staffordshire, and Northamptonshire relating to the estates of the Earl of Middlesex, the Earl and Countess of Dorset and the Countess of Bath, 1645–1687 (Charles and Francis Agard, John and Edward Raynes, Christopher Smith, George Peacock, Martin Capson, Arthur Walker, William Lynne, Richard Pollard, H. Carter, Robert Hawdon, Thomas Brome, John Warren), 251 letters; there are also useful sets of accounts for the Sussex and Warwickshire estates (1667–70, 1680–1, 1695–1713 for the former and 1643–50 for the latter). Held in Kent RO.

LORD LECONFIELD ARCHIVES, COCKERMOUTH CASTLE

Correspondence relating to the West Cumberland estates of the Earl of Northumberland, 1663–70 (Hugh Potter) and the Duke of Somerset, 1695–1707 (Joseph and Edward Relfe), 62 letters consulted. Obtainable through Cumbria RO (Carlisle).

DUKE OF PORTLAND ARCHIVES

Correspondence of Andrew Clayton, chief steward to the Earl (subsequently first Duke) of Newcastle (1659–70); miscellaneous estate correspondence of Lord Haughton, Gilbert Holles, Earl of Clare, and first and second Dukes of Newcastle (1602–1705) (and see also *The Letters of John Holles 1587–1637*, Thoroton society, 31 (1975)); Ralph Gowland, steward of the Newcastle estates in Northumberland (1700–16); amounting to 177 letters in all. Held in Nottingham University Library.

RADNOR PAPERS

Correspondence of John Snow, steward of Downton, Wiltshire, with Sir Joseph Ashe, Lady Ashe and Sir James Ashe (1665–1702), 115 letters; accounts of John Snow and Leonard Snow (1686–1702). In Radnor Papers, Wiltshire RO.

BARRETT-LENNARD PAPERS

Estate correspondence concerning the Horsford estate, Norfolk, 1654–1720 (Robert Carne, Thomas Barnham, Robert Britiffe, Robert Caudell), 89 letters; collection also contains accounts of John Lancaster, 1685–7, and Thomas Featherstonhough, 1703–11, stewards of the Earl of Sussex's Cumbrian estates. Held in Barrett-Lennard, Essex RO.

ST JOHN'S COLLEGE, CAMBRIDGE

Correspondence concerning Ospringe, Kent (1700–8) Marlborough, Wiltshire (1704–16); Furness, Lancashire (1693–1701), approximately 60 letters. Held in St John's College archives.

NICHOLAS PAPERS

Thomas Greene at Gillingham, Dorset to Sir John Nicholas (1698–1701), 61 letters. In John Rylands Library, Manchester.

DUKE OF SUTHERLAND (LEVESON-GOWER) PAPERS

Lord Gower estates (1673–1720), 59 letters; accounts (1685–7). Held in Staffordshire RO.

ISHAM OF LAMPORT PAPERS

Miscellaneous estate correspondence (1670–97), 62 letters; account of Edward Morpett (1710–16). Held in Northamptonshire RO.

GALWAY PAPERS

John Cocke of Redruth to Lady Arundel of Trerice (1704–18), 30 letters; Dr Richard Berrie to Marmaduke Monckton, Yorkshire (1649–51), 66 letters. Held in Galway, Nottingham University Library.

OTHER COLLECTIONS CONSULTED

The following collections contain 50 stewards' letters or less: *Devonshire*: correspondence of James Whildon, Chatsworth (1698–1707), 50 letters; Chatsworth muniments; *Paget*: correspondence of John Swynfen and Lord Paget of Beaudesert, Staffordshire (1669–83), 37 letters, Staffordshire RO; *Fielding*: Castle Rising estate correspondence, 1696–1709 (Matthew Cusande, David Hilman, Thomas Wilkinson, successive stewards to Lady Diana Fielding, née Howard), 29 letters; Norfolk RO; *Cardigan*: correspondence concerning Northamptonshire estates (William Lynwood, John Massey), 27 letters with Lynwood's accounts for 1689–96; Northamptonshire RO; *Howard*: James Maxwell, Naworth Castle, Cumberland, to Earl of Carlisle (1693–6), 10 letters consulted, Castle Howard muniments; *Northampton*: there are a few examples of stewards' correspondence in the Marquess of Northampton archives relating to Compton Wynyates, Warwickshire. While the originals are among the muniments at Castle Ashby, Northamptonshire, photocopies are held in the Warwickshire RO.

MISCELLANEOUS ACCOUNTS, NOTEBOOKS, AND OTHER DOCUMENTS

Accounts of John Bennett, steward to Lord Arundel of Wardour (1663–76); Arundel of Wardour, Wiltshire RO; Adam Sedgwick: an autobiographical memoir of Sedgwick's service with Lady Anne Clifford, Countess of Pembroke, preserved in copy in the Fleming Papers, Cumbria RO (Kendal), entitled 'A Steward's Autobiography'. Sedgwick was more man-of-business, perhaps a page, on Lady Anne's household staff rather than a steward as such; 'Thomas Jackson's Diary' c.1681–1701, Tabley Estate papers, Cheshire RO. (Jackson was steward of the Tabley estate, but this is not strictly a diary but rather a rough running-account book which he also used as a commonplace-cum-memoranda book for news and information of both local and national significance.)

Two further useful sources, which came to hand too late to help this project, are the several hundred letters on general estate business concerning the Essex, Yorkshire and Isle of Wight estates of Sir Francis Barrington and his successor Sir Thomas Barrington from the 1630s to the 1670s, Egerton MS: Barrington, BL (and with them Arthur Searle's admirable edition of *Barrington Family Letters 1628–1632*, Camden, 4th ser., 28 (1983)), and the stewards' correspondence of Colonel James Grahme of Levens Hall from the 1680s through the reign of Queen Anne, held at Levens Hall, Cumbria, but now available on microfilm in the Cumbria RO (Kendal).

INDEX

Cambridge Studies in Early Modern British History

Titles in the series

*Also published as a paperback